D0845919

Jigsaw Puzzle Politics in the Sunshine State

Florida Government and Politics

UNIVERSITY PRESS OF FLORIDA

Florida A&M University, Tallahassee
Florida Atlantic University, Boca Raton
Florida Gulf Coast University, Ft. Myers
Florida International University, Miami
Florida State University, Tallahassee
New College of Florida, Sarasota
University of Central Florida, Orlando
University of Florida, Gainesville
University of North Florida, Jacksonville
University of South Florida, Tampa
University of West Florida, Pensacola

JIGSAW PUZZLE POLITICS
IN THE SUNSHINE STATE

EDITED BY

SETH C. MCKEE

Foreword by David R. Colburn and Susan A. MacManus

University Press of Florida
Gainesville · Tallahassee · Tampa · Boca Raton
Pensacola · Orlando · Miami · Jacksonville · Ft. Myers · Sarasota

A Florida Quincentennial Book

Library of Congress Cataloging-in-Publication Data
Jigsaw puzzle politics in the Sunshine State / edited by Seth C. McKee ; foreword by David R. Colburn and Susan A. MacManus.
pages cm — (Florida government and politics)
Includes bibliographical references and index.
ISBN 978-0-8130-6071-2
1. Apportionment (Election law)—Florida. 2. Election districts—Florida. 3. Florida—Politics and government. 4. Political culture—Florida. I. McKee, Seth Charles, 1974–editor. II. Colburn, David R., author of introduction, etc. III. MacManus, Susan A., author of introduction, etc. IV. Series: Florida government and politics.
KFF420.85.A6J54 2015
328.759'073455—dc23
2015003594

The University Press of Florida is the scholarly publishing agency for the State University System of Florida, comprising Florida A&M University, Florida Atlantic University, Florida Gulf Coast University, Florida International University, Florida State University, New College of Florida, University of Central Florida, University of Florida, University of North Florida, University of South Florida, and University of West Florida.

University Press of Florida
15 Northwest 15th Street
Gainesville, FL 32611-2079
http://www.upf.com

Contents

Figures

Tables

Foreword

Florida has long been considered a bellwether state, a microcosm of the nation at-large demographically, socioeconomically, and politically. The Sunshine State's decades-long population growth has also put it at the forefront of major redistricting issues that have emerged in each redistricting cycle since the 1960s when Congress passed major civil rights legislation and the U.S. Supreme Court ruled states must adhere to the "one person, one vote" principle when drawing legislative districts. Florida's experiences with redistricting in the 2012 cycle, as in years past, will certainly be of interest to other states as their populations diversify.

Tracking the State's Evolution into a Bellwether State

Historically, reapportionment and redistricting battles in Florida reflect its evolution into one of the nation's most racially and ethnically diverse states and *the* most politically divided. As noted by the Florida House of Representatives Committee on Reapportionment in January 1991, "Reapportionment has been inextricably linked with the political history of the state, at one time or another affecting every issue of state government, serving to bring into sharp focus the divisions within Florida's political makeup, and exposing the tension of rapidly changing demographic and social forces."[1]

Beginning with the end of World War II and continuing into the 2000s, the state's population boomed. The influx of newcomers from the Northeast, Midwest, and Latin America markedly transformed Florida economically and politically. By 2010, just 35 percent of its residents were born in Florida. As Florida historian David Colburn has observed, the state changed "[f]rom one of the least appealing, most racially polarized, and poorest states to one of the most desired, most diverse, and most prosperous; from a state that had been anything but a bellwether of the nation to one that . . . is 'the whole deal, the real deal, a big deal.'"[2] However, the transition has not come without growing pains.

For the first part of the growth spurt, the state's legislative politics remained stuck in the politics of the "Old South." Florida's politics was best described as white, conservative, segregationist, and one-party Democratic. Political power rested in the northern tier of counties with the "pork choppers," who dominated the state legislature as well as the Cabinet and the courts. The "one person, one vote" principle ultimately imposed by a U.S. Supreme Court ruling was not yet in effect. "Equal" representation was county-based, rather than population-based, thereby inflating the power of rural areas at the expense of urban areas. To put things in perspective, in 1950, 13.6 percent of the state's population elected more than one-half of the state senators and 18 percent of the population elected more than half the members of the Florida House of Representatives. It was an all-white male legislature, with no women or minorities.

Ultimately, it took several U.S. Supreme Court rulings to force Florida to reapportion both houses of its state legislature on a population basis. In 1964, the Court ruled that each state was to draw its U.S. congressional districts so that they were approximately equal in population (*Wesberry v. Sanders)* and that the equal population principle applied to the drawing of districts in each house of a state legislature (*Reynolds v. Sims*). It was three years later (1967) when the U.S. Supreme Court finally ordered the reapportionment of Florida to reflect "one man, one vote" (*Swann v. Adams).*

Prior to the *Swann* ruling, the state had failed to revamp its legislative redistricting process in spite of the efforts of some state leaders like Governor LeRoy Collins (1955–61). Collins was elected with substantial backing from the urban regions of the state and with especially strong support from South Florida, so it was not surprising that he pushed for reapportionment in each legislative session, only to see it blocked by rural legislators. The rural-dominated legislature continued to fight redistricting reform even after the Supreme Court rulings in 1964 and passage of the 1964 Civil Rights Act and the 1965 Voting Rights Act (VRA). In retrospect, the 1967 court-ordered redistricting of Florida was deemed by some historians and political scientists to be a critical starting point for the state's modernization and its eventual transformation into an intensely partisan-competitive state and a powerhouse on the national stage.

Perennial Redistricting Schisms

In virtually every redistricting cycle, several schisms have been evident, although the intensity of each has fluctuated depending on the prevailing politics at the time:

- *Geographical*: North Florida vs. South Florida, more recently, coastal areas vs. interior areas, unincorporated vs. incorporated areas, rural vs. urban areas
- *Partisan*: Democrats vs. Republicans
- *Ideological*: conservatives vs. liberals
- *Executive vs. Legislative branch*: governor vs. legislators
- *Legislative vs. Judicial branch*: state legislature vs. federal and state courts: legislative vs. judicial branch
- *House-Senate*: state representatives vs. state senators
- *State Legislature-Congressional Delegation*: state legislators vs. members of Florida's congressional delegation (U.S. Senators; U.S. House members)
- *Racial/ethnic*: non-whites vs. whites; minorities vs. minorities (African Americans vs. Hispanics)
- *Old-timers vs. Newcomers*: native Floridians vs. new in-migrants
- *Gender*: women vs. men (especially among state legislators)
- *Age*: the generational division, often retirees vs. younger constituents and their advocates

In 2012, the deepest schisms were partisan, racial/ethnic, geographical, and legislative vs. judicial branch disagreements. These were, in large part, attributable to the new constitutional redistricting (the "Fair Districts") requirements, especially the Tier 1 standards. These standards *prohibit* the drawing of a plan or district:

(1) "With the intent to favor or disfavor a political party or an incumbent" (political gerrymandering).
(2) "With the intent or result of denying or abridging the equal opportunity of racial or language minorities to participate in the political process *or* to diminish their ability to elect representatives of their choice" (racial gerrymandering). At the time, this new standard effectively extended federal Section 5 retrogression standards to the entire state, rather than to just the five counties (Collier, Hardee, Hendry, Hillsborough, and Monroe) subject to Section 5 federal VRA

preclearance requirements. "Florida now has a statewide non-retro-gression requirement independent of Section 5" of the federal Voting Rights Act.

(3) That is not "contiguous" defined as "being in actual contact; touching along a boundary or at a point." Inclusion of contiguity as a Tier I standard was proof to the Court that "voters made clear their intention to establish that the section 21(b) [Tier 2] standards of compactness, nearly equal population, and utilizing political and geographical boundaries are subservient to the contiguity requirement."

In the words of the Florida Supreme Court, "With the recent addition of section 21 to article III of the Florida Constitution, the Legislature is governed by a different and more constitutional measurement than before—the *limitations* (emphasis added) on legislative authority in apportionment decisions have increased and the constitutional yardstick has more measurements."[3] The overall effect of the new standards was to create a more difficult redistricting process, requiring legislators to balance the rights of minorities and political parties.

Recurring Elements of Redistricting and New Controversies

Each redistricting cycle, Florida, like other states, has tussled with the U.S. Census Bureau over the timing of the release of key population data, the accuracy of the data, and its comprehensiveness. For example, in 1990, Florida along with a few other states sued the Bureau to release undercount statistics from the 1990 Census. In addition, in 2012, Florida and other southwestern border states heavily criticized the Census Bureau for failing to provide them with block level data on the number of non-citizens.

With each successive redistricting, technological advancements have made data more accessible to the general public. Legislative requests for citizen input via submission of their own maps for legislative consideration sharply escalated in 2012. According to the chair of the House Redistricting Committee, the committee received 177 public submissions of redistricting plans—up from only four in 2002. However, these new technologies and software programs have not gone without criticism. They have been criticized by some citizens for being overly confusing, difficult to access and manipulate, and a challenge to submit online.

New technologies, especially statistical software, have also permitted more sophisticated statistical analyses, often yielding intense methodological debates between opposing sides' expert witnesses. In 2012, the Florida Supreme Court even purchased and utilized additional software programs to do its own independent data analysis.

Pressures to solicit and incorporate citizen input have intensified as well. Public hearings designed for this purpose (and for establishing a record for expected litigation) have been an integral part of the redistricting process since 1992. However, it was not until the 2002 redistricting that citizen reform groups began demanding another round of public hearings *after* the proposed congressional and legislative maps were released. The drumbeat for such post-map release hearings got even louder in 2012, but the legislature turned instead to social media as the vehicle for gathering citizen reactions and recommendations regarding the proposed maps. As in past legislative redistricting cycles, tweaks to the initial proposals did not forestall litigation by dissatisfied groups and individuals convinced that the legislature had engaged in gerrymandering of some kind.

There have also been perennial debates over how to empirically measure broad, but critically important, concepts like "fair," "minority representation," "legislative intent," "structural impact," "compactness," and "retrogression," to name a few. In 2012, the new Fair District standards resulted in particularly heated debates between Democrats and Republicans and between the attorney general and the Republican legislators and the Florida Supreme Court on how to measure partisan and incumbent neutrality, retrogression, and compactness. The Florida Supreme Court in its ruling on the constitutionality of state legislative plans (the court has no role in validating congressional plans) provided detailed definitions of these terms. The definitions emanated from the new constitutional redistricting standards, along with federal and state court rulings and laws.

Another common pattern observed in the redistricting process has been for partisan and racial/ethnic minorities to band together to push for drawing single-member districts with sizable minority populations. The Republican-black coalition was strongest through the 1992 redistricting cycle. Up to that point, each group was underrepresented in the Florida Legislature. The coalition weakened a bit thereafter but there were still some vestiges of it in 2002 and 2012, as evidenced by voting patterns on specific districting plans and alignment on some litigation efforts. (U.S. representatives Corrine Brown-D and Mario Diaz-Balart-R challenged the constitutionality of Amendment 6—spelling out congressional redistricting standards. The court rejected their constitutional challenge.) However, the days of defining race in black and white terms are long gone in Florida, with its increasingly multi-racial/ethnic population and the presence of key language minorities (Hispanics, Haitians). Citizen commentary at redistricting hearings in 2012 revealed different representational preferences among various Hispanic groups, along with emerging political schisms in South Florida between African American and Caribbean blacks.

Just as with redistricting processes, there have been some outcome-related commonalities and controversies. For years, each party in power has engaged in incumbent, or "turf" protection, which, prior to the new constitutional standards adopted in 2010, was not inherently illegal. (Democrats controlled the governorship and both chambers of the legislature through the 1992 redistricting; Republicans held similar control over the governor's office and both chambers of the state legislature in 2002 and 2012.) However, by 2012, incumbent protection had been rendered unconstitutional by the Fair Districts Amendments 5 and 6. Too much incumbent protection in the legislature's initial senate redistricting plan prompted the Florida Supreme Court to reject it and order the redrawing of several districts. The house plan was cleared.

Legal challenges have been another "given" outcome of redistricting. Most of these challenges have raised the fairness issue and generated claims of racial gerrymandering. The same issues were litigated in 2012, but with one new additional claim—partisan gerrymandering, which was made more justiciable by the new constitutional standard. Compactness- and community of interest–related debates (mostly geographical, related to splitting neighborhoods, cities, and counties) have escalated with every redistricting cycle, beginning most dramatically in 1992. Yet, the weight of these measures lessened in 2012, with both elements defined as Tier 2 standards.

Finally, Florida's reapportionment and redistricting history shows that structural changes may produce short-term, but not necessarily permanent, representational gains. For example, while the 1982 switch to single-member legislative districts in both houses increased the number of women legislators, subsequent post-redistricting seat gains for women have been less substantial. The 2012 redistricting saw no change in female representation in the U.S. House, and minimal changes in the state senate (-2) or the state house (+1). The weak link between structural change and long-term representational gains is also evident in other research tracking the impact of legislative term limits.

The Importance of *Jigsaw Puzzle Politics in the Sunshine State*

This brief review of the evolution of redistricting standards, processes, and outcomes underscores the importance of scholarship examining the dynamics of each redistricting cycle. *Jigsaw Puzzle Politics in the Sunshine State,* edited by the highly respected political scientist Seth C. McKee, chronicles the redistricting controversies that emerged during the 2012 cycle. The volume follows in the path of MacManus's previous edited books detailing redistricting processes and outcomes in Florida over multiple decades.[4]

Jigsaw Puzzle Politics gives readers a comprehensive look at the hows, whens, whys, and consequences of the most recent redistricting wars. Specifically, the chapters contributed by prominent political scientists illustrate how two new state constitutional amendments adopted by Florida voters in 2010 created and prioritized new and existing redistricting standards. There is also a rich discussion of how heightened pressures for citizen input, the availability of more detailed and easily accessible data, more demands for process transparency, and litigation affected the process and outcomes. Overall, *Jigsaw Puzzle Politics* affirms that redistricting remains *the* most political of political undertakings, but also one of the most important tasks in a representative democracy.

David R. Colburn and Susan A. MacManus
Series editors

Introduction

Redistricting in Florida

SETH C. MCKEE

Perhaps nothing in the realm of politics is more consequential, anxiety producing, and just plain political as the act of redistricting. Indeed, one of the
contributors to this volume recently published a book titled *Redistricting:
The Most Political Activity in America*.[1] And consider this graphic assessment by a member of Congress who obviously found the changes to his
district unfavorable: "Only one thing would make me feel worse than this
last redistricting—to have my testicles laid on a stump and hit with a mal-
let."[2] Redistricting is worthy of such pronouncements because it strikes at
the heart of political power and the representational relationship. How the
lines are drawn not only establishes the basis of how economic resources
are allocated[3] and which party governs, but also, on many occasions, which
candidates will have the opportunity to win public office and which incumbents will be able to sustain their political careers.

Florida sticks out as a state with a notorious reputation for cutthroat redistricting battles, a reputation cultivated and seasoned over many decades
that have witnessed the transition from a one-party Democratic position
to a currently Republican-dominant status in district-based elections. Prior
to the reapportionment revolution brought forth by the one-person, one-
vote principle laid out in the 1962 *Baker v. Carr* decision, the rural Democrats of North Florida ruled Sunshine State politics. These "pork choppers"
maintained their political clout primarily through inaction with regard to
redistricting, because failing to redraw district boundaries fostered gross
malapportionment, most notable in the case of sparsely populated districts in North Florida versus extremely populous districts in the booming
southern half of the state.[4]

Compared to its Southern peers,[5] Florida was the worst offender in terms of malapportioned state legislative districts. In the 1950s, the disparities between the largest and smallest Florida House districts and Florida Senate districts, respectively, were remarkable. The largest state house district was over 108 times more populated than the smallest state house district. In the state senate the situation was not much better, with the most populous district 98 times larger than the smallest. Just as stunning is that it only took about 17 percent of the Florida population to seat a legislative majority in either chamber.[6] Clearly the malapportionment of Florida legislative districts sustained a political status quo enjoyed by rural North Florida Democrats, one of whom boasted, "I believe in collecting taxes where the money is—in the cities—and spending it where it's needed—in the country."[7]

Although not close to rivaling the situation in the Florida Legislature, congressional districts were also nowhere near equal in population. Following the 1960 decennial census, because of its unmatched population growth, Florida gained four seats through reapportionment, with a total of twelve for the 1962 U.S. House elections. District 9, located in the Panhandle with the state capital of Tallahassee as its major city, contained 237,235 inhabitants, making it the least populated Florida congressional district. By comparison, District 6, running from Fort Myers and other parts of the southwest coast across to the southeast coast and encompassing major metropolitan areas north of Miami (like Palm Beach), was the largest congressional district with a population of 660,345 or 2.78 times larger than District 9.[8]

However, *Baker v. Carr*, and subsequent rulings applicable to the enforcement of the equal population standard (e.g., the 1964 *Reynolds v. Sims* ruling in state legislative elections and the 1964 *Wesberry v. Sanders* opinion in congressional elections) delivered an abrupt end to the political reign of Florida's Democratic Pork Chop Gang. Because of the decision handed down by the U.S. Supreme Court in the 1967 case of *Swann v. Adams*, Florida held state legislative elections again under new maps with more equal district populations. With a massive redistribution of voters into a much larger number of metropolitan-based and growing urban centers in Central and South Florida, Republican ascendancy in Florida politics commenced. In 1964, Republicans accounted for 4.5 percent of the Florida Senate (2 out of 44 seats) and 8.9 percent of the Florida House (10 out of 112 seats). Three years later, Republicans comprised 41.7 percent of the Florida Senate delegation (20 out of 48 seats) and 32.8 percent of the Florida House (39 out of 119 seats).[9]

After implementation of the equal population mandate, the next major change affecting Florida redistricting stems from another court ruling, which also served to advantage Republicans.[10] In the 1986 North Carolina case of *Thornburg v. Gingles*, the Supreme Court established criteria (see chapter 3) for the creation of majority-minority districts and these took effect in the 1990s redistricting round. With pressure applied by the Department of Justice (DOJ), many Southern states like Florida, which were covered by the Section 5 preclearance provision of the Voting Rights Act, drew new majority-minority districts for the 1992 congressional and state legislative elections.[11]

Thanks to their legislative majorities and occupying the governorship, Florida Democrats were in charge of redistricting and their new maps "included eight house and two senate districts with a black voting-age majority and nine majority-Hispanic districts in the house and three in the senate."[12] The congressional map, which was ultimately drawn by court intervention (and redrawn in 1996), created three majority black districts and two with Latino majorities.[13] As became evident in most settings, and particularly in the South, where the lion's share of majority black districts were created, the net effect was to benefit African American Democrats contesting these districts and Republican candidates running in adjacent districts with lower black populations.

Packing minority voters into a smaller number of districts where it was possible to further descriptive representation on the basis of race, proved a steep electoral tradeoff for the Democratic Party, because Republicans benefited the most in terms of their aggregate seat gains, as demonstrated by a host of studies.[14] In addition, unlike other states (i.e., California and Texas) where the Hispanic population favors Democrats, in Florida, the large presence of Cuban Americans aligned with the GOP, meant that most of the state's Latino majority districts were won by Hispanic Republicans. As was the case in other Southern states, and stated by Tom Slade, Florida's Republican state party chair: "The blacks and Republicans have joined together in an unholy alliance to do in the white Democrats, and we have succeeded. We have been spectacularly successful."[15]

Making matters even worse for Florida Democrats was that the installation of new maps occurred at a time when political conditions greatly favored the Republican Party.[16] In the 1990s, the combination of racial redistricting and favorable partisan tides ended Democratic rule. Republicans won a majority of seats in the Florida Senate in 1994 and took control of the Florida House in 1996. Republicans have been the majority party in the Florida U.S. House delegation since 1989, but from the mid-1990s to the present, the GOP's hold on Florida's legislative and congressional districts has never been challenged. With Republicans in control of the 2002 redistricting and another favorable short-term political climate in the wake of the 9/11 tragedy, the Florida GOP made electoral gains across-the-board in U.S. House, state senate, and state house elections (see appendix table A.4).

In the last election prior to the next round of redistricting, Florida Republicans and the GOP in general were riding high in the 2010 midterms thanks to a Republican tsunami that delivered impressive majorities in the U.S. House and in numerous state legislatures previously controlled by Democrats.[17] Yet, in the midst of an election that even President Obama deemed a "shellacking," Florida voters easily met the 60 percent threshold required for approving two constitutional amendments that, whether recognized or not, were designed to curtail Republicans' liberty to further a partisan gerrymander. Thus, with the approval of Amendments 5 and 6, Florida has embarked upon the most recent major change to its redistricting process, a reform whose consequences are the focal point of this book.

Restraining partisan gerrymandering, an unlikelihood based on the lofty standards outlined in the 1986 Supreme Court case *Davis v. Bandemer* and reinforced by the more recent 2004 ruling in *Vieth v. Jubelirer*, came to fruition in Florida because of the successful grassroots lobbying efforts undertaken by the Fair Districts Coalition and their various Democratic-leaning supporters (see appendix table A.1). These reformers managed to secure the requisite number of signatures (see chapter 4) for two constitutional amendments to be placed on the Florida ballot in 2010 that have the potential to institute sweeping changes with respect to how Florida lawmakers design district boundaries.

Among other things, the most striking part of the redistricting reform, which applies in the exact same manner to state legislative (Amendment 5) and congressional districts (Amendment 6), are the restrictions against furthering partisan and incumbent gerrymanders (for the complete language see chapters 2 and 6). Codified in the Florida Constitution under Article III, Sections 20(a) and 21(a) (applicable to congressional and state legislative redistricting, respectively) state that, "No apportionment plan or district shall be drawn with the intent to favor or disfavor a political party or an incumbent." Simply put, this language places unprecedented restrictions on the power of partisan line drawers. Nevertheless, the question remains and it drives the motivation for this study: How did the newly

Table I.1. Comparing median redrawn percentages in 2002 and 2012

Median redrawn voting age population by office and district type

2002 REDISTRICTING	U.S. HOUSE	STATE SENATE	STATE HOUSE
All incumbents	33% (21)	24% (27)	31% (92)
Democrats	34% (7)	25% (9)	39% (35)
Republicans	31% (14)	19% (18)	25% (57)
2012 REDISTRICTING	U.S. HOUSE	STATE SENATE	STATE HOUSE
All incumbents	30% (22)	34% (24)	42% (80)
Democrats	22% (6)	36% (8)	42% (20)
Republicans	37% (16)	34% (16)	42% (60)

Notes: The 2002 data were computed by the author using GIS software to calculate district population overlays before and after redistricting. The 2012 data were made available online at the Florida Senate Redistricting website: http://www.flsenate.gov/session/redistricting/.

enacted restrictions shape the process, politics, and effects of redistricting in 2012?

One straightforward expectation of how the 2012 redistricting would be impacted stems directly from the prohibition on incumbency protection. If a plan (and districts) cannot be constructed in a manner that either favors or disfavors incumbents, then surely we should find that the typical incumbent seeking reelection in 2012 will receive a higher percentage of redrawn constituents—residents they did not represent prior to redistricting—vis-à-vis the redrawn percentages inherited by incumbents in the 2002 redistricting (prior to the Fair Districts reform). In other words, incumbents generally benefit when their district populations remain the same; therefore, substantial changes to district populations are evidence of not favoring incumbents.

Table I.1 displays the median percentage redrawn voting age population (VAP) for incumbents seeking reelection in 2002 and 2012 for the U.S. House, state senate, and state house. The data make it apparent that the 2012 redistricting manifested itself quite differently in legislative races and in terms of the partisan distribution of redrawn constituents. First, the median percentage redrawn VAP jumped 10 points in Florida Senate districts (from 24 percent in 2002 to 34 percent in 2012). In addition, in Florida House districts the median percentage redrawn VAP increased 11 points between 2002 and 2012 (from 31 percent to 42 percent). Second, whereas Democrats in the legislature inherited a higher median percentage redrawn VAP in 2002 (25 percent versus 19 percent in the Florida Senate and 39 percent versus 25 percent in the Florida House), in 2012 the rates by party were equal in the state house (42 percent apiece), and senate Democrats had only a slightly higher median percentage redrawn VAP (36 percent versus 34 percent).

With respect to state legislative races, then it is fair to conclude that incumbents were afforded less protection in 2012 and the distribution of a higher median percentage of redrawn VAP was more equitably dispersed across the two parties.[18] By comparison, the differences between 2002 and 2012 for the U.S. House are curious. First, similar to state legislative districts, in 2002 Democratic incumbents inherited a higher median percentage redrawn VAP (34 percent versus 31 percent)—this pattern seems easy enough to explain as evidence that it was a component of Florida Republicans' furtherance of a partisan gerrymander.

However, unlike state legislative districts, the median percentage redrawn VAP for U.S. House districts actually declined by three points in 2012 (from 33 percent in 2002 to 30 percent in 2012). This fact alone signals a lack of wholehearted compliance with the Fair Districts reform. Finally, it is very interesting that despite an overall reduction in the median percentage redrawn VAP in 2012, with respect to partisan distribution, Republicans inherited significantly more redrawn constituents (37 percent versus 22 percent). Of course, this type of analysis does not address the characteristics of these redrawn populations and thus a greater percentage of redrawn constituents in Republican districts can be partially offset by including a higher portion of registered Republicans in these districts.

Table I.2 shows the list of incumbents who were defeated in the general elections in 2002 and 2012 for the U.S. House, state senate, and state house. In addition, each incumbent's redrawn VAP is included. A quick look at the data makes it clear that most of these defeated incumbents were saddled with a redrawn percentage considerably above the median in 2002 and 2012, respectively. Barring a multivariate analysis, however, the data are admittedly suggestive, but they do reveal an obvious pattern. Prior to the Fair Districts reform, in 2002, when Republicans faced few obstacles to implementing partisan gerrymanders, all four of the vanquished incumbents were Democrats. By contrast, in 2012, with the redistricting reform on the books, seven incumbents lost their general election contests and they were all Republicans. Because of space limitations it is not possible to go into detail on each of these incumbent's unsuccessful reelection bids, but nonetheless in several of these contests redistricting contributed to their defeats.[19]

Table I.2. Redrawn percentages for defeated incumbents in 2002 and 2012

Redrawn voting age population for defeated incumbents

2002 REDISTRICTING	OFFICE	REDRAWN VAP
Karen Thurman (D)	U.S. House	53%
Richard Mitchell (D)	State senate	42%
Perry C. McGriff, Jr. (D)	State house	60%
Sara Romeo (D)	State house	39%
2012 REDISTRICTING	OFFICE	REDRAWN VAP
David Rivera (R)	U.S. House	33%
Allen B. West (R)	State senate	77%
Ellyn Bogdanoff (R)*	State house	51%
Chris Dorworth (R)	State house	61%
Shawn Harrison (R)	State house	38%
Peter Nehr (R)	State house	42%
Scott Plakon (R)	State house	55%

Notes: The 2002 data were computed by the author using GIS software to calculate district population overlays before and after redistricting. The 2012 data were made available online at the Florida Senate Redistricting website: http://www.flsenate.gov/session/redistricting/.
*Ellyn Bogdanoff ran against another incumbent, Democrat Maria Sachs in District 34.

The substantial and equitable partisan distribution of redrawn constituents in the 2012 state house plan goes a long way in explaining why there was little opposition to this redistricting plan. However, this was not the case for the state senate and U.S. House maps, which both became the subject of litigation before and after the 2012 elections (see the maps in appendix D). Indeed, the original Florida Senate plan was declared unconstitutional primarily because of its protection of incumbents and the map that eventually passed before the election has also been challenged in the courts. Democrats and their allies have also pursued litigation to overturn the current congressional boundaries.

In the summer of 2014, in the case of *Romo v. Detzner* the congressional map was struck down even though it was allowed to remain in place for the midterm elections. Districts 5 and 10 were deemed in violation of the provisions outlined in Article III, Section 20 of the Florida Constitution. Thus, a new U.S. House plan will be used for the 2016 elections. And even though the 2012 map was overturned, one thing remains clear, interpreting what constitutes a violation of the Fair Districts reforms is a moving target.

It is pure naiveté to assume that in the face of ambiguous language, Republicans would not proceed to take advantage to the extent possible in crafting redistricting plans that generally benefited their party. In addition, without guidance from the courts it simply is not obvious what does or does not violate the Fair Districts provisions. For instance, since political parties and incumbents cannot be favored or disfavored in the redrawing of district boundaries, might anything short of 50 percent redrawn constituents and evenly balanced party registration (an equal portion of registered Democrats and registered Republicans) amount to an unconstitutional map? Further, given the language protecting against retrogression of majority-minority districts, there seems to be a direct conflict with prohibiting favoritism toward a party or incumbent since these districts often violate both proscriptions. In addition, how should the Florida House and Florida Senate weigh the need to draw compact districts (a concept measured in numerous different ways and Florida possesses anything but a "compact" shape) and preserve so-called "communities of interest"? In short, redistricting reform has ushered in a legal mess that benefits a bevy of lawyers and may end up taking years to sort out.

Despite the legal morass created by partisan maneuvering in the face of new, but unclear redistricting guidelines, elections did take place in redrawn districts in 2012. When the dust finally settled, not a whole lot changed, but Democrats made marginal gains in all three district-based offices. With the results of the 2010 elections as the point of comparison, the Republican percentage of seats in the U.S. House went from 76 percent to 63 percent in 2012 (see appendix table A.4). The GOP majority in the state senate dropped from 70 percent in 2010 to 65 percent in 2012 and the 68 percent Republican state house seats in 2010 was reduced to 62 percent after the 2012 elections.

Perhaps the most remarkable finding with respect to the 2012 Florida redistricting is just how few incumbents faced each other given such considerable alterations to district boundaries. Table I.3 provides data on the universe of Florida incumbents who ran against each other in either a primary or general election in 2012. There were a total of six primaries that included dueling incumbents: two in the Florida House, three in the Florida Senate, and one in the U.S. House. In addition, there were an equal number of Democratic and Republican dueling incumbent primaries (Democrats: one house primary and two senate primaries; Republicans: one house primary, one senate primary, and one U.S. House primary). In the three state senate primaries all of the dueling incumbents were house incumbents seeking to make a jump to the upper chamber. In all of these dueling incumbent primary contests, the winner went on to win the general election. Most

Table I.3. Dueling incumbents in the primaries and general election in 2012

Dueling incumbents	Party	District	2010 district	Vote share	Winner
STATE HOUSE PRIMARIES					
Jose Felix Diaz	Republican	116	House 115	66.0%	Yes
Ana Rivas Logan			House 114	34.0%	No
John Patrick Julien	Democrat	107	House 104	49.9%	No
Barbara A. Watson			House 103	50.1%	Yes
STATE SENATE PRIMARIES					
Mack Bernard	Democrat	27	House 84	49.9%	No
Jeff Clemens			House 89	50.1%	Yes
Jeff Brandes	Republican	22	House 52	56.7%	Yes
Jim Frishe			House 54	43.3%	No
Dwight Bullard	Democrat	39	House 118	35.3%	Yes
Ron Saunders			House 120	30.3%	No
U.S. HOUSE PRIMARY					
Sandy Adams	Republican	7	U.S. House 24	38.8%	No
John Mica			U.S. House 7	61.2%	Yes
STATE SENATE GENERAL					
Ellyn Bogdanoff	Republican	34	Senate 25	47.2%	No
Maria Sachs	Democrat		Senate 30	52.8%	Yes

Notes: The vote share is the percentage each incumbent garnered when facing another incumbent in that particular contest. The last column designates whether the incumbent won the general election and hence every incumbent who managed to beat an opposing incumbent won the general election for that district in 2012. All of the dueling incumbents in the senate primaries were house incumbents in 2010.

notable is that there was only one general election contest where a Democrat and Republican squared off. In the reconfigured senate District 34, Republican senator Ellyn Bogdanoff lost a close race to Democratic senator Maria Sachs. As noted, redistricting proved a detriment to Bogdanoff (see endnote 19) and most likely was a net benefit for those dueling incumbents who retained a greater percentage of their old constituencies vis-à-vis their opponents in the aforementioned six primary contests (see chapters 9 and 10).

Like several other states that got caught up in the term limits craze of the early 1990s, Florida restricts its state legislators to eight consecutive years in office (two four-year terms in the senate and four two-year terms in the house).[20] Term limits create the incentive to institutionalize and routinize the timing of moves from one legislative chamber to the other, with, of course, the most common trajectory being a move from the state house to the state senate. Further, whether a specific legislator is in a term-limited

Table I.4. State legislators running for election in a different chamber in 2012 primaries

FROM THE STATE HOUSE IN 2010 TO STATE SENATE PRIMARY IN 2012

Name	Party	House district 2010	Senate district 2012	Winner in 2012	Vote share 2012
Abruzzo, Joseph	D	85	25	Yes	100.0%
Bernard, Mack	D	84	27	No	49.9%
Brandes, Jeff	R	52	22	Yes	56.7%
Bullard, Dwight	D	118	39	Yes	35.3%
Burgin, Rachel V.	R	56	24	No	40.7%
Clemens, Jeff	D	89	27	Yes	50.0%
Frishe, James C.	R	54	22	No	43.3%
Grimsley, Denise	R	77	21	Yes	100.0%
Hukill, Dorothy	R	28	8	Yes	100.0%
Legg, John	R	46	17	Yes	62.5%
Saunders, Ron	D	120	39	No	30.3%
Soto, Darren	D	49	14	Yes	100.0%
Stargel, Kelli	R	64	15	Yes	63.5%
Thompson, Geraldine	D	39	12	Yes	55.9%
Weinstein, Mike	R	19	4	No	35.8%

FROM THE STATE SENATE IN 2010 TO THE STATE HOUSE PRIMARY IN 2012

Name	Party	Senate district 2010	House district 2012	Winner in 2012	Vote share 2012
Fasano, Mike	R	11	36	Yes	83.1%

Notes: All of the house incumbents chose to run in open-seat senate primaries in 2012, but three of these senate primaries included dueling house incumbents (Brandes vs. Frishe in District 22, Bernard vs. Clemens in District 27, and Bullard vs. Saunders in District 39; see table I.3). House District 36 was open in 2012. Winner in 2012 designates if the candidate won the general election. Vote share 2012 is for the primary contest.

year or not also has to be factored into whether the seat they desire is or is not open because the current officeholder is in their term-limited year. With this complicated decision calculus in mind, not surprisingly, numerous Florida legislators ran for election in a different chamber in 2012. As shown in table I.4, a total of 16 state legislators ran in a different chamber's primary in 2012; 15 house incumbents ran in senate primaries (seven Democrats and eight Republicans) and one Republican senate incumbent (who was in fact term-limited) ran in a house primary.

The strategic behavior of these incumbents is evident in their decisions to run in a different chamber. Beyond the significance of term limits and their direct and indirect influence on these decisions, none of these "chamber switching" legislators took on a sitting incumbent. However, because of the desirability of these seats, as noted previously, some of these house incumbents had to beat a fellow incumbent for the right to compete in the senate general election (senate Districts 22, 27, and 39). Additionally, with the exception of one legislator (Republican John Legg running in senate District 17, which contained none of the constituents he represented in his old house District 46), the remaining 15 legislators all ran in districts that contained a healthy number of the constituents they previously represented in their old districts (Republican senator Mike Fasano ran in house District 36, which wholly contained residents he represented previously in his old senate District 11; see chapter 8). Finally, all of the incumbents who won their primary contest (11 out of 16, 69 percent) went on to win the general election.

Overview of the Book

Jigsaw Puzzle Politics in the Sunshine State is the definitive account of the 2012 Florida redistricting. As such, it examines multiple facets of the redistricting process. To further this objective, the book is divided into three broad sections: (I) process, (II) politics, and (III) effects. The first section fittingly begins with an assessment of reapportionment, a necessary step before congressional districts can be altered. In chapter 1, Jeffrey Ladewig examines congressional reapportionment in historical perspective, beginning with an explanation of the various methods that have been employed since the founding of the Republic. The chapter then turns specifically to reapportionment in Florida. Different reapportionment methods affect the total number of congressional districts granted Florida and this is important because counts are affected by inclusion/exclusion of overseas populations and the relative size of the state, which of course was once one of the smallest in population and is now the fourth largest (2010 Census).

In chapter 2, Aubrey Jewett provides a comprehensive overview of Florida redistricting, particularly concentrating on how the process transpired in 2012 for both state legislative contests and congressional races. Containing a little bit of everything relevant to the ensuing chapters, chapter 2 truly sets the table for all that follows and serves as a primer on the latest round of Florida redistricting. Chapter 3, by Mark McKenzie, examines the legal issues surrounding Florida redistricting, clearly an important focus given the enactment of the Fair Districts amendments. Beyond including a summary of legal requirements for Florida legislative and congressional redistricting, chapter 3 examines judicial decision-making in redistricting cases impacting the Sunshine State. Partisan biases are rarely evident in these judicial rulings, but it is the case that African American judges consistently rule in a manner that safeguards the provisions of the Voting Rights Act as they apply to redistricting.

Part II begins with an assessment of public opinion on Fair Districts Amendments 5 and 6. In chapter 4, Joseph Eagleton and Daniel Smith seek to find if there is notable variation in public support for redistricting reform. Perhaps surprisingly, they generally find a negligible variation in public support for redistricting reform. In other words, Floridians' support for the Fair Districts reforms was far reaching, showing little differences across demographic and partisan groups. Put plainly, the campaign for redistricting reform was incredibly successful, viewed as an almost uniformly popular political issue both by the coalition of supporters lobbying for the change and most media outlets that, whether leaning conservative/liberal or Republican/Democratic, almost uniformly backed the Fair Districts agenda. The only definitive and sizable opposition group was elected Republicans, who obviously knew they stood the most to lose from such reforms.

In chapter 5, Susan MacManus, Joanna Cheshire, Tifini Hill, and Susan Schuler undertake a novel examination of public involvement in the redistricting process in Florida. Although there exist many studies that look at the role of the public in complicated issue areas, MacManus et al. are the first to make such an assessment in the case of redistricting. Whereas the 2002 redistricting was for all intents and purposes a closed process, in 2012, Florida Republicans opened up the process by holding numerous public hearings throughout the state before redrawing the new districts for the state legislature and Congress. Thousands attended these hearings and hundreds of citizens drew their own preferred redistricting plans. Although there was a high level of public skepticism (mainly because lawmakers only wanted feedback and offered no plans of their own), the survey data uncovers Floridians' greatest priorities regarding redistricting, such as district compactness and preserving communities of interest.

It has almost become an accepted truism that geography explains why Florida exhibits a curious disconnect in the level of partisan competitiveness displayed in statewide elections versus district-based contests. Since 1992, the Sunshine State has been the nation's largest and hence most coveted battleground in presidential politics and yet Republicans from the mid-1990s forward, have dominated district-based elections in the U.S.

House and the state legislature. What is the reason for this curious electoral inconsistency? The most common (and accepted) explanation is that Democratic voters are spatially concentrated in dense urban areas with the effect of diluting their influence in districts that by law must contain equal populations. In other words, Republicans benefit from a natural gerrymander in district-based elections because their voters are more equally dispersed across rural, urban, and suburban settings.

This issue is the subject of chapter 6, authored by Micah Altman and Michael McDonald. Let me preface this by issuing a spoiler alert about Altman and McDonald's findings and conclusions. The two scholars examine various congressional redistricting plans (some submitted by the public) and demolish the myth of a spatial gerrymander. Their analysis makes it apparent that Florida congressional districts could be drawn to reflect its present status as a competitive two-party state, but instead, Republican gerrymandering accounts for the marked electoral imbalance favoring the GOP.

Part III starts with an examination of how redistricting conditions candidate emergence. In chapter 7, Cherie Maestas and Travis Braidwood explain that by reallocating voters across reconfigured districts, redistricting creates a great deal of uncertainty among incumbents and aspirants to elective office. In this political milieu, candidate decisions become extremely complex because there is a highly interdependent relationship among those seeking office. For instance, some candidates will only run for political office if incumbents retire, because they see their best hope of winning as tied to an open seat. Likewise, some incumbents will only retire if their district is greatly altered, and others will run in another district as a consequence, or instead run for another office. Thus, certain moves are dependent on prior moves by other people.

Maestas and Braidwood find that strong candidates (those with previous elective experience) are driven by one factor more than any other, whether or not a seat is open, since they rarely contest districts with an incumbent seeking reelection. Finally, the interconnectedness of candidate emergence decisions in the face of redistricting places a heavier burden on non-incumbent candidates, who end up waiting much longer before filing to run (incumbents appear to be the "first movers" in the candidate emergence process).

Chapter 8 examines what if any role redistricting plays in the decision to participate in voting. Danny Hayes, Trey Hood, and Seth McKee look at whether the dislocating effect of redistricting negatively impacts voting.

Based on their previous work illustrating voters drawn into a district with a different incumbent are less likely to be familiar with their new incumbent and leading, in turn, to a greater propensity to abstain from voting for that particular race, Hayes et al. examine voter roll-off in Florida congressional and legislative elections. Confirming their previous findings, which were limited to U.S. House contests, Hayes et al. find that with one exception (Florida House elections), voter roll-off in redrawn Florida precincts is significantly higher than that found in precincts that remained in the same incumbent's district. Finally, the analysis is extended to an examination of contests with chamber switching incumbents. Since all but one of the Florida legislators who ran in a different chamber retained precincts they represented previously in 2010, it was expected that there would not be notable roll-off in these precincts and the results comport with the authors' expectations.

Chapters 9 and 10 analyze the role of redistricting in state legislative and congressional elections, respectively. These chapters nicely complement each other. In chapter 9, Jonathan Winburn presents a detailed examination of the leading factors shaping the partisan outcomes in the 2012 Florida Senate and Florida House elections. Party registration, the percentage of constituents retained after redistricting, and the degree to which districts have been split into other districts all have a notable effect on influencing candidate decisions and the partisan outcomes of Florida's 2012 state legislative elections. Similar to chapter 9, in chapter 10 Charles Bullock provides a detailed account of Florida's congressional elections and how redistricting factored into the win/loss column for Democrats and Republicans. With a smaller number of contests, Bullock is able to offer a rich account of some of the more high profile and just plain nasty fights for the U.S. House (e.g., see his account of the Republican primary battle between Sandy Adams and John Mica in District 7 and the general election contest between Republican Allen West and Democrat Patrick Murphy in District 18).

The book concludes with a brief statement on the significance of redistricting in Florida politics and its more general importance to the functioning of a representative democracy. The effects of redrawing political boundaries are far reaching and often go unobserved, but the ramifications are substantial. This work provides valuable new insight on the redistricting process for scholars of American politics, and perhaps most importantly, to the citizens and leaders of the Sunshine State, because we analyze and reveal numerous political consequences that are sure to impact Floridians for the next decade or even longer.

I

PROCESS

1

Before the Lines Are Drawn

Congressional Apportionment in Florida

JEFFREY W. LADEWIG

Scarce any article, indeed, in the whole Constitution seems to be rendered more worthy of attention, by the weight of character and the apparent force of argument with which it has been assailed.

James Madison, *Federalist Paper*, no. 55

The equitable apportionment of seats in a legislature—whether at the state or national level—is one of the more vexing political endeavors a democracy can undertake. Even in the most well intentioned situations, the equal distribution of indivisible representatives among any kind of geographically bounded districts—be it single-member or anything short of a pure nationwide proportional representation—raises difficult, and maybe even unresolvable, philosophical, mathematical, and political issues. These range from the practical questions of who is counted and how to round fractions to the more normative questions of what does equality and fairness mean.

In the United States, apportionment has been a central focus point for, at least, the first 150 years of the Republic. In fact, the Great Compromise— without which the Constitution most likely would not have passed—is premised on the interstate equality in the U.S. House of Representatives helping to balance the interstate inequality of the U.S. Senate. In this way, a fair apportionment in the U.S. House is meant to influence not just representation within the chamber, but also public policy overall and even presidential elections. Moreover, a fair division of U.S. representatives is at the heart of the intrastate malapportionment revolution spawned by *Baker v. Carr* (1962).

Despite—or maybe because of—the centrality of congressional apportionment in the American constitutional structure, there is little constitutional direction on how it should be conducted. An institutional choice of such importance but with so few guidelines is a situation typically ripe for intense politics. American congressional apportionment is no exception. Furthermore, as with other aspects of congressional structure, its historical development mirrors—sometimes more of a circus mirror—the historical development of the nation. Similarly, as a microcosm of the nation as a whole, the state of Florida offers an enlightening and intriguing case study of congressional apportionment.

Brief Survey of Congressional Apportionment

Apportionment for the U.S. House of Representatives is calculated using three main components: (1) the state populations to be apportioned, (2) the overall number of seats to be apportioned in the chamber, and (3) the apportionment method. The choice of each can have—and has had—a profound effect on the distribution of seats allocated. Given the resulting potential for considerable changes in a state's representation and political power, it is not surprising that each of these components has been extensively debated and revised throughout U.S. history.

Apportionment Populations

During the Constitutional Convention, the Framers were provided with rough estimates of each state's population. Accordingly, in Article 1, Section 2 of the Constitution, each state was then allotted a number of seats in the U.S. House of Representatives that was loosely proportional to these estimates. One of the first tasks mandated by the Constitution, however, was to produce an accurate population count. As such, the U.S. Census was constitutionally empowered. The census's primary function is the "actual enumeration" of the U.S population for the purposes of apportionment.

Although the Constitution required that the apportionment population be calculated on the "respective numbers" of individuals within each state, it is also stained by the original sin of slavery and bigotry. Enslaved persons, otherwise considered property, were counted as three-fifths of a person for the sole purpose of apportionment. This compromise allowed the slave states to maintain the legal order of slavery while still deriving representational benefits from their presence. Non-taxed Native Americans were not counted at all, much less included in the apportionment populations.

These constitutional curtailments to the apportionment population persisted throughout the antebellum period. With the Union victory in the Civil War as well as the ratification of the Thirteenth, Fourteenth, and

Fifteenth Amendments to the Constitution, slavery was ended and all persons, except "non-taxed" Native Americans, were fully included in the apportionment enumerations. The 1860 Census was the first census to even consider that there might be Native Americans other than those "not taxed." Natives Americans "who have renounced tribal rule, and who under state or territory laws exercise the rights of citizens"[1] were considered eligible for enumeration. Few, though, were counted. The average across the states and territories included in the 1860 Census was 1,190 Native Americans. However, the distribution is highly skewed due to a handful of states: for example, 17,798 Native Americans were counted in California; while, most states counted a few dozen to a couple hundred Native Americans.[2] It was not until 1940 that all Native Americans were considered taxed in some way and thus should be included in the census's enumeration.[3]

There have been additional changes and challenges to the apportionment population since 1940. Because of the large number of individuals living abroad in 1970, primarily due to the military and civilian personnel involved in the Vietnam War, the U.S. Congress authorized the inclusion of these overseas individuals and their dependents to be included in their home states' apportionment populations.[4] Without an active war, the overseas population decreased in 1980[5] and was not included in the apportionment enumeration for each state. By 1990, however, there was bipartisan support to re-include these populations; and, they have continued to be included since then.[6] Today, debates persist about the apportionment population. For instance, recent Supreme Court cases have questioned the inclusion of undocumented immigrants in the apportionment population[7] as well as the potential use of statistical measures for a more accurate count.[8]

House Size

Given that the apportionment of the First Congress was set in the Constitution, U.S. House size was also predetermined at 65 seats—but just for this one Congress. Afterward, the Constitution offers only limited guidance on the size of the U.S. House. There are two constitutional restrictions to the size of the House. First, it cannot be smaller than one representative per state. Second, it cannot be larger than a House size that would generate an average district size smaller than 30,000 persons.

For the members of the First Congress considering the first reapportionment, the lower limit was clear: there were 15 states in 1790, thus, 15 congressional districts would be the smallest number of districts possibly created in the House. The upper limit was more controversial. Alexander

Hamilton showed that a House of 120 seats apportioned according to his method would produce a National Ideal District Size (NIDS), which is the sum of the state apportionment populations divided by the chamber size, of 30,133. A House size of 121 would dip the NIDS below the constitutional threshold.

Thomas Jefferson, however, argued that the Constitution did not refer to the NIDS; instead, he argued that each State Ideal District Size (SIDS), which is each specific state's apportionment population divided by its number of assigned U.S. representatives, had to be 30,000 or greater. Hamilton's 120-seat solution did not meet this criterion (see table 1.1, discussed in the next section). Even though the Hamilton apportionment bill passed Congress, President Washington agreed with Jefferson[9] and issued the first veto in American history. As an alternative, Jefferson then proposed an apportionment of 105 seats distributed according to his apportionment method, which kept all of the SIDS larger than 30,000 (see table 1.2, discussed in the next section). Washington signed this bill, and it became the first reapportionment of the House.

The point being, the size of the U.S. House could have consisted of anywhere from 15 members to 105 members—or maybe 120 members. Clearly, the First Congress could have stayed with 65 seats, but the Framers decided to enlarge the chamber. The major reason rests with their theories of representation. Most of them believed that the U.S. House should reasonably increase in size as the U.S. apportionment population increases and that the district sizes should be kept reasonably small. Evidence for this can be found in multiple places.

First, there was considerable debate about apportionment and the district size in the Constitutional Convention.[10] The concerns consisted, primarily, of what district size would best control corruption, allow for reasonable governance within the chamber, and maximize the influence of localities. The delegates at the Convention were considering a minimum population threshold of 40,000. On the last day of the Convention, September 17, 1787, George Washington verbally endorsed—the first time that Washington had spoken on any policy during the entire Convention—a change from a 40,000 threshold to a 30,000 threshold.[11] It passed. Many of these Framers' arguments are reviewed in Federalist Papers, no. 54, no. 55, and no. 56.[12]

Once the Framers were in position to act on these arguments, they followed suit. The best guess at the national apportionment population provided at the Constitutional Convention was 2,568,000. The first census revealed that actual national apportionment population, which included the additional states of Kentucky and Vermont, was 3,615,922. With a larger population, it would require a larger House to maintain more localized representation. Thus, the increase from 65 seats set in the Constitution was enacted.

Similarly, most members of the First Congress believed that periodic increases to the U.S. House size were so important that they passed a constitutional amendment to try to ensure it. The amendment was among the 12 passed by the First Congress, 10 of which later became known as the Bill of Rights. *Article the First*, as it was called, required the size of the House to continue to increase, but at a diminishing rate, along with any increase in the U.S. population. This amendment, along with *Article the Second*, which concerned congressional pay and later become the Twenty-seventh Amendment to the Constitution, was passed by 10 states—one state short of ratification. Although the United States grew much more rapidly than envisioned in the amendment, and as such, it quickly would have provided little additional guidance to a specific House size, the amendment clearly indicated the Framers' belief that the House size should be adjusted in some relation with the apportionment population.

In practice, this largely occurred throughout the nineteenth and early twentieth centuries. During this period, the U.S. apportionment population grew exponentially. By 1910, the U.S. apportionment population was just over 91 million. Accordingly, each decade through the nineteenth century, the size of the chamber changed—with it decreasing only once in 1840. In 1910, the U.S. House was set at 433 seats—with the expectation that New Mexico and Arizona would soon be added to the Union and each given one seat, thereby having a U.S. House with 435 seats. The 1920 Census was the first to show that a majority of Americans lived in urban areas, and the country was becoming increasingly diverse. This was a threat to the traditional political power base—rural white America.[13] Their response was a systematic effort to protect their political power, and in a move similar to the silent gerrymander, no apportionment and no change to the House size were made in 1920. In fact, with the 1930 Census and reapportionment, the size of the House at 435 seats was set in statutory law.[14] As such, the current U.S. House size of 435 seats—in place since 1910—certainly meets the minimum constitutional requirements, but it may not meet the intentions of the Framers of the Constitution.

Apportionment Methods

The history of the apportionment population and U.S. House size are filled with debates, changes, and politics. So too is the history of the apportionment methods. Throughout U.S. history, six apportionment methods have been seriously considered and/or used. Interestingly, they all share an initial basic form.[15]

Each begins by dividing each state's apportionment population by a single Target Ideal District Size (TIDS). The resulting value is the state's quotient[16] and is the exact ideal number of U.S. representatives for each state. This quotient, though, includes a whole number of representatives and, almost always, an additional fraction of a representative. A fractional remainder is generated because any state's—much less every states'—apportionment population is very likely not a precise whole number multiple of the TIDS.

The differences among the apportionment methods are found, then, in the technique that each method uses to translate the fractional remainders of the quotients into positive whole numbers necessary to assign indivisible representatives. For instance, if a state deserves exactly 1.5 representatives, it must receive either one representative or two, but which number should be mandated? Does the size of the state and, thus, the relative increase in representation that an additional seat would offer, influence the political answer to this difficult representation question? Furthermore, for a fixed House size, if one state's apportionment is increased, then another state's must be decreased. For example, if a chamber consists of two states, three seats, and each state has a quotient of 1.5, what is a fair distribution of seats? One state must receive two seats and the other state must receive one seat.

For a fixed House size, this means that the six methods will typically have to employ different TIDSs, and thus, they will typically generate different quotients and different apportionments for the states—even for the same set of state apportionment populations. Either way, no matter the outcome, any apportionment will not be "ideal." All methods are imperfect. In other words, some states will be advantaged (i.e., overrepresented) and others will be disadvantaged (i.e., underrepresented) by a given apportionment method, but different methods will often advantage and disadvantage a different set of states. Herein, contains one of the primary points of contentions among the apportionment methods. Which states will win and which will lose? There has been no apportionment method ever devised that avoids this dilemma. Therefore, the circumstances are ripe for states to engage in a considerable amount of politics as they jockey for an advantage.

To better understand the differences among these six methods, they can be divided into one of two major types. For all of them, though, there are three primary variables to be considered. The two major types are the "ranking methods" and the "rounding methods." In addition, the three variables are the apportionment populations, the chamber size, and the TIDS. In the United States, the apportionment populations are determined prior to any attempted apportionment. Only the ranking methods, however, allow the house size and the TIDS to also be determined before the actual apportionment. The rounding methods are only able *a priori* to set one of these two latter variables—but not both.

For the ranking methods, there is a direct relationship between the size of the chamber and the TIDS. Specifically, the TIDS is set at the known National Ideal District Size (NIDS). As such, the number of legislative seats awarded to a state is directly proportional to the state's apportionment population vis-à-vis the national apportionment population. Because of this unique and desirable quality, the ranking method's quotient is also called a state's quota.[17]

For any given House size and apportionment populations, the quota for each state is always a constant. Balinski and Young argue that this constant value defines a state's "fair share" number of seats.[18] A state's "fair share" apportionment is its quota either rounded down or rounded up. These two values are also called a state's lower share and its upper share, respectively. The "fairness" of any apportionment method is often assessed by whether—or how often—it assigns a state either its lower or upper share, in other words whether—or how often—it "stays within the quota."[19]

The basic form of the ranking methods is that each state's quota is calculated. Then, in the first stage of apportioning, each state is given the whole number of representatives as assigned in the quota. Because the fractional remainders are dropped at this point, the sum of the assigned representatives is usually less than the total number of representatives needed to fill the chamber. Then, the fractional remainders are ranked, and in the second stage, an additional seat is apportioned to the states according to their rank until the chamber is full.

The Hamilton method is the only ranking method that has been seriously considered and/or used in the U.S.[20] Alexander Hamilton devised this method and argued for its use for the first apportionment after the

Table 1.1. Hamilton's method: 1790 apportionment, 120 seats

State	Apportionment population	Quota	1st stage	Fraction remainder	Fractional rank	Final stage	State ideal district size
Connecticut	236,841	7.860	7	0.860	3	8	29,605
Delaware	55,540	1.843	1	0.843	5	2	27,770
Georgia	70,835	2.351	2	0.351	11	2	35,418
Kentucky	68,705	2.280	2	0.280	12	2	34,353
Maryland	278,514	9.243	9	0.243	14	9	30,946
Massachusetts	475,327	15.774	15	0.774	7	16	29,708
New Hampshire	141,822	4.707	4	0.707	9	5	28,364
New Jersey	179,570	5.959	5	0.959	1	6	29,928
New York	331,589	11.004	11	0.004	15	11	30,144
North Carolina	353,523	11.732	11	0.732	8	12	29,460
Pennsylvania	432,879	14.366	14	0.366	10	14	30,920
Rhode Island	68,446	2.271	2	0.271	13	2	34,223
South Carolina	206,236	6.844	6	0.844	4	7	29,462
Vermont	85,533	2.839	2	0.839	6	3	28,511
Virginia	630,560	20.926	20	0.926	2	21	30,027
Total	3,615,920		111			120	
House size	120						
NIDS	30,133						

Source: U.S. Census.

Notes: NIDS = National Ideal District Size; Quota = State Apportionment Population / NIDS.

1790 Census (see table 1.1). This is the apportionment vetoed by President Washington because, in part, some of the SIDS were less than 30,000. In the first stage of apportionment, the quotas are calculated and each state is given the whole number of its quota. Because this would only assign 111 seats of the 120-seat chamber, the fractional remainders are ranked. In the final apportionment stage, the states with the nine largest remainders are given an additional seat.

For the rounding methods, a quotient is generated by one of two ways. The first way is to use the states' given apportionment populations and first fix the House size and then find the TIDS to generate the appropriate House size. The second way is to first fix the TIDS and then allow the

Table 1.2. Jefferson's method: 1790 apportionment, 105 seats

State	Apportionment population	Quotient	Final apportionment	State ideal district size
Connecticut	236,841	7.177	7	33,834
Delaware	55,540	1.683	1	55,540
Georgia	70,835	2.147	2	35,418
Kentucky	68,705	2.082	2	34,353
Maryland	278,514	8.440	8	34,814
Massachusetts	475,327	14.404	14	33,952
New Hampshire	141,822	4.298	4	35,456
New Jersey	179,570	5.442	5	35,914
New York	331,589	10.048	10	33,159
North Carolina	353,523	10.713	10	35,352
Pennsylvania	432,879	13.118	13	33,298
Rhode Island	68,446	2.074	2	34,223
South Carolina	206,236	6.250	6	34,373
Vermont	85,533	2.592	2	42,767
Virginia	630,560	19.108	19	33,187
Totals	3,615,920		105	
House size	105			
NIDS	34,437			
TIDS	33,000			

Source: U.S. Census.
Notes: TIDS = Target Ideal District Size; Quotient = State apportionment population / TIDS; any TIDS between 32,139 and 33,158 would generate a house with 105 seats.

House size to become whatever quantitative outcome is produced by using this second process. Regardless of whether House size or the TIDS is set *a priori*, the TIDS will likely not be the same as the NIDS. Therefore, it is also likely that the rounding methods will not stay within the quota. The difference among the rounding methods is the fractional point at which they round the remainders to the next higher whole number or not.

The Jefferson method, for example, always rounds down the fractional remainders. Thomas Jefferson devised this method and argued for its use for the first apportionment after the 1790 Census (see table 1.2). This is the apportionment signed by President Washington. Specifically, a TIDS was chosen that would produce a 105-seat apportionment once all of the states' quotients are rounded down.[21] All states, in this way, will receive fewer representatives than their quotients suggest. This tends to cause a relatively greater degree of underrepresentation for smaller states.

During the few decades following the 1790 apportionment and the legislative victory by Thomas Jefferson, the Congress continued to be reappor-
tioned according to his method. As the United States grew and expanded
through the rest of the nineteenth and early twentieth century, however,
heated debates continued to erupt over the apportionment method.[22]
For instance, the traditional power bases of the colonial states began to
be awarded relatively fewer representatives, and thus, they had less political power—this was particularly the case for the New England states. The
large-state bias of the Jefferson method exacerbated this effect. As such,
there was deep interest and pressure from these states, in particular, in devising new apportionment methods that would provide them with relatively larger apportionments.

Specifically, three new rounding methods were introduced and seriously considered during the 1830s. They were created and advocated by
John Quincy Adams (W-MA), Daniel Webster (W-MA), and James Dean
(a professor of astronomy and mathematics at the University of Vermont).
Near the turn of the twentieth century, Joseph A. Hill (the chief statistician
of the Division of Revision and Results, Bureau of the Census) introduced
another rounding method.[23] Each of these additional rounding methods
can be calculated similarly as the Jefferson method—but with rounding the remainders at different fractional points. The Jefferson method,
again, never rounds up; the Adams method always rounds up; the Webster
method rounds to the nearest whole number—in other words, at or above
the arithmetic mean of the quotient rounded down and rounded up; the
Dean method rounds up for fractional remainders at or above the harmonic mean; and the Hill method rounds up for fractional remainders at
or above the geometric mean.

Despite the plethora of apportionment methods, none are able to produce an ideal apportionment. They also all have other problems as well.
Specifically, although all of the ranking methods stay within the quota, they
all lack "house monotonicity." This makes ranking methods susceptible to
disturbing paradoxes, such as the Alabama paradox. This occurs when the
house size increases but a state actually loses a seat that it had at the smaller
house size. This and other paradoxes of the ranking methods were discov-
ered in the late nineteenth century and fatally undermined their use.

Alternatively, all of the rounding methods have House monotonicity,
but—to varying degrees—they do not stay within the quota.[24] The Jefferson
and Adams methods tend to more frequently stray from the quota—with
the Jefferson method tending to favor larger states and the Adams method

tending to favor smaller states. The Dean, Hill, and Webster methods tend to stray less frequently, and the Dean and Hill methods have a slight bias in favor of the smaller states. Since the early twentieth century, the rounding methods have been the only apportionment type considered as a viable option.

Even though all of the rounding methods contain some degree of bias, each also minimizes a different measure of malapportionment among the states. There are many ways to measure the inequality that is invariably generated from a system that cannot be perfectly ideal. In addition, there is no clear consensus—legally, mathematically, politically, or philosophically—on what that measurement should be. The measurement that the Supreme Court has tended to emphasize is the maximum deviation between the two most extreme districts sizes as a percent of the ideal district size. This measurement is often minimized, ironically, by one of the more biased (in favor of small states) apportionment methods: the Adams method.[25] Alternatively, the method that tends to be most biased in favor of large states (the Jefferson method) may better fulfill the rationale of the Great Compromise, if the U.S. House is meant to balance the extreme small state bias of the U.S. Senate.[26] The other three rounding methods—the Dean, Webster, and Hill—minimize other measures of malapportionment.[27] Balinski and Young argue that the Webster method is the most unbiased rounding method and the one most likely to stay within the quota.[28]

Throughout the nineteenth and early twentieth centuries, all of these methods had strong advocates and were seriously considered at one point. Each apportionment method can be supported by persuasive reasons for using it, and each method has persuasive reasons that argue against utilizing the method. It may not be surprising, then, that the history of apportionment has been highly political and has generally bounced among these methods. The Jefferson method was used from 1790 through the 1830 apportionment. The Webster method was used in 1840. From 1850 to 1890, a House of Representatives size was chosen so that both the Hamilton and Webster methods agreed. The Webster method was exclusively used again in 1900 and 1910. No apportionment was made in 1920. Both the Webster and the emerging Hill method produced the same result in 1930 for a 435-seat House. Then, in the Apportionment Act of 1941, the Hill method was set in statutory law and is still currently the method being used.[29] As before, politics was likely central to this choice. The Hill method in 1940 would provide an extra seat to Arkansas at the expense of Michigan; the Webster method would provide the opposite. President Roosevelt advocated for the

Hill method and the Democratic majorities in the Congress agreed—perhaps, to get an additional seat in the House from the Democratic Solid South.

The Case of Florida

Florida offers an enlightening case study of congressional apportionment. The apportionment history of Florida exemplifies all three components of the apportionment process as well as their historic dynamics. Florida has been a small state and is now a large state; Florida, at times, has been overrepresented, and at other times, it has been underrepresented; Florida's apportionment population has been significantly affected by both the Three-Fifths Clause as well as the much more recent inclusion of overseas individuals in a state's count; and, Florida would have benefited from some of the apportionment methods, but not others. The remainder of this essay will address each of these points.

Florida: A Small State Grows Up

On February 22, 1819, the United States signed the Adams-Onís Treaty. The treaty ceded Florida from the control of Spain to that of the United States in exchange, primarily, for $5 million and the United States renouncing any claim to Texas.[30] Afterwards, settlers came "pouring in."[31] Yet even though Florida was still not a state in 1830, this census documented 34,730 resident individuals within its borders. Native Americans were not included in the census count. Of these individuals, nearly half (16,345) were African Americans; and of these, only 844 were free, the rest were slaves. Florida was the most populous of the four territories included in this census—Wisconsin was the smallest with just 3,635 individuals. In addition, Delaware had the smallest population of any state in the Union in 1830; but with 76,748 resident individuals, it was more than twice as large as Florida. New York was the largest state with 1,918,608 resident individuals.

The rest of the antebellum censuses document large increases (all about 60 percent) in Florida's resident population, growing to 140,424 individuals in 1860. This growth occurred roughly equally among whites as well as African American slaves. On the eve of the Civil War, Florida's total population had a slight majority of whites (55.4 percent) and a large minority of African American slaves (44.0 percent). In 1860, Florida's African American slave population was relatively small in absolute terms. For example, in 1860, Florida had the fourteenth most slaves out of the 17 states that had

Table 1.3. Florida's populations

Year	Total resident population	White	African American			American Indian, Eskimo, and Aleut	Asian and Pacific Islander	Hispanic origin (of any race)
			Total	Free	Slave			
1830	34,730	18,385	16,345	844	15,501	(NA)	(NA)	(NA)
1840	54,477	27,943	26,534	817	25,717	(NA)	(NA)	(NA)
1850	87,445	47,203	40,242	932	39,310	(NA)	(NA)	(NA)
1860	140,424	77,746	62,677	932	61,745	1	-	(NA)
1870	187,748	96,057	91,689			2	-	(NA)
1880	269,493	142,605	126,690			180	18	(NA)
1890	391,422	224,949	166,180			171	122	(NA)
1900	528,542	297,333	230,730			358	121	(NA)
1910	752,619	443,634	308,669			74	242	(NA)
1920	968,470	638,153	329,487			518	312	(NA)
1930	1,468,211	1,035,390	431,828			587	406	(NA)
1940	1,897,414	1,381,986	514,198			690	540	24,966
1950	2,771,305	2,166,051	603,101			1,011	1,124	(NA)
1960	4,951,560	4,063,881	880,186			2,504	3,699	(NA)
1970	6,789,443	5,719,343	1,041,651			6,677	14,067	(NA)
1980	9,746,324	8,184,513	1,342,688			19,257	56,740	858,158
1990	12,937,926	10,749,285	1,759,534			36,335	154,302	1,574,143
2000	15,982,378	13,132,438	2,468,576			53,541	274,881	2,682,933
2010	18,801,310	14,989,355	3,172,720			71,458	467,107	4,223,806

Source: U.S. Census.

Notes: (-) Not applicable. (NA) Not available. Not all race categories shown. Hispanic origin is not exclusive of the race categories.

Table 1.4. Florida's populations—percentages

Year	Change: Total resident population	White	African American			American Indian, Eskimo, and Aleut	Asian and Pacific Islander	Hispanic origin (of any race)
			Total	Free	Slave			
1830		52.9%	47.1%	2.4%	44.6%			
1840	56.9%	51.3%	48.7%	1.5%	47.2%			
1850	60.5%	54.0%	46.0%	1.1%	45.0%			
1860	60.6%	55.4%	44.6%	0.7%	44.0%	0.0%		
1870	33.7%	51.2%	48.8%			0.0%		
1880	43.5%	52.9%	47.0%			0.1%	0.0%	
1890	45.2%	57.5%	42.5%			0.0%	0.0%	
1900	35.0%	56.3%	43.7%			0.1%	0.0%	
1910	42.4%	58.9%	41.0%			0.0%	0.0%	
1920	28.7%	65.9%	34.0%			0.1%	0.0%	
1930	51.6%	70.5%	29.4%			0.0%	0.0%	
1940	29.2%	72.8%	27.1%			0.0%	0.0%	1.3%
1950	46.1%	78.2%	21.8%			0.0%	0.0%	
1960	78.7%	82.1%	17.8%			0.1%	0.1%	
1970	37.1%	84.2%	15.3%			0.1%	0.2%	
1980	43.6%	84.0%	13.8%			0.2%	0.6%	8.8%
1990	32.7%	83.1%	13.6%			0.3%	1.2%	12.2%
2000	23.5%	82.2%	15.4%			0.3%	1.7%	16.8%
2010	17.6%	79.7%	16.9%			0.4%	2.5%	22.5%

Percent of total resident population

Source: U.S. Census.

Notes: Not all race categories shown. Hispanic origin is not exclusive of the race categories.

any slaves. Yet, Florida had the fifth largest slaves-to-whites ratio at 0.79. The largest in the nation at that time was in South Carolina at 1.38, and it was the first to secede from the Union.

For the rest of the nineteenth century and early twentieth century, Florida's population steadily grew, but slightly more slowly than its antebellum rate. Throughout this period, the white population in Florida grew at a slightly faster rate than the African American population. Nonetheless, African Americans were always more than 40 percent of the entire population for the entire nineteenth century. By 1910, the ratio between the two races was about 3:2 in favor of whites, and the total population stood at 752,619 individuals. In the fifty years since 1910, Florida's population increased over 6.5 times to almost 5 million individuals. This growth was even more predominantly white—as the percent of African Americans in between those censuses fell from about 41 percent to about 18 percent. The decade of the 1950s, in particular, was a period of tremendous growth as the state's population nearly doubled (78.7 percent) from about 2.8 million people to about 5 million.

Not surprisingly, throughout the twentieth century Florida steadily climbed the ranks of the largest states. Throughout these sixty years since 1950, though, the percent of African Americans stayed roughly the same. Meanwhile, it is evident from the recent censuses, which include Hispanic ethnicity as an option, that those who identify themselves as Hispanic has dramatically increased. By 2010, about 22.5 percent of the resident population—regardless of their racial identity—is Hispanic. Moreover, this census shows that Florida had increased it resident population to about 19 million individuals.

Overall, Florida was a relatively small state throughout the nineteenth century with a large percentage of African Americans. Today, Florida looks different. Its percentage of whites has increased considerably to about 80 percent of the total population, but nearly a quarter of Floridians are Hispanic. Florida is also the fourth largest state in the nation—just barely behind New York. Even though the growth in the 2000s was generated by the lowest decennial growth rate in Florida's history, 17.6 percent, it was still nearly double the national rate. In addition, New York had just 520,282 more individuals in 2010 than Florida did, and a growth rate from 2000 of just 2.2 percent. As such, Florida will very likely be the third largest state in the 2020 Census.

Table 1.5. Florida apportionment populations, 1850–2010

Year	National apportionment population	Florida apportionment population	Florida apportionment population percent of national population	Florida population rank	Change in national apportionment population	Change in Florida apportionment population
1790	3,615,823					
1800	4,879,820				35.0%	
1810	6,584,231				34.9%	
1820	8,972,396				36.3%	
1830	11,930,987	28,530			33.0%	
1840	15,908,376	44,190			33.3%	
1850	21,766,691	71,721	0.33%	31st of 31 states	36.8%	
1860	29,550,038	115,726	0.39%	31st of 34 states	35.8%	61.4%
1870	38,115,641	187,748	0.49%	33rd of 37 states	29.0%	62.2%
1880	49,371,340	269,493	0.55%	34th of 38 states	29.5%	43.5%
1890	61,908,906	391,422	0.63%	32nd of 44 states	25.4%	45.2%
1900	74,562,608	528,542	0.71%	32nd of 45 states	20.4%	35.0%
1910	91,603,772	752,619	0.82%	33rd of 46 states	22.9%	42.4%
1920	105,210,729	968,470	0.92%	32nd of 48 states	14.9%	28.7%
1930	122,093,455	1,468,191	1.20%	31st of 48 states	16.0%	51.6%
1940	131,006,184	1,897,414	1.45%	27th of 48 states	7.3%	29.2%
1950	149,895,183	2,771,305	1.85%	20th of 48 states	14.4%	46.1%
1960	178,559,217	4,951,560	2.77%	10th of 50 states	19.1%	78.7%
1970	204,053,025	6,855,702	3.36%	9th of 50 states	14.3%	38.5%
1980	225,867,174	9,739,992	4.31%	7th of 50 states	10.7%	42.1%
1990	249,022,783	13,003,362	5.22%	4th of 50 states	10.3%	33.5%
2000	281,424,177	16,028,890	5.70%	4th of 50 states	13.0%	23.3%
2010	309,183,463	18,900,773	6.11%	4th of 50 states	9.9%	17.9%

Source: U.S. Census.

Notes: The apportionment population for 1830 and 1840 are the values that would have been used if Florida had been a state.

Florida: A Mirror of the Nation

On March 3, 1845, Florida officially entered the Union. It was paired with the non-slave state of Iowa.[32] Of the two states, Florida was smaller with 70,961 resident individuals.[33] Florida was given one seat in the U.S. House of Representatives, which then consisted of 224 total seats. Later that year, Texas was annexed and also added to the Union. Based on its resident population of 212,592 individuals, it was given two seats in the U.S. House.

The first time that Florida was included in the apportionment process as applied to the entire nation was during the 1850 Census. The total population of Florida in 1850 was calculated as 87,445 resident individuals. However, as nearly half of these individuals were African American slaves, the Three-Fifths Clause would prohibit their full inclusion in the apportionment population count. By applying the condition of the clause, Florida's apportionment population in 1850 was 71,721. This ranked Florida as the smallest state among the 31 states in the Union in 1850, and it amounted to just 0.33 percent of the entire apportionment population of the United States.

For the 1850 apportionment and the rest of the nineteenth century, the Hamilton method was the method set by statutory law. For that apportionment, Florida, given its relatively small size, received only one seat. Interestingly, Florida's 1850 quota was just 0.768. As such, it may have been necessary to assign Florida its one district because of the constitutional requirement that all states must have at least one representative. Nevertheless, Florida's fractional remainder happened to rank as the fifth largest; as such, Florida was awarded its one seat through the regular application of the Hamilton method.

It is not surprising, given the above, that Florida was considerably overrepresented in the 1850s. The national apportionment population was 21,766,691 and the chamber was set at 234 seats; as such, the NIDS was 93,020. Florida's SIDS is easily calculated to be 71,121. Thus, Florida was overrepresented by 21,299, which is 29.7 percent of the NIDS. Even though this deviation percentage is large and represents considerable interstate malapportionment, it is not unusual even by modern comparisons.[34] However, with only one member, there were no issues of intrastate malapportionment, like those found before the redistricting revolution of the 1960s.

Saying that these later nineteenth century apportionments had "a method" is, however, a bit of a stretch. The final apportionments for 1850, 1860, and 1870 do not match any apportionment method. The Hamilton

Table 1.6. Florida actual apportionments, 1850–2010

Year	House size at apportionment	Florida apportionment	National ideal district size (NIDS)	Florida ideal district size (SIDS)	Over-/underrepresented	Over-/underrepresented percent of NIDS
1790	105		34,436			
1800	141		34,609			
1810	181		36,377			
1820	213		42,124			
1830	240		49,712			
1840	223		71,338			
1850	234	1	93,020	71,721	21,299	29.70%
1860	241	1	122,614	115,726	6,888	5.95%
1870	292	2	130,533	93,874	36,659	19.53%
1880	325	2	151,912	134,747	17,165	6.37%
1890	356	2	173,901	195,711	-21,810	-5.57%
1900	386	3	193,167	176,181	16,987	3.21%
1910	433	4	211,556	188,155	23,401	3.11%
1920	435	4	241,864	242,118	-254	-0.03%
1930	435	5	280,675	293,638	-12,964	-0.88%
1940	435	6	301,164	316,236	-15,072	-0.79%
1950	435	8	344,587	346,413	-1,826	-0.07%
1960	435	12	410,481	412,630	-2,149	-0.04%
1970	435	15	469,087	457,047	12,041	0.18%
1980	435	19	519,235	512,631	6,604	0.07%
1990	435	23	572,466	565,364	7,103	0.05%
2000	435	25	646,952	641,156	5,797	0.04%
2010	435	27	710,767	700,029	10,738	0.06%

Source: U.S. Census.

Notes: Over- and underrepresented = NIDS—SIDS. Positive values indicate overrepresented; Negative values indicate underrepresented.

and Webster methods were used to establish a baseline, but then a few states were given additional seats. In 1850, for instance, the House size was set to 233 seats and the methods were applied to all of the states' apportionment populations. After the initial apportionment, however, California was given an extra seat—its second, despite a quota of just 0.991—because of the anticipated population increases that were beginning with the Gold Rush of 1849.

Florida also benefited—somewhat notoriously—from the practice of giving additional seats after the initial apportionment. In 1870, Florida had a quota of 1.394 and was initially awarded one seat. However, its apportionment was later boosted to two seats in a nine-seat giveaway. If the initial apportionment was left alone or if the Hamilton or the Webster method was applied to the final chamber size of 292 seats, Samuel J. Tilden would have won the presidency in 1876—even with the disputed ballots counted as they were.[35]

Similar to Florida's nineteenth century growth in total population, its apportionment population also increased over the decades—just much more gradually. Even though Florida's apportionment population grew at almost twice the rate of the nation as a whole, its number of representatives was still only two in the 1890 apportionment. Throughout this period, Florida was never as overrepresented as it was in 1850. After the 1870 Census, Florida was overrepresented by 19.53 percent of the NIDS, but after the 1890 Census, it was underrepresented by 5.57 percent of the NIDS.

These types of variations in interstate malapportionment were and are not uncommon. But, they are particularly prevalent when the NIDS was smaller and among small states that have fewer districts over which to distribute their number of individuals that they are either over- or underrepresented. Specifically, the smaller the NIDS, the larger percentage a constant deviation would be. In addition, smaller states tend to gain or lose by a relatively greater percent. For example, a state with a quota of 1.5 that is rounded down will lose 50 percent of its fair share number of representatives; whereas a state with a quota of 20.5 that is rounded down will lose only 2.5 percent of its fair share.

This is further evident by comparing, for example, Florida's apportionment statistics in 1860 and 1980. In 1860, Florida was overrepresented by 6,888 individuals. This entire amount applied to the sole district that Florida had, and it was 5.95 percent of the NIDS. In 1980, Florida was in a similar position when it was overrepresented by 6,604 individuals. This latter

Table 1.7. Florida overseas apportionment population, 1970–2010

Year	National apportionment population	Florida apportionment population	National overseas population	Florida overseas population
1970	204,053,025	6,855,702	1,737,836	66,259
1980	225,867,174	9,739,992	995,546	—
1990	249,022,783	13,003,362	922,819	65,436
2000	281,424,177	16,028,890	576,367	46,512
2010	309,183,463	18,900,773	1,042,523	99,463

Year	National overseas population percent	Florida overseas population percent	Percent of national apportionment population from Florida	Percent of national overseas population from Florida
1970	0.85%	0.97%	3.36%	3.81%
1980	0.44%	—	4.31%	—
1990	0.37%	0.50%	5.22%	7.09%
2000	0.20%	0.29%	5.70%	8.07%
2010	0.34%	0.53%	6.11%	9.54%

Source: U.S. Census.

deviation, though, was distributed equally among Florida's 19 districts, and it was only 0.05 percent of the much larger NIDS.

Despite the greatly increasing NIDS over the twentieth century—which is in no small part due to the U.S. House being frozen at 435 seats since 1910, Florida's tremendous growth in its apportionment population has provided it with a similarly tremendous growth in the number of seats apportioned to it. Since the 1950s apportionment, each decade Florida has gained at least two—and as many as four—seats in the U.S. House. Currently, Florida has 27 members in its U.S. House delegation, the same number as the state of New York.

These recent apportionments, as briefly mentioned above, are based on another change in how the apportionment population is calculated. All of the state apportionment populations since 1970, except in 1980, include overseas individuals—primarily those associated with the military—in their home state's count (see table 1.7).

In 1970, for instance, there were more than 1.7 million individuals counted in the overseas population, or about 0.85 percent of the national apportionment population. In that year, Florida had 66,259 individuals living abroad, which was 0.97 percent of its apportionment population. Over the decades since its re-inclusion, the percent of the nation's overseas population has consistently been less than Florida's. In addition, by 2010, almost 10 percent of the national overseas population was from Florida. In other words, each time that the overseas population had been included in the apportionment population, Florida's apportionment population increased more relative to the whole nation's apportionment population. As such, the inclusion of these individuals has been relatively beneficial to Florida's apportionment.

Florida: Apportionments that Could Have Been

Florida also offers an informative case study of the variations produced by the different apportionment methods. Using the final apportionment House sizes as well as the state apportionment populations from each census, the apportionments for each of the six methods that were seriously considered and/or used throughout U.S. history can be generated. Table 1.8 provides these values for Florida.

For the Hamilton method, the NIDS was used as the TIDS. However, because the rounding methods do not allow for the TIDS to be *a priori* determined—that is, if the House size is *a priori* determined as it is here, the TIDS had to be found through a process of trial and error. In addition, a range of TIDSs will produce the identical apportionment distribution among the states. As such, the quotients can change slightly without changing the distribution. Because of this, only the quotas are displayed—as well as because of the quotas' ability to project a state's fair share. All of the grayed cells indicate the apportionment method(s) that was actually used for that decade's reapportionment. Moreover, the rounding methods are aligned by the degree to which they tend to advantage large states—beginning with the Jefferson method.

For the smallest states, like Florida in 1850 with a SIDS smaller than the NIDS, all of the apportionment methods are likely to provide the same apportionment—a single seat. In fact, it is not until the 1870s apportionment that any of the methods begin to assign Florida a second seat. The three methods that tend to advantage small states the most (i.e., Adams, Dean, and then Hill methods, respectively) each did so. As Florida continued to

Table 1.8. Florida possible apportionments, 1850–2010

Year	Apportionment population	Actual number of members of Congress	Quota	Hamilton	Jefferson	Webster	Hill	Dean	Adams
1850	71,721	1	0.771	1	1	1	1	1	1
1860	115,726	1	0.944	1	1	1	1	1	1
1870	187,748	2[a]	1.438	1	1	1	2	2	2
1880	269,493	2	1.774	2	1	2	2	2	2
1890	391,422	2	2.251	2	2	2	2	2	3
1900	528,542	3	2.736	3	2	3	3	3	3
1910	752,619	4	3.578	4	3	4	4	4	4
1920	968,470	4[b]	3.989	4	4	4	4	4	4
1930	1,468,191	5	5.231	5	5	5	5	5	5
1940	1,897,414	6	6.300	6	6	6	6	6	6
1950	2,771,305	8	8.042	8	8	8	8	8	8
1960	4,951,560	12	12.063	12	12	12	12	12	12
1970	6,855,702	15	14.615	15	15	15	15	15	14
1980	9,739,992	19	18.758	19	19	19	19	19	18
1990	13,003,362	23	22.715	23	23	23	23	23	22
2000	16,028,890	25	24.776	25	26	25	25	25	24
2010	18,900,773	27	26.592	27	27	27	27	27	26

Source: U.S. Census.

Notes:

Gray cells indicate the method employed for census. During 1870, 1880, and 1890, U.S. House size was chosen so that the Hamilton and Webster methods would provide the same values.

a. Florida was initially apportioned a single seat. It was given a second seat retroactively.

b. With no apportionment following the 1920 Census, all states maintained their 1910 apportionment values.

Hamilton method: ranks all fractional remainders of the quotas.

Jefferson method: rounds down all fractional remainders of the quotients.

Adams method: rounds up all fractional remainders of the quotients.

Webster method: rounds all fractional remainders of the quotients on the arithmetic mean.

Dean method: rounds all fractional remainders of the quotients on the harmonic mean.

Hill method: rounds all fractional remainders of the quo-

gain population—both in absolute and relative terms—all of the methods except the Jefferson method would assign Florida two seats in 1880. It was not until the 1890 apportionment that all methods once again agreed and would have awarded Florida two seats.

As Florida quickly moved up the ranks of the most populous states throughout the twentieth century, it continued to be advantaged in its apportionment figures by the different biases of the evolving apportionment methods. Specifically, Florida achieved an apportionment advantage in its early state history under methods which favored smaller states, like Adams's, and was able to maintain its relative apportionment strength vis-à-vis other states once it became a relatively larger state because apportionment methods that favored larger states, like Jefferson's method, were employed by the federal government. In fact, in the 2000 apportionment, the Jefferson method would have advantaged Florida so much that it would not have stayed within the quota. In 2000, Florida's quota was 24.776, and the Jefferson method would have assigned Florida 26 seats. For the current apportionment based on the 2010 Census, all six methods would have stayed within the quota. In addition, all of the methods agreed in awarding Florida with 27 seats, except the Adams method that would have awarded 26 seats.

Conclusion

Florida has a rich history. When it first entered the Union, it was a small fledgling state and almost half of its population was slaves. After the Civil War, Florida rapidly grew. While doing so, the portion of African Americans began to dip, and recently, there is evidence that the Hispanic population is rapidly increasing. This population history is mirrored in the state's apportionment history. Florida was once a single-member state advantaged by the apportionment methods that are more biased in favor of the small states. Today, Florida is one of the largest states and therefore is advantaged by the methods that are more biased in favor of the large states. Furthermore, as the country tried to overcome its original sin of slavery and rise to a global superpower so too did the apportionment population similarly change. Florida's apportionment population was once reduced by the Three-Fifths Clause, whereas today it is currently enlarged because of the inclusion of overseas personnel associated with the military.

It seems appropriate that the development of the United States' most representative institution, the U.S. House, corresponds with many of the most important developments in the country. Moreover, Florida, in many ways, exemplifies many of these dynamics. The rich history of apportionment is mirrored in the rich history of Florida.

2

New Rules for an Old Florida Game

The 2012 Legislative and Congressional Redistricting Process

AUBREY JEWETT

The 2012 redistricting process in Florida can be viewed as a serious game with control of the Florida Legislature and potentially the United States Congress at stake over the next decade. This chapter reviews the history of Florida reapportionment and redistricting, looks at the changing playing field and rules (especially the Fair Districts Amendments), analyzes the goals, strategies and decisions of the major players (especially the Republican majority), and evaluates the outcomes of the new legislative and congressional redistricting process in the Sunshine State.

An Overview of the Game: The Playing Field, Rules, Players and Outcome

The playing field for the redistricting game in Florida changed as it has every ten years between redistricting cycles. Population continued to grow to almost 19 million people (with especially heavy growth in Central and Southwest Florida) and resulted in Florida gaining two new congressional seats. Florida continued to become more diverse as Hispanics grew to 22.5 percent of Florida's population and blacks to 16.0 percent. Hispanics continued their growth in South Florida where Cubans have long dominated politically, but also grew rapidly in Central Florida where Puerto Ricans are the largest subgroup.

The biggest change in the 2012 redistricting game was the adoption of new standards seeking to establish guidelines for the redistricting process. The Fair Districts Amendments were proposed through the initiative petition process and approved by Florida voters in a November 2010 referendum. The amendments (one for legislative and one for congressional redistricting) prohibit the drawing of new district lines with the intent of favoring or disfavoring political parties or incumbents or with the intent or result of diminishing minority representation and require districts to be compact and follow existing geographic and political boundaries where feasible. In addition, previously established rules concerning equal apportionment (one person, one vote) and minority access (the Voting Rights Act and numerous U.S. Supreme Court decisions) were still in effect.

The major players in the process were Republicans, Democrats, and good government groups (collectively, the combatants) and the Florida courts and U.S. Justice Department (collectively, the referees). Here is a quick rundown of their goals and strategy.

- Republicans—The GOP controlled the Florida redistricting process for the first time in 2000–2002 and did so again in 2010–2012. However, unlike 2002 when the GOP could gerrymander overtly (and successfully) to help favored incumbents and especially the Republican Party, in 2012 they would be restrained by the new requirements in the Fair Districts Amendments. Their overall strategy was to comply with the letter of the law while still crafting maps that would give them a partisan advantage. In brief, they packed black minority districts with large numbers of Democrats, which left surrounding districts more white and Republican.
- Democrats—Since Democrats were in the minority they had little input or impact in the drawing of the new districts. Their overall strategy was to change the rules of the process by supporting Fair Districts and then seek to enforce the new rules through the courts. Their goal was to increase the number of districts where Democrats could be competitive and ultimately to take back control of the legislature.
- Good Government Groups—There were several, but the Florida League of Women Voters was the most visible, vocal, and effective. They supported the adoption of the Fair Districts Amendments, put pressure on the GOP to abide by the new standards, and used the courts to try and force changes in the newly drawn districts. Their goal was to have districts drawn that more fairly represented Floridians in the state legislature and in the congressional delegation.
- Referees—The Florida Second District Court, Florida Supreme Court, and the Justice Department sought to make sure that the rules were followed. The Justice Department had to review the new districts for compliance with the Voting Rights Act and give preclearance before

the new maps could be used. The Florida Supreme Court had mandatory review of the new legislative maps and the Florida Second District Court reviewed the new congressional map when a lawsuit was filed. Their goal was to ensure compliance with existing and new laws concerning redistricting.

Ultimately, the Justice Department and Florida courts approved the maps that were drawn by Republican legislators, and candidates ran in those new districts for the 2012 election. However, the Florida Supreme Court did require substantial changes to the originally drawn senate map and lawsuits continue over the senate and congressional plans. Overall, the new process worked fairly well compared to previous redistricting efforts in Florida and compared to other states where partisan legislatures draw the lines. The new legislative and congressional districts were more compact, kept more counties and cities whole, protected minority voting rights, and did not favor or disfavor incumbents (although there were some signs of incumbency protection in the senate). However, Republicans were able to maintain an overall partisan advantage in the new districts and keep firm control of the legislature and congressional delegation despite the Democratic edge in statewide registration of more than 4 percent (or more than 500,000 registered voters).

The History of the Game: Previous Reapportionment and Redistricting

Previous to 1962, the Florida Legislature was malapportioned—that is there were unequal numbers of people in each district.[1] Each county got at least one seat in the Florida House regardless of population size. Because of Florida's rapid but unequally distributed population growth, this allowed just 18 percent of Florida's population to elect a majority to the state legislature.[2] Malapportionment reinforced almost total Democratic control of the legislature (there was frequently zero or only one Republican member), and it gave the Panhandle legislators, called "pork choppers," enormous power to bring money and programs to rural communities at the expense of the growing urban and suburban areas.[3] Many attempts were made and many special sessions held in the 1950s and early 1960s to reapportion Florida's electoral districts fairly, but the pork choppers in the legislature were able to defeat every meaningful reform.

The U.S. Supreme Court decision in *Baker v. Carr* (1962), and the subsequent decisions mandating one-person, one-vote in legislative and congressional districting,[4] had a profound effect on the Florida Legislature.[5] Reapportionment broke the grip of the rural North Florida pork choppers and redistributed legislative power to Central and South Florida.[6] It allowed African Americans to win state legislative office for the first time since Reconstruction. It brought a new generation of urban Democratic legislators to Tallahassee like Bob Graham who later served as governor. Reapportionment also dramatically increased Republican representation in the Florida House from less than ten members to thirty-nine members in the special election in 1967 that instituted fair reapportionment in Florida under the direction of a federal court[7]—and in the subsequent decades, it helped translate growing Republican strength in Florida's urban and suburban areas into more Republican legislative[8] and congressional seats.

In 1972, the issue of multimember districts caused the most contention during redistricting.[9] Florida gained three congressional seats through reapportionment (bringing it to 15), but while each congressional district held just one member, Florida House and Senate districts in more urban areas often held more than one. Republicans, Cuban Americans, and blacks fought for single-member districts because it is difficult for minority groups to elect minority legislators in multimember districts. However, the districting plan approved by the Democratically controlled legislature included five six-member, five five-member, and twenty-one single-member districts in the Florida House and seven three-member, seven two-member and five single-member districts in the Florida Senate. The Florida Supreme Court upheld the use of multimember districts despite some reservations and attempts to change the Florida Constitution also failed.

Finally, however, the adoption of single-member districts in the 1982 redistricting helped create a more representative legislative body whose membership more closely mirrored the diverse demographics of the state. With Democrats again firmly in control of the process, Republicans actually lost seats in the 1982 election but then began gaining ground in subsequent elections. However, blacks and Hispanics both gained a number of legislative seats in 1982 as single-member districts allowed the creation of districts with larger and more concentrated populations of minority groups. However, there were still no minorities in the congressional delegation (which grew by 4 more seats in 1982 bringing the delegation to 19 members) until Hispanic Republican Ileana Ros-Lehtinen won a special election in a South Florida district (FL-18) in 1989. Subsequently, in the

1990 midterm elections, Republicans won a majority of the congressional delegation seats (10–9) for the first time in Florida since Reconstruction.

Increased political competition in the state and the lack of minorities in the congressional delegation made redistricting a "full contact sport" in 1992 as members fought over how to create the majority-minority districts required by the 1986 U.S. Supreme Court ruling in *Thornburg v. Gingles*.[10] The legal skirmishing began when Dade County Republican representative Miguel DeGrandy filed suit in federal court asking the court to draw both legislative and congressional districts to ensure that minority voters, including Hispanics, were given maximum opportunities to elect representatives. Republicans were interested not only in creating Republican-leaning, heavily Cuban American districts in Miami-Dade County, but also in "packing" Democratic African American voters into urban districts in order to give Republican candidates a better opportunity to win in surrounding suburban districts. Black legislators and groups joined forces with Republicans and Hispanics to increase the number of majority black districts. Despite the disagreements, lawmakers succeeded in adopting a joint resolution creating the house and senate districts, and the Florida Supreme Court declared these plans constitutional.

However, the U.S. Justice Department objected to the senate redistricting plan. The legislature was unable to agree on how to fix the problem and so the Florida Supreme Court redrew it, creating an additional majority black district in the Tampa-St. Petersburg area. This senate plan and the house plan created by the legislature were reviewed by a three-judge panel from the federal district court in the *DeGrandy* case that had been combined with lawsuits filed by the NAACP and others. The federal judges approved the plan drawn for the senate but redrew the house boundaries in 31 districts and created five more favorable Hispanic (and thus Republican) districts in South Florida. But the state appealed that decision and ultimately the U.S. Supreme Court overturned the lower court and reinstated the house plan approved by the state legislature and the senate plan drawn by the Florida Supreme Court.[11] In the end, the house plan included 13 districts with majority black populations and nine with majority Hispanic populations and the senate plan included three districts with majority African American populations and three with majority Latino populations.[12] The creation of these minority access districts helped Republicans take control of the Florida Senate in 1994 and the Florida House in 1996.

The political infighting in the 1992 legislature over congressional redistricting created total gridlock despite the Democratic majority in both the house and senate and control of the governor's office. The federal district court was obliged to draw the state's congressional district map after the legislature failed to approve a map. It did so by creating three heavily African American districts, subsequently won by black Democrats, and two heavily Hispanic districts, subsequently won by Cuban American Republicans. Overall, Florida gained four more congressional seats after the 1990 Census and Republicans picked up three of these new seats for a total of 13 out of 23 seats in the delegation. Florida was a key component of the nationwide Republican victory in the 1994 congressional elections when, for the first time in forty years, Republicans captured control of the U.S. House of Representatives. The GOP won fifteen seats in Florida in 1994 in part due to the racial gerrymandering that created the districts in 1992. In 1996, a three-judge federal panel ruled that Florida's U.S. House District 3 (extending over 250 miles from Jacksonville to both Orlando and Gainesville in order to create an African American majority) was unconstitutional based on the U.S. Supreme Court decisions in *Shaw v. Reno* in 1993 and *Miller v. Johnson* in 1995.[13] The legislature responded by redrawing congressional districts in Northeast Florida in time for the 1996 election. Despite a drop in black voters from 50 percent to 41 percent, African American Corrine Brown won reelection in District 3 by relying heavily on the advantages of incumbency.

Florida redistricting in 2002 brought a new twist: complete Republican control of the process due to strong GOP majorities in both the Florida House and Senate and GOP control of the governor's office and cabinet. Democrats had controlled all previous redistricting since shortly after the Civil War Reconstruction era. The GOP-controlled redistricting in Florida in 2002 was based on three guidelines: the constitutional obligation to create districts of relatively equal size based on Florida's 2000 population of 16 million; the civil rights law prohibiting dilution of black and Latino voting strength; and the desire to create as many Republican leaning districts as possible by packing Democrats together in relatively few districts. With the aid of sophisticated software, Republicans were able to bring partisan gerrymandering to new heights (or new depths depending on one's point of view).

Florida gained two more U.S. House seats after the 2000 Census and the congressional redistricting plan created one new Republican district in East Central Florida for House Speaker Tom Feeney and one new Republican Cuban district in South Florida for State Senator Mario Diaz-Balart,

Table 2.1. Florida district statistics, 2002

	Congress (25 seats)	State house (120 seats)	State senate (40 seats)
Target population	639,295	133,186	399,559
Range	0%	2.79%	.03%
Black majority	3	13	3
Hispanic majority	3	11	3
Republican majority	2	18	5
Republican plurality	13	47	15
Democratic majority	7	38	13
Democratic plurality	3	17	7

Notes: Compiled by the author from data found at http://www.flsenate.gov/senateredistricting/.

chair of the committee in charge of congressional redistricting. The plan also greatly altered Democratic congresswoman Karen Thurman's district that ran from Gainesville to the Tampa area from moderately Democratic to slightly Republican for State Senator Ginny Brown-Waite. Republicans won all three of these seats, kept the 15 seats they already had, and took a commanding 18 to 7 majority of the Florida congressional delegation. Table 2.1 displays Republican effectiveness in achieving their goals. At the congressional level, three black and three Hispanic majority districts were drawn. Based on party registration, two districts had a Republican majority and 13 had a Republican plurality while seven districts had a Democratic majority and three had a Democratic plurality.

Legislative redistricting followed the same strategy as congressional redistricting and produced similar results. Minority districts were created for black Democrats, and white Democrats were packed into relatively few districts to leave surrounding districts leaning Republican. In South Florida, minority districts were also created for Cuban Republicans. The end result: in a state where Democratic registration actually outpaced Republican registration by 3.5 percentage points, Republicans took an 81–39 seat lead in the Florida House and a 26–14 lead in the Florida Senate.

While the Department of Justice (DOJ) reviewed all of the 2002 redistricting plans, and several interested parties filed lawsuits in state and federal court, in the end, only a small change to three state legislative districts in South Florida was required. However, the process did drag on until July 2002, less than two weeks before the qualifying deadline for candidates to file papers to run for office. The DOJ objected to a reduction in the number of Hispanics in a Collier County-based house district. House Speaker Tom Feeney took the unusual step of redrawing the map himself rather than calling a special session to try and get the new Florida House map approved without delaying the election timeline. A federal district court three-judge panel accepted the proposed "Speaker's fix" mandating that the legislature adopt the revised map permanently shortly after the 2002 elections and resubmit the plans for final verification (the state senate and congressional district maps had been approved by the DOJ and the panel of federal judges about two weeks earlier).[14] While the last minute alterations and unusual process added drama to the 2002 redistricting cycle, the relatively few changes required were a drastically different result from 1992, when multiple changes were required by the Justice Department, Florida Supreme Court, and various federal courts.

The Rules of the Game: New Constitutional Standards, Federal Requirements, and the Formal Legislative Process

Democrats, some independents, and even a handful of Republicans complained bitterly about the overt partisan and incumbent gerrymandering that occurred in 2002.[15] However, both Florida and federal courts had long held that political gerrymandering might be unfair, but it is constitutional. Thus, a coalition of good government and Democratic affiliated groups began an effort to change Florida's constitution through initiative petition and statewide referendum to make the redistricting process "more fair." The Committee for Fair Elections first tried to take redistricting out of the hands of the Florida Legislature altogether. The Fair Districts group circulated a petition calling for an amendment to the Florida Constitution that would have turned the responsibility over to an independent redistricting commission, similar to the process in place in some other states. The proposal almost made the 2006 ballot, but it was rejected by the Florida Supreme Court because it did not comply with the constitutional requirement of a single-subject and the ballot summary was misleading.[16]

Somewhat reluctantly, the group abandoned the idea of the independent commission, went back to the drawing board, and crafted two new amendments focused more on setting clear standards than on who would do the drawing. These were referred to as the "Fair Districts" amendments, and both initiatives obtained the necessary number of signatures, cleared Florida Supreme Court review, and then were handily approved by the voters (each got 63 percent "yes" votes) in November 2010. A lawsuit was immediately filed by U.S. representatives Corrine Brown and Mario Diaz-Balart (and later joined by the Florida House under the direction of Republican Speaker Dean Cannon) to block the congressional amendment, arguing it was improperly enacted by voters instead of lawmakers and intruded upon the power of Congress to regulate elections and the legislature's constitutionally delegated power to draw congressional lines. However, a federal judge and federal appeals court panel rejected these challenges and upheld the new standards.[17]

One amendment sets the standards for drawing the congressional districts, the other for creating the state legislative districts (senate and house) although the standards for both are identical. (Two separate amendments were needed to comply with Florida's single subject rule for initiatives proposing changes to the Florida Constitution.) The specific Florida Constitutional standards[18] for drawing congressional redistricting boundaries include:

(a) No apportionment plan or individual district shall be drawn with the intent to favor or disfavor a political party or an incumbent; and districts shall not be drawn with the intent or result of denying or abridging the equal opportunity of racial or language minorities to participate in the political process or to diminish their ability to elect representatives of their choice; and districts shall consist of contiguous territory.

(b) Unless compliance with the standards in this subsection conflicts with the standards in subsection (a) or with federal law, districts shall be as nearly equal in population as is practicable; districts shall be compact; and districts shall, where feasible, utilize existing political and geographical boundaries.

(c) The order in which the standards within subsections (a) and (b) of this section are set forth shall not be read to establish any priority of one standard over the other within that subsection.

The standards listed in (a) are often referred to as Tier 1 standards, while the standards listed in (b) are often referred to as Tier 2 standards.

In addition to these new state standards, Florida must follow federal law as well when crafting its districts. So for instance, as mentioned earlier, under the *Baker v. Carr* ruling, voting districts must be of equal population size to comply with the one person, one vote standard. The federal Voting Rights Act (VRA) also lays out quite explicit rules that state and local governments must adhere to when engaging in redistricting to protect the voting power of minorities. Section 2 and Sections 4 and 5 of the VRA have been especially important tools in protecting the voting rights of racial, ethnic, and language minorities in Florida.[19]

Section 2 of the VRA applies to all states and localities and helps to ensure that minority voters have an equal opportunity to influence the political process and elect representatives of their choice. Section 4 of the VRA was overturned in 2013 by the U.S Supreme Court in *Shelby County v. Holder*, and had the effect of nullifying Section 5 as well, although both sections did apply to the 2010–2012 redistricting cycle.[20] Section 5 applied only to covered jurisdictions with a history of discrimination and required those areas to seek preclearance from the Justice Department or federal courts before adopting any electoral changes that might affect minority representation including redistricting plans. Section 4 of the VRA established the formula for determining which jurisdictions would be required to seek preclearance under Section 5 based on old data from 1975 that was the legal foundation for the Supreme Court decision. In Florida, the Section 4 formula identified five counties that would need Section 5 preclearance because of past discrimination against Hispanics: Collier, Hardee, Hendry, Hillsborough, and Monroe. Nevertheless, because redistricting plans in one part of the state affect the districts in other parts of the state, preclearance was required for the entire legislative and congressional redistricting plans.

In summary, under the VRA, Florida cannot adopt any practice or procedure that would deprive minorities of an effective vote, cannot dilute minority votes, cannot adopt a plan that makes minorities worse off than they were under existing plans (called retrogression), and until 2013, had to seek approval (preclearance) for new redistricting maps from the Department of Justice or the federal court in Washington, D.C. before the new maps could go into effect. Civil rights advocates have called for Congress to update the formula for Section 4 that would fix the problems identified by the U.S. Supreme Court, but unless legislation is passed, Section 5 preclearance will not be required in future redistricting battles for any jurisdiction.

Since the Fair Districts Amendments are election laws that affect minority voting rights, they also had to receive preclearance from the Department of Justice after they were passed by Florida voters. Outgoing governor Charlie Crist submitted the request for preclearance after the 2010 election. However, incoming Republican governor Rick Scott pulled the request a few days after taking office, leading to Democratic charges of obstruction and a lawsuit that sought to force the governor to put the request back to the Justice Department.[21] Eventually on March 29, 2011, the legislature itself formally submitted the amendments for preclearance. In the submission, the legislature warned that the amendments were potentially regressive, and thus supported the preclearance of the new standards only under the proviso of not constraining the legislature's ability to craft minority districts under the VRA:

> Properly interpreted, we (the Florida House of Representatives and the Florida Senate) do not believe that the Amendments create roadblocks to the preservation or enhancement of minority voting strength. To avoid retrogression in the position of racial minorities, the Amendments must be understood to preserve without change the Legislature's prior ability to construct effective minority districts. Moreover, the Voting Rights Provisions ensure that the Amendments in no way constrain the Legislature's discretion to preserve or enhance minority voting strength, and permit any practices or considerations that might be instrumental to that important purpose.[22]

The Fair Districts amendment language received approval from the Department of Justice without comment on May 31, 2011.

The redistricting process in Florida is governed by the state constitution, state statute, and legislative rules. The process can be divided into two parts: (1) the steps leading up to the 60-day legislative session; and (2) the steps after legislative enactment. As a preliminary step in 2010, the legislature developed and released a web-based district building application that was made available to the public. In December 2010, Florida received official notification of the apportionment of 27 congressional seats. In March 2011, Florida received the 2010 census data from the U.S. Census Bureau. During the summer of 2011 the legislature hosted 26 public meetings around the state to receive public input to help the legislature in the creation of the new districts. About 5,000 people attended the meetings and over 1,600 spoke. In addition, at the invitation of the legislature, over 150 proposed maps were submitted by the public (only four maps were submitted by the public in 2002), including 54 complete congressional maps.[23]

Members of the Fair Districts Committee and their Democratic supporters criticized the legislature for not presenting legislative proposals for the public to discuss and analyze, for seeming uninterested in what the public was saying, and for rarely speaking at the meetings (a strategy designed to reduce the chance that a legislator might say something that could be used in the expected lawsuits over redistricting).[24] Republican

Table 2.2. A comparison of the legislative and congressional redistricting process

2012: After legislative enactment			
Legislative (state house and senate) redistricting plans		Congressional redistricting plan	
January 10–March 9	Legislature approves legislative plans	January 10–March 9	Legislature approves congressional plan
15 days	Attorney general submits legislative plans to Fla. Supreme Court	7 or 15 days	Governor signs congressional plan into law
30 days	Fla. Supreme Court upholds the legislative plans	NO AUTOMATIC COURT REVIEW	
60 days	U.S. DOJ preclears the legislative plans	60 days	U.S. DOJ preclears the congressional plan
June 4–8	Qualifying for state and federal elections in Florida	June 4–8	Qualifying for state and federal elections in Florida

Notes: Table reproduced from the Florida House of Representatives, "The Language of Redistricting: Key Concepts and Terminology," 2011. Available at http://www.floridaredistricting.org.

legislators fired back that most critics had failed to submit their own plans that they believed would satisfy the new Fair District standards. Moreover, Republican legislators asserted that it was appropriate to gather redistricting information first so the public would not think that the legislature had already decided what to do. Finally, from October to December 2011, the legislative redistricting committees and subcommittees began reviewing public input and drafting plans.

While the normal 60-day legislative session in Florida runs from March to May, the Florida Legislature moved the 2012 legislative session from January 10 to March 9 to help ensure that the entire redistricting process would be finished in time for candidate qualifying in June. The processes and timetable for adopting new congressional and legislative lines differ somewhat (see table 2.2).

Once approved as joint resolutions, the legislative plans were sent to the attorney general who had to submit them within 15 days to the Florida Supreme Court for review. The Court then had 30 days to approve the plans or require changes. For the congressional plan, once approved as a bill by both houses of the legislature, the governor had 7 or 15 days to sign the plan into law or veto it.[25] Both the legislative and congressional plans then had to be submitted for preclearance by the U.S. Department of Justice. Finally, if all went well, the maps were also cleared of remaining court challenges before the end of May so that qualifying for state or federal elections in Florida could take place from June 4 to June 8.

The Legislative Game: Goals, Strategy, and Passage

Despite the 41 percent to 36 percent Democratic edge in statewide voter registration, Republicans held a supermajority in both the Florida House (81–39) and Senate (28–12) after the 2010 elections. Thus they controlled all facets of the legislative process concerning redistricting in the 2012 session including subcommittees, committees, the calendar, and floor action. In addition, because of Governor Scott's GOP affiliation, it would be highly unlikely for him to level a gubernatorial veto threat of the congressional redistricting plan. However, according to the Fair Districts Amendments, the Republicans could not draw district lines with the *intent* of favoring the Republican Party or incumbents as they had in 2002. In addition, they also had to make the districts more compact and follow political and geographic boundaries where feasible unlike in 2002. However, just like 2002, Republicans did have to protect minority voting rights because of the VRA and because of the new Fair Districts Amendments. Given these parameters, GOP legislators devised a strategy to follow these standards and still end up with a partisan advantage in the new redistricting plans that they hoped would withstand review by the DOJ and the legal challenges sure to be filed by their Democratic opponents.

Republicans involved in the redistricting process publicly stated repeatedly that they were committed to following the new standards and having the most open and transparent redistricting process in state history.[26] They prohibited any discussion concerning incumbents' preferred districts or residences, promised not to meet with congressional lobbyists and did not include member addresses on the maps[27]—a huge change from all previous redistricting efforts in Florida when lobbying by incumbents was rampant and often successful. In addition, the Republicans refused to entertain any public discussion of the partisan makeup of the new districts and did not publicly provide summary data or statistics for party registration or electoral behavior in the new districts. (In 2002, this political information was plainly listed online and in hard copy alongside the demographic district information.)

Republicans also repeatedly stated that minority voting rights would have to take precedence over the other new standards because of federal requirements, and that they would not allow retrogression in existing minority districts or minority vote dilution in any of areas of the state with fast growing minority populations.[28] Thus, by creating a number of majority-minority, minority-influenced, and minority coalition districts, the surrounding districts were "bleached" and became more Republican. Furthermore, legally, Republicans claimed that they did not draw the lines with the *intent* of helping their political party, but rather the Republican redistricting advantage that occurred was a result of the newly drawn district lines that simply followed the required standards quite faithfully. Moreover, since the Fair Districts Amendments only forbid intentional partisan gerrymandering, Republicans felt they had a strong legal case.

The legislature moved quickly to pass the new maps once the legislative session began on January 10. The Senate Redistricting Committee passed senate and congressional maps for consideration by the full chamber on January 11 after voting down a Democratic alternative. The full senate approved the plans in a bipartisan 34–6 vote on January 18. The House Redistricting Committee passed their house and congressional plans on February 3 and the full chamber approved them later that same day on a party line vote 80–37. After some discussion the senate agreed to some minor changes requested by the house in its congressional redistricting plan to increase minority strength and reduce the number of counties and cities split in several different districts. On February 8, the Florida House voted on final versions of the plans and on February 9th the final version of the redistricting maps was approved by the Florida Senate: the congressional map CS/SB 1174 by a party line vote 80–37 in the house and a bipartisan vote 31–7 in the senate.

Because they were heavily outnumbered, Democrats had no meaningful say in the drawing of the district lines or the passage through the legislature. Thus, their strategy was to amass evidence of impropriety by the Republican majority and present that evidence in court in hopes of having the lines redrawn. Under Florida law, the house and senate district maps would be automatically reviewed by the Florida Supreme Court, while a lawsuit would have to be filed to challenge the congressional districts. Democrats also hoped that at the federal level the U.S. Justice Department might require changes when the maps were reviewed for preclearance.

The Referees Make Their Calls: Court Battles, Senate Revision, and U.S. Justice Department Approval

On the same day as final passage, the Democratic Party filed suit in state court to invalidate the congressional plan and a coalition of interest groups who supported the Fair Districts Amendments announced they would file a separate lawsuit challenging the congressional maps after they were signed into law by Governor Scott. Florida Democratic Party chairman Rod Smith said the maps "fail to meet the plain meaning of Fair Districts" regarding partisan and incumbent gerrymandering. The coalition, including the League of Women Voters, Common Cause, and the National Council of La Raza, claimed the congressional map was "intentionally enhanced" and accused Republican U.S. representatives Dan Webster of Winter Garden and Mario Díaz-Balart of Miami of taking "affirmative steps to influence members of the legislature and its staff to 'improve' the composition of their new districts to make them more favorable." It also accused the legislature of "packing artificially high numbers of minorities into certain districts"—singling out the Jacksonville-to-Orlando district of Democratic U.S. representative Corrine Brown—to "diminish the influence" of minorities in surrounding districts by rendering them more white and more likely to vote Republican.[29] A week later, Governor Scott signed the new congressional map into law on February 16 and soon after, the second lawsuit was filed.

The two lawsuits were combined and heard on an expedited basis in the Second Judicial Circuit in Tallahassee. The plaintiffs asked for a summary judgment declaring the new map to be unconstitutional on its face, or as an alternative, for a temporary injunction maintaining the existing districts until final resolution of all claims. However, on April 30, after reading the motions and responses, hearing the arguments, and weighing the evidence, Judge Terry Lewis denied both requests.[30] In a very detailed response to each of the eight allegations covering a total of 23 out of the 27 districts, Judge Lewis repeatedly stated that there was insufficient evidence to declare any of the disputed districts unconstitutional. He declared that evidence of intentional partisan or incumbent gerrymandering, lack of compactness, or crossing county or city lines could be explained by constitutionally appropriate decisions concerning minority districts or by valid policy choices concerning local geographic boundaries.

Judge Lewis went on to add that replacement maps proposed by the plaintiffs would either make minorities worse off (and in several instances lead to retrogression in some of the five Florida counties covered specifically by Section 5 of the VRA), or would be only as or even less compact than the original district maps, or would impermissibly divide as many or more cities and counties than the legislatively approved district maps. Judge Lewis concluded that, "the new map appears on its face to be an improvement over the one it replaces."

Democrats had somewhat better luck with the mandatory Florida Supreme Court review of the two legislative maps because while the house map was upheld, the senate was forced to redraw. Attorney General Pam Bondi formally requested the review as soon as the maps were approved by the legislature on February 9 and the Florida Supreme Court heard oral arguments on February 29. Republican supporters of the newly drawn maps asked for the court to approve the maps without change and insisted that the process complied with the new Fair Districts Amendments. They also argued that the court should give the new districts the presumption of constitutionality and only examine them in a cursory fashion as the Florida Supreme Court had always done in previous decades when undertaking the mandatory review—with a more detailed examination only coming if a challenge worked its way up through the trial courts at a later time. Democratic opponents asked the court to strike down both maps for unconstitutionally engaging in partisan and incumbent gerrymandering and violating standards of compactness. They also asked for a thorough vetting of the proposed maps since the Fair District Amendments had changed the court's traditional "rubber stamp" role assumed in previous decades.

The Florida Supreme Court made clear they were going to engage in a more extensive review of the proposed maps through their many requests for information before the hearing and detailed questioning during oral argument. The 234-page decision, released on March 10, found the plan for the house districts constitutional, but found the plan for the senate districts unconstitutional with violations in eight districts.[31] The Court declared that the senate map was "rife with objective indicators of improper intent" including: favoring all 19 incumbents who were not term-limited (districts were renumbered so that 16 senators previously eligible for eight years would be able to serve ten and the other three senators previously eligible for nine years would be able to serve eleven); favoring Republicans (most Republican performing districts were underpopulated and thus overrepresented compared to Democratic leaning districts); drawing many districts that were not compact or that did not follow existing geographic or political boundaries where feasible (the eight senate districts singled out as unconstitutional: 1, 3, 6, 9, 10, 29, 30, and 34, were specifically cited for one or both of these legal defects in conjunction with partisan or incumbent gerrymandering).

The legislature convened in special session on March 14 and the senate approved a new map eight days later. In order to ensure that they would not be accused of renumbering districts for incumbent advantage the senators held a lottery using green and white bingo balls and two brass tumbling machines to randomly assign districts to either two year or four year terms.[32] The house approved the senate map without changes on March 27 and the Florida Supreme Court held the 2nd round of oral arguments on April 20. Democratic opponents once again argued that the new maps had the intent of favoring Republicans while Republicans insisted they had followed all Fair District standards and conformed to the judgment of the court. On April 27, after reviewing the new maps, listening to the arguments of both sides, and even considering the alternative plans proposed by the Florida Democratic Party and coalition of interest groups, the Florida Supreme Court ruled that the newly drawn senate districts were constitutional.[33]

In addition to the court battles, the state also needed preclearance from the U.S. Department of Justice (DOJ). The state submitted the congressional and legislative plans in March and sent additional information on the revised senate districts in late April. A few days later, the Civil Rights Division of the DOJ approved the new proposed congressional and legislative district maps without requiring any changes. In a brief letter to the attorneys representing the state of Florida dated April 30, the same day as Judge Lewis's decision in Tallahassee, the Assistant U.S. Attorney General wrote, "The Attorney General does not interpose any objection to the specified changes."[34] The decisions by the Florida Supreme Court, a Florida circuit court, and U.S. Justice Department cleared the way for the 2012 elections to be held on time using the maps drawn by the legislature (although other legal challenges continue as of the writing of this chapter). Appendix D displays the final congressional and legislative district maps.

Evaluating the Game Based on Compliance with Fair Districts Standards

This research now turns to assessing the process of the 2012 redistricting game based on the outcomes it produced.[35] It can be argued that the most important part of the 2012 process is how well the new districts comply with the Fair Districts requirements. The standards to be evaluated include: equal district population size, compactness, contiguity, following geographic and political boundaries where feasible, prohibiting drawing lines with the intent of favoring or disfavoring incumbents, prohibiting drawing lines with the intent of favoring or disfavoring political parties, and ensuring that racial, ethnic, and language minorities have the equal opportunity to participate in the political process and the ability to elect the representatives of their choice.

Evaluating Process Outcomes: District Geometry and Geography

With one exception (population range/deviation), the new process under Fair Districts produced as good or better results in 2012 compared to 2002 when considering population size, compactness, contiguity, and following geographic and political boundaries where feasible. Table 2.3 displays summary statistics for the 2002 and 2012 congressional and state legislative districts for size, shape, and political boundaries.[36]

Because of population growth, the target population for the average district increased. For the 2012 congressional districts the target population was 696,345 residents (an increase of over 57,000 from 2002). Because of U.S. Supreme Court requirements, population range from smallest to largest district and total population deviation stayed exactly the same compared to the 2002 congressional districts: 1 and 0 percent respectively. However, population range and deviation actually grew for the house and senate districts. In 2012, the ideal district population for each district in the 120-seat house was 156,677 (up by over 23,000 from 2002). The actual district population ranged from 153,745 (-1.87 percent deviation) to 159,978 (2.10 percent deviation) for a total population deviation of 3.97 percent (up from 2.79 percent in 2002).

In the 40-member senate the ideal population was 470,032. The actual population ranged from 465,376 (-0.99 percent deviation) to 474,728 (0.99 percent deviation) for a total population deviation of 1.98 percent (up from just 0.03 percent in 2002). The increased deviations for both legislative plans provide evidence of either the tradeoffs that occur under the Fair Districts process or the legislature's failure to follow the guidelines (or perhaps both). The deviations may have increased because of the goal to reduce the number of cities and counties split among different districts. On the other hand, when forced by the U.S. Supreme Court, the legislature created exact minimum deviation for the congressional districts while also seeking to reduce splitting local governments.

Table 2.3. Florida districts, 2012 versus 2002: size, shape, and political boundaries

Criteria	Congressional (27 seats–25 in 2002)	State house (120 seats)	State senate (40 seats)
Target population (2002)	696,345	156,677	470,0032
	(639,295)	(133,186)	(399,559)
Total population range (2002)	1 (1)	6,233 (3716)	9,352 (120)
Total population deviation (2002)	0% (0%)	3.97% (2.79%)	1.98% (.03%)
Total miles base shape perimeter (2002)	8,120 (10,064)	12,378 (16,491)	8,934 (11,470)
Average miles to drive (2002)	31 (38)	14 (17)	25 (32)
Average minutes to drive (2002)	41 (48)	22 (26)	35 (41)
Counties split out of 67 (2002)	21 (30)	46 (30)	45 (24)
Cities split out of 411 (2002)	27 (110)	170 (75)	126 (47)

Notes: Florida House staff analysis of 2012 congressional, house, and senate final redistricting plans. Total census population: 2010 = 18,801,310 vs. 2000 = 15,982,378.

In contrast, the process created districts for all three offices that are more compact and follow political boundaries more faithfully compared to the 2002 districts (all districts were also contiguous in 2012 as they were in 2002). The new congressional and state legislative maps reduced the total perimeter of all districts, width and height of districts, and distance and driving time to travel the average district. In terms of political boundaries, the new districts reduce the number of Florida's 67 counties split and the number of its 411 cities split for all three maps. In addition, given Florida's peninsular shape, it is no surprise that many district descriptions also include a natural geographic boundary such as the Gulf of Mexico, the Atlantic Ocean or a river. In terms of overall numbers, it is clear that the new congressional and legislative maps have more compact districts that split less counties and cities than the previous 2002 maps. However, because legally mandated minority districts required some element of gerrymandering, the minority districts and the surrounding districts are less compact and split more counties and cities than a plan without gerrymandered minority districts.

Evaluating Process Outcomes: The Treatment of Incumbents

How did the new process work in terms of drawing district lines without the intent to favor or disfavor incumbents? While intent is difficult to infer from results, the actual tenuous status of many incumbents (particularly

Table 2.4. The status of Republican incumbents in the 2012 redistricting

GOP incumbents who	Congressional	State house	State senate
• were placed with another incumbent or in a worse district	8	20	2
• retired rather than move or face a party colleague	0	2	0
• moved to a new district rather than face a party colleague or run in a worse district	3	4	1
• lost in the primary against a party colleague or in a new district	2	1	0
• lost in the general election in an existing or new district	2	2	1
• sought but lost another office rather than move or face a party colleague	0	2	0

Notes: Data collected by the author.

Republican incumbents since the GOP controlled the process) in the new congressional and state house maps seems to bolster the legislative contention that the districts were drawn without intent to favor or disfavor incumbents. In contrast, few incumbents of either party were put at risk in the new state senate districts (and in the original senate map, submitted to and rejected by the Florida Supreme Court, incumbents were given clear advantages) leaving the question open as to whether this was intentional or accidental. Table 2.4 presents the status of Republican incumbents under the new plan.

By one count, almost half of the congressional incumbent legislators were either drawn out of their district, were given a district that was worse for their reelection chances, were drawn into a district with another incumbent, and/or sought to run in a different geographic district than the one they were previously in.[37] For instance, Republican representatives Sandy Adams and John Mica were drawn into the same district, decided to run for the same seat, and engaged in a brutal Republican primary (see chapter 10) where Mica defeated Adams. (This would normally be unheard of in a state that gained two seats for members of the majority party.)

Republican representatives Rich Nugent and Cliff Stearns were also drawn into the same district but worked out an agreement to run for different seats. However, running in an unfamiliar district, twelve-term incumbent Stearns went on to lose a multi-person primary to Tea Party-backed political newcomer Ted Yoho. South Florida Republican Congressmen Dan Rooney and Allen West both saw their districts become more Democratic and both decided to run in new districts—West eventually lost his bid for reelection. Panhandle Republican Steve Southerland and South Florida Hispanic Republican David Rivera both received districts that were slightly more Democratic than before, and Rivera, mired in scandal, went on to lose reelection.

Overall, eight out of a possible 19 congressional Republican incumbents were put in districts with other incumbents. This caused three congressional Republican incumbents to move to new districts and contributed to two losing in the primary and two more losing in the general election. This level of congressional incumbent majority party inconvenience and loss is unprecedented in the history of Florida redistricting.

What do the results of the new state house and senate districts suggest about the degree to which the legislature drew the maps without the intent to favor or disfavor incumbents? The house seems to have followed this standard quite well while evidence from the senate is decidedly more mixed.

Florida House Speaker Will Weatherford claimed that it was the first time in the country that so many lawmakers were drawn into districts with other incumbents in maps created by a legislature. The fact-checking site PolitiFact Florida rated this claim mostly true: one newspaper reported 35 such cases not including term-limited members; the Florida Democratic Party put the total number at almost half the legislature, 58, in a brief filed with the state court; and the Florida House said at least 40 members, one-third of the house, had been put in districts with other members.[38]

Many members of both parties were forced to scramble for new seats, but more impressive, as far as gleaning the intent of the Republican majority from the results, is the fact that so many Republican house members were moved into districts with other Republican members. For example, one source found 10 cases of Republican house incumbents being forced to run in the same district as other Republican house incumbents and six cases where Democrats faced that same fate. Moreover, three of these 16 cases, overall, actually involved three members of differing parties who now faced the more daunting task of running in the same new district rather than the less formidable challenge of competing against one another in two newly created districts.[39] In addition, while some of the affected house members overcame the political challenges posed by redistricting by moving to different, more politically favorable districts or by achieving election to different state and county offices, a number of these GOP members decided not to run again or were defeated for reelection. The massive alterations to the state house map were unprecedented in Florida politics and in state politics around the country when a partisan legislature is in charge of drawing the lines.

For instance, in West Florida, GOP house members Brad Drake and Marti Coley were drawn into District 5, and Drake decided to wait two more years to run again until Coley was term limited out. In Jacksonville, Republican representatives Mike Weinstein and Charles McBurney were drawn into District 16 and Weinstein decided to run for the senate but lost in the Republican primary. Tampa area Republican James Grant moved to a new district rather than face off against fellow Republican incumbent Shawn Harrison in District 63. In St. Petersburg, Republican representatives Larry Ahern and Jim Frishe and Democratic representative Rick Kriseman were all drawn into District 69 and Frishe decided to run for the senate but lost in the Republican primary. In Sarasota, GOP members Doug Holder and Ray Pilon were put into District 71, and Holder moved to a different district. In Lakeland, Republicans Seth McKeel and Kelli Stargel were drawn into District 40 and Stargel decided to run for the senate.

In Orlando, Representative Scott Plakon moved to a much more competitive district to avoid a primary fight with fellow Republican Speaker-elect Chris Dorworth in District 29. Plakon eventually lost in the new district to Democratic challenger Karen Castor Dentel, despite outspending Dentel by about five-to-one. Moreover, shockingly, in perhaps the biggest upset in the Florida 2012 election, Speaker-elect Dorworth also ended up losing to a Democratic challenger after a recount in his newly drawn district. (While Dorworth's ethical, financial, and personal problems were largely to blame, there is little doubt that in previous decades his district would have been drawn safer than it was in 2012.) In addition, in Orlando, Republicans Eric Eisnaugle and Steve Precourt were drawn into District 44 with Democrat Geraldine Thompson, and Eisnaugle decided to retire from politics rather than move or run against his colleague. In South Florida, GOP representative Eddy Gonzalez moved and rented a home in Hialeah rather than run against fellow Republican Jose Oliva in District 110. In Miami, Republicans Jose Felix Diaz and Ana Rivas Logan ended up facing off in a nasty primary in District 116, and Logan lost her bid for reelection.

This evidence suggests that the Republican-controlled house largely redistricted without the intent to favor or disfavor incumbents and the

Florida Supreme Court did approve these districts without change and lauded the house for its efforts and results. In contrast, however, eight of the originally drawn Florida Senate districts were flagged by that same court as being egregious examples of favoritism towards incumbents. While the Florida Supreme Court did approve the second set of senate districts once those eight districts were redrawn and new district numbers had been assigned to all 40 districts by lottery so that every incumbent was no longer given an opportunity to serve for a longer term (as was the case under the original map), there is little additional evidence from the final outcome of the redistricting process to suggest that the senate followed the judicial mandate not to favor or disfavor incumbents.

Unlike the numerous examples from the congressional and state house maps where incumbents (and especially majority party incumbents) were placed together, there is apparently only one Florida Senate district that placed two incumbents against each other, and this was created only as a direct result of the Florida Supreme Court objecting to the bizarre shape of the districts in the first plan designed to keep these two incumbents apart. In Central Florida, Republican state senators Andy Gardiner and David Simmons were both placed in District 13, but Simmons announced even before final court approval that he would simply "move one mile into Seminole County" to run in a neighboring district that was favorable to Republicans and had no other obvious Republican challengers.[40] Further, a Republican amendment that altered the second redistricting plan was criticized for stopping two other Republican senate candidates, state representative Denise Grimsley from Sebring and former state representative Bill Galvano from Bradenton—both of whom went on to win seats in the senate—from being placed in the same senate district.[41]

In the general election, one other senate race ultimately pitted two incumbents against each other, but the senate did not actually draw the incumbents into the same district, although senate leaders initially thought that they had, so charitably this might be considered a second example.[42] In South Florida, Republican senator Ellyn Bogdanoff ran against, and eventually lost to, Democratic senator Maria Sachs in District 34. The district was drawn with a Democratic advantage in registration, but Sachs was actually placed in a neighboring district "just ten feet" from the boundary line of the new district and had to move to the district to be in compliance with Florida residency law.[43]

Ultimately then, the senate had only one district where Republican incumbents were placed in the same district, one district where a Republican and a Democrat were almost placed in the same district (and did face off with the Republican losing), and one district where critics accused the Republican senate majority of protecting two Republican senate candidates from running against each other. So while the Florida Supreme Court did approve the redrawn senate map (citing lack of concrete proof of intentional incumbent protection), the state senate redistricting does not compare well with the state house or congressional redistricting in terms of incumbent placement or incumbent defeat. This is especially true when compared to the congressional map that had just 27 seats to the senate's 40, and yet the congressional redistricting plan ended up with almost half of the incumbents being placed in districts with other congressional members or in less favorable districts and with four incumbent Republicans actually losing their bid for reelection (as opposed to just one in the senate). Still, despite the shortcomings of the senate redistricting process compared to those of the state house and the congressional districts during this cycle, the redistricting process involving the state senate represented a relative improvement over previous decades because at least some of the majority party incumbents in the senate were not unduly favored and politically protected by the composition of new senate districts. Moreover, the fact that the district lines drawn by the state senate during this cycle were less overtly favorable to the majority party represented an exceptional development, when compared to most other states where the legislature draws the district lines.

Evaluating Process Outcomes: Favoring or Disfavoring Political Parties?

The new Fair Districts Amendments also prohibit drawing district lines with the intent of favoring or disfavoring a political party. What partisan results emerged from the new process? Intent concerning partisanship is also difficult to infer from the results of the maps, but like incumbency, the results may possibly shed some light on partisan intent. Four pieces of evidence are weighed to evaluate the congressional and legislative districts on this criterion: party registration of the new districts, past partisan performance of the new districts, the actual 2012 election outcomes, and potential or actual competitiveness. Table 2.5 displays some statistics concerning partisanship for the new districts.

The 2012 congressional map has 16 districts out of 27 that have a GOP registration advantage (with only one greater than 50 percent) and 11 with a

Table 2.5. Partisanship in the 2012 Florida redistricting

Number of districts with a	Congressional (27 seats)	State house (120 seats)	State senate (40 seats)
Republican registration advantage	16	61	21
Democratic registration advantage	11	59	19
Republican registration 50% or more	1	6	0
Democratic registration 50% or more	5	24	8
Party registration within 5%	10	34	10
Republican margin: 2010 governor	17	71	25
Democratic margin: 2010 governor	10	49	15
Republican margin: 2008 president	17	67	22
Democratic margin: 2008 president	10	53	18
Party Vote within 5%: 2010 governor	5	19	3
Republican district winner 2012	17	74	26
Democratic district winner 2012	10	46	14
Party vote within 5%: 2012 districts	2	11	0

Notes: Table compiled from data found at the Florida Division of Elections and Florida Legislature's redistricting websites and from data provided by Aaron Deslatte of the *Orlando Sentinel*.

Democratic advantage (with 5 over 50 percent). As of 2010, the 25-seat congressional map had a 15 to 10 Republican registration advantage. Overall, state registration as of November 2012 gave Democrats a 40 to 35 percent lead over Republicans out of 12.0 million registered Florida voters.

The congressional delegation makeup before the 2012 election was 19 Republicans to six Democrats. (The GOP had an 18–7 lead during the early part of the decade with Democrats winning 10 seats in 2008 and then losing four of those in 2010.) After the 2012 election, the Democrats gained four seats but Republicans still held a 17–10 lead in the delegation. This margin matches the performance of the proposed districts in statewide elections: 17 out of 27 new districts voted for Senator John McCain over Senator Barack Obama (who won the state by about 2 percent) in the 2008 presidential race in Florida and 17 out of 27 also voted for Republican candidate Rick Scott over Democratic candidate Alex Sink in the 2010 gubernatorial race, which Scott won by about 1 percent. Only two districts performed differently compared to their previous performance: long-serving St. Petersburg Republican Bill Young won reelection in Congressional District 13 despite its small margin for Obama and Sink, and Miami Democrat Joe Garcia won over scandal ridden Republican incumbent David Rivera in the Cuban Congressional District 26 despite its very narrow margin for McCain and Scott.

In the house, 61 out of 120 districts have a Republican registration advantage with a high of 57.6 percent in District 4 (Northwest Florida) to a low of 9.7 percent in District 108 (Southeast Florida). Conversely, 59 districts have a Democratic registration advantage with a high of 73.4 percent in District 109 (Southeast Florida) and a low of 22.6 percent in District 4. There are only 6 districts with more than 50 percent GOP registration but there are 24 districts with at least 50 percent Democratic registration (of these 24, three districts have greater than 70 percent and 13 have between 60–69.9 percent). Republicans fare even better when looking at electoral performance with 71 districts voting for GOP governor Rick Scott and 67 districts going for GOP presidential candidate John McCain. After the 2010 elections Republicans held an 81–39 advantage in the house, but running in the new districts with a victorious Barack Obama at the top of ticket, Democrats picked up 7 seats in 2012 to reduce their deficit to 74–46.

In the senate, Republicans have a party registration advantage in 21 seats with a high of 49.1 percent in District 1 (Northwest Florida) and a low of 11 percent in District 36 (Broward County). Democrats have an advantage in 19 seats with a high of 69.3 percent in District 36 and a low of 26.6 percent in District 23 (Southwest Florida). While no Republican districts have a 50 percent majority in party registration, eight districts have a Democratic registration of more than 50 percent (of these, three have between 60–69.9 percent). Republicans again have a slightly better advantage when looking at election performance from the 2008 presidential and 2010 governor's race with McCain winning 22 districts and Scott winning 25 districts. Going into the 2012 election, Republicans held a 28–12 lead in the senate, but with the new districts and some modest Obama coattails, Democrats managed to pick up two seats to narrow the gap to 26–14.

Overall, what can be observed about the potential and actual competitiveness of the 2012 congressional and legislative districts? Based on party registration, 10 out of the 27 congressional districts (37 percent) might be considered competitive as the difference between Republican and Democratic registration is 5 percent or less (ten districts also met this standard in 2010). In addition, 34 Florida House districts (about 28 percent of all seats) and 10 Florida Senate districts (25 percent of all seats) might also be considered potentially competitive using the 5 percent registration difference standard.

However, the actual electoral performance of these districts shows far less competitiveness. Only five congressional districts were competitive in the 2010 governor's race based on a vote margin of 5 percent or less between Republican Rick Scott and Democrat Alex Sink, and only 19 house and just three senate districts met that standard. Further, in the actual 2012 district races, only two congressional contests were actually competitive based on a final vote margin of 5 percent or less between the winning and losing candidate. In addition, just 11 house races and no senate races were competitive using this standard.

What can be concluded about the partisan results and what can be inferred about the intent to favor or disfavor a political party in the most recent congressional and legislative redistricting process (keeping in mind that intent is what matters constitutionally)? For the congressional seats and both legislative chambers, the partisan election results stemming from the 2012 redistricting process is quite clear, but the evidence for intent to favor or disfavor a political party is more mixed and elusive. Democrats had a half million more registered voters and a 4.4 percent advantage in statewide voter registration and yet Republicans created a majority of districts in the congressional delegation and both houses of the legislatures with a GOP advantage in registration and a strong majority of districts with a GOP advantage based on past electoral performance. In addition, while Democrats in 2012 picked up some seats in all three bodies, Republicans still have a strong majority in the congressional delegation and in the Florida House and Senate.

Republican critics, primarily Democrats and an array of good government groups, argue that it is logical to assume that the partisan results must have resulted from partisan intent. However, Republican legislative leaders deny any partisan intent. Moreover, they counter that the necessity to protect minority voting rights under federal and state law, the tendency of racial and ethnic groups to self-segregate, and the need to split fewer local communities under Fair Districts largely explains their redistricting decisions. Ultimately, the Florida Supreme Court, in its mandatory facial review of the state legislative districts, and a Florida U.S. District Court, in its facial review of the congressional districts, agreed that the partisan composition of the new districts could be explained by these legally permissible factors, upholding, respectively, the constitutionality of the newly drawn state legislative and congressional districts. (Subsequent legal challenges to the senate and congressional districts, which relied on more detailed evidence, not raised in the time-limited facial review, remain to be adjudicated by the court.)

Evaluating Process Outcomes: Protecting Minority Voting Rights

While intent is the important legal standard for favoring or disfavoring incumbency and partisanship, both the VRA and new Fair Districts standards make it clear that the actual ability of racial and language minorities to participate equally and elect representatives of their choice is what matters constitutionally, regardless of the partisan intent or favoritism shown to incumbents in drawing congressional and state legislative districts. Florida Republicans, in both the house and senate, embraced that goal and took the position that no retrogression was allowed by the VRA as part of their strategy to abide by the Fair Districts rules but still gain a partisan advantage. This allowed them to draw a number of minority districts with heavy concentrations of black and Hispanic voters who then elected a large number of minorities into office (see table 2.6).[44]

Because blacks in Florida tend to support the Democratic Party at the 90 percent level on average according to exit polls, packing black voters created districts with heavily Democratic registration and left surrounding districts more white and Republican, which helped the GOP win sizable majorities in the congressional delegation and legislature. Packing Hispanic voters into even higher concentrations of particular districts did not have the reverse effect of creating surrounding districts beneficial to the Democratic Party. Even though Cuban Floridians have tended to be Republican (particularly elected officeholders), the Hispanic population in Florida overall, actually leans Democratic in voter registration (a trend that started in the mid-2000s) and is closely divided in statewide elections according to recent exit polls.

The congressional maps have three black majority seats (District 5 in North to Central Florida, District 20, and District 24, both in Southeast Florida) and two black-influence seats (District 2 near Tallahassee and District 14 near Tampa), with African Americans totaling at least 20 percent of each district's population. There are also three Hispanic majority seats that are predominantly Cuban (Districts 25, 26, and 27, which are all in the Miami-Broward area of Southeast Florida and are all near or over 70 percent Latino) and four Hispanic-influence seats: three with Hispanics representing at least 30 percent of the population (District 9 in the Orlando area and Districts 23 and 24 in Broward and Palm Beach Counties) and one district (District 14 in Tampa) in which Hispanics represent at least

Table 2.6. Minority access in the 2012 Florida redistricting

Number of districts with a	Congressional (27 seats)	State house (120 seats)	State senate (40 seats)
Black VAP of 20%–29.9%	2	5	2
Black VAP of 30%–39.9%	0	4	3
Black VAP of 40%–49.9%	0	2	1
Black VAP of 50%–59.9%	3	11	2
Black VAP of 60% or more	0	1	0
Black district winner: 2012	3	22	4
Black district winner: 2010	4	18	3
Hispanic VAP of 20%–29.9%	1	10	5
Hispanic VAP of 30%–39.9%	2	5	2
Hispanic VAP of 40%–49.9%	1	3	0
Hispanic VAP of 50%–59.9%	0	5	2
Hispanic VAP of 60%–69.9%	1	4	0
Hispanic VAP of 70%–79.9%	2	1	0
Hispanic VAP of 80% or more	0	6	2
Hispanic district winner: 2012	3	15	6
Hispanic district winner: 2010	3	13	6

Notes: Data collected by the author from the Florida Division of Elections and Florida Legislature websites and from Aaron Deslatte of the *Orlando Sentinel*.

20 percent of the population. Note that District 14 is a minority coalition district with about a 25 percent black and a 25 percent Hispanic voting age population.

Overall, the six majority-minority districts and five of the six minority-influence districts more or less emulate what was in place under the previous district plan. The one exception, District 9 in Orange and Osceola Counties, is the first Hispanic-influence congressional seat in Central Florida. District 9 has a 41 percent Hispanic voting age population, and the dominant Hispanic group in the district is Puerto Rican (about 25 percent of the district) giving voters in that district an excellent opportunity to elect the first Puerto Rican Hispanic to Congress from Florida. However, that opportunity was lost in 2012 when two Puerto Rican Republicans split the Latino vote in the Republican primary, allowing a conservative non-Hispanic white candidate Todd Long to finish first and ultimately lose against the only announced Democratic candidate in the race: controversial former congressman Alan Grayson, who is white, Jewish, and non-Hispanic returned to Congress after losing his congressional seat in 2010.

In the end, three black and three Hispanic congressional representatives were elected from Florida in 2012. Although this equals the minority membership of the delegation for most of the decade, the 2012 congressional contests resulted in the election of one less black congressman compared to 2010, as black conservative Republican U.S. representative Allen West lost his reelection in 2012 when, following the redistricting, he found himself running for Congress in a new, less politically favorable district (see chapter 10).

In the Florida House, 12 districts were created with more than 50 percent black voting age population (VAP) including one urban South Florida district with over 60 percent: District 108 with 62.9 percent (at the opposite end of the scale, the whitest house seat—District 74 in Sarasota—had just 1.4 percent black VAP). In addition, two districts had 40–49.9 percent, four districts had 30–39.9 percent, and two districts had 20–29.9 percent black VAP. The house also created 16 seats with a majority-Hispanic VAP, with most of these house seats concentrated in South Florida, including one with 93 percent VAP (District 111 in Miami), 5 with 80–89.9 percent, 1 with 73 percent, and 4 with 60–69.9 percent. In addition, 3 districts were formed with 40–49 percent, 5 with 30–39 percent, and 10 with 20–29 percent Hispanic VAP—at the opposite end of the spectrum, the most Anglo house seat was District 25 in Daytona Beach with just 3.5 percent Hispanic VAP.

In the senate, two districts were created with 50–59.9 percent black VAP (with District 36 in South Florida the highest with 58.3 percent), one with 40–49.9 percent, and 3 with 30–39.9 percent (the whitest seat was again in Sarasota—District 28 with just 4.2 percent black VAP). The senate also created 2 South Florida seats with over 80 percent Hispanic VAP (with District 38 the highest at 86.9 percent) and two other Florida Senate seats with more than 50 percent Hispanic VAP (including one in Central Florida)—the most Anglo senate seat was District 2 in Pensacola with just 4.0 percent Hispanic VAP.

Ultimately, a record number of minority lawmakers were elected to the Florida Legislature: 37 in the house and 10 in the senate. The number of black representatives increased from 18 to 22 (an all-time high) and the number of Hispanics from 13 to 15 (also a record high). While the number of black senators remained at six members (equaling the record high), the number of Hispanic senators grew from three to four (a record high). All of the black legislators are Democratic except for one: Mike Hill elected as a Republican from District 2 in Pensacola. The Hispanic membership remains largely Cuban, Republican, and from South Florida, but there are four Hispanic Democrats in the house (Janet Cruz from Tampa, Ricardo Rangel from Osceola, Jose Javier Rodriguez from Miami, and Victor Manuel Torres from Orange) and one in the senate (Darren Soto from Osceola).

Overall, the evidence presented here strongly suggests that the new process did protect minority voting rights. The congressional and legislative maps complied with the requirement to allow minorities to participate in the political process and elect representatives of their choice. Mapmakers created more minority districts than in the past and both legislative bodies ended up with a record number of blacks and Hispanics. Although the congressional delegation actually lost one black member (Allen West) because incumbents were not protected, the three black and three Hispanic members equal the total for most of the previous decade. Further, when compared to the voter registration of these groups in Florida, the legislature is actually quite proportional: 13.6 percent of all Florida registered voters were black in 2012 compared to 17.5 percent of the legislature (up from 15 percent in 2010); and 13.9 percent of all Florida registered voters were Hispanic in 2012 compared to almost 12 percent of the legislature (up from 10 percent in 2010). The congressional delegation is just slightly less proportional with 11 percent African American and 11 percent Latino membership.

Democrats and the coalition of groups supporting Fair Districts argue that Republicans have gone well beyond what is required in creating minority districts to ensure that minority voters have an equal chance to participate and elect representatives of their choosing. They argue that several of the black-majority districts are so packed with African American residents that minority voters are actually hurt by the redistricting in violation of the Voting Rights Act and the Fair Districts standards (in essence arguing that black votes are wasted and that blacks are denied their statutory and constitutional rights to have additional Democratic representatives in Congress from Florida). Democrats also insist that intentionally packing extra Democrats into those minority districts also violates the Fair District standards prohibiting intentional partisan gerrymandering.

Democrats point to the fact that the three black majority-minority districts have in excess of 60 percent Democratic registration (Congressional District 5 with 60.7 percent, Congressional District 20 with 65.2 percent, and Congressional District 24 with 69.3 percent) as one illustrative example of how Republicans have been successful in intentionally packing superfluous Democrats into these black-majority districts to dilute their overall Democratic representation in Congress from Florida. Moreover, Democrats also point to the fact that the two black-influence districts have over 50 percent Democratic registration (Congressional District 2 with 54.3 percent and Congressional District 14 with 51 percent) to support their allegation of intentional partisan gerrymandering. On the flip side, only one proposed congressional seat is even 50 percent Republican: District 1, isolated in the Western Panhandle, with 50.9 percent.

By comparison, none of the South Florida majority Hispanic districts are even over 41 percent Republican (although each has a slight GOP edge in partisan registration), and each has an approximately 70 percent Latino population. Of course, Republican legislators counter that black districts contain more Democrats than Cuban American districts contain Republicans because about 83 percent of registered African Americans in Florida identify with the Democratic Party while Florida Hispanic voter registration is more evenly split between the parties. (31 percent of registered Hispanics identify as Republican while 38 percent identify as Democratic.)

Conclusions: Who Won? Is the Game Over? How Did the New Process Work Overall?

In legislative reapportionment, there are always winners and losers. In past decades, the usual winners of the redistricting game were the majority party, incumbents, and (since the 1982 redistricting) minorities (previous to 1982, minorities almost always lost). The usual losers were the minority party, challengers, and the public who got gerrymandered districts with odd shapes splitting local boundaries that were usually drawn for a particular political party. The adoption of the Fair District Amendments not only changed the process, but also changed the usual won/loss record in some ways.

One thing did not change. The biggest winner continued to be the majority party. Republicans adapted to the new rules, controlled most of the process, created maps that favored their party but that were also able to pass legal muster, and ended up maintaining control of the congressional delegation and the legislature by comfortable, though somewhat smaller, margins. Democrats, by contrast, were clearly the biggest loser—although they kept the game closer than in the past. They had hoped that by pushing through the Fair Districts Amendments they might avoid the drubbing they took in the 2002 redistricting process that marginalized their party for the rest of the decade. Relatively speaking, they did better in 2012 because they gained some seats. However, if Democrats could not regain the majority in 2012 when Democratic presidential candidate Barack Obama's money, organization, and personal popularity spurred Florida Democratic registration and turnout to high levels, it is unlikely that Florida Democrats will be able to do so anytime soon.

Incumbents were the biggest losers in 2012, especially relative to previous redistricting years. The political losses suffered by incumbents represented, perhaps, the biggest change in the game. This was particularly true for incumbents in the congressional delegation and the Florida House of Representatives. In previous decades, incumbents of both parties were usually protected from serious competition or even inconvenience. In contrast, in 2012, a large number of incumbents were put in different districts, or given worse districts, or placed in the same district as other incumbents— and this included many Republican members. In addition, a relatively large number of congressional and Florida House incumbents chose not to run or were actually defeated—thus challengers in these districts became big winners under the new process. In the Florida Senate, however, whether by luck or by design, most incumbents were still given a relatively easy path to reelection.

Florida minorities were also winners in terms of descriptive representation, as has been the case in the last few decades with the advent of affirmative racial gerrymandering. Record numbers of black and Hispanic representatives and senators were elected to the Florida Legislature. The congressional delegation contained three black and three Hispanic members, which is the same number as most of the past decade, but less than the seven minority congressional representatives that Florida had going into 2012. Ironically, the congressional delegation became slightly less diverse with the loss of black Republican Allen West, who ran in a different, less favorable district because his incumbency status was not protected under the new redistricting procedures. Of course, for African Americans, the win is not unconditional when taking into account political party. While there were record numbers of blacks elected, almost all are Democrats serving in a Republican-controlled congressional delegation or state legislature. Critics argue that "unpacking" blacks into less concentrated districts might reduce African American representation marginally, but increase the chances of a Democratic majority more favorable to black interests.

Finally, the Florida public can also be considered a qualified winner relative to previous redistricting cycles. Congressional and legislative districts were drawn more compactly, split far fewer cities and counties, and based on party registration had a relatively large amount of competitive districts ranging from 25 percent to 37 percent of all seats. On the other hand, the overall partisan balance of the legislature and the congressional delegation (still firmly Republican) does not match statewide voter registration preferences (still comfortably Democratic). On the other hand, as Republicans like to point out, there are a large number of Florida voters with no party affiliation (almost 3 million or 24 percent) who seem to lean Republican in many statewide contests (indeed Republicans have dominated governor and cabinet races since 1998). In addition, Republicans have done better with state party organization, candidate quality, and fundraising, which also helps explain their dominance in Tallahassee and in the congressional delegation.

While winners and losers can be identified based on the process and results of the 2012 cycle, it is important to note that the redistricting game is not over in Florida. While Florida Circuit Judge Terry Lewis refused to replace the congressional maps in April 2012, so that elections could be held as scheduled, he did allow the lawsuit to move forward.[45] Moreover, although the Florida Supreme Court ruled the legislative districts facially valid during their mandatory 30-day review, their findings did not preclude additional lawsuits bringing up new evidence for a detailed review that was impossible to give under the constraints of time forced on the court by candidate filing deadlines for the 2012 election cycle.[46] Thus, lawsuits continue in state court arguing that the congressional and state senate districts violate the Fair District standards. Specifically, the Democratic Party of Florida, a number of individuals, and a coalition of good government groups (led by the Florida League of Women Voters) allege that the legislature had specific intent to favor or disfavor political parties and incumbents and that they have a "smoking gun" to prove it in the form of e-mails discussing redistricting plans between Republican legislators, staffers, and outside consultants.[47]

However, even if the lawsuits are successful, it is unlikely to change the overall partisan balance of the Florida Senate or congressional delegation. The Democratic Party of Florida and the coalition groups have suggested alternative maps that would likely improve Democratic fortunes.[48] Nevertheless, these alternative state senate and congressional district maps would not likely increase Democratic political representation in the Florida Senate and in Florida's congressional districts for three reasons.

First, the alternate plans may not stand up to federal scrutiny since they may violate the VRA. These alternate plans seek to help Democrats by reducing the number of blacks in some districts below the level of the previous 2002 plan (potentially viewed as retrogression) or by diluting growing Hispanic strength in Central Florida (potentially denying a minority group the ability to elect representatives of their choosing). Second, the Democratic alternate plans may not withstand state court scrutiny since they may also be challenged as demonstrating improper partisan intent under the Fair Districts standard. Third, even if found to be constitutional, the new maps would only improve Democratic fortunes, at best, marginally. Under the current political conditions in Florida, these new maps would most likely fail to provide sufficient political benefits to Democrats and allow them to close the current party gap in the senate, let alone facilitate their achieving majority party status in the state legislative chamber.

The intent of the Fair Districts Amendments was to apply standards to what had been a fairly unregulated process, to balance a number of conflicting but worthwhile goals, and to end up with districts that fairly represented Floridians in their state and national legislatures. In analyzing the history of the reapportionment process in Florida, the novel and ongoing process to draw electoral districts for the 2010–2012 redistricting cycle, and the recent outcomes of that revised process, the overall conclusion is that the new process worked fairly well. On average, the new process produced districts that were more compact, split far fewer cities and counties, protected minority voting rights, and did not favor or disfavor incumbents. (Although, with respect to this last outcome it was prevalent to a lesser degree in the state senate than it was with the redistricting results for the redrawn state house and congressional districts.) The new process fell a bit short on producing districts that were neutral towards political parties. On the one hand, Democrats were able to make some gains at all three levels; on the other hand, Republicans maintained solid majorities despite the statewide Democratic advantage in voter registration.

This part of the process might be improved by allowing the Florida Supreme Court to review the congressional districts and grant more time to review all three maps, as it was difficult for the court to do a thorough review in the 30-day window they currently are permitted. In addition, reformers might rethink the "intent" standard when it comes to incumbency and partisanship, since intent is extremely difficult to ascertain. Instead, they might want to look into establishing a more objective standard for those criteria. Still, while the Fair Districts Amendments may not have created a perfect redistricting "game" in Florida, they largely have succeeded in improving the process and outcome compared to all previous redistricting cycles in the Sunshine State.

3

The Law and Politics of Florida Redistricting in State and Federal Court

MARK JONATHAN MCKENZIE

The law of redistricting in Florida underwent dramatic change in the 2010 redistricting cycle. This change was the result of Florida voters passing two new state constitutional amendments that altered the legal criteria by which the state legislature could redraw electoral lines for both Congress and the state legislature. Amendments 5 and 6 gave the state supreme court new weapons to deploy in their decennial tussle with the legislature over redistricting (also legally referred to in Florida as the process of "apportionment"). In every decade since the 1960s, when the U.S. Supreme Court altered the legal landscape of redistricting, Florida courts, both state and federal, have entered this political thicket and dabbled in politics. In fact, the Florida Constitution, adopted in 1968, constitutionally compels the state supreme court to review new state legislative reapportionment plans, thus ensuring regular court participation in this very political process. Though the state and federal courts have been quite active historically in overseeing Florida apportionments, the political wrangling amongst judges in these decisions has been low compared to other states.[1]

Ironically, in an effort to take politics out of the process in the state legislature with the new constitutional amendments 5 and 6, the voters may have inadvertently shifted some of that partisan politics into the state supreme court, as evidenced by the court's behavior in their 2012 decision. In one of the Florida Supreme Court's decisions, a justice indecorously charged his colleagues on the bench with engaging in partisan politics. Another justice lamented about the court's new political role as mandated by the two constitutional amendments. The new amendments add to what is already a complicated federal legal fabric operating in Florida, and this new state of affairs offers more opportunities and challenges for federal and state courts operating in this area. Will the changes in Florida redistricting law, designed to take partisan politics out of the state legislature, simply transfer some of those politics to the judicial deliberations and decisions of the Florida state and federal courts?

This chapter analyzes the current state of the law of apportionment in Florida, taking into account the state and federal requirements that the 2011–12 Florida Legislature was operating under. Other chapters in this book are investigating the political effects of Florida redistricting, and certainly, the new legal landscape and the state supreme court played a role here. This chapter will also cover the history of federal and state court oversight of redistricting in Florida since 1962, focusing in particular on the behavior and politics of federal and state supreme court judges in these cases. With these decisions placed in context, the chapter concludes with an examination of the 2012 state supreme court decisions on apportionment and some observations about the future of Florida court activity in redistricting.

The Law of Redistricting in Florida

In November 2010, Florida voters approved two constitutional amendments (5 and 6) that altered the legal criteria employed by the legislature to reapportion congressional and state legislative seats. Though the new rules are somewhat similar to redistricting requirements in a few other states, the wording of the amendments—coupled with the circumstances that Florida has found itself historically under the federal Voting Rights Act (VRA)—create a number of potential legal pitfalls for the legislature.

This section details the current legal rules of Florida redistricting, and these rules provide some perspective on the constraints that the Florida Legislature was operating under whilst drawing their lines in 2011–12. This section also specifies what redistricting rules were in place in previous decades before the new amendments. It also outlines changes to federal voting rights law in the wake of the recent 2013 Supreme Court decision *Shelby County v. Holder*. Redistricting is governed by state and federal law, and the law sometimes treats congressional apportionment differently from state legislative apportionment (see table 3.1). The three main federal requirements for the Florida Legislature are equally populous districts (based on the Fourteenth Amendment to the U.S. Constitution), compliance with the federal Voting Rights Act, and proscriptions on unconstitutional Four-

Table 3.1. The law of redistricting at the federal and state levels in Florida

	Federal requirements	State requirements
Equal population	Congressional plans cannot exceed a maximum deviation of more than .69% from the ideal district (i.e., the deviations should be close to zero) State legislative plans cannot exceed a maximum deviation of more than 10% from the ideal district	The new amendments to the state constitution note in Sections 20(b) and 21(b) of Art. III that congressional and legislative "districts shall be as nearly as equal in population as is practicable" unless such compliance "conflict[s] with the standards in subsection (a). The problem with this language is that equal population requirements under the U.S. Constitution cannot be subservient to other redistricting requirements. Thus, it's unclear how these sections of the state constitution would ever be enforced.
Voting Rights Act	VRA Section 2: This portion of the Act applies to the entire country and prevents discrimination in voting practices, including redistricting. A litigant must satisfy three threshold factors before proceeding to a final test of the totality of the circumstances: Minority group must constitute a majority of the population in a geographically compact area. Minority group must show that it is politically cohesive. Minority group must show that the white majority votes sufficiently as a bloc to enable it usually to defeat the minority's preferred candidate. The court must consider all the factors in the Senate report of the 1982 amendments as well as the proportionality of minority seats to the overall minority population. VRA Section 3: This section allows courts to require states to obtain preclearance of plans from judges. The U.S. Department of Justice (DOJ) is currently attempting to apply this little-used section of the statute to Texas and North Carolina, and if successful, this same strategy could be employed against Florida redistricting and other election laws. VRA Section 5: Before the Section 4 coverage formula was struck down by the U.S. Supreme Court in 2013, there were five counties in Florida that were covered by Section 5, requiring the state to seek prior approval from the DOJ before implementing any statewide redistricting plan.	Florida Constitution Art. III, Sec. 20(a) and Sec. 21(a): The language in this section states that "districts shall not be drawn with the intent or result of denying or abridging the equal opportunity of racial or language minorities to participate in the political process or to diminish their ability to elect representatives of their choice." In 2012, the state supreme court interpreted this language to essentially incorporate the federal Voting Rights Act into the state constitution.

(continued)

Table 3.1—*Continued*

	Federal requirements	State requirements
Racial gerrymandering (*Shaw v. Reno*)	The U.S. Supreme Court has held that under the 14th Amendment, states cannot use race as the predominant factor in drawing electoral lines. These claims often involve white litigants who are complaining that a state went too far in trying to draw majority-minority districts.	N/A
Partisan gerrymandering	In theory, a state can violate the 14th Amendment equal protection clause by engaging in extreme partisan gerrymandering of districts. In practice, however, no statewide redistricting plan has ever been struck down solely based on this claim.	Florida Constitution Art. III, Sec. 20(a) and Sec. 21(a): The language in this section states that the legislature is prohibited from drawing lines with the "intent to favor or disfavor a political party or an incumbent." Though the legal rule focuses on intent, courts can use the partisan "effect" of a plan, along with other data, to infer illicit intent in drawing lines.
Mandatory judicial review	N/A	The state supreme court is required to review all newly enacted statewide redistricting plans to ensure their legality.
Contiguity	N/A	Fla. Constitution, Article III, Sec. 16, Sec. 20(a), and Sec. 21(a): all plans must be composed of contiguous territory. No plan has been struck down based on this clause, though the clause has been subject to some litigation. The State Supreme Court has interpreted the clause to allow for multi-member districts and for districts to jump over bodies of water.
Compactness	There is no federal requirement of compactness. However, in racial gerrymandering *Shaw v. Reno* claims, courts may look to traditional redistricting principles, such as compactness, in order to help them infer whether a district was drawn primarily on the basis of race.	Fla. Constitution, Article III, Sec. 16, Sec. 20(b), and Sec. 21(b): The 2012 Florida State Supreme Court said it would test compliance with this constitutional provision by employing "a visual examination of a district's geometric shape [as well as] quantitative geometric measures of compactness."

	Federal requirements	State requirements
Political and geographic boundaries	There is no federal requirement of following traditional political or geographic boundaries. However, in racial gerrymandering *Shaw v. Reno* claims, courts may look to traditional redistricting principles, such as the extent to which a district crosses political boundaries or ignores geographic features, in order to help them infer whether a district was drawn primarily on the basis of race.	Fla. Constitution, Article III, Sec. 16, Sec. 20(b), and Sec. 21(b): "districts shall, where feasible, utilize existing political and geographical boundaries." The state supreme court interpreted this language to be more flexible than other clauses in subsection (b) and found that considerations of political boundaries or geography must give way to compactness standards.
How to weigh redistricting rules	N/A	Fla. Constitution, Article III, Sec. 16, Sec. 20(c), and Sec. 21(c): "The order in which the standards within subsections (a) and (b) of this section are set forth shall not be read to establish any priority of one standard over the other within that subsection." This language suggests that the Florida State Supreme Court cannot treat compactness standards as more important than political and geographic standards in subsection (b). Yet, in the first 2012 redistricting case, the Florida State Supreme Court elevates compactness standards above these other two requirements, in spite of the express language of subsection (c). On the other hand, "where feasible" suggests that political and geographic standards are subservient to compactness if they are not feasible to implement. The language is thus a bit contradictory in its commands.

teenth Amendment racial gerrymandering claims of the *Shaw v. Reno* variety.

Theoretically speaking, states could be sued for engaging in unconstitutional partisan gerrymandering, but since the Supreme Court has never found an unconstitutional partisan gerrymander or created a workable standard to find one, this federal requirement is rather toothless and won't be discussed here.[2] Most of Florida's state law requirements arise directly from the new amendments to the state constitution adopted by voters in 2010. These new amendments, set forth in Sections 20 and 21 of Article III of the Florida Constitution, deal with intentional partisan gerrymandering, incumbency protection, racial and language minority discrimination, contiguity, compactness, equal population, and adhering to political and geographic boundaries. A synopsis of these state and federal rules are outlined in table 3.1.

Federal Law Requirements

1. Equal Population

U.S. Supreme Court precedent in equal population cases is well settled. Generally, a redistricting plan for the state legislature will be in compliance with the Equal Protection Clause if the plan does not deviate more than 10 percent from the ideal district.[3] For example, if the state of X has a population of 1,000 people and has 10 seats in a state senate, then the ideal (or perfect) district size for a state senate district would be 100 people. This means that when the state of X redraws the lines for its state senate, the difference between the lowest and highest populated districts cannot total more than 10 percent in absolute distance from above or below the ideal district. Thus, if state X's state senate plan contained one district with 95 people and another district with 105 people, the plan would pass this threshold constitutional test for equal population. This law does not mean that all state plans in excess of 10 percent will be struck down by the courts. Plans that deviate more than 10 percent may survive judicial scrutiny if the state is able to come up with important rational reasons for justifying the deviations.[4] However, a state that sticks within the judicially sanctioned 10 percent leeway is almost completely insulated from constitutional attacks based on equal population.[5]

The U.S. Supreme Court has much stricter equal population requirements for congressional districts. The Court has said that differences in populations among districts should be minimal and near zero.[6] Though normally the Court has upheld maximum deviations that are less than 1 percent, at least one overzealous federal district court made the nonsensical decision to strike down a state's congressional plan because it had a maximum deviation of 19 people, even though the amount of people who had moved, died or were born from the time the census was taken until the time the plan actually went into effect surely exceeded 19 persons. Still, such is an aberration, and normally federal courts (as well as state courts following federal constitutional law) will look beyond very small deviations in congressional plans, particularly if the state legislature asserts reasonable justifications for minor deviations.

2. The Voting Rights Act, Sections 2, 3, and 5

In addition to federal equal population rules, Florida must also comply with the Voting Rights Act. The scope of this compliance changed dramatically in 2013 when the Supreme Court struck down Section 4 of the Act, thus making Section 5 inoperative.[7] The Court left Sections 2 and 3 of the VRA untouched, and those provisions are still enforceable. Section 2 of the VRA applies throughout the entire country.[8] One of the seminal U.S. Supreme Court cases explicating Section 2 was a case out of Florida called *Johnson v. DeGrandy* (1994).[9] The other major Supreme Court case interpreting this portion of the VRA is *Thornburg v. Gingles* (1986).[10]

In order to sue successfully the state of Florida (or any state or political subdivision) for discrimination in redistricting under this section of the act, there are two steps a minority litigant[11] has to satisfy according to *Gingles* and *DeGrandy*. The *Gingles* case lays out three threshold factors a litigant must demonstrate.[12] First, the minority group subject to alleged discrimination must be able to constitute a majority of the people in a geographically compact area. If the minority group is too widely dispersed or is not sufficient enough numerically to constitute a majority, then the state is not required by federal law to try to create such a district.[13]

The U.S. Supreme Court has never directly settled the question about whether states are required under Section 2 to create coalition districts, where two different minority groups (such as African Americans and Latinos) are combined together in one district in order to construct a majority-minority district. However, the Eleventh Circuit U.S. Court of Appeals, which covers the state of Florida, has answered this question, allowing plaintiffs to sue the state for failure to draw a district combining two or more minority groups that are located in a sufficiently compact area, as long as those minority groups are politically cohesive.[14]

The second criterion of *Gingles* requires that the minority group alleging discrimination show that their group is "politically cohesive."[15] In the most simplistic terms, this means that if the group consistently scattered its votes across several candidates for office, it would not be politically cohesive and not meet this threshold criteria. Third, the minority group must demonstrate that the "white majority votes sufficiently as a bloc to enable it . . . usually to defeat the minority's preferred candidate."[16] The proper mathematical method one should use to measure polarized voting is still in dispute among the different federal circuit courts, and the Supreme Court has never definitively answered this question.[17] If any of these three conditions noted above is not proven with sufficient evidence, the court must dismiss the case.

These three *Gingles* criteria do not end the inquiry. Assuming one fulfills all three conditions mentioned above, the court must then proceed to a "totality of the circumstances" test, as outlined in greater detail by the Supreme Court case of *Johnson v. DeGrandy* (1994). If the three conditions are satisfied, "courts must also examine other evidence in the totality of circumstances,"[18] and this additional relevant evidence is outlined in the senate report that was published with the passage of the 1982 amendments made to the Voting Rights Act.[19] In applying this test to Florida's redistricting plan, the *DeGrandy* Court focused on proportionality as one important piece of additional evidence. The justices in *DeGrandy* dismissed the VRA case against Florida because they thought it was legally significant that the state drew a plan where the number of majority Latino districts were roughly proportional to the size of the Latino population as a whole. Thus, even though the plaintiffs met all three preconditions, and even though more compact Latino districts could be created in the Florida state house plan, the Court ruled that the state was not required to maximize Latino representation, because "reading §2 [of the VRA] to define dilution as any failure to maximize tends to obscure the very object of the statute and to run counter to its textually stated purpose."[20]

However, the Court also noted that a state could not use proportionality as a defense to insulate a redistricting plan from legal attack by discriminating against minority voters in districts in one part of the state and making up for that discrimination in representation in another part of the state.[21] In some respects, this scenario that the Court warned against is a bit like what Texas tried to do in 2003 in their "re-redistricting" plan—diluting the

Latino vote in Laredo, Texas to shore up Republican congressman Henry Bonilla's district, and then trying to make up for that vote dilution with a non-compact drawn Latino district in another part of the state.[22]

In practice, by expressly declining to adopt a bright-line rule, the Supreme Court's interpretation of the VRA and this totality of the circumstances test opens the door for lower federal courts and state courts to engage in partisan mischief, as current research suggests.[23] Assuming federal judges can agree on how to apply the *Gingles* preconditions, federal judges still have tremendous discretion to decide the case based on their own perception of evidence under this vague "totality of the circumstances" test, and with such vague guidelines for judges trying to follow the Voting Rights Act, this provides an opportunity for judges' own partisan and ideological biases to creep into the decision making process.

Although Section 5 is no longer operative, a review of its parameters is important for three reasons. First, the provision was in effect at least through the most recent redistricting cycle and thus is important for helping us understand the conditions under which the legislature and the courts have been operating. Furthermore, Section 5 precedent could have some influence on how federal courts resolve Section 3 challenges. Third, the Florida State Supreme Court claimed in 2012 that both Section 2 and Section 5 principles will govern interpretations of the new state constitutional amendments, and the constitutionality of Section 4 may not change this view.

Section 5 of the act required certain states, based on a particular formula in Section 4,[24] to seek prior approval of any election-law changes from the U.S. Department of Justice, including changes to a state's electoral lines in redistricting. Five counties in Florida[25] came under the ambit of Section 5 in 1975 when Congress added language minority groups as a class protected from voting discrimination. In the jurisdictions covered by Section 5 in Florida, the federal law did not allow a state to draw apportionment plans that would lead to a retrogression in minority voting power.[26] In short, the term retrogression assumed that minorities would not be in a worse position electorally after the change in the apportionment plan.[27] Section 5 thus prohibited plans that would have a discriminatory effect, but it also prohibited plans created with "any discriminatory purpose."[28]

Section 3 of the VRA allows for federal courts to order a state or locality to submit to preclearance of specified voting laws, irrespective of the coverage formula laid out in Section 4.[29] Under this section, courts have enormous flexibility to set the boundaries regarding which voting laws in the jurisdiction will need to get preclearance (either from the court or the Department of Justice), and thus, relief under this section is typically directed at specific voting laws rather than a wholesale preclearance of all voting laws as provided for in Section 5. Courts also have flexibility in setting the length of time under which the jurisdiction must obtain preclearance. Unlike Sections 2 and 5, where discrimination can be proven by looking at the effects or the product of a redistricting plan on minority representation, litigants in Section 3 lawsuits must prove intentional discrimination on the part of the state or locality. As litigants are finding out in the 2013 Florida case involving the League of Women Voters, proving intentional discrimination—in that case partisan discrimination—can be quite difficult and costly.[30]

On the other hand, proving intentional discrimination becomes unnecessary in Section 3 litigation if the plaintiffs can get the defendant jurisdiction to agree to preclearance requirements in a consent decree. For example, the state of New Mexico entered into a consent decree to undergo Section 3 preclearance, whereas Arkansas was forced into Section 3 preclearance after plaintiffs presented evidence of intentional discrimination in court.[31] Federal courts have rarely deployed Section 3 preclearance provisions in the past, and only two states and a handful of localities have been required to get preclearance based on Section 3.[32] The Obama Justice Department, at the time of this writing, is attempting to bring North Carolina and Texas within these Section 3 preclearance measures,[33] and thus the possibility remains in the future that Florida could also be brought back under preclearance provisions of Section 3 for redistricting laws.

3. Shaw v. Reno *Racial Gerrymandering Claims*

The last major federal requirement constitutes a proscription on racial gerrymandering practices of the *Shaw v. Reno* (1993) variety.[34] The *Shaw* case involved white plaintiffs who challenged a North Carolina African American majority district which was non-compact, spanning parts of the I-85 corridor, and in many places constituted a width no larger than the interstate highway itself. The Supreme Court ruled that the state, in its attempt to maximize the number of African American districts to comply with what it thought was required under the VRA, went too far and violated the U.S. Constitution's Equal Protection Clause since the state only focused on race as a criteria for drawing district lines while ignoring other traditional districting principles such as compactness, political boundaries, and geography. As some legal scholars noted, these cases seemed at times to contradict the requirements of the VRA, thus placing tremendous legal uncertainty on state redistricting practices.[35] In the latter part of the 1990s, the Court backpedalled somewhat, ruling that as long as race was not the "predominant" factor in the drawing of lines, such districts could withstand judicial scrutiny.[36] Today, racial gerrymandering lawsuits have become less successful avenues of legal attack in the federal courts because states have become more adept at avoiding these claims (by drawing less bizarrely-shaped majority-minority districts) and because federal courts have been loath to find racial gerrymandering claims with the same zeal and frequency as they had in the 1990s.[37]

Florida State Law Requirements

Historically, Florida law provided few redistricting rules for the state legislature and state supreme court to follow. During the heady days of the reapportionment revolution of the 1960s, begun by the U.S. Supreme Court's ruling in *Baker v. Carr* (1962), the state of Florida was beset by a number of lawsuits challenging various attempts at redistricting. After a few trips to the U.S. Supreme Court,[38] in which the High Court struck down Florida's handiwork as violating the equal population requirements of the Equal Protection Clause, the lower federal court in Florida finally drew the plan that lasted until after the next census in 1970.[39] Partly in an effort to prevent judicial mapmaking and keep redistricting lawsuits out of the hands of federal judges, the state of Florida adopted the 1968 Constitution, which instituted a new set of rules for redistricting.

1. 1968 Florida Constitution and the pre-2010 State Law Requirements

Though limited in their scope and nature, the redistricting rules that were born of Article III, Section 16 of the 1968 Florida Constitution instituted two major reforms. First, all state legislative plans are now subject to mandatory review by the state Supreme Court. Once the state attorney general files the plan with the Supreme Court, the court has *only* 30 days to consider protests to the plan and rule on the plan's constitutionality. In previous cases, including most recently in 2012, justices on the court have complained that the 30-day window is not enough time for them to adequately review claims involving complicated fact-intensive issues. Given the short window for review, the court has typically stated that its review of plans in these proceedings are cursory at best—that they are merely reviews of the facial validity of the redistricting plans, and that if facts later surface that challenge the constitutionality of a plan, those fact-intensive issues can be initiated in the trial courts.[40]

If the state legislature fails to apportion itself, the state supreme court assumes the duty of redrawing state house and state senate lines. The second major requirement imposed by the 1968 Constitution in Article III Section 16 calls for state legislative districts "of either contiguous, overlapping or identical territory." The court has subsequently expounded on this phrase in two important ways. First, the language permits the state to create either single-member or multimember districts.[41] Second, the court has interpreted the contiguity requirements to allow the state to connect districts over bodies of water (even a large lake such as Lake Okeechobee), though the court has warned about taking this liberty over water too far.[42]

Until the most recent amendments adopted in 2010, there were no other significant state constitutional rules for the Florida Legislature to follow. Before the new amendments, the court had noted more than once that "requirements under the Florida Constitution are not more stringent than the requirements under the United States Constitution."[43] In other words, for example, Florida's Constitution does not require equal population rules that are stricter than the federal guidelines. Finally, nothing in the constitution before 2010 referred to any state rules about congressional redistricting. There is no automatic state supreme court review of Florida's congressional redistricting plan. However, nothing prevents a state court from reviewing congressional plans, if the state legislature fails to redistrict congressional lines. Such a failure would most likely fall to a federal court to remedy under federal law.

2. New Amendments 5 and 6

Most of the state-level requirements that the legislature had to follow in the 2012 redistricting cycle arose out of the 2010 passage of Amendments 5 and 6 (codified as Sections 20 and 21 of Article III of the Florida Constitution). Though one section refers to congressional district lines and the other refers to state legislative lines, both sections are in every other respect identical in language. They are divided into two primary subsections, with a third subsection dealing with how the rules should be prioritized. In the state supreme court's 2012 review of the new amendments, it offered extensive interpretation as to the meanings of these new sections. The Florida Supreme Court made clear that the new amendments provided redistricting rules that were more stringent than the U.S. Constitution.[44] The following exposition relies heavily on the court majority's initial interpretation of these amendments in its 2012 case *In re: Senate Joint Resolution of Legislative Apportionment.*[45]

Subsection (a) prohibits the legislature from drawing lines with the "*intent* to favor or disfavor a political party or an incumbent." Though perhaps not intended by the authors of this amendment, this language is somewhat limiting in terms of the Court's power to address partisan gerrymandering. As the majority opinion in *In re: Senate Joint Resolution of Legislative Apportionment* (2012) notes, since "intent" is the standard, evidence of whether the plan actually favors a political party or an incumbent (i.e., the effect of the plan) is less relevant to the inquiry.[46] Rather, the complaining party must show that the line-drawers intended to favor or disfavor a political party or an incumbent. Of course, in proving intent (i.e., *mens rea*—the subjective mental state of the mapmaker), the court has stated that it will consider objective circumstantial evidence (such as "the effects of the plan, the shape of district lines, and the demographics of an area").[47] Nevertheless, the intent clause poses less of a constraint on the legislature as compared to some other states, like Arizona, which affirmatively require the drawing of competitive districts.[48]

The second clause in subsection (a) tracks the language of the Voting Rights Act by prohibiting the state from denying racial or language minorities an equal opportunity to participate in the electoral process. In the 2012 state supreme court case of *In re: Senate Joint Resolution of Legislative Apportionment*, the court ruled that this language essentially incorporates the federal Voting Rights Act, both Sections 2 and 5, as a state constitutional requirement.[49] In fact, the court stated directly in its opinion that it would look to U.S. Supreme Court precedent on the VRA for guidance in applying this state constitutional provision.[50]

Most significant about the court's interpretation of this clause was the view that this state constitutional clause applied the federal principles of VRA Section 5 (non-retrogression) to the *entire* state. Thus, this interpretation places far greater legal responsibilities on the state legislature beyond the former federal requirements of Section 5, where only five Florida counties fell under the provisions. As noted earlier, it is unclear whether the Florida Supreme Court will continue in the future to interpret the state constitutional amendments as requiring compliance with the now obsolete Section 5, given that the U.S. Supreme Court declared Section 4 unconstitutional.

The Florida Supreme Court declared in its initial 2012 opinion that the state provisions were "[c]onsistent with the goals of Sections 2 and 5 of the VRA" and that "all the parties" to the 2012 case "agree[d] that Florida's constitutional provision now embraces the principles enumerated in Sections 2 and 5 of the VRA."[51] Consequently, since the "principles" of the VRA were essentially incorporated into the state amendments by the Florida Supreme Court, and since Section 5 was never declared unconstitutional by the U.S. Supreme Court but was only rendered inoperative due to the unconstitutionality of Section 4, one could argue that irrespective of the current legal status of Section 5 in terms of federal law, the Florida Legislature still has to comply with Section 5 principles in any future redistricting effort in order to comply with state constitutional law.

Finally, subsection (a)'s third clause mandates that territory be contiguous—a requirement that was already listed in Section 16 and for which the court says should be interpreted no differently than the Section 16 language.[52] All three of these clauses in subsection (a) are to be enforced with equal importance.

Subsection (b) of the two amendments deals with traditional redistricting principles—namely equal population; compactness; and the utilization of political and geographic boundaries (see table 3.1). The rules in this subsection are subservient to subsection (a).[53] In terms of equal population requirements, the 2012 Court seemed to suggest that they are no stricter than the federal requirements. For making determinations as to whether districts comply with the compactness provisions, the court said it would employ "a visual examination of a district's geometric shape [as well as] quantitative geometric measures of compactness."[54] Finally, subsection (b) states that "districts shall, where feasible, utilize existing political and geographical boundaries." The court found the words "where feasible" provided the legislature with "more flexibility" than the compactness standard.[55] In other words, it seems as though the Court is suggesting that geographic and political boundaries can be ignored at the expense of compactness standards. Interestingly, the last subsection of these amendments, subsection (c), states that no priority should be given to requirements within each subsection. Yet, the Court seems to ignore this language, suggesting that more compact districts can come at the expense of districts that follow political and geographic boundaries. Thus, these new amendments contain somewhat contradictory language as well as a certain level of vagueness.

Redistricting in Court: 1962 to 2003

As the above account indicates, the legal minefield of congressional and state legislative redistricting in Florida for most of the last five decades has resided in federal law with few state law restrictions placed on the legislature. During this timeframe, how has the legislature fared in avoiding this legal minefield when their plans have been challenged in the state and federal courts of Florida? Moreover, what do the past actions of these courts say about the future of redistricting in Florida under the new state constitutional rules? This next section analyzes the multitude of state supreme court and federal court cases from 1962 to 2003 in order to bring some clarity to the important factors governing judicial decision making in past Florida disputes. By separately analyzing court cases before the new amendments, we gain some perspective and context in understanding the dynamics of the 2012 state supreme court cases and the future of redistricting disputes in the Florida courts.

How Courts Behave in Redistricting: Partisanship, Ideology, and the Law

Since the redistricting revolution in the 1960s, the public law community has produced an innumerable amount of research into the doctrinal and theoretical issues confronting courts that regulate politics. Setting aside doctrinal and theoretical issues to some extent, a 1995 study of federal court regulation of state legislative plans by Randall Lloyd brought a more statistically based understanding of the political influences affecting judges in redistricting cases. He found that federal judges of one political party tended to strike down at higher rates legislative plans that had been passed by a legislature controlled by the opposite political party.[56] It was not until after the U.S. Supreme Court decided *Bush v. Gore* (2000) that more political scientists began to take a more quantitative look into how courts systematically regulate partisan-charged electoral disputes.[57]

From a theoretical perspective, it seems logical to suspect that a judge's partisan leanings might influence her thought processes in partisan legal disputes. We have long understood that ideology influences judicial decisions.[58] But ideology is not the same as partisanship. For example, a conservative Republican judge who has a tendency to be skeptical of claims about discrimination might nevertheless find discrimination and strike down a redistricting plan drawn by Democrats if that judge were influenced more by partisan concerns. Thus, in partisan-charged legal disputes, partisan influences do not always work in the same direction as ideological influences, though certainly they can.[59]

Moreover, political scientists have shown that people often process information through a partisan lens,[60] and since judges often arise from political backgrounds, it seems Pollyannaish to expect them to be able to totally divorce themselves from their partisan leanings when a case presents a decision with a clear partisan outcome.[61] On the other hand, judging in general is more than a mere partisan or ideological decision, and thus it is equally naïve to believe that judges completely ignore the law in their decision making, particularly when the law is quite unambiguous.[62] Finally, one must also consider the fact that supreme courts operate differently from lower courts. A state supreme court (or the U.S. Supreme Court, for that matter) might also view a partisan legal dispute as a separation of powers issue,[63] taking into consideration a more strategic horizon. Strategic motivations offer a fruitful explanation for previous research that has shown that states with appointed judiciaries are less partisan and less willing to invalidate a state's redistricting plan when compared to partisan-elected judiciaries.[64]

Florida Courts and Redistricting

What explains previous decisions of the Florida Supreme Court in redistricting? This study begins in 1962—shortly after the landmark U.S. Supreme Court case of *Baker v. Carr*—and ends in 2003. The most recent state supreme court cases of 2012 are addressed in the last section of this chapter. The study focuses on all published cases that represent final decisions on the merits and involve disputes about the validity of a state legislative or congressional redistricting plan in either the state supreme court or the federal courts in Florida. In sum, between 1962 and 2003, there are twelve cases in the state supreme court and twelve cases in the Florida federal courts. To be sure, there are other published decisions that indirectly involve redistricting issues or entail preliminary matters in a particular case, but this study focuses only on the final outcome of a plan by the courts.

Tables 3.2 and 3.3 provide some descriptive statistics of the types of redistricting disputes encountered by previous courts (before 2012) and the outcomes of those disputes. Not surprisingly, perhaps, the federal courts in Florida are slightly more willing to strike down state plans and challenge the state government when compared to the Florida Supreme Court. In all cases before 2012, the Florida high court appears to be a rather compliant branch of government, unwilling or uninterested in using political capital to challenge the legislature on this issue. In fact, the only time the state supreme court "struck down" a plan was in 1992, after the U.S. Department of Justice (DOJ) had already effectively denied preclearance to the state senate plan. When the legislature failed to reconvene to fix the problems interposed by the DOJ for the state senate plan, the high court merely stepped in and made some corrections itself to satisfy the DOJ. By doing so, the state supreme court had to formally declare the existing plan invalid—but that was a moot point anyways since the plan had already been denied preclearance by the DOJ and would not go into effect. Thus, the high court's action in 1992 really was not a direct assault to a plan passed by the state legislature.

Before 2012, the state supreme court typically only examined the validity of state legislative plans, whereas the federal courts have reviewed both congressional and state legislative plans. Before the new redistricting amendments, no state constitutional rules governed state supreme court oversight of congressional lines. Moreover, there is still no required mandatory review of congressional lines by the state supreme court. Since only federal law governed the legislature's drawing of congressional districts before 2012, most parties decided to resolve congressional plan disputes in federal court, though the state courts do have concurrent jurisdiction.

Of course, federal legal issues dominate the federal court cases, but interestingly enough, they also dominate the state cases in the Florida Supreme Court. State law issues regarding contiguity also arose somewhat frequently in previous Florida high court cases (five times), but this is due in large part to the fact that the 1968 Constitution had a contiguity requirement. Thus, with the state court's mandatory jurisdiction following each decennial redrawing of lines (1970s–2000s), they are bound by the state constitution to examine plans for potential contiguity problems.[65] Contiguity issues never gained much traction in these cases. Typically, the complaints derived from districts that were only connected in places by bodies of water, though that concern has been definitively resolved by the high court.[66] Though the 1968 state constitution did not explicitly mention equal population requirements, part of the reason for including state supreme court review in the constitution was to avoid having the federal courts draw the state's legislative lines. Consequently, each decade that the state supreme court has assumed mandatory jurisdiction to review the state

Table 3.2. Florida Supreme Court redistricting cases, 1962–2003

State supreme court	Plan upheld?	State senate (S), state house (H), or congress (C)	VRA case	Equal population
In Re: Constitutionality of House Joint Resolution 25e (2003), 863 So. 2d 1176	Yes	H		x
The Florida Senate v. Charles R. Forman (2002), 826 So. 2d 279	Yes	S		
In Re: Constitutionality Of House Joint Resolution 1987 (2002), 817 So. 2d 819	Yes	H, S	x	x
In Re: Constitutionality of Senate Joint Resolution 2g (1992), 601 So. 2d 543	No	S	x	
In Re: Constitutionality of Senate Joint Resolution 2g (1992), 597 So. 2d 276	Yes	H, S	x	x
In Re: Apportionment Law Appearing As Senate Joint Resolution 1 E (1982), 414 So. 2d 1040	Yes	H, S	x	x
Milton v. Smathers (1980), 389 So. 2d 978	Yes	H	x	
Cardenas v. Smathers (1977), 351 So. 2d 21	Yes	H	x	
In Re: Apportionment Law . . . Futch v. Stone (1973), 281 So. 2d 484	Yes	S		
In Re: Apportionment Law . . . Edward Tohari (1973), 279 So. 2d 14	Yes	S		
In Re: Apportionment Law Appearing As Senate Joint Resolution (1972), 263 So. 2d 797	Yes	S, H	x	x
Lund v. Mathas (1962), 145 So. 2d 871	Yes	C		x
TOTAL CASES	11 yes, 1 no		7	6

[a]This dissent includes Justice McCain, the lone Republican on the court at that time.

Political gerrymander	Contiguity issues	Communities of interest	Other issues	Number of dissents
	x			0
x		x		0
x	x	x	x	0
				2
x	x			1
	x			2
				3
				2
		x		0
		x		0
	x		x	3[a]
				0
3	5	4	2	13

Table 3.3. Redistricting cases in three-judge federal courts in Florida, 1962–2002

Three-judge federal courts	Plan upheld?	State senate (S), state house (H), or congress (C)	VRA case	Equal population	Political gerrymander
Martinez v. Bush (2002), 234 F. Supp. 2d 1275	Yes	H, S, C	x		x
Fouts v. Harris (1999), 88 F. Supp. 2d 1351	Yes	C			
Johnson v. Mortham (1996), 926 F. Supp. 1460	No[d]	C			
De Grandy v. Wetherell (1992), 815 F. Supp. 1550	No	H, S	x		
De Grandy v. Wetherell (1992)[c], 794 F. Supp. 1076	No	C	?[c]	x	
Wendler v. Stone (1972), 350 F. Supp. 838	Yes	C			x
Wolfson v. *Nearing* (1972), 346 F. Supp. 799	Yes	H, S	x	x	x
Swann v. Adams (March 1966), Supplemental Opinion, 258 F. Supp. 819	Yes	H, S		x	
Swann v. Adams (December 1965), 258 F. Supp. 819	Yes[a]			x	
Sobel v. Adams II (1963), 214 F. Supp. 811	Yes	H, S		x	
Sobel v. Adams (September 1962), Supplemental opinion, 208 F. Supp. 316	Yes	H, S		x	
Sobel v. Adams (July 1962), 208 F. Supp. 316	No	H, S		x	
TOTAL	8 Yes, 3 No[d]		3	7	3

Shaw v. Reno, racial gerrymander	Contiguity issues	Other issues	Dissent?
x			0
x			1
			0
			0
	x	x	1[b]
			0
			0
			0
			0
			0
			0
2	1	1	2

Notes: [a] The plan was upheld, but only on an interim basis. The U.S. Supreme Court later reversed the lower court's decision and ordered a new plan be drawn up immediately. See *Swann v. Adams*, 383 U.S. 210.
[b] The lone dissenter in this case, Norman C. Roettger Jr., is a Nixon appointee and the only Republican on the three-judge panel. He wanted to give more validity to the plaintiffs' complaints about lack of compactness and contiguity among districts.
[c] In *De Grandy v. Wetherell* (congressional districts), the court gives much discussion to the Voting Rights Act. However, I don't classify this case as such. The court declared the state plan invalid because the legislature had failed to draw new congressional lines after the census. Thus, the illegality of the existing plan was premised on malapportionment grounds. Faced with a legislature that failed to act, the federal court had to draw up a new plan, and they relied on Voting Rights Act jurisprudence in guiding their construction of new congressional districts. But, this plan was later struck down by another federal court.
[d] The plan struck down in *Johnson v. Mortham* was drawn by the DeGrandy federal court. Thus, I don't count this case in the totals regarding the number of state plans struck down by federal courts. The DeGrandy court drew a congressional plan before it had the benefit of the precedent of the U.S. Supreme Court's *Shaw v. Reno* (1993) case, which frowned upon using the VRA to maximize African-American representation. Two of the federal judges in Johnson also served on the DeGrandy court.

legislature's redistricting, the court has reviewed the plans for federal equal population compliance—even if there are no parties complaining about equal population violations.

Political gerrymandering claims have arisen in several cases in both the state and federal courts in Florida; but these claims were dismissed in every case. It is likely they are added to the pleadings by plaintiffs in an attempt to color the facts, particularly in claims regarding equal population[67] and compactness. Finally, it is interesting to note how many times plaintiffs raised complaints about either communities of interest or compactness in cases litigated before the new 2012 amendments went into effect (see table 3.2). Pre-2010, compactness claims were not a state constitutional require-ment, and post-2010, there are still no requirements for the legislature to consider communities of interest.

Dissents in these redistricting cases are also tabulated in tables 3.2 and 3.3. Rates of dissent in the federal cases in Florida were somewhat below the norm that we should expect to see in the average set of redistricting cases in the federal courts.[68] However, the rate of dissent witnessed in Florida state supreme court cases (table 3.2) is about the same as in redistricting cases before other state high courts.[69] From a statistical standpoint, dissents are significantly more likely in cases involving Voting Rights Act claims. The higher rate of dissents in VRA cases points to the potential uncertainty and ambiguity obtaining in that area of redistricting law. Clearly, VRA cases are the most challenging in terms of maintaining collegiality and unity.

The Individual Votes of Judges in Redistricting

Moving to more micro-level understandings of court behavior in Florida redistricting, one goal of this study is to investigate how partisanship, ide-ology, and the law govern the behavior of Florida judges in state and fed-eral court. The study examines two related judicial behaviors: dissents and votes upholding or striking down a state plan. In controversial political cases, we might expect dissents to run higher than average cases. If judges are dividing along partisan lines, then dissenters should typically include judges who make up the minority political party on the bench. For a very long time, Republicans have always held a minority of seats on the Florida Supreme Court. However, on three-judge federal panels in Florida, Dem-ocrats have occasionally been the minority party on the panel. Table 3.4 divides votes by whether the dissenting judge is a member of the minor-ity party on the panel. Very little statistical evidence exists suggesting that

Table 3.4. Rates of dissent among judges in the minority and majority party on the panel

	All state court cases		All federal cases		All cases combined	
	Dissent votes	Majority votes	Dissent votes	Majority votes	Dissent votes	Majority votes
Member of majority party	16% (12)	84% (65)	0% (0)	100% (25)	12% (12)	88% (90)
Member of minority party	20% (1)	80% (4)	18% (2)	82% (9)	19% (3)	81% (13)

dissents in these cases divide along partisan lines. A more sophisticated multivariate statistical analysis also fails to show that either political party or ideology is driving dissent in these cases.

Partisanship also appears to be of little help in explaining why judges in Florida have voted for or against previous redistricting plans. Though previous studies have found partisan motivations as a factor in some redistricting cases in both state and federal courts across the country, the evidence of partisan judicial action in Florida *before* 2012 is sparse and anecdotal. Table 3.5 provides some insight on the lack of partisan action by judges in past redistricting disputes.

The table illustrates voting records for three types of judicial situations. Judges who faced a redistricting plan drawn up by a legislature controlled by the opposite party of the judge should, in theory, be more likely to strike down those plans (opposing party judges). Meanwhile, judges that are of the same party as the legislature should be more willing to uphold such plans if they are taking party into consideration in their vote. Finally, there is a third scenario. In a couple of cases, judges faced plans drawn up by another court and thus devoid of any partisan content (judges facing nonpartisan plans).

As table 3.5 illustrates, there is no pattern of partisan voting in Florida redistricting cases before 2012. In fact, among judges facing their own

Table 3.5. Casting partisan votes in redistricting cases in the state and federal courts of Florida

Type of judge situation	Vote to strike down a plan	Vote to uphold a plan
Opposing party judges	21% (7)	79% (27)
Same party judges	25% (18)	75% (53)
Judges facing nonpartisan plan	33% (2)	66% (4)
TOTAL	24% (27)	76% (84)

party's plans, they voted at slightly higher rates to strike those plans down when compared to judges facing opposing party plans (though these slight differences are not statistically significant). In other words, judges appear not to favor their own party's plans or disfavor the other party's plans to any particular degree when deciding these cases.

To provide additional evidence on the effects (or lack thereof) of partisan influences in these Florida cases, I employ a multivariate logistic regression analysis that models the judge's vote to uphold (1) or strike down (0) a redistricting plan in a case.[70] When a dependent variable is dichotomous, as in this case, logistic regression is an appropriate technique to model a judge's vote choice. The independent variables in this model (i.e., the factors that might influence a judge's vote) include whether the judge was an opposing party judge (1) or not (0), whether the court was a state court (1) or federal court (0), whether the case was a VRA case (1) or not (0), and finally, whether the judge was of African American descent. It is a little bit problematic placing the votes of federal judges (three-judge courts) in the same statistical analysis as votes of state supreme court justices (seven justices per case) because modeling behavior together for these different courts is like mixing apples and oranges. However, with so few judicial votes and cases to analyze, combining all judge votes into one large analysis is necessary to better test some propositions. In this respect, the statistical model is exploratory, and thus the results should be read with caution.

The regression results are listed in table 3.6. Judges reviewing opposing party plans appear to show no party favoritism and vote no differently than judges reviewing other plans.[71] However, state plans suffer a reduction in favorable judicial votes in cases dealing with the Voting Rights Act. Finally, judges who are African American are significantly more likely to vote against Florida redistricting plans compared to other judges.

Testing the ideology of judges in this first model is difficult for a couple of reasons. First, conservatives and liberals tend to react differently to different types of legal claims, and thus ideology effects could cancel out. Furthermore, there are no comparable ideology scores for federal judges and state supreme court justices, so including an ideology variable in the first model accounting for both federal and state judges is impossible. In order to test any possible ideological effects more directly, I examined a subset of my observations, containing only state supreme court justice votes in Voting Rights Act cases. In VRA cases at the federal level, previous research has found that liberals are more likely to strike down plans that are suspected of violating the VRA. In this second model, I use PAJID ideology

Table 3.6. Modeling judicial votes for and against state plans in redistricting cases

	All cases	Only VRA cases in state court
Opposing party judge	.255 (.531)	—
Voting Rights Act cases	-1.49*** (.435)	—
Cases in state court	1.38* (.557)	—
African-American judge	-1.24** (.439)	-2.10*** (.531)
Pajid scores (ideology)	—	.005 (.017)
Constant	1.17** (.425)	.695 (.792)
Log—likelihood	-54.9891	-27.34308
Pseudo R^2	.107	.058
N	111	46

Notes: Standard errors in parentheses; *p ≥.05; **p ≥ .01; ***p≥ .001 (two-tailed).
Dependent variable, first four models: vote to uphold state plans in a case (1); vote to strike down a plan (0).

scores of state supreme court justices developed by judicial scholars Paul Brace, Laura Langer, and Melinda Gann Hall.[72] This smaller subsample of VRA cases should also provide a better opportunity to explore the effects of race on judicial votes. The results of this regression indicate that ideology has no effect on Florida justices' votes in past VRA cases. However, race has a highly significant impact, and the substantive effect is quite large—being an African American judge decreases the chances of a favorable vote for the state in a VRA case by about 50 percent.

In short, previous court action in Florida indicates no systematic partisan or ideological influences on judicial votes either in the state supreme court or in the federal courts. There is anecdotal evidence of perhaps 1 vote (out of over 100) that might have been swayed by partisan feelings. In the 1972 three-judge court case of *Wendler v. Stone*, Judge Norman C. Roettger, a Nixon appointee, voted against a Democratic congressional plan in which political gerrymandering was one of the claims against the legislature. It is difficult to say whether Roettger's vote was influenced somewhat by partisan feelings for his party who undoubtedly was slighted in the redistricting process by Democrats.

Putting this one instance aside, what is remarkable is the lack of systematic or even anecdotal evidence of partisan favoritism in the Florida cases. On the other hand, Florida's problematic past with racial discrimination clearly played a role in influencing the diverging votes of African Americans versus other judges, particularly in VRA cases. Finally, the large number of plans upheld by Florida state and federal courts before 2012 may very well point to the limited nature of redistricting requirements in place in Florida before the new amendments.

Consider many of the claims in table 3.2. None of the contiguity claims offered clear rationales for the courts to step in. Some of the other claims by litigants, such as a failure to maintain communities of interest or compactness, were not even explicitly or implicitly listed in the 1968 state constitution. Political gerrymanders, also present in a number of these Florida cases, were not justiciable at the federal level until 1986 (and even after 1986, no statewide plan has been declared an unconstitutional partisan gerrymander by the U.S. Supreme Court). After the 1960s, the Florida state plans never came close to having equal population problems. Thus, one could reasonably argue that many of the judges in these cases were simply applying a cautious, judicial restraint interpretation of the law. In many cases, the law clearly militated against striking down a state plan. The only cases where one sees large numbers of dissents appear in VRA and racial gerrymandering cases.

The 2012 State Supreme Court Cases and the Future of Redistricting Litigation

Per the state constitution and its new amendments, the state supreme court assumed its mandatory jurisdiction to judge the new state legislative house and senate plans passed after the 2010 decennial census. The new amendments added a host of legal requirements in redistricting for the legislature to follow in crafting state legislative and congressional lines. The state supreme court, with four Democrats and three Republicans, would scrutinize a plan drawn by a Republican-controlled legislature, a political dynamic not unlike the situation after the 2000 redistricting round, where a Democratic-controlled state supreme court upheld challenges to a Republican-drawn legislative redistricting plan. However, the legal differences between the 2002–3 cases and the 2012–13 cases were the new state constitutional requirements. There were also differences in voting among Florida justices. While no justices on the Court dissented in the 2002–3 cases, there were clear partisan disagreements within the Court as to the outcomes of the 2012–13 cases. Did the new state constitutional requirements inject partisanship into the state high court's behavior?

In the first court review after the new amendments, in the case of *In Re: Senate Joint Resolution Of Legislative Apportionment 1176* (2012),[73] the Florida Supreme Court upheld the state house plan. Regarding the state senate plan, the Court found no evidence of minority vote dilution, equal population violations or contiguity problems. However, a majority of justices—four Democrats and one moderate Republican—struck down the state senate plan, claiming that it suffered, in various forms, from unconstitutional partisan intent, lack of compactness, utilization of inconsistent political and geographical boundaries, and incumbency favoritism. At one point in the opinion, the majority accuses the state legislature of drawing a non-compact senate district that "resembles an upside-down alligator."[74]

Two conservative Republican justices dissented in the case. What was remarkable for this opinion compared to previous Florida cases was the fact that one of the justices charged his colleagues with playing politics with their votes. Democratic justice Fred Lewis, in his concurrence, accused the two conservative Republican dissenters of engaging in "political rhetoric" against the majority opinion, asserting that the Republican opinions did "not assist an intelligent analysis and discussion."[75] This overt politicization of disagreement within judicial opinions is not uncommon in redistricting cases in other states such as Texas and Illinois,[76] but it is the first evidence of heated political disagreements influencing the written opinions of state supreme court justices in redistricting cases in Florida. For his part, Justice Canady, a former Republican congressman, lamented what he claimed was the majority's failure to provide a sufficient presumption of validity to the senate plan, stating, "Failing to adhere to that precedent creates the risk of having our decisions adjudicating the validity of redistricting plans decline into a species of 'it-is-so-because-we-say-so jurisprudence.'"[77]

A few months later, after the state legislature had revised the senate plan, the Supreme Court reviewed the new plan in the case of *In Re: Senate Joint Resolution of Legislative Apportionment 2-B* (2012),[78] and a majority of the court (five justices) signed off on the new plan; but Justices Perry and Quince, the Court's two African American justices dissented, arguing that one of the redrawn districts would dilute African American votes. Table 3.7 shows the breakdown of judicial votes in the most recent Florida Supreme Court cases.

After these initial 2012 rulings on the facial validity of Florida's legislative plans, the League of Women Voters and other groups filed more fact-intensive lawsuits in a Florida trial court challenging both the state senate and congressional plans. The state supreme court's behavior in these subsequent lawsuits helps bolster the notion that partisanship is starting to creep into the justices' decisions on redistricting after passage of the new amendments. For example, as these subsequent lawsuits proceeded to trial,

Table 3.7. Votes of justices for or against the GOP legislature in recent Supreme Court cases

Florida Supreme Court justices	In Re: Senate Joint Resolution of Legislative Apportionment 1176 (2012), 83 So. 3d 597	In Re: Senate Joint Resolution of Legislative Apportionment 2-B (2012), 89 So. 3d 872	The Florida House of Representatives v. The League of Women Voters of Florida (2013), 118 So. 3d 198
Barbara J. Pariente (Democrat)	Vote against	Vote for	Vote against
R. Fred Lewis (Democrat)	Vote against	Vote for	Vote against
Peggy A. Quince (Democrat)	Vote against	Vote against	Vote against
James E. C. Perry (Democrat)*	Vote against	Vote against	Vote against
Jorge Labarga (moderate Republican)**	Vote against	Vote for	Vote against
Charles T. Canady (Republican)	Vote for	Vote for	Vote for
Ricky Polston (Republican)	Vote for	Vote for	Vote for
Totals	2 for, 5 against	5 for, 2 against	2 for, 5 against

*Justice Perry was appointed by Republican governor Charlie Crist, but news accounts at the time stated that Perry is in fact a Democrat, and he is treated as such in this analysis.
**Justice Labarga is often referred to in the news media as a moderate Republican on the court.

the Republican-controlled legislature appealed to the state supreme court to dismiss the case against the state senate plan, claiming that the Florida Supreme Court already approved the revised map and no further review in lower trial courts was allowed under the state constitution. On a nearly pure partisan vote of 5 to 2, four Democratic justices and one moderate Republican justice voted to allow the trial against the Republican's revised senate plan to proceed while the two conservative Republican justices wanted the litigation dismissed (see table 3.7).[79]

In September of 2013, the Florida Supreme Court held a hearing on a preliminary issue in these cases. The plaintiffs in the lawsuit appealed to the supreme court seeking to have legislators deposed and documents produced of unfiled maps and other items during the pretrial process. The plaintiffs argued such evidence is necessary to prove intent. In oral arguments, Justices Lewis and Pariente, two liberal Democratic justices, seemed open to deposing Republican legislators, while moderate Republican justice Labarga seemed more skeptical of such a claim in light of separation of powers concerns.[80] Clearly, these recent cases since 2010 illustrate that race continues to influence justices' views on the Court with respect to redistricting and voting rights, while partisan influences on their decisions appear to have increased.

In the quest by voters in Florida to curtail the partisan, ideological, and self-serving motivations of state legislators, they may have inadvertently shifted some of the partisan politics into the judicial branch. The new amendments create a host of rules, and as other chapters in this book address, these new rules may have substantively changed the behavior of the legislature and its ability to gerrymander districts. Nevertheless, these new rules, while having the potential to constrain crass partisan mapmaking by the legislature, also bring the state supreme court into a tangled web of legal uncertainty that may very well inculcate partisan impulses into future decisions.

The Voting Rights Act, which is the most ambiguous of federal redistricting law,[81] has been incorporated into Florida's state constitution. Compactness requirements may be helpful in preventing a legislature from engaging in partisan mapmaking, but in the legal world, there is no standard mathematical measure of compactness that has been uniformly accepted by courts in other states. Furthermore, it would seem that the constitutional requirement stating that lines follow political and geographic boundaries—"where feasible"—has the potential to work at cross-purposes with compactness requirements, because geographical features and political boundaries seldom ever form nice circles or squares, shapes that measure high in compactness scores. Finally, the constitutional requirement prohibiting partisan "intent" in the drawing of lines, rather than a more objective standard of partisan effect, invites justices to arrive at the facts of how the legislature constructed a plan by relying on their own partisan prejudices. In sum, these new constitutional requirements are quite ambiguous and are open to partisan manipulation by the next Florida State Supreme Court called upon to review a new redistricting plan. With these new amendments, voters may have achieved what they wanted in the way of constraining legislative behavior in redistricting, but fixing this political problem might have yielded unexpected political problems in future Florida court cases.

II

POLITICS

4

Drawing the Line

Public Support for Amendments 5 and 6

JOSEPH T. EAGLETON AND DANIEL A. SMITH

In the November 2010 general election, both Amendment 5 and Amendment 6 received nearly 63 percent support from Florida voters, easily surpassing the state's constitutional requirement that at least 60 percent of the electorate must vote in favor of a proposed constitutional amendment in order for it to pass. The two constitutional ballot initiatives, dubbed by supporters as "Fair Districts," were designed to curb legislative gerrymandering. Following their passage, the initiatives were codified in Article III of the Florida Constitution, prohibiting the legislature from drawing, respectively, state legislative and congressional districts favoring or disfavoring any incumbent or political party, and requiring districts to be contiguous, compact, and as equal in population as feasible.[1] Comparing the long-held redistricting process in Florida to "foxes guarding hen houses" and "robbers guarding banks,"[2] the sponsor of the two citizen initiatives, Fair Districts Florida, sought to place stricter redistricting standards on the state legislature before its decennial task of carving up congressional and state house and senate seats.

In this chapter, we examine public support for these two constitutional ballot initiatives by analyzing pre-election survey data as well as precinct-level election results from the November 2010 general election. In contrast to other statewide redistricting ballot measures that have enjoyed considerable pre-election support—at least in the abstract—but nevertheless performed poorly at the polls, Amendments 5 and 6 managed to overcome the rational self-interest of many voters.[3] The electoral support for Amendments 5 and 6 was substantial both across the state of Florida and across partisan and demographic groups. We argue that the backers of Fair Districts Florida successfully framed the two initiatives as a fair, common sense solution to the inherently partisan process of drawing district boundaries, which engendered considerable support, even among those who might otherwise have been predisposed to oppose the measures. Indeed, our analysis of individual-level and aggregate-level data reveals that the two amendments appealed not only to Democrats and nonpartisans—who well could benefit from having partisan politics removed from a redistricting process controlled by the GOP majority in the state legislature—but also to Republicans and racial and ethnic minorities, notwithstanding the fact that the redistricting reforms could possibly harm these groups' immediate strategic representational interests.

Making the Case for Redistricting Reform

There is little question that "[p]olitics and political considerations are inseparable from districting and apportionment," as Supreme Court justice Byron White opined in 1973, writing for the majority in *Gaffney v. Cummings*.[4] In Florida, the Republican-controlled state legislature made it quite clear following the 2000 U.S. Census that they would gerrymander state legislative and congressional districts to advantage their party and incumbent lawmakers. In 2002, a federal court found that with regard to the 25 congressional districts drawn by Republican lawmakers during that year's reapportionment process, "[t]he legislature's overriding goal . . . was to adopt plans that would . . . maximize the number of districts likely to perform for Republicans."[5] Indeed, the court stated that it had "no trouble at all finding that the intent of the Florida Legislature, comprised of a majority of Republicans, was to draw the congressional districts in a way that advantages Republican incumbents and potential candidates."[6] Looking ahead to the reapportionment and redistricting process following the 2010 U.S. Census, there was therefore little expectation among reformers that the even more Republican-controlled legislature, with a 42-seat advantage in the 120-member house and a 16-seat advantage in the 40-member senate, would act any differently.

Realizing that redistricting reform in Florida was not politically feasible, a coalition that would eventually emerge to become known as Fair Districts Florida decided to take its case directly to the citizens of Florida. Despite the considerable public outcry against lawmakers jiggering their own districts that dates at least to the time of the eponymous Elbridge Gerry—a signer of the Declaration of Independence who would go on to be governor of Massachusetts and vice president of the United States—the effort to reform partisan gerrymandering would not be easy. In most states, with Florida being no exception, the path to amend the state constitution is lined with significant roadblocks.[7] The prospect of a majority of state lawmakers referring voters to a constitutional amendment to alter redistricting was out of the question, as any reform might compromise the reelection chances of those very legislators. It was clear that the majority party in Florida was unsurprisingly not interested in divesting itself of its power to draw legislative districts to protect its members.

As such, Fair Districts Florida took an alternate approach to redistricting than reform efforts undertaken in other states. In July 2005, Floridians for Fair Elections registered with the Florida Division of Elections as a political committee, with the intention of qualifying two initiatives on the 2006 general election ballot. Soon after the group received approval by the Florida Division of Elections, its members began circulating their original petitions for the initiatives—one of which would have created "a commission of 15 citizens appointed by legislative leaders and the state supreme court chief justice to draw the boundaries for legislative and congressional seats." The other initiative would have required "that the commission convene in time to draw new boundaries for the 2008 elections." By August 2005, the group had already collected more than 200,000 signatures on each petition, well on its way to meeting the 611,009 signatures needed to qualify the initiatives for the 2006 general election. However, the group's efforts would be thwarted by a simple counting error: unbeknownst to the coalition (as well as to the Division of Elections), the summary of their ballot initiative to create a citizen commission to draw districts exceeded the 75-word limit by six words.[8]

Following the Florida Supreme Court's decision to disqualify the one initiative because of the excessive word count in its summary language, Fair Districts Florida decided to scrap the two ballot measures and begin anew. This time, the coalition would use very different ballot language that was functionally distinct from reform efforts in other states, which like its earlier iteration in Florida, often sought to create a citizen commission to draw district lines.[9] The ballot title of Amendment 5, "Standards for Legislature to Follow in Legislative Redistricting," was followed by a 74-word summary:

Legislative districts or districting plans may not be drawn to favor or disfavor an incumbent or political party. Districts shall not be drawn to deny racial or language minorities the equal opportunity to participate in the political process and elect representatives of their choice. Districts must be contiguous. Unless otherwise required, districts must be compact, as equal in population as feasible, and where feasible must make use of existing city, county and geographical boundaries.

The language for Amendment 6 was nearly identical, merely substituting "congressional" for "legislative" in the title and the text. Under Amendments 5 and 6, the decennial redistricting process in Florida would not be removed from the hands of state lawmakers. Instead, the intent of the amendments was to place limits on the majority party controlling the state legislature; lawmakers would still be tasked with drawing district lines for themselves and for members of Congress. Fair Districts Florida ended up easily qualifying the two measures by the February 1, 2010, signature collection deadline.[10]

The new ballot language, which changed the functionality of redistricting from a citizen commission to placing reasonable limits on drawing districts for partisan or incumbent advantage, would become critical to how the coalition would frame the public debate over reform. Rather than having to convince voters that a citizen commission would do a fairer job of drawing district lines than state legislators, Fair Districts Florida instead only had to persuade voters to place reasonable restrictions on self-interested lawmakers who, in their opinion, have always "rigged districts to keep themselves in power." Asserting that under the current system, "[e]ach district was rigged to accomplish a particular result," and that "[v]oters did not have a real choice in selecting their representatives because the elections were rigged before they even started," Fair Districts Florida sought to convince voters that without serious redistricting reform, Florida would continue to suffer from unrepresentative and unaccountable government. Specifically, the coalition endeavored to win over voters by arguing that Amendments 5 and 6 would introduce a sense of reasonableness into the redistricting process through the removal of partisan and incumbent protections in the geographical crafting of district boundaries.[11]

Although the Fair Districts Florida coalition was comprised of a broad array of more than 50 nonpartisan organizations, including voting rights groups, labor unions, and individuals, and even though its board contained some prominent Republicans, including the incumbent Republican governor, Charlie Crist, Amendments 5 and 6 were backed and primarily funded by traditional Democratic-leaning groups.[12] The political committee hauled in more than 7,000 contributions totaling nearly $9 million between 2006 and Election Day in 2010. In addition, the NAACP, the ACLU, and the American Trial Lawyers Association, while not contributing directly to the coalition, actively campaigned for the passage of Amendments 5 and 6.[13] A few organizations accounted for the bulk of the contributions to Fair Districts Florida, with roughly two-thirds of the donations arriving in checks greater than $25,000. Fair Districts Florida received over $1 million from the National Education Association, $600,000 each from the Florida Education Association and the Service Employees International Union, and $400,000 from the Washington, D.C. political action committee America Votes. Progressive activists George Soros and Christopher Findlater provided additional financial aid in support of the amendments.[14] According to an analysis conducted by the *Orlando Sentinel*, more than three-quarters of the contributions to Fair Districts Florida flowed from "Democrats and their traditional allies."

Ellen Freidin, a Palm Beach attorney, served as the campaign chair for Fair Districts Florida, spearheading the effort. Freidin argued that Florida's gerrymandered districts deterred new candidates from running, as incumbents "actually designed their districts specifically for themselves." "They know how many registered voters in the district are Republican or Democratic," Freidin contended, "so someone from the other side can't win because they stack it that way."[15] Instead of having politicians pre-select their voters by gerrymandering districts, the coalition argued that district boundaries should be drawn in a way that gives voters a real choice in selecting their representatives. The two amendments, 5 and 6, the coalition contended, would stymie elected leaders from drawing legislative boundaries to benefit themselves or their political parties. "Instead of keeping voters together in more rational districts, Florida citizens have been cherry-picked by politicians as they drew voting districts to ensure they got the votes they need to get re-elected,"[16] Deirdre Macnab, coalition member and the president of the League of Women Voters of Florida, penned in a June 2010 editorial criticizing opponents of the measures.

The coalition received plenty of earned media, which undoubtedly bolstered support for the initiatives among the public. Every major newspaper in Florida supported Amendments 5 and 6. The *Palm Beach Post* wrote that "politicians in Florida try to pick voters, rather than let voters pick them," the more conservative *Tampa Tribune* noted that the Fair Districts Florida Amendments would "bring sanity to a loopy reapportionment process," and the largest newspaper in Florida, the erstwhile-named *St. Petersburg*

Times, explained that voters had "a historic opportunity to level the playing field by rewriting the rules for drawing political districts."[17] Even columnists for the conservative *Florida Times-Union*, based in Jacksonville, editorialized in favor of the measures, opining that "[party] bosses are fighting the amendments as are some minority elected officials, including our own U.S. Rep. Corrine Brown, whose sprawling district was designed to keep her in office and is the best example of why these amendments are needed."[18]

Not everyone, of course, was a fan of Fair Districts Florida's proposed reforms. Republican Kurt Browning, who served as Florida secretary of state under Governors Jeb Bush and Charlie Crist, was the spokesperson for the opposition, "Protect Your Vote." Browning claimed that the measures would create unachievable standards for the redistricting process, which would undoubtedly lead to lawsuits. "I believe it's just not good for Florida," Browning stated, as "[the] last thing that Florida needs is another election season filled with litigation."[19] Browning's political committee ran a series of television ads, asking voters to "[t]ake a close look at Amendments 5 and 6. They are a con job and a power grab." The ads claimed that "[l]iberal out-of-state special interests are spending millions on [Amendments] 5 and 6 to change the way Florida draws its congressional and legislative districts so they can elect more liberals to support the Obama-Pelosi agenda."[20] These ads charged that the Fair District standards would be impossible for the state legislature to achieve and that the amendments were "designed to elect more Democrats." More disingenuously, they claimed that the amendments would hurt minority representation by making it more difficult to draw majority-minority districts.[21]

Established only a few months before the November election, Browning's political committee received a total of nearly $4 million, but from fewer than 20 contributors. Protect Your Vote was financed largely by the Republican Party of Florida, which pumped more than $2.6 million into the campaign.[22] Other contributors included the Florida Association of Realtors ($278,000), the Florida Chamber of Commerce ($100,000), and former Florida Marlins owner H. Wayne Huizenga ($100,000). The majority leader of the Florida House, Republican Adam Hasner, described Amendments 5 and 6 as "a stealth agenda funded by the left to do in the courts what they can't do at the ballot box."[23] To Hasner and other Republican leaders, the unstated goal of Fair Districts Florida was to increase the number of Democrats among Florida's congressional and legislative delegations. Although there were approximately 600,000 more registered Democrats than Republicans in Florida in 2010,[24] since 1996, Republicans have controlled the Florida Legislature, usually by a healthy margin. As such, Republicans saw the two Fair Districts Florida amendments as a way for Democrats to undermine their stranglehold on Florida politics.

The Republican legislative leadership was dead-set against the constitutional amendments. "There are few things more hazardous in politics than a bad idea that sounds good," incoming House Speaker Dean Cannon told a crowd of more than 200 Florida Chamber of Commerce members following the passage of Amendments 5 and 6. A vociferous opponent of Fair Districts Florida, Cannon claimed that the premise of Fair Districts Florida "is flawed and the structure is flawed."[25] As Speaker, Cannon would squirrel away millions in "discretionary" funds to legally challenge the amendments, refuse to appoint legislators to the House Redistricting Committee, and join a lawsuit challenging the changes to congressional redistricting.[26] Prior to their passage, senate president-elect Mike Haridopolos asserted that the amendments would make it "mathematically impossible" for the legislature to draw districts that conformed to the constitutional requirements, thus forcing the courts to make the final decision.[27] Referring to the Fair Districts Florida Amendments as "full employment for lawyers," Haridopolos would go so far as to have the senate legislative staff draft a counter-amendment, what would become constitutional Amendment 7, in the spring 2010 legislative session.[28] Amendment 7, according to most observers, would have undermined Amendments 5 and 6 by stating that any redistricting plan need only be rationally related to the standards in the state constitution to be valid.[29] A circuit court judge eventually tossed Amendment 7 off the ballot, finding that its intended effect was unclear and that it would be confusing to voters, and the Florida Supreme Court later affirmed the lower judge's ruling by a 5–2 vote, striking Amendment 7 from the November ballot.[30]

In addition to the formal opposition by the Republican Party of Florida and Republican state lawmakers, two members of Congress—Democratic representative Corrine Brown, an African American whose majority-minority district wiggled from Jacksonville to Orlando, and Republican Mario Diaz-Balart, a Latino representing a majority-minority district in Miami who chaired the 2002 Florida House Redistricting Committee during the previous redistricting process both challenged Amendment 6. These two members of Congress claimed that the amendment was "riddled with inconsistencies" and would dilute minority representation.[31] They also argued that it violated protections under the Voting Rights Act, which they claimed allowed legislatures to carve out majority-minority districts, or districts where traditional minorities such as African Americans or Latinos make up a majority of the district's population.[32] Of course, both Brown and Diaz-Balart had another important reason to oppose redistricting reform: they were winners under the current system of gerrymandering. The two would later file a lawsuit in federal district court claiming that Amendment 6 was "unworkable" and would "have a devastating effect on minorities" by "bleaching the state of Florida."[33]

Representatives Brown and Diaz-Balart, whose opposition was echoed by other minority politicians like U.S. representative Alcee Hastings, state senators Gary Siplin and Alfred Lawson, and Republican U.S. Senate candidate Marco Rubio, claimed that Amendments 5 and 6 would make it virtually impossible for minorities to elect representatives of their choice. Specifically, by requiring legislators to make use of existing geographical boundaries and attempting to impose less arbitrariness in drawing districts, these minority elected officials argued that state lawmakers operating under the Fair Districts Florida standards would be unable to preserve communities of interest, which do not necessarily fall neatly along city or county lines. Notwithstanding language in both amendments stating that districts "shall not be drawn to deny . . . minorities the equal opportunity to . . . elect representatives of their choice," opponents of the Fair Districts Florida measures maintained that Amendments 5 and 6 would cause minority voters to lose their ability to elect minority legislators.[34]

The Voters Decide

On Election Day, November 2, 2010, Amendment 5 received a supermajority of 62.59 percent of the over five million votes cast, with Amendment 6 tallying slightly more, passing with 62.93 percent of the vote. For many seasoned observers of redistricting reform, the success of the measures came as somewhat of a surprise. When faced with election reform measures on the ballot, voters often make strategic choices to support or oppose redistricting reform based on whether they are electoral "winners" or "losers" under the current institutional system.[35] In the same way that elites who benefit from the way districts are gerrymandered are unlikely to favor any reform proposal that changes the status quo, voters who perceive that they benefit from the status quo are likely to resist any change to the current standards.[36]

In light of the many arguments made on both sides of the Fair Districts Florida debate, we examine public opinion on Amendments 5 and 6 prior to the election as well as election results to gauge whether or not voters shared some of the same sentiments on redistricting reform expressed by elected officials during the run up to the election. Specifically, we expect, consistent with the views expressed by party leaders, that registered Republicans and minorities were less likely to support the Fair Districts Florida initiatives. Since Republican lawmakers drew the current districts and consistently won both state legislative and congressional elections during the 2000s under those districts, we suspect that it would have been in the self-interest of Republican voters to oppose redistricting reform from a purely instrumental rationale.[37] Under the status quo, Florida Republicans are clear "representational winners." Conversely, Democratic voters, who are governed statewide by a majority of Republican lawmakers, are "representational losers" in the current system; accordingly, we suspect that they should have been more likely to support institutional change.[38] Indeed, Democrats in Florida have been statewide legislative "losers" since 1996, when Republicans gained control of the state legislature for good and registered Democrats likely began to feel underrepresented in Tallahassee. Considering that Democrats comprised less than a quarter of Florida's twenty-five-member congressional delegation in 2010, Democratic voters might also have valid reasons to feel underrepresented in Washington.

More difficult to predict is the public support of racial and ethnic minorities for Amendments 5 and 6. There is evidence that many African Americans and Hispanics view the redistricting process as unfair. Specifically, an analysis of opinions on districting included in the 2006 Cooperative Congressional Election Study revealed that blacks (36 percent) and Hispanics (42 percent) were more likely than whites (29 percent) to think districting is done unfairly.[39] Yet, in keeping with the arguments made by several minority elected officials regarding the possibility that the Fair Districts Florida amendments might dilute minority representation, support for reform among minority voters might very well be offset by these concerns. More subtly, though, it is possible that minority voters' views about redistricting reform may be shaped by whether they live in a legislative or congressional majority-minority district. Traditionally, these districts have been some of the most gerrymandered in Florida, as they have been carefully designed to ensure that racial and ethnic minorities have the ability to elect representatives of their choice, thereby enhancing their descriptive representation in legislative bodies.

Public Support and Votes for Redistricting Reform

What follows is our examination of who supported Amendments 5 and 6. Did Democrats support and Republicans oppose the reforms? Did minority voters share their elected officials' ostensible commitment to descriptive representation and hence retaining the status quo? While we expect Republicans and minorities to be less supportive of redistricting reform generally, the evidence suggests that support for Amendments 5 and 6 was widespread.

Initially, the Fair Districts Florida amendments did not facially appear to advantage any one political party over the other. Rather, the new standards were designed by their proponents to appeal to reasonable notions about how districts should be drawn by lawmakers in a nonpartisan fashion. Given the stature of the Republican majority in both chambers of the state legislature and in the state's congressional delegation, reform-minded Republican voters may have felt comfortable supporting the measures, or they may simply have underestimated the importance of district lines in maintaining their party's majority. Alternatively, they may have supported reform based on their long-term strategic interests, knowing full well that Republicans would still control the redistricting process in 2012 but be less sure of what the future might hold. By voting in favor of Amendments 5 and 6, Republicans could ensure that they would be protected from Democrats in future redistricting plans.

Second, African American voters may have had an incentive to support reform, contrary to the arguments made by elite minorities, if these voters, despite being represented by a black lawmaker, felt like "representational losers" from a more global perspective. Since African American voters are more likely to be registered Democrats, they might consider themselves on the short end of Florida politics, as electing a black Democrat to the legislature unlikely yields many tangible substantive benefits. Because of the Democratic Party's perennial minority status in Tallahassee, descriptive representation for many black Floridians might mean little in terms of substantive representation, so reforming the redistricting process might be seen as beneficial to their interests as a whole. This may have been especially true since the ballot summaries for Amendments 5 and 6 specifically contained language indicating that minorities would not lose their ability to elect representatives of their choice. For many minority voters, then, the Fair Districts Florida amendments might have looked like the best of both worlds, where majority-minority districts would be maintained while the entire districting process was made fairer.

Unfortunately, no exit polling on Amendments 5 and 6 was conducted. Instead, we make use of two different sources to explore voters' opinions on redistricting reform. First, we take advantage of a survey by the national political polling firm Harstad Strategic Research, conducted prior to the election to gauge voter opinions on the Fair Districts Florida Amendments. Second, we supplement these individual-level findings with aggregate election results from over 3,000 Florida precincts spanning 12 counties. Our results reveal broad-based support for redistricting reform.

Survey Results

In September 2010, Harstad Strategic Research surveyed 1,209 likely voters to gauge their opinions on Amendments 5 and 6 ahead of the November election.[40] The survey, which was conducted between September 12 and 16, oversampled about a hundred African Americans and Latinos,[41] making it particularly useful for examining minority opinions on redistricting reform. A split sample was used to query respondents about Amendments 5 and 6, with 609 respondents randomly asked how they would vote on Amendment 5 and the other 600 respondents randomly asked about their opinion on Amendment 6.[42] We then coded all "definitely" and "probably" yes respondents as 1, and all other respondents as 0.

Overall, 65.7 percent of respondents supported Amendment 5 and 64.8 percent of respondents supported Amendment 6. These numbers closely parallel the final election results, where over 63 percent of the statewide electorate voted in favor of the initiatives, lending strong external validity to the survey results. Among Democrats surveyed, 68.4 percent supported Amendment 5 and 66.8 percent supported Amendment 6. Although not overwhelming support, this is consistent with what we would expect given Democrats' status as "representational losers" in Florida politics. In line with other expectations, Republicans were less supportive than Democrats—but were only slightly so—as Amendment 5 garnered 63.4 percent support and Amendment 6 gained 62.4 percent. Perhaps surprisingly, support among Republicans was only marginally less than that of surveyed Democrats. In short, there was overwhelming bipartisan support for redistricting reform.

Breaking down the results of the September 2010 statewide survey by race and ethnicity reveals similar findings. White respondents were quite supportive (68.6 percent) of Amendment 5, placing restrictions on the redistricting of state legislative seats, but African Americans (62.7 percent) and Latinos (62.8 percent) were not far behind, challenging some of the assumptions that minorities may have wanted to hold onto intentionally gerrymandered majority-minority districts. The results for Amendment 6, regulating the drawing of congressional districts, were strikingly similar, with Latinos (66.7 percent) actually more supportive than either black (64.1 percent) or white (65.4 percent) respondents.

More importantly, the survey allows us to test whether living in a majority-minority district represented by a minority lawmaker had any impact on a likely voter's support for redistricting reform. Because the survey contained information on the state legislative (house and senate) as well as congressional districts in which the respondents lived, we were able to create six new variables, adding them to our dataset. We coded each respondent 1 if he or she lived in an African American majority-minority congressional district and 0 if he or she did not.[43] We did the same for those living in African American majority-minority state senate and house districts,[44] as well as for those residing in majority-minority Latino districts for each jurisdictional level.[45]

The level of support for Amendments 5 and 6, broken down by whether or not the respondent resided in an African American majority-minority district, is summarized in tables 4.1 and 4.2. As table 4.1 shows, 61.5 percent of all respondents living in African American majority-minority state senate districts supported Amendment 5. Among all those respondents living in African American state house districts, 66.7 percent indicated that they would vote yes on Amendment 5. It is conceivable, of course, that white voters residing in majority-minority districts—perhaps they felt trapped or underrepresented by a majority-minority legislator—may have been particularly supportive of redistricting reform, thereby driving up the overall level of support for Amendment 5. To test for this effect, we interacted a respondent's race with his or her residence in a majority-minority district. Although the number of respondents in each cell is low, table 4.1 shows that, while black voters in these districts were somewhat less supportive than the overall levels of support, almost 58 percent of black respondents residing in African American majority-minority state senate districts and 62.5 percent residing in African American majority-minority state house districts supported reform. Table 4.2's results with respect to Amendment 6 reveal substantively the same pattern of support.

Table 4.1. Support for Amendment 5, respondent residing in African American majority-minority senate or house district

	Yes on Amendment 5
All Respondents in state senate district (N=52)	61.5%
Blacks only in state senate district (N=38)	57.9%
All respondents in state house district (N=60)	66.7%
Blacks only in state house district (N=40)	62.5%

Table 4.2. Support for Amendment 6, respondent residing in African American majority-minority congressional district

	Yes on Amendment 6
All Respondents in congressional district (N=59)	64.4%
Blacks only in congressional district (N=27)	59.3%

Table 4.3. Support for Amendment 5, respondent residing in Latino majority-minority senate or house district

	Yes on Amendment 5
All respondents in state senate district (N=25)	52.0%
Latinos only in state senate district (N=17)	52.9%
Latino Republicans only in state senate district (N=7)	57.1%
All respondents in state house district (N=35)	48.6%
Latinos only in state house district (N=19)	42.1%
Latino Republicans only in state house district (N=7)	28.6%

While black voters showed strong support for Amendments 5 and 6—whether residing inside or outside of majority-minority districts—there is reason to believe Latino voters may have been less supportive of the reforms. Since many Latinos who reside in majority-minority districts are also Republicans, many of these voters may be "dual winners" under the current institutional scheme. That is, they might be having their cake (a Latino representative) and eating it too (receiving substantive representation). Accordingly, these voters should have been opposed to redistricting reform. Tables 4.3 and 4.4 reveal that this appears to be only partially true: a majority of Latinos living in majority-minority senate and congressional districts favored, but those residing in smaller majority-minority house districts opposed, the Fair Districts Florida proposals.

Table 4.4. Support for Amendment 6, respondent residing in Latino majority-minority congressional district

	Yes on Amendment 6
All Respondents in congressional district (N=52)	65.4%
Latinos only in congressional district (N=25)	56.0%
Latino Republicans only in congressional district (N=11)	45.5%

As with African Americans living in a majority-minority district, there is good reason to expect Latino voters residing in Latino majority-minority districts might be more inclined to oppose reform. Table 4.3 reveals that these voters were indeed the least supportive of the two ballot initiatives among the respondents surveyed. Only 42.1 percent of Latino voters in majority-minority Latino state house districts supported Amendment 5. This relationship, compared to the level of support of 48.6 percent among voters of all races and ethnicities in those districts, yielded a significant chi-square statistic—the only significant one among all the relationships we tested. Furthermore, although the subsample is quite small, just 28.6 percent of Republican Latino voters living in majority-minority state house districts indicated that they planned to vote yes on Amendment 5. The same opposition was not apparent, however, with respect to majority-minority state senate districts, as over 57 percent of Latino Republicans in these districts supported Amendment 5. Similarly, table 4.4 reveals that 56 percent of Latino residents supported Amendment 6, but support for reform among Latino Republicans living in majority-minority Latino congressional districts dropped to 45.5 percent.

Overall, the survey results reveal that support for reform, by and large, was broad-based and consistent across demographics.[46] The relationship between party identification and support for Amendments 5 and 6 was in line with our expectations, but both Democrats and Republicans were more than 60 percent supportive of reform. With respect to race, the relationships were generally in the expected direction, with Latino Republicans in Latino majority-minority districts—the "dual winners" under what was the current districting system—manifesting the lowest levels of support. Ultimately, however, the results indicate strong support for redistricting reform across the board.

Election Results

To supplement our individual-level survey data, we also examined 2010 election results for Amendment 6 at the precinct level across three congressional districts. Specifically, we gathered official Amendment 6 results from every county included in the majority-minority congressional districts of Corrine Brown and Mario Diaz-Balart, as well as the congressional district of C. W. Bill Young, as a control case.[47] We then aggregated the results for each representative, coding precincts in counties within these members' districts as 1, and all other precincts as 0. By comparing precinct-level support for reform among voters living within a set of counties, we can determine whether voters who were gerrymandered into majority-minority districts were more or less likely to support Amendment 6 relative to fellow voters who resided in non-majority-minority districts.

We chose Representatives Brown and Diaz-Balart since these two representatives were the most vocal leaders of the effort to defeat the Fair Districts amendments, and because their districts gave us a chance to examine voting patterns in an African American and a Latino majority-minority district. We chose Congressman Young's district because it is the only district in the state wholly contained within one county, Pinellas. In this way, it provides some validity for the cross-county precinct-level results for the other two members of Congress.

Table 4.5 shows strong overall support for Amendment 6 across all 12 counties that fall within the boundaries of the three members' districts. Given Representative Brown's adamant opposition to the Fair Districts amendments, we might expect voters residing in the 257 precincts that comprised District 3 to be significantly less supportive of reform than voters living in the 1,008 precincts in the same nine counties not contained in District 3. Yet, 56.6 percent of voters in her district nevertheless voted "Yes" on Amendment 6. Though close in geographic proximity, the level of support for reform among voters not living in Brown's majority-minority district was only slightly higher, at 60.1 percent. These results reveal that a clear majority of voters—including the bulk of African Americans living in the majority-minority district—did not support Congresswoman Brown's opposition to redistricting reform.

A similar pattern of support for redistricting reform was evident in Congressman Diaz-Balart's precincts falling within District 21. While voters residing in his majority-minority district did not give quite as much support for Amendment 6 compared to other voters living in the remaining

Table 4.5. Majority-minority congressional districts precinct support for Amendment 6

Counties	Precinct	Yes on Amendment 6
Alachua, Clay, Duval, Lake, Marion, Orange, Putnam, Seminole, and Volusia	All (N=1,265)	59.4%
	Brown precincts (N=257)	56.6%
	Non-Brown precincts (N=1,008)	60.1%
Broward & Miami-Dade	All (N=1,574)	70.5%
	Diaz-Balart precincts (N=191)	62.3%
	Non-Diaz-Balart precincts (N=1,383)	71.7%
Pinellas	All (N=372)	67.6%
	Young precincts (N=255)	66.8%
	Non-Young precincts (N=117)	69.3%

precincts in Broward and Miami-Dade counties, a sizeable 62.3 percent of voters in Diaz-Balart's district supported the reform measure. By way of comparison, Pinellas County voters living outside and within long-time Congressman Young's District 10 strongly supported reform. Pinellas voters residing outside of the district supported Amendment 6 with 67.5 percent of the vote, and those living within Representative Young's District 10 supported the initiative with 66.8 percent of the vote.

Conclusions

Fair Districts Florida touted Amendments 5 and 6 as a common sense, practical fix to a complex problem. By establishing additional standards for drawing congressional and legislative districts, proponents of Amendments 5 and 6 sought to make government more representative. On Election Day, a supermajority of Floridians apparently agreed. There was extensive support for redistricting reform in both the statewide pre-election survey and at the precinct level across partisan and racial and ethnic lines, indicating that a broad array of Florida voters strongly supported institutional change.

Immediately following the passage of the two Fair Districts Florida amendments, Representatives Brown and Diaz-Balart filed a lawsuit challenging the amendments' validity.[48] Although Brown and Diaz-Balart, joined by the Florida House of Representatives as a plaintiff-intervener, continued to argue that Amendments 5 and 6 were unconstitutional, their legal arguments proved to be unsuccessful in federal court. In September 2011, a Miami federal district court judge ruled that the new redistricting standards for the congressional seats passed constitutional muster.[49] Judge Ursula Ungaro rejected the challengers' argument that Amendment 6 removed redistricting powers granted to the state legislature under the U.S. Constitution. The state constitutional amendment "does not supplant the Florida Legislature," Ungaro ruled, but rather, "it attaches a series of conditions, adopted in accordance with the state constitution, to eventual legislative action on redistricting." In January 2012, the Eleventh Circuit Court of Appeals upheld the amendment, finding that the reform did not usurp the state legislature of its power to draw districts. "It's sad that Floridians had to hire an army of lawyers to protect themselves from their own elected officials," said former Democratic state senator Dan Gelber, the general counsel for Fair Districts Now, following the federal district court's decision. "It's the Florida Legislature's constitutional obligation to draw a map," he continued, saying "they need to draw it fairly and they need to draw it soon. . . . It is silly for them to say they're waiting for somebody else to do their job."[50]

Despite the heated rhetoric of some elected officials in opposition to Amendments 5 and 6, there is no doubt that the voters spoke clearly on Election Day. Support for reform was strong across all partisan and demographic groups. Whether approval was driven by the straightforward language of the initiatives themselves, the more effective campaign run by Fair Districts Florida, or perhaps the broader anti-incumbent mood of the 2010 midterm elections, a clear majority of Floridians wanted to reform the state's redistricting process. Given the overwhelming public support, opposing arguments to derail Amendments 5 and 6 amounted to little more than political posturing, especially by incumbents fighting to cling to power in the face of obvious public opinion to the contrary.

5

Redistricting in Florida

Loud Voices from the Grassroots

SUSAN A. MACMANUS, JOANNA M. CHESHIRE, TIFINI L. HILL,
AND SUSAN C. SCHULER

This process was the most transparent and open in Florida's history.
Rep. Will Weatherford (R), Chair, House Redistricting Committee, February 9, 2012

Now the courts have to step in to implement the will of the people, a job the GOP
in Tallahassee failed to accomplish.
Rod Smith, Chair, Florida Democratic Party, February 9, 2012

On Thursday, February 9, 2012, the Florida House and Senate approved the
state's congressional and legislative maps, thereby concluding the requisite
legislative approval of each plan. The vote "culminated a seven-month exercise that included *unprecedented public input* (emphasis added), through
the aid of technology, and was driven by Florida voters demanding a fairer
process of redrawing political boundaries."[1] According to statistics released
by the Florida Senate, 4,797 attended public hearings and 1,637 spoke at
hearings.[2] "Thousands more Floridians participated in the [Redistricting
Public Outreach Tour] using social media and tuned in via the live meeting
broadcasts provided by the Florida Channel."[3] Interested citizens submitted 175 redistricting maps; fewer than ten were submitted during the 2002
redistricting process.

Republicans argued emphatically that the plans adhere to the public's
will expressed through a series of 26 public hearings held across the state
from June 20 to September 1, 2011 and another period for public input in
the form of e-mailed comments, recommendations, and proposed maps
following committee release of map drafts. The Florida Democratic Party
and a Fair Districts-supportive coalition believed just the opposite. In their
eyes, the Republican-controlled legislature largely ignored the public's will

as spelled out in new redistricting standards approved by 63 percent of Florida voters on November 2, 2010 (constitutional Amendment 5 for the state legislature and constitutional Amendment 6 for congressional districts in Florida). The same day the Florida Legislature adopted the 2012 congressional and legislative maps, each entity filed a lawsuit in Leon County Circuit Court challenging the constitutionality of the congressional map, "claiming lawmakers didn't do what voters told them to."[4] Shortly thereafter, the same plaintiffs filed legal complaints against the house and senate legislative maps in the Florida Supreme Court.

The purpose of this research is two-fold. First, it is designed to examine empirically public input into the redistricting process: (1) the participants—how many, who, when and where, and why (concerns and recommendations), and (2) the degree to which there was consensus among the many "voices from the grassroots" regarding both the process and the actual line drawing. Second, it analyzes the effectiveness (outcome) of citizen input—the extent to which specific citizen voices were heeded by the legislature.

The major focus is on citizen input into the map drawing—first, before *any* drafts were circulated and, second, *after* map drafts were released by the senate and house redistricting committees. The effectiveness of citizen input at each stage—pre- and post-legislative map-drawing—will be examined with regard to both the process and the line-drawing. *"Authentic participation requires . . . [a] focus on both process and outcome."*[5]

While a plethora of studies (many conducted at the local level) have empirically examined citizen participation in policy areas such as planning, education, law enforcement, health and social services, civil rights, transportation, housing, urban renewal, and the environment, few have focused on citizen participation in the redistricting policy arena, particularly at the state legislative level. Previous research has documented the role of citizen participation in a democratic society, spelled out the strengths and weaknesses of citizen input, and highlighted the difficulties of measuring the effectiveness of citizen participation on the policymaking process. The 2012 redistricting in Florida affords scholars a rare opportunity to conduct such an analysis in the nation's third largest state, with its very racially and ethnically diverse population and highly partisan electorate.

Why Citizen Input and How to Structure and Measure It

Scholars and practitioners agree that citizen participation is a key component of democracy[6] and that "decision making without public participation is ineffective."[7] Since the 1960s, citizen input in some form has been solicited by governments at all levels because it has become so intertwined with democratic principles.[8] "Direct citizen participation is pervasive."[9] "Despite the warnings of its dangers, limitations, impracticality, and expense, especially in large, complex, heterogeneous, technologically advanced 21st-century societies, [direct citizen participation] remains an ideal that animates many of our theories and beliefs."[10]

Traditional forms of citizen input, such as public hearings and town hall type meetings, have been married with "revolutionary forms of connectedness—media, adaptations of information and computer technology, and the Internet . . . to support the deliberative process."[11] In 2012, Florida utilized all of these "connectedness" tools in its efforts to involve more citizens in the redistricting process both before and after initial maps were drawn by legislative committees.

The Price of Inadequate Citizen Input

Inadequate citizen input can contribute to unrepresentative views, the stifling of divergent voices, particularly those of society's disadvantaged. It can also lessen citizen trust of public officials and increase voter apathy and alienation if the public's input is ignored: "Citizens . . . are rendered cynical or apathetic by vacuous or false efforts to stimulate participation that ask for, yet discount, public input."[12] In fact, one study of the impact of redistricting on voters whose congressional districts were greatly altered found that voter turnout rates were lower after the new districts were drawn.[13] Two major consequences of inadequate citizen input are that it can result in ineffective and inefficient[14] public policy and it contributes to a lack of public transparency and accountability.[15]

Key Impediments

Because of the severity of inadequate citizen input, scholars have expended a great deal of intellectual capital on identifying key impediments to participation. In addition, scholars have recommended ways to avoid or overcome these impediments, particularly those impediments associated with public hearings.[16] Impediments can stem from decisions related to: hearing timing (day/hours); location; participant recruitment and access, pre-hearing publicity; pre-hearing transmission of critical information to potential participants; participatory rules (time limits, subject limits, permissible forms of interaction with moderator and other decision makers); stage of the policymaking process (formation, implementation, evaluation); clarity of goals and objectives of the hearings for both the citizens and the law-makers (transparency); and cost. It is important to note that demographic, socioeconomic, and political differences across states and communities often yield divergent assessments of these common barriers to citizen input.

Differences of opinion appear to be most common with regard to how to structure input on highly complex and technical policies, how broad a net should be cast to "recruit" participants, how to avoid accusations of non-inclusiveness, at what stage citizen input in the policymaking process should occur, and how to gauge citizen input effectiveness. Measuring effectiveness has always been a rather elusive task, especially with regard to complex issues with extensive legal requisites and constraints such as redistricting, when raised in politically divided areas such as Florida.

Recommendations to Boost Citizen Input

Generally, recommendations for enhancing citizen input, particularly in public hearings, cluster around improving: (1) access; (2) the quality of information and assistance; (3) representativeness and inclusiveness; (4) procedures; and (5) the likelihood of inputs impacting policy decisions— including measurements of effectiveness. An examination of suggestions made by scholars shows a high level of agreement on how to better structure citizen participation opportunities. Efforts at each are evident in Florida's 2012 redistricting cycle.

Access. The two recommendations of scholars concerning suggestions about improving access are: (1) varying hearing times to better accommodate workers; and (2) selecting geographical locations with easy access and proximity to the targeted participants. Two sessions were conducted in three of the larger cities hosting hearings (Tallahassee, Jacksonville, and Orlando). Eleven hearings were held in the morning, four in the afternoon, and 14 in the evening, giving the public 29 total opportunities to speak (see appendix table A.2).

Information and assistance. The primary recommendation of scholars concerning enhancing information and assistance is to improve advance publicity of citizen participation in the redistricting process. This can be accomplished by utilizing multiple media and providing these multiple media outlets with enough lead time to transmit critical, understandable information and instructions to potential participants.[17] Government officials need to "employ more advanced publicity and information programs that reach affected people in language understandable to them and in time for them to prepare [comments]."[18] At the hearings, knowledgeable staff should be available to explain input procedures, highly technical concepts, software programs (redistricting) and online input techniques. The purpose of the hearing must be clearly communicated to potential participants,[19] as well as what will and will not be discussed and how the results will be used.[20]

Beginning in 2009 with pre-census preparations, key legislators and staff members adopted the approach of "first educating, then engaging" the public in the redistricting process. This "strategic communication effort" created websites (http://www.floridaredistricting.org and http://RedistrictFlorida@flsenate.gov), Facebook pages, two blogs, and an e-mail subscriber option. At the 26 public hearing sites, staffers were available to demonstrate the redistricting software and answer technical questions. A YouTube channel featured video tutorials on how to draw maps and use the software.[21] At the public hearings, state legislative leaders, such as Senator Don Gaetz and Representative Will Weatherford, distributed informative brochures, made staff available, and stressed the importance of citizen input. Senator Don Gaetz at the Jacksonville redistricting hearing stated:

> Before, during and after this hearing, senate and house professional staff are available to show anyone the simple steps to getting on-line, building districts and submitting a plan now or in the weeks to come, and you can submit a plan for Northeast Florida, for your county, for your neighborhood or for the whole state.[22]

State representative Will Weatherford offered similar advice for citizens at the same Jacksonville redistricting hearing:

> It is important, and the sole purpose of what we are here for is to hear from you and to give your input and to hear what you think the legal standards that are set before the legislature and how those can be applied to districts that represent you here in Northeast Florida.[23]

Representativeness and inclusiveness. The recommendations for improving representativeness and inclusiveness in the citizen participation in the redistricting process are: (1) structure participant recruitment and hearing opportunities in a way that all participants have equal footing and one group is not privileged over the other;[24] and (2) contact key stakeholders and advocacy groups representing the oft-excluded. Typically "excluded or oppressed groups" include ethnic and religious minorities, indigenous peoples, women, the old, gays and lesbians, youth, the unemployed, underclass and recent immigrants."[25]

Florida's redistricting committees reached out to a wide array of groups—"representatives of advocacy organizations (e.g., Fair Districts coalition members), city and county commission members, representatives of regional planning councils, school board members, colleges and universities, student government associations, and supervisors of elections, among others."[26] Special outreach efforts were made to racial and language minorities.

The Florida House redistricting website (http://www.floridaredistricting.org) featured a downloadable publication entitled, "The Impact of Redistricting in YOUR Community: A Guide to Redistricting" by NAACP Legal Defense and Education Fund, Asian American Justice Center, and Mexican American Legal Defense and Educational Fund. The website also included a link to a YouTube video of a Spanish-Language Video PSA about redistricting.

The legislature's Joint Committee on Redistricting was comprised of 48 state senators and representatives. The sex, ethnic/racial, and party affiliation breakdown was: 33 percent female and 67 percent male; 71 percent white, 21 percent black, and 8 percent Hispanic; 35 percent Democratic and 65 percent Republican.

Procedures. The reality is that some citizens are inhibited by certain procedural rules—microphones, videotaping, walking to the front of a large room/audience to speak, and time limits.[27] They become flustered when there is no provision for interaction with the moderator or policy-makers present. "They get this egg timer, time to grab the microphone and speak. There's no follow-up. You don't even get to ask them questions. . . . There's no give and take."[28] Such structures produce "one-way transmissions of information from . . . citizen to public officials rather than citizen engagement in dialogues and deliberations over public policy.[29]

In spite of these legitimate criticisms, procedural rules are unavoidable. They must be in place to ensure input equity and to maximize the number of participants, particularly on contentious issues (redistricting) that will generate large crowds. The key is to publicize the rules, with explanations as to why they are needed, and how they enhance fairness. (As will be discussed later in the paper, failure to explain the rationale for the one-sidedness of public input at redistricting hearings early on quickly put hearing moderators on the defensive and created extensive bad publicity for Florida legislators.)

At each of the 26 hearing sites, attendees and speakers were asked to sign-in for the purpose of the public record. Those wanting to speak were asked to complete a sign-up card listing their name, address, and affiliation.

The time limit for speakers varied depending on the number of speakers that were signed up to testify at each hearing, although on average, speakers were given about three minutes each. Speakers were called in the order in which they signed up. If they were out of the room when their name was called, their card went to the end of the stack to be called again time permitting. They used welcoming language to help citizens coming to the microphone to feel at ease. Staff was available to adjust the microphone, display the citizen's map should they have brought one, et cetera.

Moderators announced how the hearing would be conducted. Although the hearings were structured as generally one-sided (speaker to joint committee), members of the committee had an opportunity to comment after all public testimony if time permitted. In later hearings following complaints about the "gag order," moderators at the Jacksonville redistricting hearing such as Senator Gaetz, informed attendees at the session's opening that: "If after every citizen who wants to speak has had his or her say there is time remaining, if there is time remaining then before our scheduled adjournment, then, of course, any member of the committee may make any statement, offer any proposal or any suggestion."

Real policy impacts. First and foremost, citizens need to feel that policymakers are listening to them and that their input has had an impact on the process and/or the outcome.[30] "There is a critical difference between going through the empty ritual of participation and having real power."[31] There is a greater likelihood of increased cynicism toward decision makers and alienation from the political process when citizens sense they are being "used."

Scholars agree that *chances for real citizen input, particularly on highly controversial issues, are enhanced by involving the public early in the policy process*: "Public involvement is needed early to encourage consensus and to legitimize the process."[32] In addition, scholars concur that "[h]igh conflict issues may require citizen participation in the development of alternatives in order for the public to accept the final outcome. Otherwise, groups may see the decision as biased against them or as not reflective of the majority opinion."[33] Irvin and Stansbury[34] recommend that public officials seek input *before* making critical decisions. They are critical of hearings where public officials decide on a policy, then introduce it to the public for review and comment. Such an approach increases the perception that the decision is already a "done deal" and that the hearing is merely "window dressing."

Ironically, early on in the redistricting process, Florida legislators had to defend themselves for seeking input via public hearings before drawing congressional and legislative maps. Later, after considerable pressure from Fair Districts coalition supporters, legislators solicited public comments and recommendations on their map drafts (released several months after the completion of public hearings) via other public input mechanisms—e-mails, Twitter, et cetera. Changing public involvement mechanisms is common and appropriate at different stages of the policy development process.[35] In later stages, timing and cost constraints often limit use of large scale public hearings. In Florida, the cost of conducting the statewide series of public hearings was a criticism some citizens made but one that lawmakers were willing to endure. As Irvin and Stansbury note: "When the political situation is volatile and top-down decision making would be unpopular (if not unworkable), the up-front cost of citizen participation may be worth the additional funding because the costs of a difficult implementation of policy might be avoided."[36]

In one of the most widely cited articles on how to measure the effectiveness of citizen participation, Rosener[37] lays out the difficulties of doing so. It is not easy to reach agreement on the purposes of citizen input and the criteria by which success or failure will be judged. A number of other scholars have also tackled the measurement issue. Checkoway[38] states that if the purpose of measuring effective citizen participation is just to increase participation, then success is simply measured by counting the number of proceedings and the number of participants. Crosby, Kelly, and Schaefer[39] are more specific in their list of what constitutes successful citizen participation:

(1) Participants are representative of the broader public and are selected in a way that is not open to manipulation.
(2) Proceedings promote effective decision making.
(3) Proceedings are fair.
(4) The process is cost-effective.
(5) The process is flexible.
(6) The likelihood that the recommendations of the participants will be followed is high.

These three scholars acknowledge, "that there are no widely accepted criteria for judging the correctness of a policy choice." That task is made even more difficult when a single policy choice (such as a redistricting plan) is the outcome of a calculation encompassing multiple criteria, which are likely to be weighted differently by various actors in the decision process. Such is the situation in Florida, where seven redistricting standards must be met, but not all of these standards are given equal weight by the various actors in the decision-making process. When in conflict, first-tier (1) standards supplant second tier (2) standards. (See chapters 2 and 6 for the detailed list of criteria, and chapter 3 for a discussion of how these standards invariably conflict.) However, even among those standards of equal standing (same tier) with no order or priority, agreement is lacking as to how each standard should be operationalized and which standards are more important than the others to individual citizens or various advocacy groups.

Sometimes real policy impacts are not observable in the short-term, but appear incrementally over time. Public hearings and town hall meetings help build or strengthen community organizations and coalitions, which ultimately are successful in changing public policy by bypassing unreceptive legislative bodies via initiative processes or even litigation. For example, a coalition of groups led a successful constitutional amendment petition-drive changing Florida's redistricting standards, participated in the public hearings conducted by the legislature, submitted alternative maps, and ultimately sued the state for failure to utilize the new standards in the 2012 redistricting (see appendix table A.1 for a listing of groups affiliated with the Fair Districts coalition). This outcome was expected. Previous research has shown that "because single-issue groups are wholly committed to their issue, they tend to be more resistant to compromise than multiple-issue groups."[40]

Research Methodology

Two databases were constructed for this study. The first (and most comprehensive) includes information gleaned from the universe of speakers appearing at a statewide series of public hearings before any redistricting maps were released. The second includes citizen responses to maps after their release but before final approval.

Public Hearing Database

Units of analysis: All 1,368 speakers at 26 public hearings held across Florida—June 20 to September 1, 2011.[41, 42]

  Questionnaire Construction: A coding sheet was constructed from:

- Redistricting standards established in two constitutional amendments approved by Florida voters in November 2010—Amendments 5 (legislative redistricting) and 6 (congressional redistricting).

- Federal Voting Rights Act minority participation and representation protections and court interpretations.
- Speaker comments as observed on videos of early public hearings posted online at http://www.floridaredistricting.com. All three researchers first independently, then collectively, provided input into the creation of questions and response categories. An "Other" category was created for each variable, thereby, enabling recoding after all speakers' responses had been entered into an SPSS file.

Data Entry: Recording of Responses; SPSS File: Public Hearings Data Set

- Researchers watched videos of each public hearing and recorded each speaker's demographics (race/ethnicity, and gender), group affiliation, and comments onto a questionnaire. Timelines were recorded for extended comments to enhance the ability of rechecking accuracy of recorded comments by re-listening or reviewing written transcripts posted online.
- Data were then entered into an SPSS file by Susan Schuler & Associates, a firm often contracted with by the Florida Institute of Government at the University of South Florida to assist with citizen opinion surveys. The Schuler firm specializes in "market research services, surveys, focus groups, focus group moderat[ing], telephone surveys, data entry, statistical analysis, and online surveys." Reclassification of "Other" responses, where appropriate, was a joint decision by Susan Schuler & Associates and the research team.

Statistical Analysis: Public Hearings Data Set

- Aggregate-level statistics (frequencies) were calculated for each variable to determine the degree of consensus among the speakers.
- Cross-tabulation analysis was used to break out responses by speaker affiliation (Private Citizen; Fair Districts Advocacy Group; Business/Conservative Group; Local Official; or Other). (Responses by gender and race/ethnicity were also analyzed, although there were fewer differences than when responses were broken down by affiliation.)

Legislative Map Drafts Reaction Database

Public comments were accepted by both chambers of the legislature between November 28, 2011 and January 31, 2012 in reaction to the release of preliminary maps drawn by the senate (congressional, senate) and the house (congressional, house). These comments were received via e-mail, YouTube, Twitter, and regular mail.[43, 44]

- Research team members analyzed each response posted on the http://www.floridaredistricting.com website to determine: (1) whether public comments were directed towards the congressional, state senate, or state house plan or intended as comments on all three plans generally; (2) whether citizens opposed a plan and if so why; and (3) whether they approved of a plan and, if so, their reasons for opposing a particular plan. Aggregate statistics comparing general support for and opposition to the outcome (plans) were calculated.
- To the degree possible, the affiliation of those commenting was included in the data set, although much of this information was missing from online postings. The analysis of these results, even though limited, is designed to give us more insight into how many citizens judged the redistricting process and outcome to be more acceptable (effective) versus those who did not.[45]

As previously noted, the best analytic approach to examining citizen input into redistricting is to first focus on their role in giving direction to legislators as to how to proceed (the process phase), then on citizen evaluation of the maps drawn by the legislators (the outcome phase).

Citizen Input: Pre-Map Drawing

Any doubts about Florida citizens' interest in the 2012 round of redistricting or their divergent opinions as to how it should be done were dispelled at the 26 public hearings held across the state from June 20 to September 1, 2011, attended by 4,797 people. According to our analyses of videotapes of the 26 public hearings held across the state, 1,368 citizens spoke.[46] They represented 55 of Florida's 67 counties.[47] Among the speakers, 58 percent were men, 42 percent women. Racial/ethnic minorities comprised 15 percent (African Americans, 10 percent; Hispanics, 5 percent). In terms of their self-reported affiliations, 60 percent were private citizens, 17 percent were associated with a Fair District advocacy group,[48] 8 percent represented a business or conservative group, 9 percent were local officials, and 5 percent were from a wide array of other groups, while under 1 percent did not self-identify with any political affiliation.

Table 5.1. The linkage between speaker affiliation, gender, and race/ethnicity

Numbers of speakers:		Speaker represents				
		Private citizen	Fair District advocacy group	Business, conservative group	Local officials	Other/ NA
Male	Black	37	15	2	7	7
	Hispanic	25	7	2	5	6
	White	403	78	77	68	39
	Other/NA	3	2	2	2	3
Female	Black	35	18	0	11	3
	Hispanic	18	9	1	1	1
	White	294	106	21	34	19
	Other/NA	4	2	0	1	0
Base		819	237	105	129	78

Percentage of speakers within each affiliation category		Speaker represents				
		Private citizen	Fair District advocacy group	Business, conservative group	Local officials	Other/ NA
Male	Black	5%	6%	2%	5%	9%
	Hispanic	3%	3%	2%	4%	8%
	White	49%	33%	73%	53%	50%
	Other/NA	0%	1%	2%	2%	4%
Female	Black	4%	8%	0%	9%	4%
	Hispanic	2%	4%	1%	1%	1%
	White	36%	45%	20%	26%	24%
	Other/NA	0%	1%	0%	1%	0%
Base		819	237	105	129	78

Notes: Analysis of all public hearing attendees making presentation in person; from videotapes posted on htttp://www.floridaredistricting.org.

Statistical significance is highest when responses are broken down by speaker affiliation than by gender or race/ethnicity comparisons because of the high correlations between the latter two variables and Fair District advocacy group status (see table 5.1). This explains why we have chosen to contrast citizen opinions and actions on redistricting by speaker association. Some speakers focused their comments on the process itself—how it was unfolding and what needed to be improved. Others recommended how, where, and why to actually draw district lines. Predictably, at this stage, there was more citizen consensus on the need to revamp the redistricting process than on the line drawing.

Comments on the Redistricting Process

The Hearing Itself. While most speakers did not comment on whether the hearings were a good or bad idea, more approved than disapproved of them (14 percent vs. 5 percent respectively). Among those expressly supportive of hearings, nearly two-thirds welcomed the chance to make their comments face-to-face to the legislators. Another 20 percent said the hearings helped inform them about how the process worked. Local officials and business groups more often cited face-to-face benefits, while Fair Districts supporters and private citizens liked the informative aspect (see table 5.2).

In line with previous research, those viewing the hearings unfavorably described them as "a sham" (54 percent) and/or complained about the cost (40 percent) or various other things (23 percent). (Percentages add to greater than 100 percent due to the multiple response nature of the variable.) In general, business groups and local officials were far less critical of the hearings than private citizens or Fair District advocacy group members (see table 5.3).

Issues of Concern. As shown in figure 5.1, the issues of greatest concern to the speakers were: (1) whether the legislature would adhere to the Fair Districts amendments standards when creating the district maps (26 percent); (2) whether the timeline for completion and court approval of the plans could be met (18 percent); (3) the state house's participation in a lawsuit challenging the constitutionality of provisions in Amendment 6 regulating the drawing of congressional districts (16 percent); and (4) the legislature's decision not to have proposed maps available at the hearings (15 percent).

Adherence to Fair Districts Standards. Among the 362 speakers who expressed concerns about this issue, nearly half (47 percent) feared that the legislators were seemingly ignoring these standards in spite of the fact that the *citizen-initiated and approved* Fair Districts amendments were ap-

Table 5.2. Public hearings are a good idea

Reason	Speaker represents				
	Private citizen	Fair District advocacy group	Business, conservative group	Local officials	Other/ NA
Base	121	14	27	14	10
Let voices be heard face-to-face	65%	64%	74%	79%	60%
Informative about process	21%	21%	19%	7%	40%
Other reason good idea	14%	.0%	.0%	7%	.0%

Notes: Analysis of all public hearing attendees making presentation in person; from videotapes posted on http://www.floridaredistricting.org.

Table 5.3. Public hearings are a bad idea

Reason	Speaker represents				
	Private citizen	Fair District advocacy group	Business, conservative group	Local officials	Other/ NA
Base	36	29	1	0	4
Costs too much	40%	45%	.0%	.0%	25%
A "sham"	56%	52%	100%	.0%	50%
Other reason bad idea	19%	28%	.0%	.0%	25%

Notes: Analysis of all public hearing attendees making presentation in person; from videotapes posted on http://www.floridaredistricting.org.

proved by 63 percent of the electorate. Predictably, Fair Districts coalition members were the most concerned about this development in the legislature (see table 5.4). Others (8 percent) worried about implementing the standards for compactness, communities of interest, and other standards contained in the Amendment 6 redistricting provisions, for which there were no clear legal definitions or saw the standards for these constitutional provisions as conflicting (5 percent).

The two standards most often mentioned in their testimony were district compactness (63 percent) and utilization of existing political and geographical boundaries (43 percent). Less mentioned were partisan neutral-

Public Hearings: Process Issues of Concern to Speakers

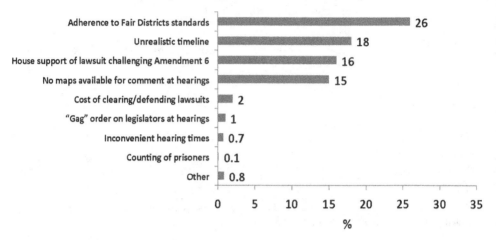

Figure 5.1. Issues of concern to speakers. Analysis of all public hearing attendees making presentation in person. Adapted from videotapes posted at http://www.floridaredistricting.org.

Table 5.4. Concern about Fair Districts adherence by speaker association

	Speaker represents				
	Private citizen	Fair District advocacy group	Business, conservative group	Local officials	Other
Base	819	237	105	129	73
Adherence to Fair Districts amendments	27%	41%	11%	9%	21%

Notes: Analysis of all public hearing attendees making presentation in person; from videotapes posted on http://www.floridaredistricting.org.

ity (26 percent), incumbent neutrality (25 percent), protecting the equal opportunity of racial or language minorities to participate in the political process (15 percent), prohibiting minorities' ability to elect representatives of their choice (13 percent), and equal population size (4 percent).

Unrealistic Timeline. By the time the public hearings began in June 2011, there had already been considerable media attention to Florida's compressed and late (by other states' standards) redistricting calendar. Indicative of citizen cynicism toward legislators' motives in the redistricting

Table 5.5. Concern about Fair Districts adherence to timeline by speaker association

| | Speaker represents | | | | |
	Private citizen	Fair District advocacy group	Business, conservative group	Local officials	Other
Base	819	237	105	129	73
Timeline is unrealistic	13%	36%	8%	21%	19%

Notes: Analysis of all public hearing attendees making presentation in person; from videotapes posted on http://www.floridaredistricting.org.

process, 23 percent of the speakers viewed the timeline as nothing more than an "intentional delay" designed to protect incumbents. Again, Fair Districts supporters more than others saw the timeline as unrealistic (see table 5.5). At the first public hearing in Tallahassee, the president of the League of Women Voters of Florida, which was part of the Fair Districts coalition, addressed this matter directly and urged the legislators to speed up the process: "Florida deserves elections where the people have time to understand their choices. This timeline benefits only incumbents and is likely to diminish competitive elections and certainly the time that our voters need to inform themselves about their choices."

Among the 239 speakers spelling out concerns about the timeline, 55 percent said it would unfairly affect potential candidates, 26 percent worried it would create massive voter confusion, and 28 percent feared it would put too much pressure on election officials. Some even saw the potential for another election system meltdown of the magnitude of the 2000 election. Deborah Clark, Pinellas County Supervisor of Elections, had this to say at the redistricting hearing in Largo:

There can be no doubt in your mind how important people's right to vote is, and how deeply they feel about the process, and how much they want to be included in the process. . . . Our [Florida State Association of Supervisors] main concern is time, and you've heard several people comment about how confusing it will be for candidates if we get those lines late next year. And it's happened before. It's our responsibility as Supervisors [of Elections] to conduct impartial and accurate elections for these folks and 11 million voters in Florida. But you have the authority to move that process along to ensure that we get those lines in plenty of time so that we can prepare for and be ready for the fall elections. We are perfectly capable of doing that. You heard a reference to the 2000 Presidential election. It would be shameful if Florida lost all the ground we've gained in the last decade, with all the efforts that have been put into election reform.[49]

As to the courts, 12 percent anticipated that there would not be enough time for the courts to clear the plans, while others (3 percent) were upset with the possibility that the courts would end up drawing the plans rather than elected representatives. With candidate qualifying for both federal and state offices beginning June 4, 2012, some worried there might not be enough time for the legislative plans to work their way through the requisite legal channels. These legal channels included obtaining approval by the Florida Supreme Court, achieving the preclearance approval of legislative plans required by the U.S. Department of Justice under federal Voting Rights Act Section 5, and overcoming the likely state and federal court challenges to the plans.

House Joining in Legal Battle Challenging Constitutionality of Amendment 6 (Congressional Redistricting). As mentioned earlier, citizen complaints (213 speakers) about this legislative action surfaced early in the public hearing cycle and forced legislators to have to "explain themselves." This criticism, too, was most frequently voiced by Fair Districts supporters (see table 5.6).

The chronology of the lawsuit was as follows:

November 3, 2010: U.S. representatives Corrine Brown (D) and Mario Diaz-Balart (R) filed a suit challenging Amendment 6 (*Brown v. Browning*) in the federal Eleventh Circuit Court of Appeals; they argued the amendment violates the federal Voting Rights Act and "represents an impermissible effort by Florida to limit the discretion directly delegated by the United States Constitution to the Florida Legislature."

January 11, 2011: Florida attorney general Pamela J. Bondi filed a motion asking a U.S. district court to dismiss the Diaz Balart-Brown lawsuit.

January 24, 2011: Florida House of Representatives formally filed to join the Brown-Diaz-Balart challenge of Amendment 6.

Many citizens (69 percent) found it ridiculous that state funds were being expended both defending the amendment (Secretary of State Browning) and challenging it (Florida House of Representatives): "How can we take

Table 5.6. Concern about Fair Districts lawsuit by speaker association

	Speaker represents				
	Private citizen	Fair District advocacy group	Business, conservative group	Local officials	Other
Base	819	237	105	129	73
Lawsuit against Amendment 6	16%	30%	4%	3%	11%

Notes: Analysis of all public hearing attendees making presentation in person; from videotapes posted on http://www.floridaredistricting.org.

taxpayer money and sue the taxpayers and that is what we are doing?" complained Wallace Haber at the Panama City hearing. Forty-eight percent saw it as wasteful; 23 percent cast it as a misplaced priority, arguing that the money spent on this case would have been better spent on schools and social services, both of which had been cut during the 2011 legislative session.

Some saw this whole lawsuit as evidence of partisanship (a Republican plot), but more saw it as legislators thumbing their nose at voter approval of Amendment 6. The issue certainly put legislative leaders on the defensive and forced them to explain their position at various hearings, which was neither an easy task nor very convincing to critics. State representative Weatherford responded to critics of the Republican lawsuit:

In regards to litigation, there were several questions about why are taxpayers fighting Amendments V and VI that have passed. Congressman Mario Diaz-Balart, who is a Republican from Miami-Dade County, along with a Democratic Congresswoman, Corrine Brown, from Jacksonville, actually are the ones who filed a lawsuit only in regards to Amendment VI, and it deals with a Federal constitutional issue. It only deals with the Congressional maps, and it is whether or not the U.S. Constitution had been impeded—has been impeded by that constitutional amendment that passed in Florida, and I won't get you into the details, but we will give you all of the information on that case if you want it. But just so it is clear, the two Congressmen, a Republican and a Democrat were the ones who originally filed that lawsuit, and I think that is very important. I think there has been some misinformation out there about that as well.[50]

Table 5.7. Concern about Fair Districts map preparation by speaker association

	Speaker represents				
	Private citizen	Fair District advocacy group	Business, conservative group	Local officials	Other
Base	819	237	105	129	73
No maps already prepared	14%	30%	10%	2%	2%

Notes: Analysis of all public hearing attendees making presentation in person; from videotapes posted on http://www.floridaredistricting.org.

September 9, 2011: U.S. District Judge Ursula Ungaro rejected the Diaz-Balart-Brown lawsuit challenging Amendment 6. The judge's decision was appealed. The House of Representatives continued as a party to the lawsuit. Speaker Dean Cannon said, "it was important as 'a matter of principle' to settle whether the citizen backed standards would apply not just to this round of redistricting but a decade from now." Cannon said "the judge's ruling was 'inconsistent' with the U.S. Constitution and case law and frankly also included some factual inaccuracies that reflect a basic misapprehension of some basic facts. Among these, according to a subsequent e-mail, the judge identified Diaz-Balart as a legislator, not a congressman.[51]

January 31, 2012: A panel of judges from the Eleventh Circuit Court of Appeals upheld Amendment 6. The State of Florida prevailed in the *Brown v. Browning* litigation. The Florida House of Representatives did not prevail.

No Proposed Maps Available for Comment at Hearings. Some citizens (15 percent) expected to be able to react to legislatively drawn maps at the public hearings and were angry when there were none, prompting accusations that the redistricting process was not fully transparent and that plans had already been drawn in "smoke-filled rooms" out of the sight of the public. This opinion was most pervasive among Fair Districts advocates (see table 5.7).

George Gonzalez, who spoke at the Largo hearing, shared this sentiment and saw it as part of a larger scheme to protect incumbents:[52]

I'm not really here today to give you my opinion about redistricting, how to draw the districts, or to plead that you create fair districts that more aptly represent the voter composition of our state because I know the money and time wasted on these meetings is only for show. *If you were truly representatives of the voters these meetings would have been held months ago, and they would surely include maps of suggested districts.*

Others felt just as passionately that soliciting citizen input first was the proper procedure. Legislative leaders repeatedly defended their "citizens first, legislature second" timetable. As expressed by Senator Gaetz at the Orlando hearing:

There should be no preconceptions created by politicians in our view, but rather public testimony should be free and unrestricted and should come first. In fact, the Chairperson for the Fair Districts campaign, Helen Freidin, testified before the House and Senate Redistricting Committees that she felt that it would be absolutely impossible to draw maps before public comment was taken and we certainly agree with Ms. Freidin with respect to that and are following that advice.[53]

Cost of Clearing/Defending Lawsuits against the Legislatively Drawn Districts. Prior to the public hearings, much criticism had been launched against legislative appropriations set aside to cover the costs of clearing plans through the Department of Justice and the Florida Supreme Court and defending the plans against lawsuits filed in federal and state courts. Thirty million dollars was a figure that was often cited by critics of the redistricting plans.[54] Similar to the criticisms of the costs involved in challenging the constitutionality of Amendment 6, some speaker critics (2 percent) characterized money spent to defend "bad plans" as a misuse of state funds. They saw it as taxpayer dollars being spent to defend actions citizens had already voted to prohibit. Atlantic Beach City Commissioner Carolyn Woods asserted:

I just want to add one brief comment to the subject of Amendments 5 and 6, and that is basically that I feel it is one thing for the people to sue the government, but it is quite another for the government to sue its people, and I am hoping that all of these workshops and public gatherings are your good faith effort to move forward with Amendments 5 and 6.[55]

And Mary Lou Woods at the St Augustine hearing voiced a similar criticism:

This is still America, right? Think about the park for a moment. If a dictator or someone, some other Third World leader spent the public's money trying to overturn its own vote, we as Americans would be appalled, but yet it is business as usual in the state of Florida.[56]

The frequency with which this criticism was made prompted legislative leaders presiding at the hearings to make a statement denying this allegation. For example, state representative Will Weatherford said at the Panama City hearing: "There is no $30 million pot of money. That doesn't exist. . . . Certainly we have to have attorneys, this process is legal in nature, we have to have staff, so resources are being addressed, but there is no large pot of money that is out there that is fighting anything."

"Gag" Order Prohibiting Legislators from Commenting at Hearings. Early on, some speakers (1 percent) expressed outrage that legislative leaders in each house had forbidden legislators to comment on proposed plans or public testimony—affirmation in the view of these speakers, of the one-way nature of the hearings. This concern prompted legislative leaders conducting subsequent hearings to rebut this claim. For example, at the Pensacola hearing Representative Will Weatherford stated: "There is no gag order. We have not asked members not to speak, simply we have reminded them that this is a listening tour. This is one of the few times I have seen in politics where you don't sit back and listen to politicians give speeches or pontificate for hours and hours on end."[57]

Time constraints dictated whether redistricting committee members addressed hearing attendees. Representative John Legg, who spoke at the Lehigh Acres hearing asserted: "If after every citizen has had his or her say there is time remaining before our scheduled adjournment, any member of the Committee may make any statement or offer any observation."[58]

Inconvenient Hearing Times. This criticism (0.7 percent) primarily came from those who spoke in locations where there was only one hearing and it was held during working hours. However, some critics also complained that an 8 a.m. start time was not optimal due to traffic congestion.

Counting of Prisoners. This concern (0.1 percent) was raised by a few speakers in rural counties in which large state prisons are located. Their worry was that because inmates cannot vote, the political clout of the community housing them would be unfairly diluted. These speakers urged legislators to count prisoners in the counties in which they are residents rather than in the counties where they are incarcerated. Jefferson County Commissioner Betsy Barfield stated at the Tallahassee hearing:

The practice of including prisons in local districting plans leads to serious distortion of political power in county and state governments. How fair is this to the people to whom we all represent and answer to? I ask you, please, do not include the prison populations while drawing the lines for districts in the State of Florida.[59]

Summary: Citizen Recommendations for Process Reforms

Over one-fourth (27 percent) of the speakers gave specific process-related recommendations for how to proceed with the redistricting process. Many reflected timeline concerns (see table 5.8). Some recommendations were more plausible than others and ended up being at least partially accepted, as will be detailed later in the discussion of citizen input effectiveness.

Public officials were the strongest advocates for speeding up the timeline. Fair Districts supporters advocated another round of public comment to respond to maps and amending the constitution to speed up redistricting, and both private citizens and Fair Districts proponents favored getting out of the litigation challenging Amendment 6 (see table 5.9).

Drawing the Lines: Key Concerns and Recommendations

At the hearings, only a small proportion of speakers expressed opinions about whether congressional (15 percent), state senate (14 percent), and/ or state house (17 percent) districts needed to be reconfigured. In each instance, the vast majority wanted to change the districts significantly. The three most common reasons were: (1) the old district lines split counties or

Table 5.8. Specific process-related recommendations

Recommendation	Percentage of speakers
Speed up timeline	54
Get out of lawsuit challenging Amendment 6	29
Hold hearings after maps officially drawn by legislature	25
Other process-related suggestions*	9
Suspend public hearings until maps drawn	3
Hold hearings at more convenient times	1
Propose constitutional amendment to permit redistricting of legislative districts in year when state receives census data	1

*Included instructions to use nonpartisan resources and experts and to simply let the computer draw the districts.

Table 5.9. Process recommendations by speaker association

Recommendation	Speaker represents				
	Private citizen	Fair District advocacy group	Business, conserva-tive group	Local officials	Other/ NA
Base	185	118	15	26	22
Speed up timeline	39%	57%	53%	77%	68%
Get out of lawsuit challenging Amendment 6	32%	31%	7%	5%	23%
Hold hearings after maps of-ficially drawn by legislature	22%	31%	20%	15%	27%
Other process-related statements	34%	24%	20%	8%	9%
Suspend public hearings until maps drawn	1%	5%	0%	0%	5%
Hold hearings at more conve-nient times	1%	0%	0%	0%	0%
Propose constitutional amend-ment to permit legislative redistricting earlier	1%	5%	0%	0%	5%

Notes: Analysis of all public hearing attendees making presentation in person; from videotapes posted on http://www.floridaredistricting.org.

cities; (2) the old district lines were tied to another part of the state that was too different from where they resided; or (3) the old district lines were ger-rymandered. These criticisms reflect perceived failures of the old configu-rations to keep communities of interest together, create compact districts, and produce more partisan balance and competitiveness.

Three percent of the public hearings speakers acknowledged they had at-tempted to redraw district lines using MyDistrictBuilder—the free software program available online that was promoted as easy to use and identical to that being used by legislators. Another 1 percent said they had tried to use the district drawing software program but had given up. Seventy-three percent of those who had used the software found it difficult to use. The instructions were confusing and assistance was not readily available or user-friendly (including the online tutorial). Key data were absent from the public use data set available via the house's MyDistrictBuilder and the senate's MyDistrict, specifically incumbent residential location and party registration information. Legislators were forthright in admitting that

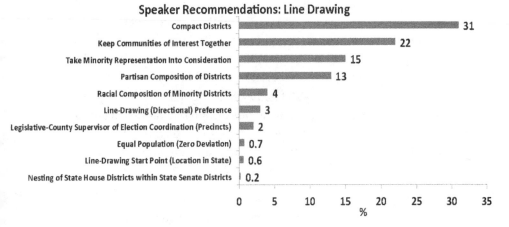

Figure 5.2. Speaker recommendations. Analysis of all public hearing attendees making presentation in person. Adapted from videotapes posted at http://www.floridaredistrict ing.org.

the exclusion of these data points from the software was intentional—to comply with Tier 1 requirements to draw partisan- and incumbent-neutral plans. Critics did not agree with this rationale, believing instead that it was another example of the lack of transparency in the process.

There was little consensus as to what factors legislators should pay close attention to when drawing district lines (see figure 5.2). All are interrelated, but the two most cited—compactness and keeping communities of interest together—are perhaps the most closely intertwined.

An excellent example of just how closely tied together are the principles of compactness and communities of interest is the testimony of Sheri Morton at the Orlando public hearing:

I live in unincorporated West Osceola County, a suburb of Orlando near Kissimmee. Osceola County is currently divided into three congressional districts with much of Osceola, including where I live in District 15. Most of the population of Congressional District 15 is from Brevard and Indian River Counties, which are far away from where I live and with which Osceola shares little in common. Brevard and Indian River Counties are focused on NASA. In contrast, the focus in Osceola is on metropolitan Orlando, including both Osceola and Orange Counties. Osceola is a majority-minority county with over a quarter of a million people, high unemployment and urban problems, including transportation, gangs, and gridlock on Interstate 4. People in Osceola generally work in the tourism industry, including theme parks and hotels. Having a congressman from far away on the east coast who is focused on NASA, I-95 and the beaches doesn't give my community the representation we need. With Osceola County broken into three congressional districts, the needs of Osceola's largely Hispanic population are easily ignored by central Florida's Congressmen. Please follow the Fair District Amendments of Florida's Constitution and keep Osceola County intact in one Congressional District. Please combine Osceola with Orange County into a Congressional District together that has similar community interests and populations.[60]

Compact Districts

The most common line drawing–related recommendation (at 31 percent) was to create more compact districts. That is easier said than done in light of the multiple quantitative measures submitted to courts to "prove" compliance with the compactness standard.[61] To the average citizen, compactness conjures up an image of a district shape that does not meander across multiple political and geographical boundaries. Among the speakers making this recommendation to state legislators, 62 percent urged that where

Table 5.10. Summary of draw compact district recommendations by speaker association

Recommendation	Speaker represents				
	Private citizen	Fair District advocacy group	Business, conservative group	Local officials	Other/ NA
Base	256	45	40	55	25
Keep counties, cities together	56%	53%	58%	76%	64%
Avoid odd-shaped meandering districts	38%	44%	23%	15%	28%
Avoid pieces being cut off into other districts	14%	9%	15%	16%	16%
Don't tie interior rural areas to coastal urban areas	6%	2%	18%	11%	0%
Other reason to draw compact districts	10%	16%	20%	22%	12%

Notes: Analysis of all public hearing attendees making presentation in person; from videotapes posted on http://www.floridaredistricting.org.

possible, counties and cities should not be split, 34 percent opposed odd-shaped meandering districts, and 16 percent argued against little pieces being cut off and placed in other districts.

Common arguments expressed by proponents of more compact districts were that they are needed to keep constituents closer to their elected representatives, reduce voter confusion, and help election officials and poll workers better conduct elections. A few even advised mapmakers not to adhere to the zero deviation (equal population size) standard if it would divide neighborhoods or precincts.

Predictably, support for keeping cities and counties together was highest among local officials. Preferences for more compact and less gerrymandered districts were highest among Fair Districts supporters and private citizens. Business and conservative affiliated speakers were more likely than others to want to keep economic communities together (see table 5.10).

Keep Communities of Interest Together

Slightly more than one in five speakers (22 percent) mentioned keeping communities of interest intact. However, the delineation of which communities should be kept together varied considerably, not surprising in a large diverse state like Florida. As shown in figure 5.3, *economic* (40 percent) and *geographically-based* (38 percent) definitions of "community" were the most prevalent, followed by socioeconomic, cultural, and political commonalities.

Among the speakers indicating the importance of protecting specific economic sectors being kept together, 56 percent cited coastal communi-

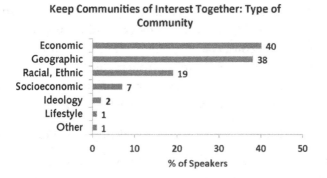

Figure 5.3. Types of communities of interest identified by speakers. Analysis of all public hearing attendees making presentation in person. Adapted from videotapes posted on http://www.floridaredistricting.org.

Table 5.11. Summary of type of community to keep together by speaker association

Type of interest	Speaker represents				
	Private citizen	Fair District advocacy group	Business, conserva- tive group	Local officials	Other/ NA
Base	168	36	46	38	25
Economic	36%	17%	54%	53%	36%
Geographic	25%	14%	34%	26%	12%
Racial, ethnic	21%	39%	4%	11%	8%
Socioeconomic	4%	6%	0%	0%	0%

Notes: Analysis of all public hearing attendees making presentation in person; from videotapes posted on http://www.floridaredistricting.org.

ties, 49 percent agriculture, 17 percent tourism, 9 percent interior (non-coastal), and 4 percent mentioned the importance of maintaining military communities of interest in the redrawn districts. Among those focused on more geographically defined communities, 52 percent wanted to keep rural areas together, 24 percent desired to maintain the compactness of metropolitan/urban areas, and 4 percent thought it vital to keep suburban areas together. Two common prescriptions were: "Separate interior from coastal areas" and "Don't tie rural counties to big cities."

Other types of communities of interest identified as important and examples singled out in each included: *Socioeconomic*: blue collar vs. wealthy; retirees vs. college town; *Racial/ethnic*: African American, Haitian, Hispanic/Latino; *Lifestyle*: GLBT (gay community); *Ideology*: Tea Party; conservative; liberal; and *Political party*: Democrat and Republican. Speakers representing business/conservative groups were more likely to define community of interest in either economic or geographic terms, while Fair Districts affiliates and private citizens saw community more in terms of race/ethnicity or socioeconomic composition (see table 5.11).

Racial/Language Minority Representation and District Composition

Among the 15 percent of the speakers urging the mapmakers to focus on minority representation when crafting the districts, 55 percent specifically mentioned Hispanics, 48 percent African Americans. (Some mentioned both.) Lawmakers were urged to adhere to federal Voting Rights

Act requirements (18 percent) and Fair District amendment requirements (11 percent) and to avoid retrogression (another term with multiple legal interpretations).

Opinions are often split as to whether creating majority-minority districts or drawing minority influence, or access, districts is the best way to provide equal opportunity for minority voters to elect their candidates of choice and to participate in the political process. Among the 4 percent of the speakers expressing a preference, 65 percent preferred minority access districts, while 47 percent favored majority-minority districts. Obviously, some preferred each approach depending on the demographic and/or political circumstance. For example, minority-influence districts were acceptable to those who wanted to keep minorities together but recognized that their population size was insufficient to make up a majority of a district. Haitian American Gepsi Metellus, at the Miami hearing, had this to say:

> I simply want to implore you to allow me an opportunity to elect someone of my choosing; elect someone who will represent my interests, my needs, my aspirations, my issues; who represents me in terms of recognizing and understanding my history, my traditions; someone who will represent me in terms of ensuring that my interests, my needs, and aspirations are not in contradiction with those of my next door neighbor; someone who will reflect the growing population of Miami-Dade County's Haitian American population. As you know, we are probably over 500,000 strong in South Florida. I believe Dr. Georges mentioned that we in fact are about 35 percent of the voters in specifically Congressional District 17. We have a 30-year presence in Miami-Dade County and [are] very much willing to work towards improving conditions for all of us. So, I ask you to ensure that you protect those political gains that we've made of the past several years. I want to implore you to indeed maintain the boundaries as they are such that our interests are protected in the manner that I've stated.[62]

And Hispanic Patrick Mantiega, at the Tampa hearing, made a similar point:

> I'm here to ask that you honor Florida's diversity. I believe that with a little extra effort the Legislature can make compact contiguous districts that respect concentrations of Hispanic and black minorities. The Hispanic community shares a mostly common heritage, culture, and cuisine. They frequent the same bodegas and sandwich shops.

Hispanic community boundaries should be as important in the redistricting process as municipal and subdivision boundaries. The census
shows that Hispanics are the state's largest minority population, but
the population of Hispanic elected officials falls far short of our population percentage. No prominent Hispanic Congressional district in
Central or North Florida. No prominent Hispanic state senate district
in Central or North Florida. The only prominently Hispanic house
district is where we currently sit in District 58. Florida's Hispanic
population has grown by leaps and bounds, but sadly the number of
elected officials that share Hispanic heritage, culture, and the love of
cafe con leche have not. Please rectify this problem.[63]

There was another reason for some, even within the black community, to
favor drawing influence districts rather than majority-minority districts.
Their view is that minority representational levels are more likely to expand
if minority populations are not "packed" into safe districts with larger minority populations than are needed to elect a person of color (on this point,
see chapter 6).

Others (14 percent) making minority representation recommendations
opposed using race as a factor and argued instead for drawing color blind
districts. According to these citizens, too much focus on keeping racial/
ethnic groups together runs counter to the broader goal of diversity and
racial integration. Creating minority districts (whether majority or access)
can sometimes be seen as confusing and symbolic of racism, particularly
when district lines give neighbors on opposite sides of the same street different representatives. A Florida State student testifying at the Tallahassee
hearing articulated this dilemma persuasively:

If I cross the street, literally 40 feet from my door I am in someone
else's district. I think that it is Representative Marti Coley's district.
So I mean, we are talking literally 40 feet and it is not like there is a
totally different community between us, it is the same community, the
same people. A lot of the folks that live on one side are predominantly
African American, the other one are students. And so if we have anything that affects us in this district that has to do with transportation,
which is Tennessee Street, a major corridor in Tallahassee, there is a
lot of transportation issues with the city, who do we go talk to? If we
are African American you talk to Alan Williams and if you are a student you go talk to Marti Coley, and that to me pits these two groups
against each other.[64]

Table 5.12. Minority representation taken into consideration and referenced by speaker association

Minority group referenced	Speaker represents				
	Private citizen	Fair District advocacy group	Business, con-servative group	Local officials	Other/ NA
Base	70	28	3	14	5
Hispanic	46%	79%	67%	57%	40%
Black	49%	32%	67%	50%	100%
All	20%	18%	33%	14%	0%

Notes: Analysis of all public hearing attendees making presentation in person; from videotapes posted on http://www.floridaredistricting.org.

Private citizens and speakers representing the Fair Districts coalition were considerably more likely to single out minority representation, especially of Hispanics, as a factor to consider when drawing district lines (see table 5.12).

Partisan Competitive Districts

Among those Florida citizens advocating paying more attention to the partisan composition of districts (31 percent), 60 percent of this subset of citizens told legislators they should focus on making them more competitive (Tier 1 standard). A majority argued for creating more Democratic and politically competitive districts—a top priority of the Fair Districts coalition. For example, Joan Carver at the Jacksonville hearing asserted:

> Mr. Chairman and members of the committee, I am here to urge you to draw the new Florida House and Senate districts and the congressional districts without consideration of protection of incumbents and for partisan advantage. I might note that most of our peer democracies that use single-member districts select their legislators through a neutral commissioner. Gerrymandered districts have long been one of the things Americans like least about their government. They have good reason for this dislike. For elections and the resulting governing bodies to have legitimacy, elections should be fair. If elections are to have legitimacy, they should reflect the divisions within the state. A review of recent election results in Florida indicates that this is not the case currently.[65]

Line-Drawing Preferences

What is the best way to draw the lines—vertically (north and south) or horizontally (east and west)? Where should the drawing begin? Should the drawing begin in core metropolitan areas or in rural areas? Alternatively, should the drawing begin at the northern and southern ends of the state (the more traditional approach)? Among the speakers proposing directional preferences, 49 percent called for using a horizontal approach, while 31 percent sought a vertical draw. Preferences here seem to be guided by whatever approach would best keep economically integrated areas together or interior areas separated from coastal areas.

While only a handful of speakers prescribed a starting point (< 1 percent), half supported the traditional start point, the ends of the state, followed by urban areas (38 percent), then rural (13 percent). Strong proponents of protecting minority representation argued for beginning in densely populated, diverse urban areas. Those focused more on zero deviation tended to support starting at the state's ends (3 percent)—similar to starting a jigsaw puzzle by constructing the outer borders.

Precinct Lines: State-Local Coordination Needed

Two percent of the public hearing speakers asked legislators to work more closely with local supervisors of elections in constructing precinct lines and to use VTDs (Voting Tabulation Districts). Some also asked for more attention to existing natural boundaries. The biggest reason for each was to minimize voter confusion (cited by 60 percent). However, savings in time (44 percent) and/or money (24 percent) were also seen as major benefits of pro-active coordination. County election officials, represented at most hearings, were the strongest proponents of this approach as well as to drawing compact districts that respect communities of interest. For example, Mary Jane Arrington, Osceola County Supervisor of Elections, stated at the Orlando hearing:

> I am not superhuman nor are any of my fellow supervisors, and the projected timeline really does not give us much time once these districts are adopted and approved. It is about two weeks, and that really isn't enough time for us to accurately draw new precinct lines, notify the voters, mail ballots, and sometimes we are probably going to have to find new voting locations. So if possible, I would love for ya'll to expedite, compress this process wherever you can so we will have more time to notify our voters. Come Election Day, if they are confused

they are not going to be mad at you, they are going to be mad at me. Also, your redistricting legislative staff and the U.S. Census staff have drawn VTD's [voting tabulation districts]. Please use them. They take into effect communities of common interest, traffic patterns, natural and physical barriers, and they also provide for compactness, and a compact district is an efficient district when it comes to operating an election. It saves money.[66]

Impact (Effectiveness) of Citizen Input into Redistricting Process: Pre-Map Phase

The 26 public hearings put a lot of pressure on the legislature to speed up the process and to add an additional period for public comment following the release of redistricting maps by each chamber. The legislative redistricting committees in both houses agreed to an earlier-than-planned release of the congressional maps in 2011[67] and to add an additional period of citizen input following the initial release of redistricting maps by each chamber. Putting a constitutional amendment before the voters to allow the legislature to begin the drawing of the state legislative districts earlier in 2012 also began to get more serious legislative attention.

Citizen map submissions steadily increased up to the original November submission deadline (see table 5.13). Over 20 percent more maps were submitted after the initial release of legislatively-drawn maps. By far, congressional district maps represented the most numerous redistricting plans submitted for consideration by the legislature.

Table 5.13. Plans submitted by public: type and date

Type/Number	Month Submitted/Number
Congress—complete plans (80)	February 2012 (1)
Congress—partial plans (27)	January 2012 (28)
Florida House of Representatives (26)	December 2011 (24)
Florida Senate (8)	November 2011 (33)
State house—complete plans (30)	October 2011 (53)
State house—partial plans (25)	September 2011 (20)
State senate—complete plans (32)	August 2011 (34)
State senate—partial plans (18)	July 2011 (17)
Updates regarding written submissions (3)	June 2011 (1)
	May 2011 (2)

Notes: Based on public comments data posted on MyDistrictBuilder blog, https://mydistrict-builder.wordpress.com/.

The state senate released maps on November 28, 2011 and state house on December 6, 2011. The plans were formally approved on February 9 (see appendix D for maps).

Public Input: Post-Legislative Release of District Maps

Round Two of public comments occurred because of citizen outrage at the absence of maps at the initial series of hearings limiting their chances to react to the maps. Legislators heard the citizen voices and reacted: "We kept hearing 'Where are the maps?'" I believe there was an important step which is missing—to take these maps back to some of those locations," said Representative Dwayne Taylor, D-Daytona Beach. "The citizen participation is, I believe, an important part of the discussion that is missing."[68]

An analysis of 830 written submissions[69] sent via e-mail, mail, fax, YouTube, Twitter, and Facebook to the Florida House, Florida Senate, and specific legislators[70] shows citizen reaction to legislative districting plans (congressional, state senate, and/or state house) was more positive (56 percent) than negative (39 percent) (see table 5.14). Among those who liked the maps, the vast majority (93 percent) did not give a specific reason. However, among those who did, the most common reasons were the respect legislators gave to communities of interest and minority representation, especially the Hispanic congressional influence district in Central Florida.

Among those critical of the initially drawn plans, 11 percent complained that the maps did not reflect communities of interest, while another 11 percent said there was still evidence of gerrymandered districts. Another 6 percent complained that the districts were not compact and 4 percent were upset that the maps did not sufficiently increase minority representation.

The two most challenging difficulties legislators faced in reacting to the citizen-generated submissions about the various maps were related to: (1) citizens' lack of specificity as to which map (congressional, senate, house) they were referring, and (2) *conflicting* citizen criticisms and preferences regarding the same district, mostly over how and which communities of interest were to be maintained. Ultimately, the revised house plan was seen by Fair District coalition members (and the Florida Supreme Court) as the most compliant with the Fair Districts amendment standards.

Democratic-leaning voting rights advocacy groups remained extremely dissatisfied with the redrawn senate and congressional maps ultimately approved by the legislature on February 9, 2012. They saw these plans as

Table 5.14. Public assessments of the newly drawn districts

Overall voter assessments of newly drawn districts	Percent response
1. Didn't like	39%
2. Like	56%
3. No clear opinion	5%
REASONS FOR POSITIVE REACTION TO LEGISLATIVE PLANS	
1. Reflect communities of interest	6%
2. Keeps counties together	0.3%
3. Likes openness of process	0.3%
4. Better minority representation	1%
5. More Republican districts	0.3%
6. No reason given	93%
REASONS FOR NEGATIVE REACTION TO INITIAL LEGISLATIVE PLANS	
1. Splits neighborhoods, cities, counties	51%
2. Violates Fair Districts standards	14%
3. Ignores communities of interests	11%
4. Still gerrymandered	11%
5. Not compact	6%
6. Insufficient minority representation	4%
7. Districts not contiguous	1%
8. Does not follow natural boundaries	1%
9. Insufficient representation	1%
10. Non-competitive districts	0.4%

Notes: Analysis of written comments submitted by the public to the Florida Legislature in the period between the initial release of maps (November 28, 2011) and the final deadline for public comment (January 31, 2012).

largely ignoring Fair Districts standards, particularly those protecting minority voters against racial gerrymandering, prohibiting partisan gerrymandering, and mandating respect for existing geographic and political boundaries. These reform proponents continued to fight the revised congressional and senate plans in court, often citing public comments made before and after the initial maps were released by the state legislature as justification for their legal complaints. In summary, loud voices from the grassroots continued to be heard long after the maps were approved in early 2012.

Conclusion: Five Lessons Learned (Re-Learned)

Citizen participation in the 2012 round of redistricting was at an all-time high.[71] As this research has shown, aggressive use of traditional forms of involvement (public hearings) in tandem with new media and free downloadable software greatly increased the number of Floridians engaged in the redistricting process *before* legislators created any maps and, then again, *after* proposals were released by each legislative chamber. There are some lessons to be learned (or re-learned) from this experience.[72]

(1) Lesson #1. *What was once thought to be a policy area of little interest to the general public due to its complexities turned out to be false.* Any doubts about Florida residents' interest in the 2012 round of redistricting or their divergent opinions as to how it should be done were dispelled at the 26 public hearings held across the state from June 20 to September 1, 2011, and attended by 4,797 people, yielding a record number of diverse citizen voices from the grassroots.

According to our analyses of videotapes of the public hearings, 1,368 citizens spoke. They represented 55 of Florida's 67 counties. Among the speakers, 58 percent were men, 42 percent women. Racial/ethnic minorities comprised 15 percent (African Americans, 10 percent; Hispanics, 5 percent). In terms of who they were affiliated with (on a self-reported basis), 60 percent were private citizens, 17 percent were associated with a Fair Districts advocacy group, 8 percent represented a business or conservative group, 9 percent were local officials, and 5 percent were from a wide array of other groups. (Fewer than 1 percent gave no affiliation.)

(2) Lesson #2. *Public input can change both the redistricting process and the outcome.* This does not necessarily mean that there will be a consensus among the citizen participants about how to do either. As this analysis has shown, on many issues there was not. What *was* evident is that legislators were eager to link their decisions and actions to public input. In addition, there was some evidence that where voices were the loudest and recommendations more plausible, legislators did make some adjustments. Over one-fourth (27 percent) of the speakers gave specific process-related recommendations for how to proceed with the redistricting process. The three that received the most support were to speed up the timeline (54 percent), get out of a lawsuit challenging Amendment 6 (29 percent), and hold hearings after the initial maps drawn by the legislators were released to the public (25 percent).

Public officials were the strongest advocates for speeding up the timeline. Fair Districts supporters advocated for another round of public comment to respond to maps and amending the constitution in order to speed up redistricting, and both private citizens and Fair Districts proponents supported dropping the litigation challenging Amendment 6. The legislature ended up speeding up the timeline and allowing for public input regarding the proposed maps. Ultimately, the courts rejected a complaint by U.S. representatives Corrine Brown (D) and Mario Diaz-Balart (R) filed in federal court challenging Amendment 6, which initially alleged that the amendment would negatively impact minority voters and subsequently, unsuccessfully sought to have Amendment 6 nullified by the federal court as an unconstitutional intrusion on the state legislature's power to draw congressional districts under Article 1, Section 4 of the U.S. Constitution.[73]

There was substantial input from citizens in response to the initial congressional and legislative map proposals released in late 2011. An analysis of 830 written submissions sent via e-mail, mail, fax, YouTube, Twitter, and Facebook to the Florida House, Florida Senate or specific legislators and posted online showed citizen reaction was more positive (56 percent) than negative (39 percent). A high percentage of those who liked the maps (and gave a reason) cited the respect legislators gave to communities of interest and minority representation, especially the Hispanic congressional-influence district in Central Florida (15 percent). Among critics of the maps, nearly one third (31 percent) complained that the maps did not reflect their notion of "communities of interest," while 29 percent said there was still evidence of gerrymandered districts. Another 17 percent complained that the districts were not compact and 11 percent were upset that the maps did not sufficiently increase minority representation.

Some adjustments to the initial maps were made in response to these complaints and reflected in the final maps approved on February 9, 2012.[74] But the adjustments were not enough to fend off lawsuits filed in state circuit court by the Florida Democratic Party and disgruntled members of the Fair Districts coalition challenging both the congressional and Florida Senate maps. They continued to believe the legislature had engaged in partisan gerrymandering and incumbent protection and ignored other constitutional requirements related to minority representation.[75]

(3) Lesson #3. An "inform, then engage" approach does bolster citizen participation. Extensive use of new communication technology and media is vital to the success of this approach as is the effective structuring

of opportunities for public input in-person or online. Beginning in 2009 with pre-census preparations, key legislators and staff members adopted the approach of "first educating, then engaging" the public in the redistricting process. This "strategic communication effort" created websites (http://www.FloridaRedistricting.org and http://RedistrictFlorida@flsenate.gov), Facebook pages, two blogs, and an e-mail subscriber option.

At the 26 public hearing sites, staffers were available to demonstrate the redistricting software and answer technical questions. A YouTube channel featured video tutorials on how to draw maps and use the software. The multi-media approach certainly contributed to greater participation in the 2012 redistricting than in any previous cycle.

(4) Lesson #4. *Citizen participation analyses yield richer insights of who favors what and why, when opinions are examined within the context of their local interest group affiliation.* Our analysis of citizen participants found that redistricting preferences were often sharper among those representing divergent local interest groups (socioeconomic, racial/ethnic, public/private sector) than different political party affiliations. It should be noted that this study of grassroots-level citizen participation in the redistricting process is the most comprehensive to date in its identification of grassroots-level interest group affiliations.

(5) Lesson #5. *Overly general, often conflicting redistricting standards, with a multiplicity of competing measures on which there is little consensus about which is best (e.g., compactness, retrogression) virtually guarantee court battles in a politically divided state.* This has been the pattern in Florida over the past couple of redistricting cycles as it was in 2012. Although state constitutional Amendments 5 and 6 had established new redistricting standards, many of the standards lacked clarity as to how adherence to them would be measured. The Florida Supreme Court, in its review of the house and senate redistricting plans, ended up establishing these measures, although the decision to do so was not unanimous among the justices.

One thing that is indisputable is that redistricting remains the most political of political decisions, whether in the legislature or in the courtroom. The 2012 redistricting process also made it clear that loud voices from the grassroots *can* affect decisions in each.

6

Paradoxes of Political Reform

Congressional Redistricting in Florida

MICAH ALTMAN AND MICHAEL P. MCDONALD

Florida's congressional redistricting has historically been conducted with no mandated state requirements, only limited federal requirements for population equality and voting rights. Within this limited regulatory environment, Florida Republicans engineered one of the four most pro-Republican congressional redistricting plans following the 2000 Census.[1] Seeking to prevent future partisan gerrymandering, reform advocates twice attempted to reform the state's redistricting process through constitutional amendment, succeeding in their second attempt. In 2010, Floridians voted by wide margins in favor of constitutional Amendments 5 and 6, providing for new state legislative and congressional redistricting criteria, respectively.

Recent experience suggests that reformers' expectations might not be met when redistricting reform is put into practice. Arizona reformers campaigned on the promise that a proposed commission would increase electoral competition. However, expectations did not meet post-2000 reality when the commission required that Latino voting rights be protected in heavily Democratic districts in a Republican-leaning state, leaving few Democrats available to form competitive districts.[2] Likewise, California reformers promised a citizen commission would increase competition, but were disappointed with the results.[3] An analysis of the 2000 Florida redistricting suggests reformers would likewise be disappointed, asserting the geographic distributional advantage for Republicans is a product not of gerrymandering, but of the inefficient concentration of Democrats in Southeast Florida that limit opportunities to produce a politically balanced plan.[4]

Our purpose here is to evaluate trade-offs among various redistricting criteria by analyzing the large number of redistricting plans proposed during Florida's recent redistricting. Scholars have used this approach to evaluate alternative plans,[5] and courts often require plaintiffs to provide a demonstration plan to show that it is possible to draw a plan that rectifies alleged violations. A technological innovation in the most recent redistricting is that web-based redistricting software has greatly expanded public participation by enabling the public to draw legal redistricting plans.[6] This has in turn greatly increased the number of plans available for analysis, allowing for a broader evaluation of the trade-offs among redistricting plans.[7] The proliferation of plans, particularly those produced by the public outside the political process, enables us to explore trade-offs among redistricting goals as they apply to Florida's recently adopted reform.

Florida's Reform Path

Prior to the adoption of the 2010 constitutional amendments, redistricting provisions found in Article III, Section 16 of Florida's constitution applied only to state legislative redistricting. In 1965, the U.S. Supreme Court voided Florida's practice of apportioning state legislative districts to counties,[8] found in the state's 1885 constitution.[9] A constitutional convention was convened, which issued a new state legislative redistricting process that was approved by voters. The newly adopted process required the state legislature to adopt state legislative districts without a governor's veto, but with mandatory review by the Florida Supreme Court, which was also tasked with drawing districts if the legislature failed to take action. State legislative districts were to be contiguous, and these districts could be single-member, multimember, and could even overlap.

Florida's constitution was silent on congressional redistricting, which was governed by statute. A statutory process implies the congressional redistricting process follows the regular legislative process, with the legislature adopting plans with a governor's approval. As late as 1962, the Florida Supreme Court refused to overturn a congressional redistricting plan for population inequalities, citing that neither the federal nor the state constitution required population equality, or any other criteria.[10]

Federal requirements also apply to Florida's congressional redistricting. In the early 1960s, the U.S. Supreme Court articulated a new federal criterion when it ruled that the Fourteenth Amendment requires congressional districts to be of equal population.[11] In 1964, a federal district court found Florida's congressional plan had constitutionally impermissibly high population deviations, but allowed the state legislature to correct the matter.[12] Two important sections of the federal Voting Rights Act of 1965 and its subsequent reauthorizations also apply to Florida. Section 2 applies to the entire country and essentially requires the creation of a minority opportunity district, if the minority community is large and compact enough, and there is the presence of racially polarized voting, and there is a past history of discrimination.[13] Prior to the *Shelby County v. Holder* decision, section 5 applied only to certain "covered jurisdictions" that had past low voter participation and a past use of a discriminatory test or device. Five Florida counties were covered—Collier, Hardee, Hendry, Hillsborough, and Monroe—for voting concerns regarding Latinos. Although only five counties were covered, section 5 required that the Department of Justice or the U.S. District Court of the District of Columbia review all statewide redistricting plans—or changes to election laws, generally—to verify that the ability for minorities to elect a candidate of their choice had not been reduced in these counties.

Florida's constitution was among the many states silent on congressional redistricting, allowing the party controlling the state government to draw congressional districts within the wide latitude provided by the federal government. In the last decade, Florida drew reform advocates' attention because its congressional plan was among the four most pro-Republican plans adopted during the 2000s,[14] thereby contributing to a geographic distributional advantage for Republicans in congressional elections.[15]

Florida provides two mechanisms to reform its constitution: citizen-initiated ballot initiative and legislative referendum. Placing a ballot initiative before Floridians requires substantial effort. Supporters must collect hundreds of thousands of signatures to qualify an amendment for the ballot (see chapter 4). Initially, they must wage a statewide campaign to educate and persuade voters to support the reform, and then they must be prepared for litigation. Reformers tried twice to amend Florida's redistricting process, succeeding on the second attempt. In 2006, after collecting signatures, the Florida Supreme Court rejected a ballot initiative that would have altered both the redistricting criteria and process, due in part to a violation of the state's single-subject rule.[16] In 2010, reformers met with more modest success, with Floridians voting by wide margins in favor of separate Amendments 5 and 6 to provide for new state legislative and congressional redistricting criteria only, respectively.

The Amendment 6 ballot initiative amended the Florida Constitution to add Article III, Section 20, which requires congressional redistricting to follow these standards (similar state legislative standards were proposed in Amendment 5):[17]

(1) No apportionment plan or individual district shall be drawn with the intent to favor or disfavor a political party or an incumbent; and districts shall not be drawn with the intent or result of denying or abridging the equal opportunity of racial or language minorities to participate in the political process or to diminish their ability to elect representatives of their choice; and districts shall consist of contiguous territory.

(2) Unless compliance with the standards in this subsection conflicts with the standards in subsection (1) or with federal law, districts shall be as nearly equal in population as is practicable; districts shall be compact; and districts shall, where feasible, utilize existing political and geographical boundaries.

(3) The order in which the standards within sub-sections (1) and (2) of this section are set forth shall not be read to establish any priority of one standard over the other within that subsection.

Once supporters collect enough signatures to qualify an initiative for the ballot, the Florida Supreme Court rules if the initiative satisfies state constitutional requirements. The court found that Amendments 5 and 6 met state constitutional requirements.[18] However, in the first signs of the legal battles to come, the court required the state to amend the financial impact statement, striking a claim that the amendments would cost millions of dollars of legal fees. The claim was not entirely without merit. Indeed, prior to the election, Congress members Corrine Brown and Mario Diaz-Balart mounted a legal challenge to proposed Amendment 6, which the state legislature attempted to join in opposing Amendment 5. The Florida Supreme Court ruled that these pre-election challenges did not raise a vital issue that was not addressed in their initial review, and thereby dismissed the case.[19]

Soon after the amendments qualified for the ballot, the state legislature voted to place a referendum, Amendment 7, before the voters that was also intended to amend Florida's redistricting process. Supporters of the ballot initiatives claimed the move "a blatant effort to fool voters," alleging Amendment 7 would relax redistricting standards and would result in the three proposals being voided if voters approved all of them.[20] The Florida Supreme Court upheld a lower court's order to remove Amendment 7 from the ballot, finding, among other issues, that the proposed title for Amendment 7 "is misleading as to the true purpose and effect of the amendment."[21]

Amendment 6 received 63 percent of the vote in the 2010 general election, and thereby reached the 60 percent threshold for adoption.[22] Voter approval of the amendment did not necessarily mean that it would take effect. In early 2011, the recently elected Republican governor Rick Scott withdrew the state's request of the Department of Justice to review the new amendment, as then-required by Section 5 of the Voting Rights Act.[23] Supporters of the amendment sued to force Governor Scott to take action.[24] Ultimately, the governor relented and the Department of Justice approved the changes to the redistricting criteria.[25]

U.S. representatives Corrine Brown and Mario Diaz-Balart continued their legal challenge to Amendment 6 in federal court. The plaintiffs argued that Article I, Section 4 of the U.S. Constitution ("[The] Times, Places, and Manner of holding Elections for Senators and Representatives, shall be prescribed in each State by the Legislature thereof.") allows legislatures the unfettered ability to draw congressional districts.[26] However, an appeals court upheld a district court's ruling that U.S. Supreme Court precedent broadly interprets "legislature" to include all facets of a state's lawmaking process, including ballot initiatives.

With the pre-redistricting litigation settled, the Republican-controlled legislature set about the task of drawing districts within the legal framework of the newly adopted criteria. The new criteria demonstrably constrained the senate. During the Florida Supreme Court's mandatory review of state legislative redistricting plans, the Court approved the state house districts, but found the senate plan violated the new criteria.[27] The revised senate plan was approved,[28] but reformers were not satisfied and pursued further litigation.[29] The Court does not automatically review congressional plans. However, similar to the senate, reformers alleged violations of the new criteria among the congressional districts in court.[30]

Public Participation

Redistricting is a data intensive task. Since the U.S. Supreme Court equal population rulings of the 1960s and the passage of the Voting Rights Act in 1965, the exacting demands for population equality and racial representation require districts be drawn at the smallest unit for which the U.S. Census Bureau reports population data, census blocks. In urban areas, census blocks roughly correspond to city blocks, but because they follow visible features, their borders sometimes also outline oddly shaped geographies such as road medians and meandering streams. A state such as Florida has nearly a half million census blocks. Without a computer, manually assigning these census blocks to redistricting plans to create legal redistricting plans would be so labor intensive as to be practically impossible.

Public participation in redistricting has evolved with technological innovations. In the past, only well-funded organizations had the resources to create mainframe computer systems and to construct redistricting databases of merged census and electoral data to meet redistricting legal requirements.[31] This effectively restricted the scope of participation to politicians, who benefited by closing the process to a public that may have different priorities. In the post-2000 round of redistricting, commercial vendors entered the market providing less expensive software that could run on a desktop computer. However, the cost was in the thousands of dollars, beyond the budget of most of the public. A decade later, high-speed data transfer capabilities of the Internet and open-source development communities created a rich and robust set of web-deployable open source geographic information system tools. These advancements enabled the development of web-based redistricting tools, thereby broadly opening redistricting to anyone with an Internet connection.[32] For example, in Virginia, open-source web-based redistricting software developed by the authors, called DistrictBuilder, was used by advocates to support a student-drawing of redistricting plans for a competition and was used by Governor Bob McDonnell's Independent Bipartisan Advisory Redistricting Commission.[33]

Florida has been a leader in public participation in the redistricting process. In the post-2000 redistricting, the two chambers of the state legislature jointly developed and deployed FREDS 2000, so-named for Florida Redistricting Software.[34] The desktop application was loaded with census and election data, prepared by legislative staff. FREDS was deployed to libraries and universities, and the public could purchase a desktop version of the software for $20. State senator Daniel Webster described how the purpose of the software was to allow interested parties "to take an active role in how their districts will look." However, the resulting public participation was modest.[35] Of the 106 congressional and state legislative plans submitted to the state legislature for consideration, the public submitted only four plans. Three of these plans were two state legislative plans and a congressional plan submitted jointly by Common Cause and the League of Women Voters. The remaining plans were submitted by state legislators or members of Congress, or were plans developed during the legislative process without a clear author.

In the post-2010 redistricting, the house and senate chambers of the Florida Legislature independently developed web-based redistricting applications. In a sign of evolutionary convergence, the house's tool was called MyDistrictBuilder;[36] and the senate's tool was called District Builder.[37] (These had no relationship to our DistrictBuilder application.) The public had access to the Florida tools, which were loaded with census and election data. The senate provided links to the 228 state legislative and congressional plans that were submitted to the legislature, which represented more than a doubling of the number of plans submitted a decade earlier.[38] Accessibility in the form of web deployment thus appears to be an important factor in facilitating public participation. The increase in the number of plans was predominantly due to greater public involvement, with 179 plans submitted by the public. At least 17 students submitted plans, with the youngest person being thirteen-years-old.[39] However, we determined that only forty-two of these public submissions might be considered legal plans. Many had population deviations well in excess of those tolerated by the federal courts, failed to assign all geography, or were not contiguous. Often, these legal issues arose when a person drew a partial plan for one or more districts, but less than the total number required for a legislative body.

Evaluating Plans

The greater number of plans produced in the post-2010 redistricting through public participation provides an opportunity to compare plans; of particular interest is how the public may approach redistricting differently than politicians. We find that in Virginia the public tends to explore a wider range of alternatives than politicians on various criteria.[40] This difference allows a more expansive exploration of the trade-offs among various redistricting criteria than what is possible by evaluating only plans developed predominantly to achieve politicians' goals. The public plans may thus be especially informative to reveal how well politicians adhered to the new redistricting requirements adopted by Floridians in the 2010 election. We caution that redistricting is such a complex mathematical problem that we can never know if any plan is *the* optimal plan on one criterion or all criteria one is interested in.[41] The observed trade-offs are thus only illustrative and not definitive, and only apply to conditions as they existed during the 2010 redistricting. However, the existence of a plan that is, say, both compact and politically fair can falsify some assertions, such as the Republican electoral advantage arising from redistricting is primarily a function of Democrats being inefficiently concentrated within urban areas.[42]

We evaluate Florida's redistricting plans with two data sources.[43] First, we obtained the U.S. Census Bureau's geospatial and demographic redistricting data prepared following the 2010 Census.[44] Second, we obtained the Florida House's database containing election data.[45] The Florida House overlaid the state's 2008 general election precincts on the 2010 census geography, enabling a merge of these two databases. Since redistricting plans are drawn from census blocks, election data must be disaggregated from the larger voting precincts to the smaller census blocks if one wishes to measure the partisan composition of districts. The state allocated votes by the percentage of the area of a census block within a precinct. In our experience, the state's approach is unusual; usually precinct election results are disaggregated into census blocks by population or the number of registered voters within the census blocks. The disaggregation method produces some oddities, such as assigning votes to large offshore census blocks, but we have no reason to suspect that the area disaggregation approach greatly affects the calculation of election results within districts.

Plans are evaluated using measures of individual districts and overall redistricting plans on various characteristics. The first set of evaluations is what is often known as "traditional redistricting principles" and which we refer to as process-based regulations.[46] These criteria govern characteristics of the districts: population equality, compactness, and respect for local political boundaries. The second set is what we refer to as outcome-based regulations that attempt to affect an electoral outcome: such as adherence to voting rights, the overall partisan balance of the plan, and overall political competitiveness of the districts. We briefly describe, in the following paragraphs, these criteria and how we measure them.

We begin with describing the process-based traditional redistricting criteria. Population equality is a federal and state constitutional requirement. As mentioned previously, the U.S. Supreme Court articulated a federal equal population mandate in the 1960s, and the federal courts have enforced this requirement upon Florida. For congressional redistricting, the courts generally tolerate a 1 percent deviation from the largest to smallest congressional district if there is a compelling state reason why a deviation should exist, such as to meet another rational goal of maintaining the integrity of local jurisdiction boundaries (see chapter 3).

In practice, states have sought a safe harbor from litigation by drawing congressional districts with an absolute minimal population deviation. The adopted Florida congressional districts embody this strategy with population deviation of only one person. The newly adopted state criteria also require population equality, but since the state strove for precise population equality, there is an open question if the state constitution provides more stringent population equality than tolerated by the federal courts. Another unanswered question is if the federal or state courts would tolerate larger population deviations to achieve better compliance with other criteria found in Amendment 6. We measure the population deviation of a plan by subtracting the population of the smallest district from the largest district, and express this as a percentage relative to the ideally sized district, which is the state's total resident population divided by twenty-seven, or 696,345 persons.

Compactness is a surprisingly difficult concept to measure. While not in the federal constitution, the federal courts sometimes regard violations of compactness as evidence for improper motives during redistricting, particularly with regard to race.[47] Amendment 6 also requires districts to be compact, but provides no further guidance. Operationalizing compactness turns out to be more complicated than it might seem. There are many ways to measure district compactness.[48] Common methods generally compare the length of a district's perimeter or the area of the district to an idealized shape, such as the most compact shape, a circle. The idea is that irregularly shaped districts should score lower on such measures. However, unless a state explicitly defines a compactness measure, and Florida's Amendment 6 does not, the courts have generally measured compactness through visual inspection. We used the ratio of a district's perimeter to a circle's perimeter with the same area as the district. This measure is commonly known as "Schwartzberg" compactness, although the algorithm was invented by Cox, and the rankings it yields are identical to other perimeter-to-area ratios—as long as they are properly normalized. Each district is scored on a scale of 0 to 1, with 1 being more compact.[49] In the table and scatterplots, plans are scored on the average compactness of all districts, such that a greater number indicates a plan with an overall greater degree of compactness.

Amendment 6 requires the districts "utilize existing political and geographical boundaries." We do not attempt to measure how well districts utilize existing geographical boundaries since there is no clear metric that we can devise; for example, we cannot devise a rule as to how large a stream must be for it to qualify as a meaningful geographic boundary. Existing political boundaries such as counties are easiest to identify since they are explicitly designated in the census geography. We count the number of times local political boundaries such as counties are split into districts.[50] A county that is entirely contained within a single district is not split, a county split between two districts is split twice, a county split between three districts is split thrice, and so on. We then sum the number of splits across all counties to calculate an overall plan score. In the scatterplots, we rescale this measure by subtracting it from zero, such that a higher number indicates a plan with fewer splits.

Turning to the evaluation of representational measures, voting rights requirements are difficult to assess. Typically, jurisdictions hire experts to evaluate patterns of racially polarized voting by racial and ethnic groups to determine the percentage of minority voting age population necessary to elect a minority candidate of choice.[51] Patterns of racially polarized voting may vary across states and localities, so the exact percentage of minority voting age population required to elect a minority candidate of choice will similarly vary. Lacking the resources to do a comprehensive evaluation of Florida's racially polarized voting, we implement a simple measure that a voting rights district must have at least 50 percent black or Hispanic voting age population.[52] For the table and scatterplots, we then count the number of such so-called "majority-minority" districts across the redistricting plan.

"Political balance" and "political competition" are two measures constructed from the same election data.[53] We begin by describing the political balance measure. First, the underlying partisan strength for the Democratic and Republican parties within districts is calculated. Votes for minor party candidates are removed from the underlying partisan strength measure to calculate a "two-party" vote measure since the two major political parties are in all but rare instances elected to legislative offices. We measure the partisan support of districts using the 2008 two-party presidential vote share.[54] We then shift the two-party vote to approximate roughly a hypothetical 50/50 election. Next, the political balance and competition measures are calculated.

For the political balance measure, each district is scored based on whether it has an underlying partisan strength measure above or below 50 percent. Thus, the score indicates which party is favored within a district. The number of districts leaning towards one of the two parties is summed across all districts. Since the statewide vote is shifted to simulate a hypothetical 50/50 election, the deviation of the percentage of districts that lean towards a party from a 50 percent baseline reveals what redistricting scholars call the partisan bias of the plan. In the scatterplots, we scale this measure so that it represents the deviation from an equal number of Democratic and Republican congressional districts, which is 27 divided by 2 or 13.5. We present two measures of partisan balance. The *Democratic Surplus* measure is scaled such that positive numbers indicate a greater number of Democratic-majority districts and negative numbers indicate a greater number of Republican-majority districts. We fold *Democratic Surplus* around 50 percent to measure *Partisan Balance*, such that a perfectly balanced plan is scored a zero and unbalanced plans favoring either party have a negative number.

Political competition starts with the same underlying partisan strength measure used to measure partisan balance. Where partisan balance provides a direction of party support in a district, political competition provides a measure of how closely contested a district may be in a typical election, absent specific candidate or campaign effects. We score a district as competitive if it has an underlying partisan strength measure plus or minus 5 percentage points from 50 percent.[55] Unlike the partisan balance measure, we do not shift the vote share to simulate a 50/50 election since we are interested in competition in a typical election. In the table below, we sum the number of competitive districts across all districts to calculate a plan level measure of competition. In the scatterplots, we report the same measure since a greater value indicates a greater level of competition.

Analysis

We analyze the adopted plan, those created by the legislature, and those authored by the public. We include only 42 plans among all 228 plans submitted to the Florida Legislature in our analysis that meet minimum legal requirements of assigning all geography,[56] being contiguous, and having an overall population deviation of less than 2 percentage points from the largest to smallest district. In addition, we include the two plans developed and later submitted to the courts by the plaintiffs in *Romo v. Scott*. The summary statistics in table 6.1 reveal how the adopted plan, the average legislative plan, plaintiff's plans, and average public plan differ overall on our measures. All plans score similar with minimal population deviations; the adopted and legislative plans all had minimal deviations of one person while only nine of the public plans had deviations larger than one-hundred persons. In terms of shape, the adopted plan has few county splits compared to the average legislative or public plan, and is slightly more compact than the average plans. In terms of political outcomes, the adopted plan was

Table 6.1. Congressional plan statistics

Statistic		Legislature	Public	Romo plaintiffs	Adopted plan
Number of plans		19	22	2	
Compactness	Mean	0.157	0.155	0.144	0.152
	Std dev	0.002	0.002	0.001	
	Max	0.164	0.175	0.145	
	Range	0.019	0.051	0.002	
Majority-Minority	Mean	5	4.091	5	6
	Std dev	0.076	0.173	0	
	Max	6	5	5	
	Range	2	2	0	
Population	Mean	0	0	0	0
Equality	Std dev	0	0.001	0	
	Max	0	0	0	
	Range	0	0.018	0	
Partisan balance	Mean	-3.29	-2.23	-1.50	-3.5
	Std dev	0.151	0.265	0.000	
	Max	-1.5	-0.5	-1.50	
	Range	3	4	0.000	
County integrity	Mean	-106	-107	-99	-105
	Std dev	0.597	2.723	1.000	
	Max	-98	-83	-98	
	Range	10	59	2	
Competitiveness	Mean	12.32	11.73	6	12
	Std dev	0.287	0.379	0	
	Max	14	14	6	
	Range	6	7	0	

Notes: Legislature and public categories summarize all legislative proposals and public submissions meeting the legal requirement. A column for the adopted plan is included for comparison. Note that the adopted plan was created by the legislature and thus *is included* among the 19 plans summarized in the legislature column.

less balanced than the average legislative or public plan, and had slightly fewer competitive districts than the average legislative plan and slightly more than the average public plan. By contrast, the plaintiff's plans were somewhat more balanced than the average public plan—although still not as balanced as the best public plan in that area, and the *Romo* plans were much worse in terms of competitiveness—having only half the number of competitive districts of the average public plan.

Finally, the adopted plan has more majority-minority districts than the any legislative or public plan. The adopted plan has six Hispanic majority districts, located in the Cuban community in the Miami area. It is the only plan to have three black majority districts, with two in the Miami area. The adopted plan's additional majority black district is District 5, represented by Democrat Corrine Brown. The district scores just slightly over 50 percent African American (when including all census racial categories including black alone or one or more combinations).

The district may not be required by the federal Voting Rights Act: it is not in an area of Florida covered by Section 5 and it is unknown to us if the district is required by Section 2. However, also unknown to us is if the district may be required under the newly adopted Amendment 6 provision congruent with federal voting rights language. (We have not performed the necessary voting analyses to make any determination.) The district stretches over one-hundred miles from Jacksonville to Orlando, with one segment following the St. John's River. The district thus figures highly when the adopted plan's statistics are compared with other plans since it splits several counties, is non-compact, and concentrates Democrats into a 71 percent (two-party vote) Democratic district. The district also affects adjacent districts as it bisects the northern part of the state in a north-to-south direction, thereby preventing the drawing of districts in an east-to-west direction that may be more compact or more amenable to creating additional Democratic-leaning districts.

Simple descriptive statistics naturally mask characteristics of individual plans. So that individual plans may be visually compared against one another, we present scatterplots of individual plan statistics in figures 6.1 through 6.3. In these plots, we label the adopted plan with an "A," the legislative plans are identified with a circle, and the public plans with a downward triangle, and the plaintiff's plan with an upward triangle labeled with a "P." We draw clouds (0.99 percent density ellipses) around legislative and public plans so that they may generally be distinguished from one another (except in figure 6.2 due to graphical constraints). When there is little variation, such as when there is minimal population deviation among the legislature's plans, these ellipses collapse to a straight line.

We note a number of generalizations from the descriptive statistics and scatterplots, with particular implications for participation in redistricting, some of which we have noted elsewhere in an analysis of Virginia plans.[57] First, we note the public is capable of creating legal redistricting plans. Seven of the public's plans had the minimal population deviation of one person, a time-consuming goal for any map drawer to achieve. While no public plan has three black majority districts, two have four Hispanic ma-

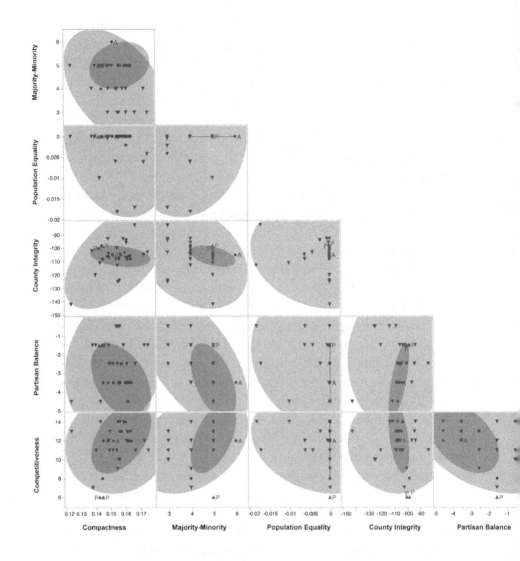

Figure 6.1. Congressional plans scatterplots. For ease of comparison, scores in these scatterplots have been transformed so that an increase on either axis reflects a substantively better score. Thus, population equality is plotted as -1 times the absolute deviation from 0 (0 is the best score); county integrity is plotted as -1 times the number of county splits (0 is the best score); and partisan balance is plotted as -1 times the absolute deviation from a 50/50 seat split (0 is the best score).

jority districts, at the apparent expense of a black majority district, since both have only one such district. Six of the public's plans had three Hispanic majority districts and two black majority districts, the same number as the modal legislative plan. While we cannot go into exhaustive detail, we suspect that the public plans demonstrate alternative configurations of majority-minority districts that may enhance minority representation, as they did in Virginia.

Second, we note that the public plans generally demonstrate a wider range of possibilities than the legislative plans. Only in the case of the additional black majority district do we see a legislative plan outside the range of those formulated by the public. In all other cases, the legislature's plans have a narrower range than the public's plans. This is of particular interest to us since by covering a greater range of possibilities the public's plans can inform us about the bounds of possibilities, in one or multiple dimensions. For example, several of the public plans have fewer county splits and are more compact than the adopted plan or any legislative plan. We observe that among the public's plans are those that score better in terms of partisan balance and competition. Indeed, we discuss in greater depth below how two of the public's plans are unbalanced in a Democratic direction, by having 17 and 16 Democratic leaning districts out of 27.

We explore the trade-offs between three substantive outcomes further in figure 6.2, where we plot partisan balance, competition, and the number of majority-minority districts against one another in a three-dimensional scatter plot. The *Pareto frontier* across this set of three criteria is highlighted in this plot. The Pareto frontier is the set of submitted plans that represent efficient trade-offs between criteria. Any plan not on the Pareto frontier can be beaten—or dominated—on *all* of the substantive criteria by plans on the frontier. In the plots on the left of figure 6.2, dark lines illustrate the frontier among pairs of criteria. Highlighted points show plans that are undominated on all three criteria simultaneously. In the plot to the right, the undominated plans are highlighted in the three-dimensional criteria space. One caution: as mentioned above, because redistricting is such a complex partitioning problem, we cannot be certain that a plan does not exist that does better than the observed Pareto frontier.

Note that the public plans covered a larger set of possible trade-offs among each criterion. Public plans covered a greater amount of the two-dimensional space defined by the pairs of criteria. In addition, with the exception of the majority-minority criterion, public plans covered a strict

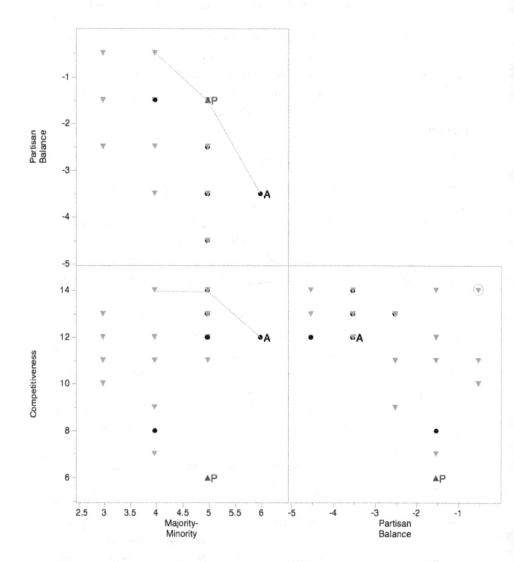

Figure 6.2. *Above and facing page*: Pareto frontier across the three political and substantively varying criteria. In the plots above, black lines illustrate the frontier among pairs of criteria, and the darkest points represent plans that are undominated on all three criteria simultaneously. In the plot to the right, the undominated plans are represented by the largest circles in the three-dimensional criteria space.

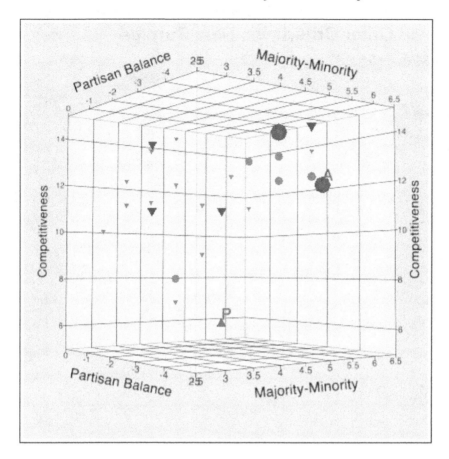

superset of the plans created by the legislature (in technical terms, the set of public plans "dominated" the legislative plans). This suggests that the public explored more substantive possibilities than the other entities. Furthermore, with the exception of majority-minority districts, the "best" plan, as ranked by each individual criterion, was a public plan. Although no plan dominated all others in every criterion, the top ranking plan in each single-criterion ranking either belonged to a public entry or was substantively tied.

The adopted plan is at the observed Pareto frontier among the three substantive criteria, due to the presence of an additional black majority district. The adopted plan creates an additional majority-minority seat against sharp reductions in both partisan balance and district competitiveness. As discussed, we have not performed any additional voting analyses to determine if this additional black majority district is legally required under Section 2 of the Voting Rights Act or under the new Florida constitutional

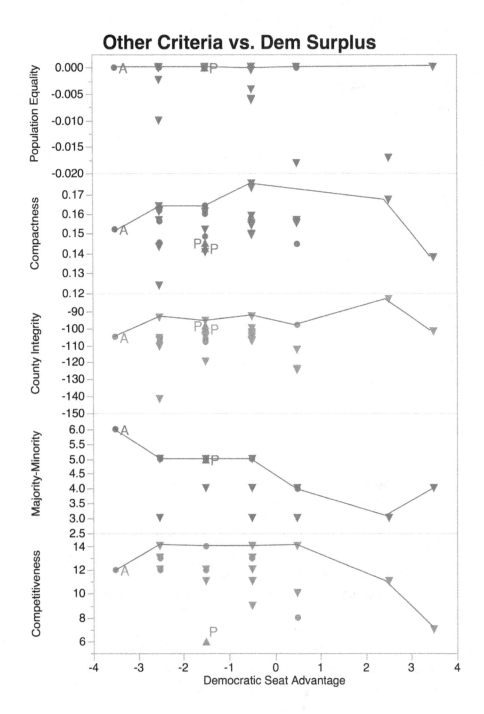

Figure 6.3. Democratic seat advantage versus other criteria.

provisions. It may be that a black-preferred candidate could be elected from a so-called influence district, which contains a sizable African American community, but below 50-percent black voting age population. This analysis helps explain why Republicans in the state legislature financially supported Corrine Brown's lawsuit against the congressional redistricting ballot measure,[58] since Republicans stood to gain substantially from this shoestring district. Different district configurations without this one black majority district enable a plan with more partisan balance and/or more district competitiveness.

Indeed, it is possible to further trade off majority-minority districts for a greater number of Democratic districts. In figure 6.3, we unfold the partisan balance measure so that it now represents the number of Democratic-leaning seats, relative to an even division of 13.5 of 27 districts. There are two plans with a majority of Democratic-leaning districts. The plan with 17 Democratic-leaning districts is perhaps of most interest since it has a minimal population deviation of two persons.[59] In contrast, the plan with 16 Democratic-leaning districts has a population deviation of 11,876, or 1.7 percent.[60] The 17 Democratic districts plan is less compact than the adopted plan, but has fewer county splits. It has significantly fewer competitive districts, with only 7 compared to 12 in the adopted plan, but has four districts just outside the cusp of our competitiveness range. It has only one black majority district and three Hispanic majority districts, whereas other plans typically have two black majority districts, aside from the adopted plan's three black majority districts. Figure 6.3 draws a line representing the Pareto frontier in two dimensions to illustrate the major trade-offs in a Democratic plan appear to be primarily along dimensions with black representation and district competitiveness.

Discussion

The reform process in Florida, catalyzed by advances in information technology, enabled a dramatic increase in public participation in the redistricting process. In turn, public participation yielded a large set of proposed plans that could be used to check the efficiency and the compliance of the adopted plan with the redistricting criteria specified. These plans also provide a counterfactual story to scholarly claims that Democrats are at a geographic disadvantage when drawing congressional redistricting plans in Florida.

Based on an analysis of all valid congressional plans, the redistricting reform process in Florida can be considered a partial success. Florida now requires that congressional "districts shall not be drawn with the intent or result of denying or abridging the equal opportunity of racial or language minorities to participate in the political process or to diminish their ability to elect representatives of their choice." The adopted plan represents one of the efficient observable trade-offs among the reformer's criteria, primarily along the lines of racial representation by creating an additional black majority district in the form of the current Fifth Congressional District. This does not mean, however, that reform was entirely successful. The adopted plan is efficient, but is atypical of the plans submitted by the legislature and public. Based on the pattern of public submissions, and on contextual information, we suspect the adopted plan was drawn for partisan motivations. The public preference and good-government criteria might be better served by the selection of the other efficient plans—that were much more competitive, and less biased, at the cost of a reduction of one majority-minority seat. At the time of this writing, it remains to be seen in ongoing litigation if the Florida courts will agree with the legislature that this district must be drawn at the sacrifice of other criteria now found in the constitution.

The public plan with 17 Democratic districts provides strong counterfactual evidence to claims that Democrats must suffer a pro-Republican bias in Florida's congressional redistricting because they are inefficiently concentrated in urban areas of the state. Similarly, in a separate analysis of redistricting plans created in Virginia, we have observed that it is possible to draw a more balanced congressional plan than what the Republican government adopted. Instead, the public plans suggest a structural trade-off of a different nature, between black majority seats and Democratic seats. This pattern is most evident when comparing the adopted plan's three black majority districts with the two black majority districts found in the typical legislative and public plan.

III

EFFECTS

7

Running with Uncertainty

Candidate Emergence during Redistricting in Florida

CHERIE D. MAESTAS AND TRAVIS A. BRAIDWOOD

Perhaps no one waits with more anticipation for the new district boundary maps than those with political ambition for legislative office.[1] This was certainly the case in the spring of 2012 in Florida as legislative incumbents and potential challengers waited for U.S. House and state legislative maps to be finalized. In routine election years, potential candidates for office decide whether to run very early in the cycle to ensure sufficient time to raise money and organize a vigorous campaign. Early organization is especially important for state legislative incumbents in Florida since they face fundraising restrictions when the legislature is in session.[2] However, during redistricting years, the uncertainty surrounding political boundaries makes it difficult to plan campaign strategies, or know which constituents to court early in the electoral cycle.

Legislative boundaries define electoral competition for office. Consequently, shifts in their locations also shift electoral fortunes. In some cases, redistricting opens up opportunities for challengers in districts that seemed guaranteed to incumbents. In others, it bolsters incumbents' natural constituencies, dashing the hopes of would-be challengers. The boundaries and patterns of candidate emergence that result from redistricting, in the aggregate, shape broader party fortunes in the state and sometimes disrupt stable majorities in the legislature. Thus, the redistricting stakes are high both for individual candidates and for partisan interests.

Florida, like most states, relies primarily on a legislative-led process to revamp district maps following each decennial census. Legislators are well aware of the personal and partisan ramifications of these district maps, so, not surprisingly, political redistricting battles tend to be lengthy and intense. Disputes over district lines in Florida stretched well into late spring, leaving candidates uncertain about where, or even if, they should run for office.[3] Dan Raulerson, for example, was hoping to win a seat in the Florida House; he filed early despite redistricting uncertainty, but this forced him into concentrating his spring campaign on areas he felt certain would remain in the district.[4] The uncertainty over boundaries left many candidates waiting in the wings rather than trying to run in districts that might not be intact when the redistricting dust settled.[5] From the outset, political activists complained that the slow legislative progress in Florida was intentionally designed to ward off challengers, starving them of the time needed to effectively campaign.[6]

The redistricting battle in Florida offers an interesting glimpse of the competing influences on candidate decision-making among incumbents and political aspirants. In this chapter, we focus on the ramifications of redistricting on the emergence of candidates for office, particularly those considered to be strong, "quality" candidates. By quality, we simply mean candidates with sufficient experience, attractiveness, and/or resources to run an effective, visible campaign regardless of whether they eventually win. Understanding how redistricting influences candidate emergence in Florida, or any other state, helps us assess the quality of democracy and the prospects for representation of public preferences. Strong candidates willing to run for office are a vital ingredient to democracy because they serve as democratic watchdogs. As James Madison noted, the solution of last resort to prevent the abuse of political power "must be obtained from the people, who can, by the election of more faithful representatives, annul the acts of the usurpers."[7]

Challengers compel incumbents who are out of step with their constituencies to comply with the wishes of voters, or face electoral defeat.[8] Moreover, challengers serve as vigorous competitors in open seat races, keeping citizens informed of relevant public debates. Strong candidates attract media, party support, and fundraising, all of which serve to inform, energize, and mobilize the electorate. As a result, when high quality, strong candidates challenge each other in the electoral arena, citizens are more aware of key political debates, and are therefore more likely to participate.[9] Similarly, elements associated with increased campaign competition, such as open seat races and political advertising, have been shown to increase candidate name recognition.[10] Candidate emergence in legislative races is essential to fostering collective representation. Replacement of legislators through the electoral process helps bring the partisan balance of legislatures and their policies into line with aggregate public preferences.[11] However, for this mechanism to function properly, the political boundaries must facilitate candidacies among ambitious individuals from both parties so that citizens have meaningful choices.

Florida in Context: A Look at Candidacies and Races Following Redistricting

Competition for legislative office can generate many benefits to society, but competitive races are not the norm in legislative elections. Instead, legislative elections are fraught with incumbent entrenchment and non-competitive races; this trend is hardly unique to Florida. Between 1970 and 2012, 65 percent of U.S. House races were won by landslide vote margins of 20 percent or more, and fully 95 percent of incumbents who ran for reelection won.[12] This is hardly surprising when one considers the plethora of official resources members have granted themselves.[13] Florida's elections mirror these national trends. Of Florida's 388 U.S. House incumbents running for reelection since 1970, only 14 were defeated in the general election.[14] Instead, partisan change in the Florida delegation has stemmed mostly from seats changing parties in open seat races. These include seat expansions from reapportionment, and strategic retirements (i.e., incumbents choosing to leave office in anticipation of likely defeat). Redistricting often serves as an impetus for strategic retirements because changes to district boundaries alter incumbents' chances of winning.

Table 7.1 shows the stark difference in the nature of candidacies and races in years following redistricting compared to normal elections. We examine data for all U.S. House districts (top of table) and compare this to Florida's U.S. House districts (bottom of table), for the years 1970 to 2012. Generally, U.S. House contests in Florida exhibit less competition. Florida had more unchallenged incumbent races and open seat races than was typical of the rest of the nation, and Florida had fewer experienced challengers running against incumbents.

Redistricting following the five decennial census periods included in the dataset had a substantial effect on the subsequent races. The second column presents the effects of districts that were changed due to redistricting in 1972, 1982, 1992, 2002, and 2012. Overall, redistricting increased the proportion of open seats and decreased the number of seats unchallenged by one of the two major parties. As table 7.1 reveals, the proportion of expe-

Table 7.1. U.S. House elections and candidate characteristics, 1970–2012

	No redistricting	Post-census redistricting
UNITED STATES		
% of All U.S. House districts		
Open seats	9.4	14.7
Unchallenged seats	13.6	11.5
Races with experienced candidates	27.1	35.1
N	6,990	2,175
% U.S. incumbent-held seats		
Unchallenged incumbents	14.8	13.3
Experienced challengers	20.4	24.7
N	6,333	1,856
FLORIDA		
Percentage of all Florida U.S. House districts		
Open seats	9.9	24.8
Unchallenged seats	34.9	19.3
Races with experienced candidates	24.8	34.1
N	335	109
% Florida's incumbent-held seats		
Unchallenged incumbents	37.8	25.6
Experienced challengers	15.4	14.8
N	302	82

Notes: Analysis of U.S. House data compiled by Gary C. Jacobson, University of California at San Diego. Analysis excludes races with mid-cycle redistricting.

rienced, high-quality challengers generally increased following redistricting. However, the increase in quality challengers resulted mostly from their entry into open seat races rather than challenges to sitting incumbents.

The national trends are exaggerated in the state of Florida, where the proportion of open seats in redistricting years jumped dramatically compared to non-redistricting years. Nearly a quarter of all races following redistricting were open compared to slightly less than 10 percent in non-redistricting years. The percent of uncontested races dropped from 34.9 percent for non-redistricting years to 19.3 percent in post-redistricting years. Although Florida incumbents were more likely to be challenged in a redistricting year, they were slightly less likely to be challenged by an experienced candidate than incumbents were in non-redistricting years.

Redistricting in Florida facilitated the dramatic shift in party fortunes, although some of the effects of district boundaries were not immediately apparent. Rather, district boundaries created the context through which national and regional partisan tides were amplified over a series of elections. Prior to 1990, Democrats controlled a strong majority of the seats in both the state legislature and the U.S. House delegation. However, the party balance was not reflective of increasing Republican support in the state. In 1980, for example, 55 percent of the state voted for Republican presidential candidate Ronald Reagan, and 38 percent voted for Democratic president Jimmy Carter, despite the U.S. House delegation being 73 percent Democratic that year. During the 1980s and 1990s, Republicans made steady inroads as district boundaries and new seats were drawn to advantage Republican candidates. By 2002, Democrats made up less than one-third of the U.S. House delegation, and they had lost majority control in the state legislature. Despite these legislative shortcomings, in 2008 Barack Obama won just over half of the statewide vote. This is hardly surprising when one considers that Democrats comprise 41 percent of registered Floridians, compared to only 36 percent registered as Republicans. Despite this registration advantage, in 2008 Republicans held nearly twice the number of seats in the lower and upper chambers of the state legislature and U.S. House delegation.[15]

Voter mandated changes in 2010 created an opportunity to lessen the imbalance by reducing partisan gerrymandering, and requiring district lines align more closely with natural political and geographic boundaries. Democrats were hopeful that the new redistricting requirements passed by Florida voters would open opportunities to break up the strong Republican majorities in the U.S. House delegation and the state legislature, but they found it difficult to recruit candidates due to uncertainty.[16] How did the new standards and resulting district lines affect the emergence of candidates? In the next sections, we examine patterns of entry in Florida's 2012 legislative elections.

The 2012 Redistricting, Strategic Choices, and Candidate Emergence

Legislative elections are dominated by the strategic decisions of individuals ambitious for higher office rather than the coordinated direction of political party leaders.[17] Parties work hard to encourage candidacies by creating a supportive environment, but it is individuals who must decide whether to bear the costs of a risky run for office.[18] Before entering a particular race, individuals seeking to gain or retain office generally weigh the benefits of holding office against the costs of running,[19] as expressed by the following equation:

$$Pr(Run)=f(E(U)), \text{ where } E(U)=pB-C$$

In this equation, the probability of running is a function of the expected utility of office; defined by, the probability of winning, B, the benefits of holding office, and C, the cost of running. The anticipated benefits of holding office, B, include the prestige, power, and pay of the office and play an important role in the decision-making process of potential candidates. However, these benefits are discounted by the chances of winning, since the potential candidate only gains the benefits from office holding by winning both the primary and general election.

The costs of running apply regardless of whether the candidate wins or loses, thus, they serve as a deterrent to entry. Direct costs of running include things like the costs of filing with the state to run for office and the time and money spent campaigning. Campaigns also involve indirect and opportunity costs such as the activities forgone by running for office, and the personal and psychological costs of a grueling race. Redistricting influences many aspects of the cost equation. For example, incumbents whose district boundaries shift dramatically must invest in advertising to introduce themselves to new constituents. Previous research shows that the incumbency advantage due to incumbents' efforts to cultivate a "personal vote" declines appreciably when district boundaries change.[20] Incumbents must compensate for this with greater campaign spending.

Florida campaign finance laws potentially increase the time and monetary costs to candidates. If candidates file early and later change the district in which they are running after the boundaries are finalized, their staff must contact each contributor who donated funds for running in the original district and ask whether they would like their money back. The only exception is when a district number changes solely for redistricting, meaning that a candidate is running in the same location for which he/she filed but under a different district number.[21] However, some candidates opt to run in an entirely different location or for a different office once boundaries are finalized.

Redistricting also has the potential to also impose significant residency costs upon candidates for state legislative office, as candidates are required to live in the district they represent upon taking office.[22] It is not uncommon for an incumbent or potential challenger to find their district residence unexpectedly redrawn into a different district leaving them scrambling to change residences mid-campaign.

Interestingly, not all aspects of redistricting are detrimental to would-be candidates. Just to qualify to appear on the ballot in Florida, candidates must either pay a qualifying fee, or collect a predetermined number of qualifying signatures to run in a specified district.[23] However, Florida senator Aaron Bean (R-District 4) noted the benefit of running during redistricting years includes an exception to the signature gathering rules that allows a candidate to procure signatures from across the state to qualify for the ballot, rather than only signatures from voters in a given district.[24] This exception prevents candidates from being disqualified as a result of boundary shifts that move some of the qualifying signatories outside of the new district boundaries.

Redistricting and the Probability of Winning

The probability of winning is considered to be the most influential aspect of candidates' calculations. If the probability of winning is very small, even potentially great benefits from office cannot overcome the costs associated with entering a race and running a campaign. Ample evidence shows that ambitious, potential candidates are likely to enter a race when the probability of winning is high, such as in open seat races, but that these contenders sit on the sidelines when the probability is low.[25] The probability of winning is a function of several things, some structural and some personal. The structural component is directly tied to the location of district boundaries because those boundaries define the racial and socioeconomic demographics of the voters in the district, including the partisan balance. Shifting the racial, economic, religious, or partisan composition of the district can erode or bolster support for a sitting incumbent.

The chances of winning also depend on a personal component, such as the skills and personal qualities of a candidate. Incumbents are well known to be high on this dimension,[26] but some of the personal vote cultivated through service to constituents dissipates as those constituents are redrawn into other districts.[27] This helps to explain why potential candidates are often emboldened to challenge incumbents following redistricting—their probability of winning rises as the probability of the incumbent winning falls. In many cases, redistricting results in minor adjustments of district boundaries that have little impact on the overall constituency and probability of winning, but in some districts the change is dramatic. This can influence the chances that a potential candidate for office can successfully unseat an otherwise safe incumbent.

District Changes and Candidate Entry Patterns in 2012

In practice, it is nearly impossible to observe the type of individual-level perceptual data required to predict candidate emergence. That said, based on prior research, we would expect to see different patterns of candidate emergence in districts that changed little during redistricting compared to those that changed a great deal.[28] For incumbents, large changes in district boundaries serve to reduce the chances of winning while raising the costs of running. When incumbents lose a large share of their current voters, they must increase their effort and expenditures to make themselves familiar to those new to the district. The personal vote advantage at the ballot box declines, leaving the door open for opportunistic challengers.[29] In contrast, potential candidates see their chances increase as they gain a more equal footing among new voters.

Table 7.2 compares the percentage of incumbents who filed to run in districts with little change versus those that changed dramatically. District change is measured as the size of the carry-forward population—the proportion of the 2012 district that is comprised of residents from the largest contributing 2010 district. For example, the 2012 Florida House District 2 was comprised of residents from three different 2010 districts, and each district's population contributed a different share of 2012 residents to the new District 2. We identify 2010's District 3 as the "parent" of 2012's District 2 because it contributed more Floridians of voting age to the new district than the other two contributing districts (its voting age population comprised approximately 55 percent of the new district's voters).

In contrast, the district that shared the same number as the 2012 district—2010 District 2—only contributed 39 percent of the 2012 District 2's voting age population (VAP). The remainder of 2012 District 2 (6 percent) came from 2010 District 1. Our measure has a theoretical range of 0 to 1, but an observable range of .31 to 1.0. In other words, no single 2012 district was composed of less than 31 percent of voters from another, while some districts underwent no change (1's), composed of 100 percent of a single 2010 district. It is in districts with a high amount of change (those closer to 0) that we expect to find higher levels of incumbent retirement and more robust candidate pools.

Table 7.2. Percent of eligible incumbents filing to run for reelection

	District change			
	High	Moderate	Low	Seats
State house	64%	73%	70%	
N	33	52	23	108
State senate	56%	69%	83%	
N	9	16	6	31
U.S. House	50%	92%	85%	
N	2	12	13	27

Notes: Analysis excludes term-limited members but includes all incumbents who filed to run regardless of later withdrawal or primary defeat.

In table 7.2, we group together districts with a great deal of change, meaning less than 50 percent of the population of the new district came from a single parent district. We compare these with districts with moderate change (.50 to .70) and those with low change (.71 to 1.0). For the purposes of this analysis, we include all incumbents who filed to run, regardless of whether they were defeated in the primary or withdrew for other reasons.[30] We do so because incumbent filing is a strong signal to potential candidates of their chances of winning. We exclude all term-limited incumbents from our analysis since they lacked the option of running for reelection.

The likelihood of incumbent retirement is greatest for high change districts in all three chambers. The number of "high change" districts is quite small for the state senate and U.S. House, so these findings are at best speculative, but they make intuitive sense. As the carry-forward population declines (i.e., district change increases), the cost of advertising to achieve name recognition among new voters increases and the incumbents' subjective probability of winning declines. For some incumbents, the anticipated costs of running exceeded the expected benefits, so they opted not to run for reelection.

It is worth mentioning that officeholders with political career ambitions for higher office assess their chances of winning and their costs of running relative to other political opportunities, which are also affected by redistricting. When desirable higher political offices shift district boundaries, this changes the chances that a lower officeholder might win a race for higher office. Although beyond the limits of our data, the combined forces of declining chances of reelection in one's own seat due to boundary shifts, on the one hand, and the increased chances of winning in a higher seat, on

Table 7.3. District changes and candidate entry

	Two party race		Democratic candidate		Republican candidate	
Carry-forward population	-2.34	*	-2.24	*	-3.33	***
	1.28		1.27		1.25	
Increase in party registration imbalance	-5.84	**				
	2.47					
Increase in Republican registration advantage			-9.99	***	5.17	**
			2.74		2.06	
Incumbent's 2010 vote margin (0 if open)	-1.87	***	-1.47	**	-0.80	
	0.54		0.60		0.59	
Republican incumbent	-0.12		-1.00	*	-2.41	***
	0.46		0.53		0.63	
Democratic incumbent	-0.06		-2.20	***	-1.60	**
	0.63		0.72		0.78	
Incumbent years in office (0 if open)	0.03		-0.01		0.07	*
	0.05		0.04		0.04	
Term-limited incumbent	-0.25		0.18		-0.19	
	0.55		0.57		0.64	
Florida House	-1.71	***	-1.84	***	0.04	
	0.64		0.69		0.51	
Florida Senate	-0.66		-1.38	*	0.73	
	0.74		0.75		0.63	
Constant	3.57	***	4.60	***	3.50	***
	1.13		1.14		1.03	
N	187		187		187	
Ll	-105.71		-91.01		-101.11	
chi2	31.46		41.68		38.44	

Notes: The table reports logit coefficients with standard errors below. The model includes open and incumbent held seats. Incumbent variables score 0 when seat is open. Carry-forward population is the share of residents in the 2012 district carried forward from the largest contributing 2010 district.
*p<.10
**p<.05
***p<.01 (two tailed)

the other, are likely to create a powerful pull and increase the number of lower office open seats.

We turn now to examine how district changes influenced the entry of non-incumbent candidates. One goal of the Fair Districts initiative was to increase competition for office, and this is best seen in whether the 2012 district boundary changes encouraged candidate entry and competitive two-party races. A comparison of the data from the presidential election of 2012 to that of 2008, reveals the raw number of candidates for office increased, particularly for the U.S. House. In 2008, a total of 65 non-incumbent candidates filed to run for the U.S. House compared to only 46 in 2008, a 41 percent increase. The addition of two new seats and considerable shifts in some district boundaries provided a venue for attractive potential candidates. In contrast, the size of the candidate pool for the Florida House grew by a modest 6 percent over 2008. The number of Florida Senate candidates more than doubled, but this is not a fair comparison since the number of seats open in 2008 was half that of 2012, when all senate seats were up for election following redistricting.

How did district changes contribute to encouraging candidacies? Table 7.3 examines this in two ways using multivariate analysis. The first model (column 1) looks at the how district boundary changes affected the likelihood of a two-party race. One key variable of interest is the proportion of carry-forward population in the district as described earlier. Higher values indicate less change in a district, and significantly reduce the probability of a two-party race. Figure 7.1 displays this relationship graphically, showing how the predicted probability of a two-party race declines as the carry-forward population increases.

The second redistricting variable of interest captures the "change in partisan balance" of the 2012 district compared to its 2010 parent district. The measure is calculated by subtracting the relative party registration balance in 2010 (the absolute value of the percent of registered Republicans minus the percent of registered Democrats) from the relative party registration balance in 2012. Values close to zero indicate little change in the party balance compared to 2010. Negative values mean the district has greater partisan registration balance than the parent district, positive values indicate that the 2012 district is less balanced. The variable ranges from -.13 to .29 with a mean and median of 0. In other words, half the 2012 districts became more balanced than their parent, while half became less. This is important because our model indicates that, independent of other factors, a shift in party registration balance is consequential for candidate entry. Districts

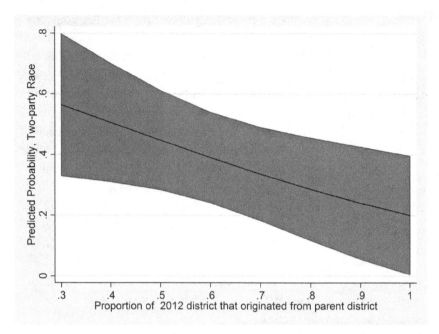

Figure 7.1. Predicted probability of a two-party race by district change. Predicted probabilities with 95-percent confidence interval based on logit model in table 7.3 with all variables set to their mean or mode.

that became more balanced were more likely to have a two-party race than those that became less balanced. The probability of having both a Democrat and a Republican file to run was .52; evenly split for those districts whose party balance increased by 10 percent (scored -.10 on our change in imbalance scale), while the probability was .26 for those whose party balance decreased by .10.

It is important to note that incumbency plays a strong role in whether non-incumbents file to run in the same district, so we control for a number of things related to incumbency, including the party of the incumbent. Here, open seat races serve as the reference category. We also include incumbent controls for number of years in office and previous vote margin, both of which were coded 0 when the race is open. Not surprisingly, the results show that it is the incumbent's prior vote margin at the polls that depresses the chances of a two-party race. Finally, since candidate entry is often correlated with prestige of the seat, we include variables indicating the chamber of the race with U.S. House as the omitted reference category.

As table 7.3 reveals, Florida House races were less likely to be two-party contests.

Models 2 and 3 (columns 2 and 3 in table 7.3) examine partisan candidate entry in an effort to determine how redistricting affected the likelihood that at least one candidate representing one of the major parties would file to run for office. The size of the carry-forward VAP depresses the likelihood of candidates from both parties filing, though it depresses the chances slightly more for Republicans than Democrats. We also include a partisan change measure that compares the party registration advantage for Republicans in 2012 to the Republican registration advantage in the 2010 parent district. Districts in which the registration advantage increased were more likely to draw a non-incumbent Republican and less likely to draw a non-incumbent Democrat. Incumbency matters greatly as well. An incumbent running in either party decreased the probability of a candidate emerging in a district, but this effect, not surprisingly, is largest on the probability of a candidate emerging in the same party as the incumbent. The incumbency effects are notable because table 7.2 showed that as the carry-forward population declined, incumbents were less likely to run. As a result, the effects of redistricting on candidate emergence are both direct, through changes in the carry-forward population and changes in party registration advantage, and indirect, through greater incumbent retirements.

Emergence of Experienced Non-Incumbent Candidates

The preceding analysis focused on the emergence of *any* candidate, but we are also concerned with whether *experienced* candidates emerge. Prior research suggests that experienced candidates fare better in the electoral arena than amateurs.[31] More competitive races translate into greater public awareness of candidates and issues during the campaign process. Table 7.4 examines the patterns of emergence by the type of race and the level of experience of the candidates. As the table reveals, an important way in which redistricting influences the quality of candidates who run is through increasing the number of open seats. Large changes to district boundaries increased the odds that a seat would be open, and open seats drew the lion's share of experienced candidates. Among the 187 races in 2012, incumbents filed to run in 130 seats, leaving 57 seats open prior to the primary election. At least one experienced candidate filed to run in 67 percent of open seat races. In contrast, experienced candidates filed to run in only 11

Table 7.4. Percent districts with an experienced challenger

	Open seat	Incumbent race
State house	53%	6%
N	38	82
State senate	93%	8%
N	15	25
U.S. House	100%	17%
N	4	23

incumbent-held districts (8.5 percent). This is not surprising since many ambitious, experienced candidates wait until their probability of winning is greatest before running, and this often correlates with an incumbent leaving office.[32]

The most common type of political experience for a candidate to have was service in the Florida House. Among all non-incumbent candidates who filed to run, 13 percent had held office in the Florida House while only 3 percent had served in the Florida Senate. Another 12 percent of candidates filing had a history of serving in local city or county government positions, such as sheriff, school board member, city or county clerk, commission members, and mayors. Overall, 24 percent of non-incumbents who filed had held at least one office prior to filing to run in 2012, and 4 percent had held more than one office.

Table 7.5 offers further evidence that the primary mechanism attracting experienced candidates to run was incumbent departure. We ran an analysis of races in all three chambers to determine which factors predicted at least one experienced candidate would file to run for office. We included the two measures of redistricting change, outlined earlier, along with controls for incumbent characteristics and chamber. The first model predicts the probability of any experienced challenger filing, while the second and third split the sample by party.

Our findings reveal that change in the party registration balance has no effect on the chances of an experienced candidate entering. Neither does the size of the carry-forward population. Rather, the presence or absence of the incumbent is the main determinant in the models, particularly the presence or absence of Republican incumbents. The coefficients in the model featuring both Democratic and Republican incumbents indicate that there is a lower probability of an experienced challenger filing when an incumbent from either party is present. For example, the predicted probability that an experienced challenger would emerge in an open Florida Senate

Table 7.5. Coefficients from logit model, predicting the emergence of at least one experienced candidate

	Any experience	Experienced Democrat	Experienced Republican
Carry-forward population (proportion of 2012 district from single largest contributing district)	0.68 1.48	-1.38 2.20	0.70 1.50
Increase in party registration Imbalance	-2.39 2.57		
Increase in Republican registration advantage		-0.48 1.75	1.84 2.00
Republican incumbent	-2.39 *** 0.84	-0.40 0.84	-3.20 *** 1.08
Democratic incumbent	-1.55 1.19	0.65 1.44	-2.37 *** 0.87
Incumbent 2010 vote margin (0 if open)	-2.30 1.35	-1.77 1.39	-2.12 1.72
Incumbent years in office (0 if open)	-0.02 0.05	-0.28 0.25	0.03 0.04
Term limited incumbent	0.09 0.81	-0.14 0.80	0.20 0.74
U.S. House district	1.34 *** 0.60	1.15 0.73	1.49 ** 0.69
Florida Senate district	1.36 *** 0.59	1.35 *** 0.55	0.65 0.58
Constant	-0.08 0.91	-0.81 1.29	-0.64 0.93
N	187	187	187
Ln likelihood	-67.53	-52.26	-55.38
chi2	51.06	21.19	31.86

Notes: The model includes open and incumbent held seats. Incumbent variables score 0 when seat is open. Carry-forward population is the share of residents in the 2012 district carried forward from the largest contributing 2010 district.
* $p < .10$
** $p < .05$
*** $p < .01$ (two-tailed)

race, holding all other variables constant, was .57, but this drops to only .11 if an incumbent Republican is running.

We also tested for potential conditional effects, such as whether the incumbent vote margin mattered more for districts in which the incumbents' carry-forward population was large; however, we found no evidence to support this expectation. Splitting races into incumbent and open seat elections also made no difference to the main results (model not shown). Modeling candidate emergence only for incumbent races found all coefficients were insignificant, except for the incumbent vote margin. We caution against making much of these results, however, since experienced challengers emerged in only 11 of the 130 races for incumbent-held seats.

Timing of Candidate Entry

We turn now to the question of whether the uncertainty about boundaries during the 2012 redistricting affected the timing of candidate entry. This is an interesting question because the timing of candidate entry marks the beginning of the candidate's campaign efforts. Although candidates may announce their intention to run for office, they may not collect donations, spend money, or obtain signatures to qualify for the ballot without filing forms with the Florida Division of Elections.[33] As a result, a delay in filing to gain certainty comes with a cost to the campaign organization. Compared to other states, Florida has a much later electoral calendar, leaving candidates ample discretion in choosing when to file. In 2012, the final date to qualify for the ballot was June 8, so candidates had the option to wait for clarity over district lines before filing to run. Did redistricting delay the initiation of campaigns in Florida?

We tackle this question in two ways. First, we simply compare the differences in candidate filing dates between 2012 and 2008. We chose 2008 as the basis for comparison since it, like 2012, was a presidential election year with a vigorous presidential primary season in the state.[34] Second, we compare filing timing across races in 2012 to see whether candidates filed later in districts that faced large changes to district boundaries. We collected data on the date that each candidate for legislative office filed with the Florida Division of Elections and calculated the number of days qualifying prior to the deadline. Overall, the mean was 284 days prior and the median was 233 days. Only 10 percent of candidates filed during the last two weeks before the qualifying deadline.

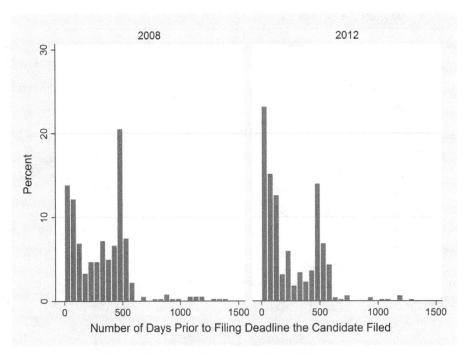

Figure 7.2. Distribution of candidate filing dates, 2008 and 2012.

Figure 7.2 shows considerable differences in filing dates when comparing 2008 and 2012. Although the distributions show two distinct groups—early filers who file over a year in advance, and late filers who file within months of the election—the percentage of candidates who were late filers is appreciably larger in 2012. A Kolmogorov-Smirnov test for equality of distribution shows that the patterns of candidate entry differ between the two years (D= .1916, < .001). In 2008, candidates filed an average of 325 days prior to the deadline while in 2012 they filed an average of 250 days before, a difference of 75 days (p < .001).

Table 7.6 shows comparisons between the two election years by candidate and chamber. This table is interesting in several regards. First, it helps illuminate the source of the bimodal distributions observed in both years. The majority of early filers are incumbents. Overall, incumbents filed on average 446 days prior to the deadline, while non-incumbents waited until an average of just 205 days before the deadline. By far, the chamber with the greatest incidence of early filing is the Florida Senate, with an average of 974 days (2 years, 8 months) before the deadline in 2008, and an average of

Table 7.6. Summary statistics on candidate entry timing

	2008			2012			Percentage decline from 2012
	Mean days	Std. Dev	N	Mean days	Std. Dev	N	
Florida House	328	206	250	249	202	261	
Incumbent	466	106	87	457	139	85	-2
Challenger	150	162	60	136	138	61	-9
Open seat	315	208	103	156	148	115	-50
Florida Senate	541	442	40	347	347	85	
Incumbent	974	256	13	615	233	26	-37
Challenger	162	224	10	99	182	17	-39
Open seat	433	381	17	282	353	42	-35
U.S. House	189	138	70	160	143	89	
Incumbent	195	145	24	124	124	24	-36
Challenger	182	137	41	166	155	37	-9
Open seat	220	143	5	181	141	28	-18

Notes: Column one reports the average days before the filing deadline candidates filed to run for office by the standard deviation in the second. N is the number of individual candidates in each category. The last column provides the percentage change in average early filing days from 2008 to 2012.

615 in 2012. This, of course, makes a great deal of sense given that the term of a Florida senator is four years. The timing is similarly long in the Florida House where members filed on average 466 days in advance in 2008 and 457 in 2012.

Part of the reason for the very early filing of incumbents in Florida pertains to campaign finance rules that prohibit legislators from raising money during the session. Filing early for a race years ahead of the election permits candidates to build a campaign war chest outside of sessions, well before potential challengers consider running for office. War chests are seen as considerable deterrents to potential challengers,[35] so early filing permits candidates to reduce the likelihood of facing an opponent, as well as prepare their coffers should one emerge. Since federal campaign finance law does not have similar prohibitions, U.S. House incumbent filing times are much later in the process, averaging only 195 days in advance in 2008, and 124 days in advance in 2012.

Notably, within each chamber, there is a considerable delay in 2012 candidate filings compared to 2008. The difference in the number of days was greatest among Florida Senate incumbents, whose average early filing days dropped by 354 days, and least among Florida House incumbents, whose average early filing days declined by 9 days. However, in terms of percentage change, the effects were most pronounced among open seat candidates for the Florida House (50 percent decline in average days) and Senate (24 percent decline), as well as challengers to Florida Senate incumbents (39 percent decline).

In an ordinary election, candidates know well in advance which incumbents will be departing due to term limits, so open seat candidates file quite early. The uncertainty surrounding district boundaries delayed early filers even when seats were expected to be open. For U.S. House candidates, the strongest declines in early filing came among incumbents (36 percent decline in average days), rather than challengers (9 percent decline) or open seat candidates (18 percent decline). Overall, our data present a picture of both incumbents and challengers waiting for the uncertainty to clear before filing to run for state legislative and congressional office.

Second, we were curious whether filings were delayed further in the subset of districts with especially large changes to their boundaries (those with low carry-forward populations). Given our variable of interest is the time delay in candidate filings we utilize a duration model, also known as a hazard model. Here we think about candidate entry as failure time process, with all would-be candidates eventually entering the fray, but with various factors affecting their individual decision calculus to file. Predicting when a candidate will file requires controlling for both candidate-specific factors, and district characteristics.

This model, unlike previous specifications, is a candidate-level analysis. We included controls for changes in district party composition and whether the district was open due to term limits. In this iteration, however, we also added controls for whether the candidate was an incumbent or a challenger (open seat is the reference category), whether a challenger shared the same party as the incumbent (if an incumbent was present), the candidate's party affiliation (Democrat = 1), race (African American = 1), and gender (male = 1). We also coded whether the candidate was running in a district with a term-limited incumbent to separate expected departures from strategic departures. We expected earlier candidate filings in the open seat reference category. Finally, since we are pooling the data across

Table 7.7. District and candidate effects on date of candidate filings

	Hazard ratio	SE
District carry-forward population	0.85	0.31
District increase in unbalanced registration	1.91	1.05
Candidate: incumbent	0.58	0.16 **
Candidate: challenger	1.28	0.24
Challenger same party as incumbent	0.82	0.18
Non-incumbent with prior experience	0.76	0.14
Democrat	1.07	0.16
Black	1.21	0.20
Male	1.33	0.17 **
Running in term-limited district	0.98	0.21
U.S. House seat	1.14	0.15
Florida Senate seat	0.57	0.10 **
Constant	0.00	0.00 ***
γ	0.002	0.00 ***
N	422	
Wald chi2	165.92	***

Notes: Gompertz regression. Standard errors clustered by district. Dependent variable is the number of days before the filing deadline the candidate filed. Coefficients are the hazard ratio of filing for office.
*$p<.10$
**$p<.05$
***$p<.01$ (two tailed)

three legislative chambers, we also included controls for the U.S. House and Florida Senate, with the Florida House as our base category.

The results of our duration model are featured in table 7.7. The analysis reveals that neither the carry-forward population variable nor the increased partisan imbalance variable was statistically significant.[36] In fact, only three of the substantive controls reached conventional levels of significance, candidate type (incumbent versus open seat versus challenger), gender, and type of office (U.S. House, Florida Senate, or Florida House). The predicted days filing prior to the deadline for incumbents was 281 compared to 180 for open seat candidates and 146 for challengers to incumbents.[37] This finding suggests that incumbents enjoyed a substantial time advantage to non-incumbent candidates in terms of organizing their campaigns.

Figure 7.3 shows the lack of a significant difference between those running in districts that faced large shifts in district VAP (the solid line representing the minimum population from the old district comprising the new), and districts with no change (the dashed line). Taken together, the evidence from tables 7.6 and 7.7 shows that during redistricting, most can-

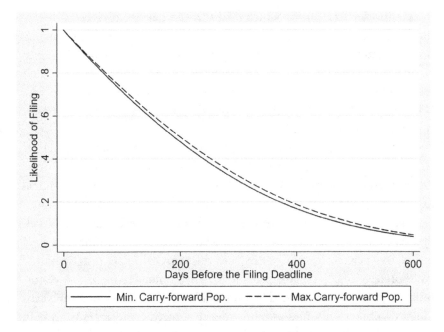

Figure 7.3. Effect of change in the proportion of the old district comprising the new district on candidate decisions to file before the deadline.

didates delay filing for legislative office regardless of whether they were running in districts that faced large shifts in district VAP. Yet, the filing delays are most prevalent among non-incumbent candidates. This is a substantively significant finding since it shows that redistricting is likely to impose greater costs on those who need more campaign time for fundraising and organization.

Summary and Conclusions

Candidates are central to the functioning of a healthy democracy. They offer citizens choices at the ballot box, they raise the visibility of policy issues facing the state and nation, and they engage citizens in the political process. Without the potential for choice, there can be no accountability for elected officials. Creating district boundaries that encourage rather than discourage candidates to run for office is an important mechanism for ensuring a responsive legislature. One concern raised by scholars and pundits in Florida is a marked absence of electoral competition in the state's legislative elections. At each level, district boundaries created over the last few decades produced a map in which the party seat balance diverged substantially from the party preferences of the state's electorate. Heavily partisan districts combined with term limits produced a system in which would-be challengers tended to wait for open seats rather than squander their resources on a race against an incumbent that they were unlikely to win. Voters were left with few options other than the incumbent running for reelection. Did 2012 change that?

We think so. The recent district boundary changes appear to have chipped away at the uncompetitive nature of Florida's races. The process differed from other years because of the voter-passed initiative designed to increase competition and district compactness. In the aggregate, Democrats gained ground relative to Republicans and the seat share at all levels of legislative races became slightly more balanced. Although the legislative seat shares per party still diverge from the aggregate state distribution of voter preferences, the changes made to district maps reduced this distortion. Such an outcome would be impossible without a slate of strong candidates willing to file, and as our evidence showed, candidates from both parties were willing to step into the ring to run, even if they waited until late to file.

The 2012 redistricting process resulted in large changes to district boundaries in some areas of the state that led to strategic incumbent retirements. As districts were subdivided and recombined to form new districts, the chances of non-incumbent candidates winning generally increased, leading to more candidates entering the race. In large part, this was due to the fact that "high change" districts produced more open seats. This was especially true for newly formed districts that reduced party registration disparities. In many ways, this is what the voter mandated changes of 2010 were meant to achieve: increased electoral competition. However, given the average district was composed of 60 percent of its parent district and only half of new districts were more balanced than their primary parent district, the effectiveness of such efforts should be taken with caution.

Finally, this chapter explored the effect of district change on an individual candidates' timing of filing for candidacy with the state. In a typical year, Florida candidates tend to file quite early. Term limits facilitates this; candidates know far in advance which seats are certain to be open. However, during the 2012 redistricting, many candidates responded to uncertainty by waiting on the sidelines—until the new maps were cleared by the courts. This resulted in considerable delays, particularly for non-incumbent candidates. These delays, in turn, delayed candidates from organizing and fielding campaigns. For incumbents, the impact of this was likely negligible. For non-incumbents, particularly those without prior political experience, the delay may have been extremely costly.

The slower than average filing of non-incumbent candidates suggests to us that the full effect of redistricting may not be felt until the 2014 races when challenger and open seat contestants have more time to organize. To be sure, the crop of 2012 incumbents will be working hard to carve out a personal vote in their new districts, but redistricting reduced the strength of the structural party advantage for at least a subset of districts. Moreover, potential challengers are likely to recognize that the incumbency advantage will only grow over time so running in 2014 should prove attractive. If previous redistricting periods are a guide, new patterns of candidate competition will persist beyond the initial redistricting election. Overall, our evidence suggests that the 2012 redistricting increased candidate emergence and voter choice, but future years will reveal whether the increase in candidacies, particularly from the Democratic Party, are a new norm or just a product of the high uncertainty of 2012.

8

The Participatory Consequences
of Florida Redistricting

DANNY HAYES, M. V. HOOD III, AND SETH C. MCKEE

In the wake of the 2012 election, redistricting became a controversial topic. Journalists, politicians, and political scientists argued vociferously over whether the redrawing of congressional district lines had allowed the Republican Party to hold the U.S. House of Representatives, despite the fact that Democratic congressional candidates collectively won the popular vote. "Redistricting drew such a GOP-friendly map that, in a neutral environment, Republicans have an inherent advantage," Aaron Blake of the *Washington Post* wrote two days after the election.[1] Political scientists Eric McGhee and John Sides suggested, however, that the Democrats' seat deficit was principally from other sources: "These claims about gerrymandering aren't as strong as they appear."[2] (On this point, see also chapter 6.)

While the particulars of these debates were new to the 2012 election, the script was familiar: debates over redistricting focus almost exclusively on electoral outcomes and seat shares in Congress. Given redistricting's importance to party competition in American politics, these exchanges are valuable to study. Nevertheless, although the emphasis on election outcomes is important, redistricting debates almost always ignore another important feature of the reapportionment process—its potential effects on voter participation. A growing body of research suggests that the drawing of district lines can influence who votes and who does not, for a specific office affected by the redrawing of political boundaries. Our task in this chapter is to investigate whether and how redistricting has participatory effects that are often given little attention.

We examine precinct-level data from congressional and state legislative elections in the 2012 Florida elections. The analysis allows us to broaden the empirical evidence on redistricting's effects on participation and to extend such an analysis for the first time beyond congressional races.

Redistricting and Participation

When congressional district lines are redrawn after every decennial census—or, as happened several times over the last two decades for partisan or legal reasons in many Southern states like Florida—the connection between some citizens and their representatives is severed. This is an unavoidable part of the reapportionment process, and it injects instability into United States elections.[3] One consequence is that citizens who are redrawn into an unfamiliar incumbent's district experience an increase in information costs, since in U.S. House elections, the identity of the incumbent is one of the few things voters know about the contest.[4] A large literature has shown that increases in information costs lead to lower rates of participation.[5] This has generated the hypothesis that, all else equal, redrawn citizens should be less likely to participate than individuals who remain in a district with a familiar incumbent.

Indeed, survey data show that people who are redrawn are less likely to know their new incumbent's name.[6] For instance, Hayes and McKee find in an analysis of 1992 National Election Studies (NES) data that citizens redrawn after the 1990 Census were 16 percentage points less likely to recall and 11 percentage points less likely to recognize their incumbent's name than those who remained with a familiar incumbent.[7] Likewise, Winburn and Wagner examine counties that are split by congressional districts and find a similar pattern in NES data from 1994 through 2000.[8] Redrawn voters evidently have less information about their new incumbent than voters who remain with the same incumbent.

The literature is less clear, however, about whether this decline in incumbent familiarity leads to lower levels of participation. Two studies have found that redrawn citizens are less likely to vote in U.S. House contests in the election following a redistricting. In an analysis of precinct-level data from Texas, Hayes and McKee report that in portions of the state redrawn before the 2002, 2004, and 2006 elections, the level of "roll-off"—the proportion of voters failing to cast a ballot in the House election after having voted in a top ticket race—was between three and eight percentage points higher than in parts of the state that were not redrawn, controlling for other factors.[9] A second study revealed the same pattern in a series of

11 post-redistricting elections from 1992 through 2006 in a larger sample of states—California, Florida, Georgia, North Carolina, as well as Texas.[10] The average roll-off effect was smaller—less than two percentage points—but the emergence of the pattern in a wider sample of states in various elections adds a measure of generalization and reliability to the initial finding that redistricting increases voter abstention in contests affected by a boundary change.

Drawing firm causal inferences, however, from such studies is treacherous. As Sekhon and Titiunik point out, such a design assumes that precincts that were redrawn are identical in politically relevant ways to those that were not redrawn.[11] If that assumption is right, any differences in participation rates can be attributed to redistricting, not some other characteristic. However, this may not be a justifiable assumption, since the parts of a state targeted for redistricting are often redrawn precisely because they have a particular demographic or political composition. If these characteristics are correlated with participation rates, then "post-treatment" differences may actually be the result of "pre-treatment" differences rather than redistricting itself.

For that reason, individual-level analyses, in which analysts can control for a host of potential confounding variables, have been a crucial supplement to aggregate-level investigations. Nevertheless, the results of these studies have been mixed. Using NES data, Hayes and McKee find that redrawn voters are less likely to know their incumbent's name, and that this lack of information increases voter roll-off, controlling for a host of other attributes such as education levels, partisanship, and various demographic characteristics.[12] Other studies, however, have not found the same pattern. For instance, Winburn and Wagner do not find a relationship between the split of a county into multiple congressional districts with either turnout or roll-off.[13] Hayes et al. find that redistricting affected turnout in the 2006 Georgia congressional elections, but, counter to the negative participation hypothesis, redrawn voters in some cases were *more* likely to vote.[14] Keele and White study a subset of redrawn and same-incumbent registered voters in North Carolina, and they find no effect of redistricting on turnout.[15]

Individual-level data carry significant advantages over precinct-level analyses, but these studies have limitations of their own. Winburn and Wagner do not actually attempt to compare redrawn and same-incumbent voters, instead focusing on the geographic overlap between a respondent's congressional district and county of residence.[16] Hence, their results cannot speak precisely to participatory-based differences or similarities in groups of voters whose information costs have been altered as a direct consequence of a change in the incumbent-constituent relationship. Hayes et al. suggest that mobilization efforts—which they do not measure—might explain why some redrawn voters were more likely to vote, while others were less likely to turn out.[17] In addition, Keele and White's use of a voter file to track individuals identified as having been redrawn is a considerable improvement.[18] Nevertheless, their approach actually eliminates many voters whose behavior might alter the results. For instance, they do not include in their analysis citizens drawn into a district with an incumbent of a different race.

This last point is particularly important because previous work suggests an interaction between the race of constituents and the race of incumbents can condition how redistricting affects participation. Hayes and McKee find that redistricting has its strongest negative effects among African Americans drawn into white incumbents' districts.[19] Redistricting can mobilize blacks, however, when they are drawn into districts represented by African Americans. Thus, accounting for the characteristics of voters as well as the electoral context—and particularly, the race of incumbents— appears central to understanding how redistricting's participatory effects manifest themselves.

All of this underscores the need for the collection of more data and better research designs to test for the purported causal relationship between redistricting and participation. Furthermore, it is imperative that research move beyond congressional elections to determine whether any relationship between redistricting and participation can be broadly generalized in political contexts outside of congressional elections.

In particular, state legislative elections are a promising area for more research. Most voters know little about candidates for state legislative offices, but many are at least familiar with their sitting incumbent. When voters are redrawn into a new incumbent's district, however, their information costs are likely to rise significantly, in large part because state legislative campaigns are very low-profile. As a result, we might expect redistricting's effect on participation to be even stronger in state legislative elections than in congressional contests.

In the analysis that follows, we use precinct-level data from the 2012 Florida congressional and state legislative elections to explore the relationship between redistricting and voter participation. This allows us to put to a test with new data, a hypothesis that has been raised by the existing literature. This analysis gives us an opportunity to broaden the investigation of redistricting's effects. All of the previous work has focused on U.S. House elections. Presently, we examine whether the same patterns are also evident in post-redistricting state legislative contests.

Data and Method

The data we analyze in this chapter were compiled from several sources. As mentioned, we have precinct-level data for both U.S. House and state legislative races for the 2012 general election. In addition to vote returns for congressional and state legislative offices, we also have returns for U.S. Senate and for president of the United States. Data for top of the ballot races, specifically for the presidential contest, is critical to the construction of our dependent variable, which is a measure of voter roll-off. Each Florida county delivered their precinct-level vote returns for various offices in electronic format to the Florida Division of Elections website, where they were made available electronically. Additionally, we merged the vote returns data with data from the Florida voter registration and history files when they were made available by the state after the 2012 general election.

The voter registration file includes important demographic data at the individual level, which we aggregated up to the precinct. We have data on party affiliation, race/ethnicity, age, and gender. The demographic data include numbers for both registration and turnout in a given precinct (e.g., the number of females who registered and voted in Precinct 1 in Alachua County). We also have district level data for several key variables like the type of contest (incumbent or open seat), whether a district was contested (Democrat versus Republican), and the total spending by major party candidates (Democrats and Republicans). Finally, we are able to code properly our primary independent variable of interest, whether or not a precinct was redrawn.

An important caveat we accounted for concerns the handful of districts where the race is technically open but includes the presence of an incumbent who previously represented a different office. These cases are all confined to state legislative races. Briefly, there was one incumbent state senator[20] who ran for the Florida House in 2012 and ten state representatives running for the Florida Senate in 2012. All but one of these state legislators ran in a district that contained a share of the constituents they represented prior to redistricting, when they served in the opposite legislative chamber.

In the descriptive analysis, we treat the precincts that these state legislators represented while serving in the opposite legislative chamber as "same" precincts as opposed to coding them redrawn and show these data separately. Similarly, in the multivariate analysis, we include dummy variables to indicate those precincts these state legislators retained after redistricting albeit while running for a different legislative office.

In keeping with previous research on redistricting and political participation,[21] our dependent variable for all the analyses that follow is a measure of voter roll-off. The roll-off measure is: 1-(N of votes cast in U.S. House/Florida state senate/Florida state house of Representatives divided by the N of votes cast for president). Taking the example from Hayes and McKee, "a precinct with 1,000 votes in the presidential contest and 900 votes in the U.S. House election has a 0.90 full voting rate and a roll-off rate of 0.10."[22] For the sake of mathematical computation, roll-off is calculated only when the total number of votes cast for the lower office (U.S. House, state senate, or state house) is greater than or equal to zero *and* the total number of votes cast for the higher office (president) is greater than or equal to one.[23]

We begin our analysis with a descriptive assessment of the relationship between redistricting and voter roll-off in Florida's U.S. House, state senate, and state house contests in 2012. The expectation is that compared to precincts retained by incumbents (same precincts), redrawn precincts (precincts drawn into an incumbent's district) will exhibit a higher roll-off rate. This is hypothesized because redrawn voters are less familiar with their new incumbent vis-à-vis voters who retain the same incumbent after redistricting, and this reduces the likelihood of voting for the specific office affected by a boundary change because of the greater propensity to abstain when one does not recognize the representative running in the district.

We then turn to multivariate analyses that further test the expectation that redrawn precincts exhibit higher roll-off rates. In addition to the presence of several demographic controls (created from the Florida voter registration file), the initial models include indicators for open seat districts and contested races in the U.S. House, state senate, and state house. In the state senate and state house models, we also include the dummy variables that identify the precincts retained by the chamber switching state legislators. Finally, we limit our assessment of the relationship between redistricting and roll-off in these three types of district-based offices, to just those districts with incumbents seeking reelection against a major party challenger.[24]

Descriptive Results

Table 8.1 presents the distribution of Florida precincts for the U.S. House, state senate, and state house, classified as redrawn, same, or open seat in the 2012 elections. Whereas the modal distribution is the same precinct category for the U.S. House (56.3 percent), in both the state senate and state house, most precincts are located in open seat districts (41 and 39.7 percent, respectively). The higher rate of open seat precincts in the state senate and state house reflects a greater number of districts compared to the U.S. House, coupled with the reality that many state legislators were term-limited. There were more redrawn precincts than open seat precincts in the U.S. House (24.2 percent versus 19.5 percent), and in all three types of offices, the proportion of redrawn precincts exceeds twenty percent (22.7 percent in the state senate and 27.7 percent in the state house). Given the number of precincts in each category ($N \geq 900$) and overall for each office, the population size for our unit of analysis is large enough to conduct multivariate tests of the effects of redistricting on voter roll-off.

Table 8.2 displays the average roll-off rate for the three types of precincts for the U.S. House, state senate, and state house in the 2012 elections. Not surprisingly, in every case the rate of voter roll-off is positive, which means that more votes were cast for president than for the corresponding down-ballot district-based office (U.S. House, state senate, or state house). Roll-off is displayed as a percentage of voters failing to cast a ballot in the down-ballot race. For example, in the U.S. House, roll-off averaged 6.5 percent in redrawn precincts. Two patterns are evident in table 8.2. First, roll-off increases as we go from the highest office (U.S. House) to the low-

Table 8.1. The distribution of redrawn, same, and open seat precincts (%) in Florida for the U.S. House, state senate, and state house in the 2012 elections

Office	Redrawn	Same	Open Seat	Total
U.S. House	24.2	56.3	19.5	100
	(1,250)	(2,911)	(1,009)	(5,170)
State senate	22.7	36.3	41.0	100
	(971)	(1,554)	(1,754)	(4,279)
State house	27.7	32.6	39.7	100
	(900)	(1,061)	(1,291)	(3,252)

Notes: Data compiled by the authors. Ns of precincts in each category are in parentheses. The state senate data exclude District 34, where an incumbent Democrat (Maria Sachs) ran against an incumbent Republican (Ellyn Bogdanoff).

Table 8.2. Roll-off rates in redrawn, same, and open seat precincts (%) in Florida for the U.S. House, state senate, and state house in the 2012 elections

Office	Redrawn	Same	Open seat	Total roll-off
U.S. House	6.5	5.1	4.6	5.3
State senate	8.1	7.3	5.9	7.3
State house	11.6	9.0	10.7	10.4

Notes: The table shows the average roll-off rate for each office in the 2012 elections. The roll-off rate is the percentage difference in the votes cast for president compared to the number of votes cast for each lower office displayed in the table. In this case, the positive roll-off rates reflect the fact that on average there were more votes cast for president vis-à-vis any of the district-based offices displayed in the table. For example, on average, there were 6.5 percent fewer U.S. House votes cast than presidential votes cast in redrawn Florida precincts in the 2012 elections. The state senate data exclude District 34, where an incumbent Democrat (Maria Sachs) ran against an incumbent Republican (Ellyn Bogdanoff). The state house and state senate data also exclude the ten districts highlighted in table 8.3, which show the cases where an incumbent state legislator ran for election in a different chamber.

est (state house), irrespective of the precinct type (redrawn, same, or open seat). Overall, the roll-off rate almost doubles when we go from U.S. House contests (5.3 percent) to state house contests (10.4 percent). This finding is consistent with the assumption that abstention rates will be higher in lower profile offices. Second, and more significant to our hypothesized relationship regarding redistricting and voter roll-off, in all three types of races, the roll-off rate in redrawn precincts exceeds the abstention rate in the same precincts. We also see that the roll-off rate is lowest in open seat races in the U.S. House and state senate (4.6 and 5.9 percent, respectively), but in state house contests voter roll-off is lowest in same precincts (9 percent).

The roll-off rates in table 8.2 exclude the ten districts where an incumbent state legislator ran for election in a different chamber and retained some of their old precincts. As mentioned previously, one state senator ran for the state house in 2012 (Senator Mike Fasano-R), and ten state representatives sought a state senate seat in the 2012 general election. Omitting the one case where a state representative (Representative John Legg-R) ran for the state senate (District 17) in a district that did not overlap with his old house seat (District 46), table 8.3 displays the roll-off rates for the ten state legislators who sought election in districts where they retained a portion of their old precincts. Since none of these ten legislators are truly incumbents by the fact that they are seeking election to a different office, in the multivariate analyses we produced, their districts are coded as open seats. These multivariate analyses also include a dummy variable that identifies

Table 8.3. Roll-off rates (%) for legislative chamber switching incumbents in Florida precincts in the 2012 elections

Switch to:	New	Same	Total roll-off
House District 36	NA	14.1	14.1
	(0)	(28)	(28)
Senate District 8	5.1	4.8	5.0
	(67)	(44)	(111)
Senate District 12	7.0	4.7	6.3
	(47)	(21)	(68)
Senate District 14	4.3	4.7	4.5
	(43)	(27)	(70)
Senate District 15	6.5	6.1	6.3
	(69)	(37)	(106)
Senate District 21	6.5	4.8	6.3
	(102)	(18)	(120)
*Senate District 22	29.9	29.0	29.7
	(120)	(30)	(150)
Senate District 25	6.1	6.5	6.2
	(188)	(51)	(239)
*Senate District 27	24.4	24.2	24.3
	(146)	(70)	(216)
Senate District 39	16.4	7.3	14.9
	(145)	(29)	(174)

Notes: Florida House District 36 completely contained all of the precincts Republican state senator Mike Fasano represented in Florida Senate District 11 before redistricting (hence zero new precincts). Ns of precincts are in parentheses.
*These state senate districts were not contested by both major parties (a Republican ran in District 22 and a Democrat ran in District 27).

all of the precincts these legislators retained from when they served in the opposite chamber before redistricting. As the heading in table 8.3 states, we refer to these candidates as "chamber switching incumbents." In addition, instead of denoting precincts as redrawn, for these state legislators seeking election to a different chamber, the districts they did not represent while serving in the opposite chamber are labeled "new"; whereas, the precincts they represented prior to redistricting are designated as "same."

In the single instance where a state legislator went from the state senate to the state house, all of the precincts in the new house district were contained in this incumbent's old state senate district. This explains why there are no roll-off data under the column for new precincts—none of the precincts in House District 36 were new to this legislator. However, the fairly high roll-off rate of 14.1 percent in same precincts reflects the fact that this legislator had token opposition in the form of a write-in candidate who collected 52 votes in the general election (compared to 54,197 for the chamber switching legislator). Consistent with the theory that candidate familiarity reduces roll-off, out of the nine cases where chamber switching incumbents ran in districts with both new and same precincts (see state senate districts shown in table 8.3), we find voter roll-off in just two instances to be lower in new precincts vis-à-vis same precincts (Florida Senate Districts 14 and 25). In the rest of the senate districts analyzed, the roll-off rates are lower in the same precincts, and this is the case by a whisker in the two state senate districts (22 and 27) lacking two-party competition. In these two senate districts we attribute their massive voter roll-off rates to the fact that these incumbent legislators faced obscure write-in opponents who collectively garnered 586 votes.[25]

So far, the descriptive data tell a consistent story in line with our theoretical expectation that redrawn precincts should exhibit higher roll-off rates versus same precincts, where in the latter, representatives have the opportunity to cultivate greater familiarity with their constituents. In fact, a simple bivariate correlation between roll-off and redrawn precincts exhibits a positive and highly significant coefficient in all three types of elections (+.133 in the U.S. House, +.074 in the state senate, and +.056 in the state house; $p < .01$, two-tailed).[26] Of course, we need to find out if the relationship remains when we control for numerous other factors that may affect voter roll-off, and hence the next section presents the findings from our multivariate models.

Multivariate Analysis of Redistricting and Roll-off

Using turnout data we created a number of demographic variables at the precinct-level relating to race/ethnicity, gender, and age. We include indicators for the percentage of blacks, Hispanics, Asians, and other [race] at the precinct-level, with non-Hispanic white turnout serving as our excluded comparison category. For gender, we include a measure of the percentage of precinct turnout comprised of female voters. Turnout by age is divided into various categories (25–34, 35–44, 45–54, 55–64, 65–74, 75–84, and 85–105), with the 18 to 24 year-old range serving as the comparison category. Also measured at the precinct-level is the percentage of turnout comprised of Republican registrants and our primary variable of interest, *Redrawn*, a dummy variable indicating that a precinct was shifted to a new incumbent during the redistricting process.

A number of district-level variables are also incorporated into the models presented. These include two election-related indicators, *Open Seat* and *Contested Seat*, which are dummy variables denoting if the district lacked an incumbent and if it was contested by both a Democratic and Republican candidate, respectively. In addition, we include a measure of the total spending (*Spending*) by major party candidates associated with each contest.[27]

For the models analyzing roll-off for state senate and state house races, we also include a set of binary indicators to denote those precincts that incumbent state legislators retained after redistricting while running for a seat in the opposing legislative chamber. For the state house model, this includes state senator Fasano running in House District 36 and for the state senate this includes the following state house members: Hukill (District 8), Thompson (District 12), Soto (District 14), Stargel (District 15), Grimsley (District 21), Brandes (District 22), Abruzzo (District 25), Clemens (District 27), and Bullard (District 39).

Since our dependent variable is a continuous measure, we utilize a panel regression model that includes a random intercept to estimate roll-off rates for the three office-holding levels of interest. Standard errors are clustered by legislative district.[28] Using this technique we are able to include both substantive district-level indicators while also controlling for district-level heterogeneity (via the inclusion of a random intercept).

The results of our multivariate analyses of roll-off are shown in tables 8.4 and 8.5. Table 8.4 includes the results for all types of contests—open, contested incumbent, or otherwise. Our primary variable of interest, *Redrawn*, is positive and statistically significant across all three types of office-holding levels analyzed: U.S. House, state senate, and state house. This is an indication that voters in redrawn precincts were more likely to roll-off (not cast a ballot for these down-ticket contests) compared with those voters whose precinct remained in the same incumbent's district after redistricting. For state house races the percentage of black voters is negatively related to roll-off and the percentage of Hispanics is associated with increased roll-off. The percentage of female voters is negatively associated with roll-off for congressional and state senate races, as is the percentage of voters in the 45 to 54 age group category in U.S. House races.

At the district level one can see that contested races featuring a Republican and a Democratic candidate are significantly less likely to experience

Table 8.4. Roll-off analysis, Florida 2012 general elections

	U.S. House	State senate	State house
Redrawn	.0140*** (.0038)	.0083* (.0034)	.0147** (.0050)
Open seat	.0070 (.0051)	.0238 (.0137)	.0145 (.0158)
Contested seat	-.0686*** (.0154)	-.1274*** (.0347)	-.1032** (.0351)
Spending	-.00006** (.00002)	-.0022 (.0017)	-.0045 (.0043)
% Female	-.0602* (.0293)	-.0854* (.0387)	-.0180 (.0651)
% Republican	-.0392 (.0227)	-.0409 (.0509)	-.1428** (.0479)
% Black	-.0398 (.0223)	-.0291 (.0287)	-.1039*** (.0327)
% Hispanic	.0136 (.0079)	.1162 (.0870)	.0870** (.0353)
% Asian	.1122 (.1316)	.0468 (.1593)	.1577 (.1805)
% Other race	.1776 (.1081)	.1229 (.2288)	.4125 (.2112)
% 25–34	.0286 (.0551)	-.1043 (.0899)	-.0434 (.0680)
% 35–44	-.0367 (.0341)	-.1023 (.0573)	-.0453 (.0789)
% 45–54	-.0925*** (.0281)	-.1821 (.1130)	-.0899 (.0773)
% 55–64	-.0252 (.0227)	-.0540 (.0644)	.0520 (.0665)
% 65–74	-.0223 (.0263)	-.0660 (.0717)	-.0503 .0673)
% 75–84	-.0253 (.0306)	-.0819 (.0632)	-.0235 (.0661)
% 85–105	-.0411 (.0338)	-.0032 (.0769)	-.0071 (.0765)
Hukill (SS 8)	—	-.0089** (.0030)	—
Thompson (SS 12)	—	-.0158 (.0161)	—
Soto (SS 14)	—	-.0103 (.0062)	—
Stargel (SS 15)	—	-.0021 (.0023)	—
Grimsley (SS 21)	—	-.0192*** (.0041)	—
Brandes (SS 22)	—	-.0064*** (.0019)	—
Abruzzo (SS 25)	—	-.0073** (.0024)	—
Clemens (SS 27)	—	.0044 (.0054	—
Bullard (SS 39)	—	-.0809*** (.0130)	—
Fasano (SH 36)	—	—	-.0386 (.0281)
Constant	.1825*** (.0241)	.3316*** (.0778)	.2504*** (.0615)
R^2	.36	.41	.25
N	4,516	3,737	2,812

Notes: Entries are regression coefficients with standard errors clustered by district in parentheses.
*p<.05
**p<.01
***p<.001

roll-off across all three types of elections analyzed. For congressional races the total amount of campaign spending is negatively related to roll-off, an indication that competitive races are more likely to maintain voter interest. As for the incumbent officeholders switching legislative chambers, we see that in five of ten cases, precincts retained by these candidates significantly

Table 8.5. Roll-off analysis of contested incumbent districts, Florida 2012 general elections

	U.S. House	State senate	State house
Redrawn	.0134*** (.0036)	.0087*** (.0025)	.0044 (.0042)
Spending	-.00005** (.00002)	-.0003 (.0011)	-.0024 (.0015)
% Female	-.0571 (.0422)	-.0951** (.0351)	-.0495 (.0509)
% Republican	-.0257* (.0129)	.0091 (.0171)	-.0171 (.0111)
% Black	-.0305*** (.0085)	-.0537*** (.0149)	-.0549*** (.0124)
% Hispanic	.0273*** (.0065)	.0655*** (.0169)	.0490*** (.0132)
% Asian	-.0648 (.1032)	-.1581 (.1598)	-.0247 (.2136)
% Other Race	.2059 (.1363)	.5589** (.2005)	.5385* (.2476)
% 25–34	.0855 (.0594)	-.2049 (.1372)	-.0992 (.0487)
% 35–44	-.0729* (.0355)	-.0360 (.0635)	-.0668 (.0724)
% 45–54	-.0494* (.0209)	-.2904 (.1814)	-.1063 (.0576)
% 55–64	-.0399 (.0236)	-.1009 (.0522)	-.0503 (.0669)
% 65–74	-.0019 (.0182)	-.1952 (.1088)	-.0530 (.0331)
% 75–84	.0083 (.0334)	-.0750 (.0832)	-.1147** (.0398)
% 85–105	-.0127 (.0461)	-.0743 (.1012)	.0189 (.0458)
Constant	.0910** (.0332)	.2394* (.0943)	.1579*** (.0477)
R^2	.13	.21	.07
N	2,885	1,677	1,115

Notes: Entries are regression coefficients with standard errors clustered by district in parentheses.
*$p<.05$
**$p<.01$
***$p<.001$

reduced voter roll-off. This is not surprising given the fact that these state legislators ran in new districts that contained some degree of overlap with their previous legislative districts in the opposite chamber.

Table 8.5 confines our analysis to contested races that featured either a Republican incumbent running against a Democratic challenger or a Democratic incumbent facing a Republican challenger. As such, a number of variables drop out, including the indicators for those officeholders switching state legislative chambers. For congressional and state senate contests we see that redrawn precincts were significantly more likely to experience roll-off compared to same precincts. The coefficient for state house races, while positive, is not statistically significant. Overall, spending in congressional races is again associated with a lower incidence of roll-off, as is the percentage of Republican voters at the precinct-level. Consistently, across the three office holding levels analyzed, the percentage of black voters at the precinct-level is negatively associated with roll-off while the percentage of Hispanics is positively related to roll-off rates. For state senate races, the percentage of female voters is also negatively related to the level of roll-off within a precinct.

Figure 8.1 summarizes roll-off rates for the six types of election contests analyzed in tables 8.4 and 8.5. Because these are regression coefficients, it is fairly straightforward to interpret the effects for our primary variable of interest—those precincts redrawn into a new incumbent's district. For each type of contest, figure 8.1 presents the difference in roll-off rates for redrawn versus same precincts. For example, in contested congressional races featuring an incumbent, the roll-off rate is estimated to be 1.3 percent higher in redrawn precincts as compared to same precincts. Since the coefficients for the redrawn indicator are all positive for the six models estimated, the difference measures are also all positive. With the exception of incumbent-contested state house contests, the roll-off rate differential between redrawn and same precincts is statistically significant. Again, this robust finding underscores the fact that voters moved to a new incumbent's district across a redistricting cycle are less likely to vote for that down-ticket contest compared to voters who remained in the same district.

Conclusion

On the firm footing of past research, this chapter demonstrates once again that redistricting has the effect of reducing participation. We are impressed by the consistency in finding that redrawn precincts increase voter roll-off. Out of six multivariate regressions that include a host of important controls, only in incumbent contested state house races do we find that the coefficient for redrawn precincts fails to reach statistical significance. In the other five models, redrawn precincts clearly have the effect of increasing voter roll-off in the 2012 U.S. House, state senate, and state house elections in Florida. We are not yet ready to contend that redistricting generally has the effect of leading to greater abstention rates in district-based contests, but the body of evidence certainly pushes us in this direction.

With a different methodology and unit of analysis (registered voters in Georgia), we conducted a previous examination that found in some cases redrawn voters were in fact more likely to turn out to vote. Nonetheless, that study was considerably different from this one because the most theoretically appropriate method for capturing the participatory effects of redistricting is to evaluate voter roll-off as opposed to turnout. This makes the most sense because it is dubious that redistricting deters people from

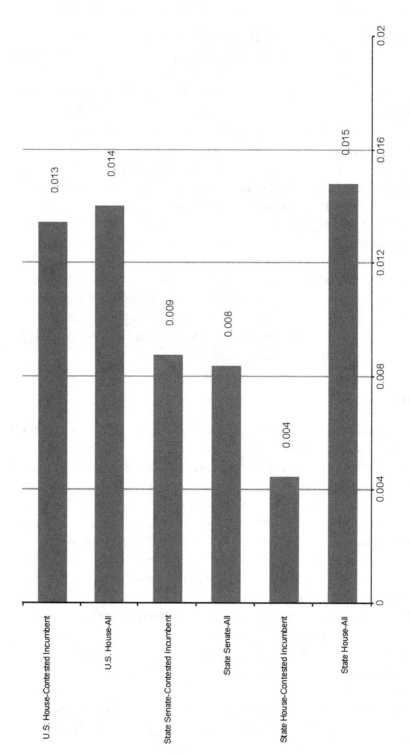

Figure 8.1. Estimated roll-off rate differentials, Florida 2012 general elections. The roll-off differential for contested incumbent races in the state house (0.4 percent) is not statistically significant.

voting (or increases their likelihood of voting), rather it affects the decision to vote for an office affected by redistricting once someone has decided to turn out to vote. Given the proper approach to measuring the effect of redistricting on voter roll-off, this chapter provides further evidence that constituents redrawn into districts with a new incumbent cast fewer votes for the office directly affected by a boundary change.

In a novel modification to the typical assessment of the influence of redistricting on voter roll-off, we were also able to determine whether chamber switching state legislators enjoyed less voter roll-off among the precincts they retained after redistricting that they represented previously, while serving in the opposite chamber. These cases are interesting because they lie somewhere between the traditional conception of incumbency and open seat contests. Given the likelihood that voters in precincts retained by these chamber switching state legislators are more familiar with these candidates, it was expected that roll-off would be less. In the multivariate analysis (see table 8.4), for the precincts retained by the ten chamber switching state legislators, there is only one instance where the coefficient is not negatively signed (a negative sign indicates less roll-off), and that is in one of the two state senate districts not contested by both major parties (Clemens in Senate District 27). For half of the chamber switching state legislators, among their retained precincts, we find that they had the negative and statistically significant effect of reducing voter roll-off, which comports nicely with our theoretical expectations.

As we stated at the outset of this chapter, the bulk of attention about redistricting concerns its expected, intended, and actual effects on election outcomes. It is only more recently that scholars have turned their focus to the possible and realized influence that redistricting has on the decision to vote for the office impacted by a boundary change. Consistent with our previous research on this topic, and for the first time extending such an analysis to district-based contests below the congressional level, we find that in the 2012 Florida elections for U.S. House, state senate, and state house, redrawn precincts exhibit a higher rate of voter roll-off than in those precincts incumbents retained after redistricting.

This finding is firmly grounded in what we know about the incumbent-constituent relationship. Incumbents typically expend a good deal of effort cultivating a relationship with their voters and especially among those whom they depend upon for reelection. Thus, it is little wonder that through this representational relationship many voters become familiar with their incumbent, and even cross partisan lines to support their member in recognition of their impartial service to district inhabitants.

The home style that so many legislative members work diligently to maintain is directly and negatively impacted by redistricting, with many of their favored constituents being redrawn into another incumbent's domain. When this happens the electoral status quo is abruptly disrupted and in addition to potentially altering the prospects for winning another term, incumbents are anxious to establish new relationships with voters redrawn into their districts. As we have shown, the precincts that contain redrawn constituents are less likely to vote in the contest affected by redistricting. It is somewhat curious that the vast majority of studies focus strictly on how redistricting influences election outcomes when a fundamental component of redrawing political boundaries is tied directly to the altered relationship between representative and voter and, hence, not just how votes are cast in a given race, but whether they are cast at all.

9

Elections in a Brave New World

Reform, Redistricting, and the Battle for the 2012 Legislature

JONATHAN WINBURN

As the Florida Legislature set out to complete redrawing their legislative districts, they faced new constraints designed to limit their ability to offer partisan and incumbent protection in the process. As discussed throughout much of this book, the so-called Fair Districts constitutional reforms, contained in Amendment 5, were enacted by Florida voters during the 2010 state general election. These constitutional reforms altered the playing field for the state legislature when the body undertook its work to complete the redistricting process. The 2012 legislative elections would be the first test of these new reforms and provide the ultimate test for their effectiveness. In this chapter, I examine the 2012 legislative outcomes with a focus on the role of redistricting in these elections.

As the dust settled on all the political and legal maneuvering surrounding redistricting, two major questions emerged heading into the 2012 legislative elections: (1) Would the so-called Fair Districts reforms create a more competitive electoral landscape that proponents pushed for, and (2) Could the Republicans retain their supermajority in both chambers that essentially rendered the Democrats procedurally useless during the most recent legislative session? The answer to both of these questions partly revolved around the fate of incumbents in the first set of maps produced under the new rules of redistricting in the state.

Brief Background on Redistricting and Election Outcomes

The fundamental goal of redistricting is to equalize population among districts to help ensure fair representation in the electoral and legislative arenas. The political controversy emerges in exactly how to achieve that goal while simultaneously protecting partisan or other political motives. In addition, there are any number of ways to equalize district populations while carving up districts for political gain in a political culture with a history of partisan gerrymandering. Moreover, there is little doubt as to why the redistricting process generates so much debate among those involved. Like athletes, politicians want to maximize any advantage they can obtain while never wanting to play in an environment where their opponents have a seemingly unfair advantage. For the parties, redistricting is an opportunity to protect themselves while taking away opportunities from the other party. According to long-time Republican redistricting expert Tom Hofeller, the goal "is to design wombs for his team and tombs for the other guys."[1]

The role of redistricting on election outcomes is an important and debated question. In the political world, good government types, pundits, and politicians (usually from the losing side) often blame redistricting for many of the ills of our electoral system. Whereas in the academic world, the power of redistricting over election outcomes, while debated, is seen as much less significant. Much of this work focuses on the effect of redistricting on electoral competition.[2] This line of inquiry dates back to the 1970s when scholars argued incumbents could use the process to protect themselves in future elections.[3] Since then, the debate has also examined the role of redistricting on overall partisan balance, mainly in Congress, with early studies showing a redistricting bump for the party in control; however, other studies have found little to no advantage in picking up seats for the party in control.[4]

The role of redistricting methods and reforms on the process is another important question. As several states have moved towards a commission format for redistricting, studies have examined the differences between commission and legislative redistricting. Commissions have differing incentives than legislators in the process; however, studies have not produced consistent results regarding the influence of commissions on electoral outcomes.[5] The move towards commissions has received most of the attention in terms of redistricting reform, but as in Florida, there are other ways to change the system.

The Florida Fair Districts reforms did not remove control of the process from the state legislature, but placed greater constraints on how they can draw the maps. It is important to consider the incentives and constraints the Republicans faced to better understand the potential influences of redistricting on the election results. The rules in place can limit the ability to gerrymander and often forces mapmakers to not put in place the type of gerrymander or, at least, as aggressive of a gerrymander as they may have preferred.[6] For the Republicans, the limits against using incumbency and partisan data clearly put new constraints on them. Given the unified Republican control of the state, the party was in a position to implement their preferred plans with little Democratic influence. However, these new rules did not allow them to follow the traditional strategy of protecting their own incumbents while perhaps targeting a few Democratic districts for their own gain.

In the Republicans' case, even without the Fair Districts rules in place, they probably could not have expected to take away too many Democratic districts given their already safe majorities that held steady throughout the previous decade and rules to protect minority representation. Clear and blatant partisan gerrymanders usually only occur under specific conditions, such as a recent change in political control and competitive electoral environments. The case of Texas during the 2000s easily comes to mind as the Republicans, once they gained control of the process from the Democrats for the first time since Reconstruction, were able to draw their own favorable maps, undoing years of Democratic designs. Over the previous decades, Texas Democrats were able to draw plans that helped them stay more competitive than changing electoral tides suggested they should have been.

While the Republicans did not need to partisan gerrymander to protect their majority, without a doubt, they wanted to maintain and build on, if possible, their legislative supermajority that left the Democrats procedurally powerless. In previous decades, the party could have attempted a subtle gerrymander that targeted specific districts within their own ranks and vulnerable Democratic seats in an attempt to add a couple of seats, or at the very least, not lose any seats during the next decade. The new restrictions on incumbent and partisan considerations took away, assuming the reforms worked as hoped, the ability to make district changes with such precision.

Data and Methods

Combining data from the 2012, 2010, and 2008 elections, along with precinct level changes in districts, I examine the role of redistricting in the 2012 elections. Before getting into the analysis, it is important to set the stage for the elections and discuss a few fundamental aspects of the 2012 redistricting plans. First, it is helpful to examine the amount of change found between the 2010 and 2012 maps and to discuss a common metric to make comparisons between old and new districts. To do this, I account for the population overlap between portions of old and new districts.[7] Since multiple old districts go into each new district, comparing individual districts between different plans can be problematic. To make these comparisons, I rely on the so-called "parent" district for each district in the new plans.

The parent district is the particular old district that adds the largest share of population to the new district.[8] Another way to think of this is in terms of a new district's intactness with its parent district. Therefore, when discussing changes to individual districts, unless otherwise noted, I am referring to changes between the new district and its parent district. Additionally, I do not base this on the numbering scheme, as this is an easy, but misleading way to compare plans. For example, House District 73 in the 2012 map is the exact same district as the previous House District 67. Whereas, the 2010 House District 73 became parts of four new districts and became the parent for District 78. This district comparison does not take into account the previous district of incumbents running in the new district since not all districts have incumbents, and it makes direct comparisons between the old and new maps difficult. That said, I consider incumbency in the analysis and discuss it when appropriate.

To get a sense of the amount of change between plans, table 9.1 provides descriptive statistics for overlap between the new districts and their parents. As table 9.1 highlights, not all old districts became a parent for a new district while some districts became the parent for multiple districts. In the house, 92 of the 120 (77 percent) districts became a parent of one new district. While 14 of these house districts shared the most population overlap with two new districts, 14 districts did not share the most population with any new district, effectively dissolving them within the new maps. In the senate, 34 of the 40 (85 percent) districts had the most overlap with one new district while three old districts became the parent with two new districts. This resulted in three old districts being dissolved by not becoming a parent in the new maps. In terms of overall intactness, the house and senate maps look quite similar as the mean population overlap between the new districts and their parent district is 60 percent, and house districts have only a slightly larger variation.

With an idea of the changes in the new plans and the establishment of parent districts to use for comparison, this analysis examines the influence of redistricting on Election Day, by doing a descriptive analysis of the re-

Table 9.1. Overlap of 2012 district population with 2010 parent districts

Population overlap	House	Senate
Mean	59.71	60.52
SD	14.89	12.63
Min	31.06	30.71
Max	100	88.99
Fate of old districts:		
No parent	14	3
1 parent	92	34
Multiple parent	14	3
N	120	40

sults followed by a multivariate analysis of a vote-share model. I take the estimates from the vote-share model to predict the partisan winners in each district and compare these to the actual outcomes. The descriptive analysis compares the results in 2012 to those in 2010 and looks at the changes in levels of electoral competition by party and incumbency. I also take a closer look at a subset of districts, namely the Republican incumbents who lost, to compare the changes caused by redistricting in their districts to their fellow Republican incumbents who won reelection.

In the multivariate analysis, I use a variant of the popular linear seat-vote share techniques to estimate the vote shares for the controlling Republicans in both chambers.[9] The results of this model allow for a check on the influence of redistricting by comparing the actual outcomes with predicted outcomes utilizing both the 2012 election setting and interesting counterfactuals, such as the elections being held with the 2010 districts or without the influence of incumbency. To predict the seat changes (displayed in table 9.9), I have constructed a statistical model predicting the percentage of the Republican vote in each district as a function of the Republican percentage of registered voters in the district and the Democratic percentage of registered voters in the district. In addition, this statistical model accounts for the presence or absence of a Republican or Democratic incumbent. The use of registration data serves as a baseline predictor of partisan support in each district. This base measure of partisanship compared to the level of partisan support of the parent district in 2010 (using 2010 registration data) captures the change between plans.[10]

Overview of Seat Changes and Partisan Control in the 2000s

As figure 9.1 shows, over the previous decade, the Republicans held safe majorities in both chambers. The Republican majority never dipped below 62 percent in either chamber throughout the decade with the number reaching a high of 70 percent in the house in 2004 and attaining a similar high watermark percentage of 70 percent in the senate in 2008. More importantly, riding the Tea Party wave in 2010, the Republicans held a supermajority in both chambers, making the Democrats virtually powerless. Heading into 2012, the Republicans had a virtual lock on the majority in both chambers, as the Democrats would have needed to pick up 22 seats in the house and 9 seats in the senate to regain control. More realistically, the Democrats hoped to pick up a minimum of two seats in both chambers to end the Republican supermajority gained in 2010.

In the following analysis, I examine the 2012 elections with a particular focus on the role redistricting did (or did not) play in influencing the partisan results for the Florida Senate and Florida House that year. The new redistricting cycle offered new political uncertainty in the Sunshine State, as it was unclear how unprecedented changes implemented under Fair Districts reforms, which were designed to limit the ability of the legislature to consider partisan or incumbency when creating the new maps, would influence the results of the state house and state senate elections in 2012.

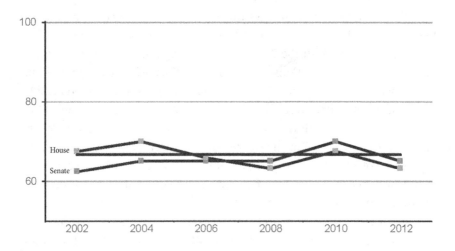

Figure 9.1. Republican seat shares in legislature (2002–2012). Horizontal line marks the supermajority threshold.

Table 9.2. Electoral decisions of 2010 incumbents in 2012

House	% (n)	Mean splits of 2010 district	Mean population with new district
Ineligible to run (termed out)	10 (12)	3.83 (1.19)	29.34 (10.30)
	% of eligible to run		
Ran for house	76.85 (83)	4.27 (1.54)	25.96 (9.25)
Did not run*	23.15 (25)	4.24 (1.23)	25.98 (8.97)
Total	100 (120)	4.22 (1.44)	26.30 (9.28)

Senate	% (n)	Mean splits of 2010 district	Mean population with new district
Termed Out	22.5 (9)	4.66 (1.5)	23.27 (6.20)
	% of eligible to run		
Ran for senate	83.87 (26)	4.04 (1.28)	27.07 (9.97)
Did not run	16.13 (5)	5 (1)	22.06 (4.32)
Total	100 (40)	4.3 (1.32)	25.59 (8.81)

Notes: In columns 2 and 3, standard deviations are in parentheses.
*Includes one member who resigned before the elections.

Heading into the elections, there was much uncertainty for incumbents and challengers alike, as candidates adjusted to the recently implemented new maps. These new maps, most significantly affected incumbents, as many had to scramble to become familiar with new districts, move to a new district to retain most of their previous constituency, or simply decide to walk away. The Speaker of the House claimed the new house map was "the first time in the nation this many members have been drawn into the same districts where it wasn't a court order."[11] As a result, dozens of house members had to choose between moving, changing their political plans, or fighting it out with another incumbent during the 2012 election cycle. Several members chose to move, and in one case, a member moved home with his mother to find a suitable district.[12] On the senate side, the map had much more stability and caused less chaos for the current incumbents.

To highlight these decisions, table 9.2 shows the choices of the incumbents heading into the elections. The second and third columns show what happened to their old districts during redistricting in terms of the mean number of new districts they were split into and the mean population overlap with these new districts.

For nine (22.5 percent) state senators and 12 (10 percent) state representatives, there was no decision to make as term limits prevented them from running for their current seats again. Of those eligible to run, 84 percent of the senators and 77 percent of the representatives ran again. Compared to 2010, there was no change in the senate, as 85 percent of non-termed limited incumbents ran. While in the house, there was an 11-point drop in eligible incumbents running, as 88 percent of those eligible ran for their house seat two years earlier.

In terms of overall district changes, there is not much difference across incumbency status. In the senate, there is little difference between incumbency status and the resulting district shifts. The five senators who did not run did have their districts carved into multiple new districts and shared less population overlap with those new districts. In the house, the splits look virtually the same between those members who ran again and those who did not. Interestingly, it appears the Republicans did not take the opportunity to systematically carve up the term-limited districts. In fact, the Republicans kept those 12 districts more intact than the non-term-limited districts by a half a seat and by over 3 percent of the population overlap.[13]

Primary Analysis

With new plans complete, the landscape for the August 2012 primaries took shape under a cloud of uncertainty because of the new redistricting rules limiting consideration of partisanship and incumbency. Ultimately, with all of the political calculations made during the summer, only three house races and no senate races saw incumbents face each other during the primaries. Despite all this uncertainty, as table 9.3 shows, there were no major changes in terms of contested primary races and in the average margin of victory in those races.

On the senate side, the number of contested primaries did not change for either party from 2010 to 2012 as only eight Republican and three Democratic seats had multiple candidates run. The Republican margin of victory actually increased by 7 percent; while, the three Democratic races were 10 percent more competitive. On the house side, the number of contested Republican primaries remained essentially unchanged and the margin of victory, like the senate, actually increased by 7 percent. Part of the reason for these two political results benefiting house and senate Republican

Table 9.3. Comparison of primary outcomes, 2010 and 2012

	Contested primaries		Average margin of victory	
	2012	2010	2012	2010
House				
Republican	37	36	31.84	24.84
Democrat	26	17	20.71	33.74
Senate				
Republican	8	8	32.46	25.47
Democrat	3	3	5.60	15.31

incumbents can be attributed to a Republican strategy of protecting incumbents who moved because of the new boundaries during the election season.[14] The Democrats saw an increase of nine contested primaries that became 13 percent more competitive than 2010. Across both chambers, it is worth noting that less than a third of the seats were contested across both 2010 and 2012, and with the exception of the three 2012 senate Democratic races, the contested races were not very competitive.

Despite redistricting causing chaos for some house members prior to the Democratic and Republican primary elections, the revised and reconstituted districts did not have a major influence on the outcomes. Generally, most districts did not have competitive primary contests, similar to the 2010 Democratic and Republican primaries. The one exception for the house Republicans was District 116, which pitted Representatives Jose Felix Diaz and Ana Rivas Logan. The candidates were both finishing their first terms in the house, and in 2010, had an almost identical margin of victory over their Democratic opponents in these neighboring Miami-based districts.

The Republicans created the new District 116 from four old districts, which were all drawn from inside Miami-Dade County. This new District 116 was also composed of 53 percent of Representative Logan's old 114th District, and Representative Diaz's old District 115 contributed 34 percent of the population in the new District 116. The remaining 13 percent of the population of this new district came from old Districts 112 and 119 (both Republican districts).

The race was particularly nasty as Representatives Diaz and Logan sparred back and forth and traded insults, ranging from accusations of defamation regarding parenting skills (or lack thereof) to competing

Table 9.4. House District 116 primary results by 2010 districts

2010 district	Percent of Diaz vote to District 116	Precincts contributed to District 116	Percent of population in new District 116
114 (Logan)	58.38	25	52.94
115 (Diaz)	71.40	14	34.06
112 and 119	53.15	4	13.00
New District 116	63	43	

claims about which candidate won the more impressive award from lobbying groups.[15] As table 9.4 shows, Diaz won the district with a comfortable 63 percent of the vote and carried each of the old districts within the new 116th District. He won the highest percentage of his votes (71 percent) in the precincts that composed his previous district. In contrast, while Diaz carried Logan's old precincts, he did so with only 58 percent of the vote.

Overall, the Fair Districts remap caused a lot of headaches for incumbents, especially Republicans in the house, but much of this had taken care of itself by the August 2012 primary elections. While some house legislators had to scramble for a new district or a new strategic plan, the primary outcomes did not change much from 2010 and despite the fear of party leaders of widespread incumbent versus incumbent battles, only three actually occurred in the house.

General Election Analysis

Heading into November, the Democrats hoped the new redistricting process would allow them to pick up a few seats and reverse a decade-long trend of losing ground to the Republican majority. According to one Democratic consultant, the goal was to win a few seats back, "We didn't lose a bunch of districts overnight and we're not going to win a bunch of districts overnight."[16] Most observers expected the Democrats to pick up a few seats in both chambers with the Democratic hope of gaining enough seats to be procedurally relevant again. Since 2010, the Republicans held supermajorities in both chambers, which essentially gave them free reign over legislative business.

The November 2012 general election went as many predicted with modest gains made by the Democrats. Most importantly, they picked up enough seats to end the Republican supermajority. As table 9.5 shows, the Democrats picked up five seats in the house, and senate Democrats gained two.[17]

Table 9.5. Republican seats in legislature, pre- and post-2012 election

Chamber	Pre-election	%	Post-election	%	Change
House	81	67.5	76	63.3	-5
Senate	28	70.0	26	65.0	-2

While the Republicans still easily controlled both chambers (76 of 120 seats in the house and 26 of 40 seats in the senate), their majority shrank to just below the two-thirds supermajority they enjoyed in the previous session.

Following the election, Republican leaders were quick to laud the Fair Districts reform for creating more competition despite the fact it cost them their supermajority. Incoming Speaker Will Weatherford summed up this view, "We knew we were making a very competitive map. I'm not happy about the fact it cost us seats, but it was the right thing to do."[18] The focus of the remainder of this chapter is to test the conventional wisdom that the new maps increased competition and fostered Democratic gains.

In terms of competition, I use two common metrics: contested races and average margin of victory in contested races. Table 9.6 highlights two different stories across chambers. Despite all the talk of increasing competition, only 47 of the 120, or just less than 40 percent of the house seats had a Republican and Democrat facing each other in the 2012 general election. This was an 11 percent drop from the 2010 elections when both parties contested half of the seats. Breaking this down by types of seats, only open

Table 9.6. Comparison of contested seats, 2010 and 2012

Contested seats	2012		2010		Difference
HOUSE	%	TOTAL	%	TOTAL	
Open seats	55.00	40	58.33	36	-3.33
Incumbents running	31.25	80	46.43	84	-15.18
Dem. incumbent	30.00	20	44.44	36	-14.44
Rep. incumbent	31.67	60	47.92	48	-16.25
Total	39.17	120	50.00	120	-10.83
SENATE	%	TOTAL	%	TOTAL	DIFFERENCE
Open seats	73.33	15	50	12	23.33
Incumbents running	56.00	25	10.71	28	45.29
Dem. incumbent	77.78	9	11.11	9	66.67
Rep. incumbent	43.75	16	10.53	19	33.22
Total	62.50	40	22.50	40	40.00

Table 9.7. Comparison of average margin of victory in contested races, 2010 and 2012

Average margin of victory	2012		2010		Difference
HOUSE	% MOV	TOTAL	% MOV	TOTAL	
Open seats	15.56	22	24.62	21	-9.06
Incumbents running	15.39	25	23.8	39	-8.41
Dem. incumbent	36.47	6	18.29	16	18.18
Rep. incumbent	8.73	19	27.63	23	-18.90
Total	15.49	47	24.74	60	-9.25
SENATE	% MOV	TOTAL	% MOV	TOTAL	
Open seats	22.32	11	27.70	6	-5.38
Incumbents running	25.76	14	18.20	3	7.56
Dem. incumbent	33.51	7	26.80	1	6.71
Rep. incumbent	18.01	7	13.90	2	4.11
Total	24.25	25	24.53	9	-0.28

seats saw less than a 5 percent drop in contested races from 2010; whereas seats with incumbents had a 15 percent decline, with both Democratic and Republican incumbents facing a similar number of fewer contested races.

In the senate, the number of contested races skyrocketed by 40 percent, to 25 of the 40 (62.5 percent) races being contested. Incumbents facing an opponent drove this increase. Overall, the number of contested races with an incumbent increased to 45 percent compared to 23 percent for open seats. While a partisan difference in the number of incumbents facing contested races was absent in the house, there was a partisan difference in the senate as seven of the nine Democratic incumbents faced a challenger in 2012, up from only two of the nine in 2010. Republican incumbents experienced a 33 percent increase in Democratic challengers. Part of this large increase in contested senate races in 2012 stems from extremely low contestation rates in 2010, especially among incumbents, where only 11 percent faced a challenger in the previous election. However, during 2010, there were no partisan distinctions, while in 2012, Republican senate challengers saw potentially vulnerable Democratic incumbents and challenged all but two of those nine seats.

A second measure of competition looks at the average margin of victory in the contested races. As table 9.7 highlights, the average race was not very competitive, with victory margins between 15 to 25 percentage points over their competitors. Florida is common in this regard, as state legislative races in most states are notorious for lacking competitive contests. In terms of potential redistricting influence, the focus in table 9.7 is on the relative difference in average margin of victory between 2012 and 2010. In this table, negative numbers indicate more competitive races occurred as the margin of victory declined.

While the house saw a decline in the number of contested races, those contested races were more competitive than the races in 2010, an average of 9 percent more competitive. Overall, incumbent races became 8 percent more competitive. However, there is a major difference between the Democratic and Republican seats. The 19 Republican incumbent-held seats had the closest races of any group, winning on average by only 9 points. As I discuss below, much of the increase in the number of very competitive house races can be attributed to the four contests involving Republican incumbents, who each failed to retain their respective seats. Democrats saw opportunities in the new maps to challenge Republican incumbents. This suggests the Fair Districts reforms may have worked to prevent the Republicans from protecting themselves and may highlight an extremely pro-Republican protection plan from the previous decade. While the Republican incumbents saw a major increase in competition, the six Democratic incumbents had a much easier time as their margin of victory increased by 18 points compared to 2010.

On the senate side, there was little change among the overall levels of competition, as the margin of victory was nearly 25 percent for the 25 contested races in 2012 and the 9 races in 2010. Incumbents improved their margin by nearly 8 points, with little difference between Democrats and Republicans. Open seats did see a modest increase in competition. Overall, the senate margins did not change much between the 2010 and 2012 elections, fitting with the theme of fewer significant changes in the senate plan.

Moving to expected seat changes, the seat predictions based on the regression results in table 9.8 show the Republicans did worse than predicted. In the house, the baseline model predicted the Republicans would not lose any seats and stay at the pre-election total of 81 seats. Taking away incumbency, the model predicts a one-seat gain for the party. However, when comparing the predictions of the new plans to those of a hypothetical election held under the old map, there is some evidence that the new redistricting plan was clearly not a Republican gerrymander. If the 2012 election was held using the 2010 map, the model predicts the Republicans would win 85 seats or gain four seats and that increased by an additional seat when removing incumbency.

Table 9.8. Models of 2012 election outcomes

Independent variables:	House	Senate
District Republican registration	1.40 (.2231)**	.913 (.3719)*
District Democratic registration	.229 (.2048)	-.535 (.3736)
Democratic incumbent	-.089 (.0297)**	-.039 (.0442)
Republican incumbent	.069 (.0226)**	.033 (.0337)
Constant	-.053 (.1530)	.431 (.2696)
N	120	40
Adjusted R^2	.78	.80

Notes: OLS regression, standard errors in parentheses.
*p < .05
** p < .01

On the senate side, the Republicans lost one more seat than predicted from the base model. There is not much evidence of redistricting having a role in the outcomes, as all three of the counterfactual situations predicted 27 victories for the Republicans, as did the base model using the 2012 map with incumbency.

These results confirm the general consensus heading into the election that the Republicans were not likely to gain many seats and that they did not have the opportunity to produce overtly favorable or gerrymandered districts. The results in tables 9.6–9.9 present an interesting picture in the house. As the levels of two-party contestation dropped, the competitiveness of those races increased, especially for Republican incumbents. This could suggest the Democrats ran quality candidates, or the Democrats strategically targeted districts that they thought the party could pick up under the new maps.

For the senate, the contested rates dramatically increased, but there was little change in the competitiveness of those races. The increase in competition for contested Republican incumbents does fit with the goals of the Fair Districts reforms. By taking away incumbency information, the party could not target their own weak incumbents for protection nor target vulnerable Democratic districts. These results also highlight the high rate of predictability of most races, as the models accurately predicted over 90 percent of the contests using only district registration and incumbency information.

While redistricting did not drastically alter the overall partisan results of the legislative elections in 2012, the Fair Districts reforms did hamper the ability of the Republicans to protect some of their notable incumbents. In most cases, the incumbents who chose to run were able to keep their seats, but four Republicans did lose their reelection bids. I now take a closer look

Table 9.9. Seat predictions

Condition	House		Senate	
	Seats	% Correctly predicted	Seats	% Correctly predicted
Previous seats	81		28	
Actual seats	76		26	
New plans	81	92.50	27	97.50
New plans, all open seats	82	91.67	27	97.50
Old plans	85	89.17	27	92.50
Old plans, all open seats	86	88.33	27	92.50

at these incumbents' districts to see how their fates were affected by district changes.

To assess the district changes these four incumbents faced, table 9.10 breaks down the partisan registration shifts between their old and new districts and then compares the changes in these four districts to all other Republican incumbents. The top portion shows each of these members lost close races with both Representatives Dorworth and Harrison losing by only a few hundred votes. These two incumbents were also the most vulnerable of the four house members as they both won relatively close elections in 2010. An examination of the district changes reveals these four incumbents did not get the "help" other Republican incumbents generally received.

There are not drastic differences between changes in partisan registration, as the four losing incumbents kept virtually the same percentage of registered Republicans (52 percent) while the other 56 Republicans saw a small increase in registered Republicans in their new districts (56 percent compared to 54 percent in 2010). When comparing district intactness however, these four losing incumbents did appear to be at a disadvantage relative to their Republican colleagues. The four members who lost reelection in 2012 kept only 51 percent of their old constituents, while the other Republicans retained 62 percent. Therefore, these four incumbents faced a similar partisan landscape, but they did so with significantly greater numbers of new constituents. Nonetheless, a closer look at voting outcomes across new and old precincts reveals little difference within these district races. Only Representative Shawn Harrison in District 63 fared noticeably worse among his new voters, winning only 47 percent compared to 52 percent among his old voters.

Table 9.10. Breakdown of changes among losing Florida House incumbents

Republican incumbent	2012 district	2010 district	2012 vote share (%)	2010 vote share (%)
Chris Dorworth	29	34	49.90	56
Scott Plakon	30	37	46.91	100
Shawn Harrison	63	60	49.45	56
Peter Nehr	65	48	47.07	61.5

	2012 reg. Rep (%)	2010 reg. Rep (%)	District intactness (%)
Chris Dorworth	55.7%	52.8	38.67
Scott Plakon	49.6%	56.6	44.85
Shawn Harrison	45.8%	44.6	61.10
Peter Nehr	57.4%	57.4	59.43
4 Losers	52.13	52.85	51.02
56 Republican incumbent winners	55.67	53.89	61.72

	% Vote old precincts	% Vote new precinct
Chris Dorworth	46.76	51.49
Scott Plakon	48.71	46.50
Shawn Harrison	51.92	46.96
Peter Nehr	47.45	46.62

When considering the role of the new Fair Districts reforms, it is worth noting the loss for Representative Chris Dorworth (District 29) in Seminole County just outside of Orlando. In "one of the most shocking upsets in Florida legislative history," Dorworth, the presumed next Speaker of the House, lost by 146 votes to local firefighter, Mike Clelland.[19] As shown in table 9.10, Dorworth faced a somewhat safer district in 2012, with a 3 percentage point increase in registered Republicans (56 percent overall) compared to his 2010 district. However, this increase in partisan safety was offset by only keeping 39 percent of his constituents from his old District 34. Yet, Dorworth actually performed better in his new precincts than his old ones, suggesting his growing political scandals had more to do with this defeat than the reconfiguration of his Seminole County-based district.

Hailed as the political story of the year in Florida, Dorworth's defeat shocked many throughout the state as he was in line to be the next Speaker and outspent Clelland by a large margin ($604,166 to $108,783).[20] Additionally, Dorworth was directly involved in the redistricting process and some claim District 29 was drawn specifically for him to cruise to reelection since he gained more Republican registrants (mostly from neighboring Republican Scott Plakon who also lost).[21] Despite the defeat of Dorworth, along with only three of his Republican colleagues in the house, the effectiveness of the Fair Districts constitutional reforms could be called into question, particularly if they were purposefully designed by their advocates to drastically alter the overwhelming Republican majorities in the legislature.

Conclusion

The 2012 legislative elections produced a few surprises and saw the Democrats pick up a small number of seats. However, proponents of the new redistricting system hoped for widespread changes in electoral outcomes and hence they were most likely disappointed. As this chapter shows, redistricting did not have a dramatic influence on the 2012 elections, at least compared to the 2010 outcomes. However, reformers could look at the maps as a victory for the new process because many incumbents were left scrambling to determine their next political move and the Republicans were not able to produce maps that significantly increased their chances of keeping a supermajority. In an ironic twist, the one member accused of manipulating the redistricting process lost in one of the closest and most watched upsets in the state. More broadly, however, both the primaries and general election produced similar outcomes in terms of electoral competitiveness compared to 2010.

Overall, these results highlight that, contrary to many pundits' proclamations, redistricting alone does not necessarily produce widely different electoral outcomes (see table 9.9). The new maps did not lead to a massive ousting of incumbents or even much of a change in the competitiveness of their races. However, these results suggest the new process slowed the Republicans down enough to allow the Democrats to pick up enough seats to be relevant again, at least marginally.

10

Effects of Redistricting
in Congressional Elections

CHARLES S. BULLOCK III

"To the victor go the spoils" has long been the celebratory cry of the triumphant but also a reality of American politics. Among the spoils enjoyed by political parties that win control of the legislative and executive branches is the decennial opportunity to redraw legislative districts. Each new census yields multiple examples of the majority party devising plans that pay it handsome and disproportionate rewards. In a particularly striking example, upon securing control of Texas government after the 2002 midterm elections, the legislature, under the goading of U.S. House majority leader Tom DeLay, reconfigured the Lone Star State so as to eliminate seven of the ten Anglo Democrats.[1] The DeLay-engineered new map came about even though less than two years earlier the state had implemented a new plan approved by federal judges.[2] In other recent examples, when Republicans, for the first time in history in 2011, achieved control of both chambers of the North Carolina legislature, they drew districts that replaced three Democrats with Republicans. In a fourth case, the Democratic incumbent won reelection in the closest contest in the nation. These developments transpired in one of the most competitive states in the nation in the 2012 presidential election. Illinois Democrats countered the Republican surge in North Carolina with a map that defeated four sitting Republicans, even as the state lost a seat due to reapportionment.

As explained earlier in this volume, Florida voters at the urging of Democratic activists sought to restrict the ability of the legislative majority to capitalize on its advantage when it went about designing districts for the next decade. Consequently, Republicans who already held 19 of 25 congressional seats had poor prospects for building on that advantage when recasting maps to accommodate two additional seats. Republicans in other Southern states that gained seats (Georgia, South Carolina, and Texas) designed plans with the intent of adding to their advantages, easily thrusting aside objections from Democratic legislators. Since Georgia and South Carolina enacted redistricting plans to protect majority-black districts, their plans quickly secured approval from federal authorities as required by Section 5 of the Voting Rights Act. The Texas plan was intended to elect Republicans from three of the four districts allocated to the state as a result of its rapid population growth but soon became the target of a court challenge. However, in Florida, the Fair Districts standards for redistricting adopted by popular vote in 2010 forced Republicans to restrain their partisan ambitions. As will be detailed in this chapter, the new plans were complicit in the primary defeat of one sitting Republican and two others in the general election. Moreover, Democrats secured the two seats that Florida picked up through the reapportionment process.

Expectations

Democrats recognized the constraints under which the majority Republicans operated in Florida and anticipated gains there as part of a strategy to take back the House in 2012. Steve Israel, chair of the Democratic Congressional Campaign Committee, expected that the new standards would so limit GOP ambitions that he said, tongue in cheek, "The only way that they could conceivably add more Republicans to Florida without violating Florida's own fair redistricting standards would be to redistrict into Bermuda and the Cayman Islands."[3] An unbiased observer speculated that if the terms of the two constitutional amendments were fully honored, Democrats might double their six-member contingent in the Sunshine State delegation. Since Florida has been among the most heatedly contested states in presidential elections and more often than not favored Democrats since 1996, winning more than a quarter of the congressional seats did not seem unreasonable. Nonetheless, Republicans coveted the two seats awarded the state as a result of its continued growth during the first decade of the new century.

Not all Democrats embraced the new standards, especially the portion that called for drawing compact districts to the maximum extent possible, using existing political boundaries. That element encouraged one of the strangest bedfellows' alignments for which politics is notorious. Corrine Brown, whose then District 3 was originally drawn by a federal court in 1992 and was characterized as the "fish hook district" and the "love bug district," had already seen the black concentration in her district reduced as the result of a *Shaw* challenge. She feared that requiring compactness would destroy the electoral security of her current district, which linked distant African American communities stretching from Orlando north to Jacksonville.[4] Brown joined Republican legal challenges arguing that stressing compactness and ignoring the fortunes of incumbents could lead to violations of the Voting Rights Act.

Brown was not the only African American incumbent who saw trouble in the new standards. Allen West, one of two African American Republicans in Congress, represented a long, narrow district designed to unite Republicans in Fort Lauderdale and West Palm Beach. Despite bringing together most of the available Republicans in the area, West's district backed President Obama in 2008 and sent a Democrat to Congress that year, but then it was overwhelmed by the GOP wave in 2010, leading the district to elect West to Congress just two years after the election of President Obama.

Primary Elections

Redistricting resulted in one pair of Republican incumbents slugging it out in the primary. Freshman U.S. representative Sandy Adams competed against ten-term incumbent and House Transportation Committee chair John Mica. In the plan implemented in 2002, Representative Mica's District 7 and District 24 represented by Representative Adams both came into the eastern side of Orlando and intersected at Daytona Beach. Mica's district ran from the outskirts of Jacksonville to Daytona while Adams's district extended further south along the coast to just north of Melbourne. Half the population in the new District 7, which Representatives Adams and Mica would contest, came from Adams's old district along with just over 40 percent from Mica's old district. Both incumbents lived within the confines of the new District 7. If the Republicans had redrawn the District 7 without taking into account the concerns for the new standards and the likelihood of a court challenge, they probably would have separated the homes of the two members into two different congressional districts.

Since a member of Congress need not live in the district he or she represents—the only requirement is residency within the state—the "death match" between Congressman Mica and Congresswoman Adams could have been avoided had one of the incumbents run in the new open District 6. The new District 6 included St. Johns and Flagler Counties, which Mica had represented for the previous decade; almost three-fourths of the constituents had been in his previous district. The Cook Political Report's

Party Voting Index for the new districts calculated that the new District 6 is more Republican than the new District 7. Barack Obama took half the vote in 2008 in the precincts included in the new District 7 but only 46 percent of the vote in the new District 6. An appealing feature of the new District 7 is its more compact design being limited to the eastern side of Orlando with no direct link to the coast.

Representative Adams quickly announced that she would seek reelection in District 7. An early assessment of the new plan even designated Adams as one of the winners who had received a district in which her party members were more concentrated in the new district than in the old district.[5] Mica took longer to indicate where he would run. During the period when Mica remained mum, one of his campaign staffers had boasted that, "Wherever he runs, we're confident he will win."[6] Once Mica decided to seek reelection in the 7th rather than the 6th District, he justified his choice, explaining that "I have lived in Central Florida for 40 years, raised my family here, was successful in business here and enjoyed strong support from this community."[7] Mica, who had helped Adams win her initial election, offered to assist with her fundraising if she would run in the 6th rather than the 7th District. Mica claimed that at some point in his career he had actually represented 93 percent of the area in the new 7th District.[8]

Representative Adams, who represented part of Seminole County for eight years, advanced to the House riding the 2010 GOP wave that enabled her to defeat an incumbent in this marginal district that gave a narrow 51 percent majority to John McCain. In 2010, Adams had Tea Party support from the outset and former Alaska governor Sarah Palin gave Adams her blessing in the general election. The pro-GOP tide coupled with the strong ties of Adams to the district where she had been a deputy sheriff for 17 years before serving in the Florida House enabled her to handily defeat freshman Democrat Suzanne Kosmas by taking 59.6 percent of the vote.

The 2012 contest featured appeals that split along generational and ideological lines. Adams remained true to her Tea Party roots and launched anti-government attacks highly critical of federal spending. In the primary she bludgeoned Mica with a Tea Party club as she berated the Transportation Committee chair for being addicted to earmarks and using his influence to gain millions of dollars to fund highways and a rail line in Florida. Concentrating her fire on the spending bills that Mica had supported, Adams asked, "How do you expect someone who's been here and helped create the mess, to be the one to fix the mess that they helped create?"[9]

Prior to the brewing of the Tea Party, one of the principal rewards for seniority and achieving the chairmanship of a house committee that had influence over the allocation of tens of millions of dollars was to use that substantial political influence to help promote one's own reelection through the ability to direct federal dollars to the legislator's district. In addition to defending his efforts on behalf of his district, in particular, and Florida in general, Mica attacked Adams's record as a state legislator asserting that she had only recently converted to the Tea Party pork-free diet. The candidates' disagreements over federal spending obscured the similarities in their overall voting records, which were well into the conservative end of the spectrum.

One ad run by Adams showed Mica standing with President Obama as the president signed a piece of legislation. The voice-over characterized the House Transportation Committee chair as the president's "best cheerleader." Mica filed a complaint against Adams for using this footage, which he said violated house rules against using materials filmed during the course of legislative proceedings.

Not surprisingly, the committee chair had greater fund raising success than the freshman congressional representative did. In announcing his reelection bid, Mica boasted that he had $900,000 on hand and almost 10,000 contributors. At the end of July 2012, Mica had raised $1.6 million, far outpacing Adams who had brought in $941,902 for that same time period.[10] For the final push, Mica had almost $1 million, more than twice what Adams had in the bank. As one would anticipate for a committee chair, the funding came disproportionately from sources having concerns before the Transportation Committee. Filings on *Opensecrets* (https://www.opensecrets.org) show more than $400,000 contributed by transportation interests along with almost $200,000 from the construction industry. Adams reported raising just under $900,000 and spending virtually all of it while taking on $100,000 in debt. Representative Adams's fundraising was impeded by the expenses involved in her initial election to Congress. Although she raised $1.3 million in 2010, her opponent raised almost twice as much. Adams held two fundraisers in 2011 designed to pay off debts remaining from her 2010 run.

In keeping with her Tea Party affiliation, Adams regularly won straw votes conducted by Tea Party enthusiasts. She also boasted of endorsements from Sarah Palin, conservative darling Allen West and even former secretary of state Condoleezza Rice. Several of her fellow freshman Republicans, including the class president Austin Scott (R-GA) kicked in money to her campaign. Mica countered with an endorsement from former

Arkansas governor and 2008 presidential candidate Mike Huckabee. Mica also could point to the support he had received from a number of mayors in the district.[11]

Despite a greater share of her former constituents residing in the new District 7 than former constituents coming from Mica's old district, Adams lost badly in the GOP primary. Mica took 61 percent of the vote and won each county handily with his smallest percentage coming in Seminole County where he nonetheless won with 60 percent.

Redistricting influenced the outcome in a second district although this one did not involve a two-incumbent duel. Cliff Stearns had represented District 6 since 1989. During the first decade of the new century, Stearns's district stretched from Ocala to Jacksonville. The new plan split his home county of Marion and resulted in Stearns's home actually being in the District 11. Rather than clash with fellow GOP incumbent, first-term congressman Rich Nugent, the more senior Representative Stearns sought reelection in the new District 3. Although the new 3rd extended westward into the Panhandle, Stearns had previously represented 65 percent of its population. In contrast, less than 30 percent of the population in the new 11th came from Stearns' old district while Nugent had represented twice as many of the constituents. In an effort to heighten his appeal in Clay County, Stearns bought a house there, when his Ocala residence ended up in Nugent's district.

Stearns's new district became less urban as it no longer went into Duval County but added seven rural counties that extended from the Georgia border to the Gulf of Mexico. Although Stearns had attracted at least 60 percent of the vote in every election since winning his third term, an early indication hinted at potential vulnerability. Congressional incumbents rarely lose their party's renomination. Consequently, in light of widely perceived invulnerability, congressional representatives face few, if any, strong primary challengers. When Congressman Stearns drew three opponents in the 2012 GOP primary, it suggested that in the new District 3, even if not in Washington, D.C., political observers sensed an opportunity to defeat Stearns. The reconfiguration of the district coupled with Stearns' age (71), encouraged multiple competitors to come forward. Nonetheless, to outsiders, Stearns appeared formidable with $2.1 million in his reelection kitty, an amount no one could hope to match.[12]

The field of challengers included a state senator, the county clerk of Clay County, and a political neophyte, Gainesville veterinarian Ted Yoho. In sizing up his opponents, Stearns took aim at the wrong target. He concentrated his attacks on Steve Oelrich, a state senator and former Alachua County sheriff. Yoho managed to stay out of the line of fire and at a time when many voters distrusted all politicians, Yoho's inexperience became an asset. Being a veterinarian, Yoho connected more easily with the rural voters added to the district.

Like Sandy Adams in District 7, Yoho sought to turn the seniority and power of his opponent from an asset into a liability. The veterinarian had a memorable ad in which he portrayed incumbents as men in business suits eating from a hog trough. Others joined Yoho in attacking the incumbent for an allegedly liberal voting record. James Jett, Clay County Clerk of Circuit Court, called Stearns a "parasite" for remaining in Congress for a quarter of a century and criticized the incumbent's repeated votes in favor of raising the debt ceiling.[13] Stearns countered by seeking to enhance his Tea Party credentials by securing endorsements from some of the rock stars of that movement. Former presidential aspirant Michele Bachmann and House Budget Committee chairman Paul Ryan signed on as supporters of their house colleague.[14] Yoho took another swipe at Stearns's long tenure by promising to serve no more than eight years—the maximum length of service permitted in Florida's state legislature.

The incumbent apparently did not see defeat lurking at his door. As one bit of evidence that Stearns felt overly secure, he left a bulging campaign treasury. Articles at the time of the primary attributed Congressman Stearns's defeat, in part, to the incumbent's failure to spend his excess campaign funds, with news reports claiming that he had $2 million still sitting in the bank. Opensecrets reports a smaller cache of unspent cash putting the figure at close to $1.6 million. Even though Stearns did not exhaust his campaign treasury, he substantially outspent Yoho by a margin of $738,048 to $163,524.[15]

Monday-morning quarterbacks claimed that Stearns got outworked by Yoho who campaigned throughout the district in contrast with Stearns, who constituents criticized for not visiting their rural counties.[16] As often happens when an incumbent ages and assumes greater responsibilities, Stearns, who chaired a house energy and commerce subcommittee, spent less time in the district. In a year in which long tenure became a liability, Stearns's efforts to parlay his work as a subcommittee chair into popular votes in his new district failed to succeed. To bolster his claims of conservatism and underscore the advantages of seniority, Stearns pointed to his efforts to investigate Planned Parenthood—a frequent target of pro-life groups—and his investigation into the Obama Administration grant of more than $500 million to the bankrupt solar panel company Solyndra. Attempting to make a mark in Washington, D.C. did not compensate for Representative Stearns's failure to appear at county fairs, fall festivals, and other local events. Especially detrimental to Stearns's reelection was his failure to connect sufficiently with the new portions of his district.

In a closely contested election contest where the unanticipated outcome did not become clear until midday on the Wednesday after the election, Yoho, the Tea Party favorite in the contest, ended Stearns's career by a margin of 875 votes with a plurality of 34.4 percent. When Stearns conceded the day after the election, Yoho, being a true Gator, immediately dropped to one knee in the style of former University of Florida football player Tim Tebow. Of the thirteen counties in the district, the incumbent won only his home county and Clay County. If the county of Marion had not been split between the 3rd and 11th Districts, Stearns could have won the election. Likewise, had Clay County Clerk of Circuit Court Jett not taken 27 percent of the vote in that county in a futile political effort that saw him get only 13.5 percent of the vote district-wide and left him $75,000 in debt, the incumbent might have won another term.

Despite winning only two of the counties, Stearns defeated Yoho by more than 3,000 votes in the portions of the district that he had previously represented. The challenger succeeded in unseating the incumbent by beating Stearns by more than 4,000 votes in the areas added to the district.[17] These largely rural areas that had less familiarity with the incumbent found the appeal of the veterinarian overwhelming.

General Elections

In terms of national attention, the reconfiguration of Republican Allen West's district stood out. Prior to entering politics, West served as a career Army officer, rising to the rank of lieutenant colonel before retiring in 2004. West left the service after being reprimanded for use of harsh techniques when interrogating an Iraqi police officer. West became a media star as one of two African American Republicans elected to the U.S. House in 2010. West and South Carolinian Tim Scott became the first black Republicans in the House since J. C. Watts retired from his Oklahoma district in 2002. Both of the newcomers arrived in Washington with strong Tea Party support. Of the two, West more often provided memorable quotes such as his accusation that 70 Democrats in Congress belong to the Communist Party. As a result of these kinds of statements, West had higher visibility and greater notoriety. By giving voice to the suspicions of some on the far right, West developed a national following.

Given West's stature as a conservative rock star, if in 2011 the legislature had drawn districts free of the redistricting constraints adopted with the enactment of Amendment 6 by Florida voters in 2010, West would likely have received a congressional district no less politically favorable than the district that elected him in 2010. To get to Congress, West had knocked off a two-term incumbent Democrat. West's victory in 2010 reversed the outcome in 2008 when he lost by ten percentage points. In 2010, West won by eight points, thanks in part to his ability to raise $6.5 million, the most accumulated by any non-incumbent House candidate.

West represented a narrow ribbon of a district along the Atlantic coast stretching from the northern boundary of Palm Beach County to south of Fort Lauderdale. In securing 54 percent of the vote in 2010, West did better than McCain in 2008 or President Bush in 2004 who won 48 and 47 percent of the vote, respectively. The new District 22, where 56.5 percent of the population came from the district West had previously represented, was more favorable to Democrats, having given President Obama 57 percent of the vote in 2008. Rather than compete in that hostile environment, West executed a strategic retreat northward to compete for the open seat in District 18. Most of the district came from the old District 18 and West could move into this district without having to battle an incumbent since Representative Tom Rooney, who had represented the 18th, moved westward and ran in the new 17th (another open seat). Although less than a quarter of the population in District 18 came from West's old district, Obama had managed only 51 percent of the vote in this area when initially elected. Rooney moved into District 17 since it was more Republican than the new 18th, having given Obama only 44 percent of the vote.

As his opponent in 2012, Representative West drew political newcomer Patrick Murphy, who had recently changed his party registration from Republican to Democrat.[18] The moderate Murphy stalked the right-wing conservative West. Murphy initially indicated he would run in District 22 but when West moved northward to District 18, Murphy followed him. Murphy explained, "The Tea Party started, you know, taking hold and people like Allen West won in my backyard. And I just decided I'm not going to sit back and complain and not do anything about it."[19]

The challenger proved a successful fundraiser as he amassed $4.3 million. West's notoriety in liberal circles helped Murphy raise campaign funds, as West became a lightning rod for Democrats outraged at what the former colonel said about them. In most congressional contests, Murphy's bank account would be viewed as impressive in its own right. Yet, West, with his ties to conservatives nationally, far exceeded Murphy's campaign fundraising totals, pulling in $19.3 million. To put the West campaign fundraising achievement in perspective, the most raised by a House candidate in 2010 was Michele Bachmann's $13.5 million. In 2010, only four U.S. Senate candidates generated more dollars than West brought in during the 2012 election cycle. On a per capita basis, West raised more than $25 for every man, woman, and child in the new district or almost $60 for every voter who participated in the 2012 contest.

West and Murphy traded body blows using their substantial treasuries to attack one another on television. In one television campaign advertisement, West contrasted his personal actions with those of Murphy on February 16, 2003. West had just received orders to deploy on the same night Murphy was arrested after being thrown out of a Miami nightclub. The West ad included Murphy's booking photo. West also charged Murphy and his family of "putting profits ahead of people" for hiring foreign workers. Murphy gave as good as he got and charged West with casting roll call votes that promoted outsourcing of jobs. Several Murphy ads featured quotes from West and one of them ended with a national journalist saying that West is the "craziest member of the House of Representatives." These kinds of back and forth allegations prompted a former Florida Democratic legislator to observe that, "Nasty is the new normal in Florida. Politics here is very gutterlike [sic]. It's like a very bad reality TV show that still gets very high ratings."[20]

Despite being awash in money, West came up short following a brutal campaign. A prolonged recount showed Murphy to have won by 1,907 votes out of more than 330,000 cast. The challenger benefited from the enthusiasm among Democrats outraged at what they considered to be irresponsible statements by West and eager to secure a second term for President Obama. While Democrats around the country contributed to Murphy's campaign, he could not have won without the support of a number of Republicans for whom West proved too extreme. West's defeat coupled with Sandy Adams' primary loss, may signal an early step towards reclaiming the Republican Party brand by moderates concerned about the image created by Tea Party enthusiasts. West also suffered from the need to establish a relationship with the 77 percent of the district's population he had not represented. When the 113th Congress convened, the 29-year old Murphy was its youngest member.

A second South Florida GOP incumbent joined West in defeat. Like West, David Rivera entered the House in 2010; however unlike West, Rivera succeeded a retiring Republican. The vacancy that opened the way for former state legislator Rivera to advance to Congress involved a retirement and a switch. Lincoln Diaz-Balart came to Congress following the addition of a second Hispanic district in the Miami area in the 1992 redistricting plan. A decade later, his younger brother, Mario, succeeded Lincoln in the Florida House after the older sibling was elected to the Florida Senate. Later, as a state senator, Mario Diaz-Balart used his position as redistricting committee chair to fashion a third Hispanic congressional district that politically benefited his brother Lincoln who had become a congressman. In 2002, Mario won Congressional District 25, which stretched from Miami west to the Gulf of Mexico, joining his brother in Congress. By 2010, District 25 had become a toss-up in which John McCain barely won, while District 21 immediately to the east was slightly more Republican. When Lincoln retired from Congress in 2010, Mario opted to seek reelection from the more compact and more secure District 21. Despite some concern that the open District 25 might go Democratic in 2010, Rivera easily defeated his Democratic opponent Joe Garcia by 11 percentage points.

In winning the seat in 2010, Rivera overcame questions about whether he had worked for the U.S. Agency for International Development, as he claimed. Once in office, questions about Rivera's past multiplied. In the 2012 Rivera vs. Garcia rematch in the reconfigured District 26, the challenger concentrated on ethical issues. Garcia's claims gained credibility when the Florida Department of Law Enforcement launched an investigation into what Rivera characterized as a consulting contract worth at least $500,000 from a dog track owner hoping to secure authority to operate slot machines.[21]

Just before the election, the Florida Commission on Ethics charged the incumbent with eleven misdeeds growing out of the alleged consulting contract, misuse of campaign funds, and incomplete campaign fund disclosures. The FBI and the Internal Revenue Service also became interested in Rivera's finances. Adding to his problems, the non-partisan Citizens for Responsibility and Ethics named Rivera as one of the dozen most corrupt members of the House.[22] The FBI investigated claims that Congressman Rivera had funded the campaign of Justin Stenard who challenged Garcia in the Democratic primary. Stenard seemed an unlikely candidate for the U.S. House of Representatives since his annual income was only $30,000 yet he reported having loaned his campaign $53,000.[23] The investigation indicated that Rivera funneled money to the Stenard campaign via Stenard's campaign manager.

Rivera might have survived the change in the district but for the ethical questions surrounding his candidacy. The district became only one point more Democratic in terms of the 2008 Obama vote. The district also shifted from having a narrow, 2,500 GOP registration plurality in 2010 to a 1,500 Democratic registration edge two years later, thanks to the Obama team's sophisticated voter mobilization efforts.[24] An incumbent can usually overcome a small partisan disadvantage through activities promoting the legislator's name such as travel throughout the district, newsletters, and casework. The district had changed politically, but Rivera had the advantage of having represented more than two-thirds of its residents. Eighteen percent of the voters added to the district came from Diaz-Balart's 21st District while the remainder came from Ileana Ros-Lehtinen's 18th District. In short, the new District 26 consisted entirely of voters who had already lived in one of the three districts represented by Hispanic Republicans.

Another element contributing to Garcia's victory involves generational changes in partisan preferences. Rivera, like the other Hispanic Republican members of Congress, maintained a hard line vis-à-vis Cuba. Garcia, who is also of Cuban heritage, favored allowing people to travel to Cuba and to send money to family members still living on the island nation.[25] Garcia's approach proved more in tune with the views of younger Cuban Americans who have no memory of the pre-Castro regime. Based on its own polling, the Garcia campaign claimed to have made inroads in the Cuban American electorate.[26] Redistricting in combination with generational replacement and ethical concerns enabled Garcia to coast to an 11 percentage point victory margin.

A second Democrat who benefited from the new map succeeded in restarting a congressional career swept away by the Republican tide of 2010. The defeat of this Democrat in 2010 bore a striking resemblance to West's loss in 2012. Like West, former Democratic congressman Alan Grayson was judged too extreme by his constituents with the difference being that Grayson had staked out a position on the left end of the political continuum in contrast with West who was far to the right. Like West, Grayson managed to attract the political spotlight even as a freshman by making statements outside the political mainstream. One incendiary Grayson attack asserted that the GOP alternative to the Obama healthcare plan for the poor was: "Don't get sick. And if you do get sick, die quickly."

Grayson initially got to Congress by defeating a four-term incumbent.

In his 2008 victory, Grayson took the same share of the vote as Obama received in the district, 52 percent. However, Grayson's high octane attacks on Republicans in general and his 2010 opponent in particular, contributed to a fourteen-point swing against him, as he was defeated by Republican Daniel Webster 56 to 38 percent. Grayson suffered this embarrassing defeat despite raising $6 million, more than three times what Webster secured.

Redistricting created a new district in the Orlando area, which allowed Grayson to stage a comeback in 2012 without having to take on the man who had defeated him two years earlier. More than a third of the population in District 9 in which Grayson competed in 2012 came from District 8, which he had previously represented. Hispanics and African Americans constituted a majority of the adults redrawn from the old district into the new one. The other major source of constituents for the new District 9 came from the old District 15 and the adult component from this district consisted predominantly of minority groups. Overall the bulk of the adults in the new District 9 were black or Latino. Much of the district Grayson won lay in Osceola County, which has experienced a dramatic increase in individuals of Puerto Rican descent who tend to give strong support to Democratic candidates. Unsurprisingly, this newly crafted district—one of the two Florida added after the 2010 reapportionment of congressional seats—sent Grayson to the 113th Congress with a comfortable vote share of more than 60 percent. As he had in the past, Grayson demonstrated his fundraising prowess, bringing in $4.5 million, which far surpassed his hapless Republican opponent's total of $147,112.

The other seat Florida gained through reapportionment went to the Gold Coast and here, as in Central Florida's 9th District, the winner had lost a previous bid for Congress.[27] In 1992, Lois Frankel joined four other Democrats seeking the newly created District 23. This district was drawn under the watchful eye of the Department of Justice then operating under a "Max Black" approach, demanding that jurisdictions subject to Section 5 of the Voting Rights Act draw as many majority-minority districts as possible. The northern portion of District 23 looked reasonably contiguous and compact, as it included much of inland Palm Beach, Martin, and St. Lucie Counties. However, the *Almanac of American Politics* described the district as "geographically grotesque" because of the narrow finger that extended southward along the Florida East Coast Railroad to attach black concentrations in Fort Lauderdale and Miami to a largely rural district.[28] Stringing together these African American populations resulted in a 52 percent black district.

Frankel, at the time a state legislator, won the first round of the 1992 primary with 35 percent of the vote. Two African Americans, Alcee Hastings and Bill Clark, were the next closest candidates to Frankel. In the 1990s, Florida still required a majority vote to win a party nomination. In the runoff, Frankel questioned Hastings's suitability, reminding voters that he had been impeached and removed as a federal district court judge, having been charged with accepting a bribe. Although Judge Hastings was acquitted in a criminal trial, the individual accused of having helped him secure a $150,000 bribe in return for the judge granting leniency in sentencing concerning a couple of cases, was convicted. Hastings responded to his opponents' attacks and rallied black support by observing of Frankel, "The bitch is a racist."[29] Hastings also chided Frankel for running in the majority black district suggesting she was an opportunist for running in this open seat rather than competing in a predominately white district.[30] The former judge easily won the runoff with 58 percent of the vote.

Bouncing back from her defeat, Frankel returned to the Florida House and then served two terms as mayor of West Palm Beach. Facing term limits, she announced her candidacy for District 22 in the spring of 2011 expecting to challenge Allen West.[31] When West opted to compete in the new District 18, Frankel had a clear shot at the solidly Democratic 22nd and in what may be an inspiration for many election losers, she got to Congress 20 years after her initial bid.

Democrats in North Florida hoped that the new districts would allow them to reclaim a seat they had lost two years earlier. In 2010, U.S. House candidate and Tea Party Republican Steve Southerland thrashed Blue Dog Democrat and seven-term Vietnam veteran Allen Boyd, to take the 2nd Congressional District. Boyd's moderate record had enabled him to hold onto this Panhandle district that shares much in common with the rural Georgia and Alabama districts just to the north, even as the two previous Republican presidential candidates took 54 percent of the vote. Boyd had managed to stay in step with his conservative voters until he got tripped up on the Obama health care bill. Although he opposed the initial version, Congressman Boyd voted for the final version and this provided the opening that Southerland used to link the incumbent with the unpopular House Speaker Nancy Pelosi and to characterize Boyd as simply her lapdog. In 2010, Boyd managed only 41 percent of the vote in a field that included two minor candidates.

The new map shifted District 2 westward and centered it on reliably Democratic Tallahassee. The old map had run a finger into Leon County to attach much of the state capital to Republican Ander Crenshaw's Jacksonville-based 4th District. Although 91 percent of the population of the new District 2 came from the previous version of the district, the inclusion of Tallahassee produced a district in which President Obama had received 47 percent of the vote, two points more than in the previous configuration. As further evidence that Democrats saw promise in this northern district, the four candidates entering the District 2 Democratic primary equaled the largest field of Democratic competitors entering a Florida U.S. House primary. University of Virginia professor and electoral guru Larry Sabato considered Southerland's hold on the seat as tenuous, categorizing it among the "Likely Republican" seats.

As the winner of the right to challenge Republican Steve Southerland, Democrat Al Lawson had a lengthy political resume. He had served 28 years in the Florida Legislature, the last decade as a senator. In 2010, Lawson took on Boyd in the Democratic primary attacking the Blue Dog Democrat for hedging his support of the Obama agenda and came within 2,400 votes of unseating the incumbent in what proved an omen of the sitting member's vulnerability.

The new District 2 has a potential electorate slightly less than 25 percent black, and these voters could be expected to support Lawson strongly, who is an African American. With the benefit of President Obama at the top of the ticket, Lawson ran better than incumbent Boyd had in 2010. Despite a stronger showing, Lawson's upset bid came up short, as he lost 53 to 47 percent to Southerland.

Assessment

Assessing the results of congressional redistricting in Florida from the GOP perspective produces familiar alternative interpretations: Is the glass half empty or half full? Florida Republicans could not control the process as the legislature's partisan majority did in many other states; they nonetheless fared reasonably well. Compared to the outcomes in states in which the districting process had been taken out of the hands of legislators and given to independent entities, Republicans might count Florida among their triumphs.

Despite the dislocations occasioned by redistricting and discussed above, 20 of the 25 Floridians serving in the 112th Congress will return for the 113th Congress. One of those who will be missing, erstwhile Republican congressman Connie Mack, could almost certainly have won another term, but instead mounted an unsuccessful challenge to Democratic senator Bill Nelson, which resulted in a historic first: a husband and wife both lost congressional elections on the same day.[32] However, in an environment in which well over 90 percent of incumbents usually renew their contracts with their constituents, the attempt to limit gerrymandering capabilities of the party dominant in the legislature may have proven less successful than supporters had hoped.

Given the disparity between the GOP's share of the congressional seats compared with the competitiveness of presidential contests in the Sunshine State, winning additional districts would have challenged Republicans' ingenuity even without the enacted prohibitions on traditional gerrymandering practices. In the face of President Obama's three-point Florida victory in 2008, Republicans held 76 percent of the state's congressional delegation in 2011. Democratic victories in the two new districts along with the defeat of two GOP incumbents, means that Democrats hold, as of 2013, 37 percent (10 total) of the delegation's seats. This is well below the majority vote given President Obama and Senator Nelson in 2012, but a substantial increase over the 24 percent (six congressional members in total) Democratic share of the delegation in the 112th Congress.

The new plan generally resulted in districts that tilted more toward the Democratic Party than the districts they replaced. An examination of the 25 districts from the 112th Congress and the successor districts, as presented in table 10.1, shows that in the six districts that reelected Democratic incumbents as well as in the two districts where a Democrat defeated a Republican, the share of the vote won by the Democrat in 2012 exceeded the Democratic vote share in 2010.[33] In contrast, all of the 17 Republican incumbent winners, except for U.S. representative Dennis Ross (who had no Democratic opponent) got smaller shares of the vote in 2012 than two years earlier. Some Republicans like Ander Crenshaw in District 4 experienced a minimal decline while others saw their vote shares fall significantly. The greatest decrease of 24 percentage points occurred for Mario Diaz-Balart who had no opponent in 2010, and in 2012 ran in a district where he had not previously represented 49 percent of the population. John Mica and Jeff Miller each experienced a 10 percentage-point drop in support; Ileana Ros-Lehtinen saw her vote share fall by 9 percentage points. The dean of the Florida congressional delegation, the late Bill Young, and Tom Rooney each got eight points less of the vote in 2012, than in their previous elections. Most of these incumbents, despite doing worse in 2012, still won with comfortable margins. However, Vern Buchanan saw popular support

Table 10.1. Comparison of the old and new congressional districts

Old district	Old district member	Party	New district member	New district member	Party	% of old CD in new CD	Vote share			Obama's 2008 vote share		New-old
							2012	2010	Difference	New district	Old district	
1	Miller	R	1	Miller	R	0.949	0.7	0.8	-0.1	32	32	0
2	Southerland	R	2	Southerland	R	0.9121	0.53	0.54	-0.01	47	45	2
3	Brown	D	5	Brown	D	0.8067	0.71	0.63	0.08	71	73	-2
4	Crenshaw	R	4	Crenshaw	R	0.8577	0.76	0.77	-0.01	37	37	0
5	Nugent	R	11	Nugent	R	0.5851	0.65	0.67	-0.02	44	43	1
6	Stearns	R	3	Yoho	R	0.6572	0.65	0.71	-0.06	40	43	-3
7	Mica	R	7	Mica	R	0.0257	0.59	0.69	-0.1	50	46	4
8	Webster	R	10	Webster	R	0.5621	0.52	0.56	-0.04	47	52	-5
9	Bilirakis	R	12	Bilirakis	R	0.568	0.64	0.71	-0.07	47	47	0
10	Young	R	13	Young	R	0.8349	0.58	0.66	-0.08	52	52	0
11	Castor	D	14	Castor	D	0.8485	0.7	0.6	0.1	66	66	0

12	Ross	R	15	Ross	R	0.5304	1	0.48	0.52	46	49	-3
13	Buchanan	R	16	Buchanan	R	0.9596	0.54	0.69	-0.15	49	47	2
14	Mack	R	19	Radel	R	0.9775	0.62	0.69	-0.07	43	42	1
15	Posey	R	8	Posey	R	0.7912	0.59	0.65	-0.06	44	48	-4
16	Rooney	R	17	Rooney	R	0.371	0.59	0.67	-0.08	44	47	-3
17	Wilson	D	24	Wilson	D	0.7979	1	0.86	0.14	87	87	0
18	Ros-Lehtinen	R	27	Ros-Lehtinen	R	0.6659	0.6	0.69	-0.09	49	51	-2
19	Deutch	D	21	Deutch	D	0.7623	0.78	0.63	0.15	64	66	-2
20	Was.-Schultz	D	23	Was.-Schultz	D	0.6559	0.63	0.6	0.03	62	63	-1
21	Diaz-Balart	R	25	Diaz-Balart	R	0.5111	0.76	1	-0.24	45	49	-4
22	West	R	18	Murphy	D	0.2311	0.503	0.46	0.043	51	52	-1
23	Hastings	D	20	Hastings	D	0.7344	0.88	0.79	0.09	81	83	-2
24	Adams	R	6	DeSantis	R	0.2257	0.57	0.6	-0.03	46	46	0
25	Rivera	R	26	Garcia	D	0.6862	0.54	0.43	0.11	50	49	1
			9	Grayson	D		0.62			61		
			22	Frankel	D		0.55			57		

in his Gulf Coast district decline by 15 percentage points as he fell into the competitive range with 54 percent of the vote.

Some of the incumbents who fared worse did so even though their new districts consisted overwhelmingly of residents from their old districts. In Buchanan's district, 96 percent of the people came from his old district. Miller's new district contained 95 percent of his previous constituents; while Young had a district composed of 83 percent of his old constituents. Some of the other incumbent congressmen experiencing a sizable loss of support got new districts in which they had previously represented relatively few of the residents. At the low end, 42 percent of Mica's constituents came from his old district. Rooney also had to get acquainted with many new people as his district contained just 37 percent former constituents.

Redistricting likely prevented freshmen Republicans from experiencing a sophomore surge. Rather than increasing the vote share in his first reelection bid, Southerland received 1 percent less support than he did in 2010. Daniel Webster, who had unseated Alan Grayson in 2010, fared even worse as his vote share declined from 56 to 52 percent. Rich Nugent, another GOP freshman, won 2 percent less of the vote in his reelection than in his initial victory. Of the other four new Republicans elected to Congress, Sandy Adams lost in the primary, and Allen West and scandal-plagued David Rivera fell in the general election—only Dennis Ross (FL-15), who had come to Congress with a 48 percent plurality, improved his position by avoiding any opposition in his new district which became three points more Republican.

The two Democratic freshmen from Florida experienced a healthy sophomore surge in their reelection to Congress. Frederica Wilson, who has an impregnable district, escaped without a challenger thereby improving on the 86 percent of the vote won in 2010. Ted Deutch bettered his initial performance, winning his Gold Coast district by 15 percentage points more than he did in 2010.

Another statistical source for illustrating and analyzing partisan voting comparisons of the old and new districts appears in table 10.1 and focuses on the share of the vote won by Barack Obama in 2008. Using this measure, no districts underwent dramatic change, with the greatest difference occurring in Webster's district in which 52 percent of the vote had gone to Obama in the old district compared with 47 percent in the new district. The district represented by Republican congressman Bill Posey became four percentage points less oriented toward Obama, as did the district represented by Diaz-Balart. Not all of the districts made less hospitable toward

Democrats belong to Republicans. Four of the districts occupied by Democrats prior to redistricting became slightly less Democratic in terms of their Obama vote while two districts experienced no change.

Focusing on the 2008 Obama vote allows one to assess whether a district has changed its party orientation during that presidential year. One congressional district in Florida stands out as an illustrative example of a district that clearly changed its party orientation during 2008. It is the congressional district represented by Republican congressman Daniel Webster, which went from being slightly pro-Obama at 52 percent to a more Republican district at 47 percent Obama support.

Congressman Dennis Ross's district became slightly more Republican as it went from a district that gave Obama 49 percent to one in which he received only 46 percent. In similar fashion, the district of Representative Posey went from one in which Obama had taken 48 percent to one where he got 44 percent. Moving in the opposite direction, Representative Mica's old district gave Obama 46 percent; while in the new District 7 Obama had taken half the vote. The district of Representative Buchanan inched towards the Democrats with Obama having gotten 47 percent in the earlier version and 49 percent in the new configuration. The congressional district represented by Ileana Ros-Lehtinen fluctuated ever so slightly with the old district having cast 51 percent of its votes for Obama compared with 49 percent in the new district. In contrast, the district that Rivera held and then lost to Garcia changed from one in which Obama obtained 49 percent to a new version that gave him half the vote.

If the GOP goal were to retain every seat it held going into the mapmaking state legislative session of 2011 and elect Republicans to the two newly apportioned congressional seats in 2012, then the 17 to 10 seat Republican advantage achieved in the 2012 elections had to be a disappointment. On the other hand, in a state in which President Obama bested Mitt Romney by almost a percentage point and in which the Democratic senator beat his GOP challenger by 13 points, Republicans retained 63 percent of the congressional seats. The GOP percentage of the seats also exceeded their share of the congressional vote by a substantial margin. If all districts for which results are reported are considered, Republicans garnered 53 percent of the vote.[34] If only districts that featured two-party competition are considered the GOP won 53.7 percent of the ballots.

If Florida Republicans had been able to draw the congressional maps after the 2010 Census in the manner they desired, they might have secured one of the new seats. They might also have created districts more hospitable for Republican U.S. representatives Allen West and David Rivera although the latter's loss was more likely the result of scandal than an inability to survive in a district made marginally more Democratic. A GOP-drawn map free of concerns expressed by Florida voters' enactment of the 2010 Fair Districts reforms would probably have responded to the political favorability concerns from John Mica and Sandy Adams and left Cliff Stearns with more of his old district.

In another effort to place the Florida congressional redistricting outcome in the context of what might have happened, the example of the redistricting process in Arizona presents the worst case scenario of what likely would have come about if the process had been taken wholly out of Republican hands rather than merely placing legal constraints on the degree to which the GOP could press their partisan advantage. In the Grand Canyon State, Republicans held the governor's office, had two-thirds of the house seats, and had an even more commanding control of the senate. Arizona leans more heavily Republican than Florida, and it has remained in the GOP category in recent presidential elections, even as Florida has become the most populous swing state that now tilts toward the Democrats.

An independent commission carried out redistricting in Arizona and the plan it devised so outraged Republican governor Jan Brewer that she tried to replace the commission chair.[35] The plan drawn by the independent commission following the 2000 Census had produced five Republican- and three Democratic-held districts as of 2011. The new plan caused as much disruption for Arizona Republicans as their fellow partisans in Florida experienced. Two sitting Republicans squared off against one another in the primary—just as had happened in Florida. A Democrat won the state's new congressional seat. Representative Ann Kirkpatrick, who had lost her reelection bid in 2010 to a Tea Party advocate, played the Alan Grayson role and managed to grab the vacated 1st Congressional District seat so that in the 113th Congress, the state in which Mitt Romney beat Barack Obama by nine percentage points will have five Democrats and four Republicans in its congressional delegation.

Although causality cannot be demonstrated, the presence of the new state constitutional constraints in Florida may have kept Republicans from practicing some of the gerrymandering tactics that a dominant majority often uses to maximize its advantage.[36] The new plan did not pair any Democratic incumbents. Instead, the new plans resulted in several instances in which two GOP members found themselves living in the same district. In addition to Representatives Mica and Adams, as discussed above, Stearns and Nugent shared a district.

Another common gerrymandering tactic involves "cracking" minority party concentrations so that they cannot dominate a district. No evidence of cracking Democratic strength was found in this study. Yet, a third gerrymandering tactic is to "pack" districts with excessive numbers of minority party supporters while spreading majority party loyalists so that the minority party wastes votes while the majority party wins a number of districts with narrow but reliable margins. Again, the evidence from table 10.1 suggests that the new plan did not disadvantage Democrats by packing them into a minimal number of districts.

Some have hypothesized that redistricting, since it creates additional open seats, works to the advantage of groups underrepresented in a legislative body because it creates opportunities that do not require the defeat of an incumbent.[37] The Florida delegation in the 113th Congress has the same composition in terms of salient member characteristics as its predecessor. No additional congressional seats in Florida were won by minorities. Although, as noted above, a Democratic Hispanic congressional candidate replaced a Republican congressional incumbent. Representative Allen West's defeat reduced the number of African Americans in the delegation from four to three. Among women, the House delegation has the same number, although Republican representative Adams has been replaced by Democratic representative Frankel.

The bottom line is that redistricting, even when complying with the Fair Districts standards, left the Florida delegation much as it had been. Ninety percent of the incumbents seeking reelection succeeded. Except in the case where hubris prompted two incumbents to run against each other rather than one of them shifting to the open District 6, explanations other than redistricting can account for defeats. Congressman Rivera's loss in 2012 was at least partially and perhaps primarily the result of corruption charges against him. Representative Stearns's defeat, while at least partially attributable to redistricting, might have been avoided had he campaigned more aggressively, spent more liberally, and concentrated his attacks on his opponent Ted Yoho. By giving Florida two additional seats, reapportionment did permit an encore opportunity for two individuals. Representative Grayson returned to Congress and Representative Frankel finally achieved her ambition that had been detoured for a generation.

The reelection of Republican Bill Young to a 22nd term in Congress and

Representative John Mica's defeat of Representative Sandy Adams indicate that seniority need not pose an insurmountable obstacle. Congressman Stearns, the delegation's second most senior member, might have survived had he worked and spent as aggressively as Congressman Mica worked and spent campaign funds. As with seniority, the interpretation of the meaning of the Tea Party is also inconclusive. Representative Mica overcame the Tea Party; while, on the other hand, Stearns was tripped up in part by the Tea Party movement. Nevertheless, Tea Party support could not save Allen West from being defeated for reelection in 2012 by Democrat Patrick Murphy.

Redistricting can often roil the usually placid waters of incumbency but need not bring in a flood of new members. If the supporters of the Fair Districts reforms had hoped to transform Florida's congressional delegation, they must have been disappointed. Far greater change took place in the two states held up as examples of partisan redistricting at the beginning of this chapter. New redistricting plans helped defeat three incumbent Democrats in North Carolina and an even greater number of Republicans fell to Democrats in Illinois.

Conclusion

The Never-Ending Story

SETH C. MCKEE

Out of a total of 8,401,203 votes cast for Barack Obama and Mitt Romney in the 2012 presidential election in Florida, the incumbent prevailed by a margin of 74,309, or a difference of 0.9 percent.[1] Although not quite rivaling the 537-vote margin of George W. Bush in 2000, the 2012 presidential contest reaffirmed the battleground status of the Sunshine State and thus it is hardly surprising that the presidential campaign sucked up most of the oxygen emitted by political reporters. Nonetheless, redistricting was far from ignored. The Fair Districts Amendments 5 and 6 were enacted by the voters in 2010 and were first made applicable for the 2012 elections. The amendments garnered plenty of ink because their possible effects were an issue of great interest to political observers and a subject worthy of scholarly examination.

This book examines the 2012 Florida redistricting from many different angles, including the behavior of the mass public and political elites alike, and it provides a comprehensive account of how the mere act of altering political boundaries reshapes the perennial struggle for partisan control and the demands for representation among a host of various groups that comprise the kaleidoscopic Florida electorate. The eminent political scientist Clinton Rossiter once averred that representative democracy would not be possible in the absence of political parties.[2] In addition to this observation, we should add that American elections cannot be understood apart from the role of redistricting. It occurs every ten years (and sometimes more frequently because of legal action), making it an institutional feature of American politics. However, unlike most structural components of the American political system, redistricting is by its very nature an unpredictable and often untamed factor in the realm of electoral politics.

To be sure, political scientists have learned a lot about redistricting and the numerous ways it impacts elections and representation, but we remain surprised by the turn of events that seemed unfathomable until they come to pass once a map is redrawn. Among the fifty states, Florida is just the sort of setting where the improbable is likely to occur. A state of in-migrants and immigrants, whose population is in a constant state of flux because of its unrivaled mixture of Yankees, Southerners, Latin Americans, African Americans, and Anglos—leading many observers of the Sunshine State to view it as a microcosm of the nation.[3] In addition, with the Great Recession finally becoming a memory, Florida is primed to once again welcome a new wave of residents who share a common characteristic with most of the "natives," which of course means they came from somewhere else.[4]

Furthermore, despite the remarkable fluidity of the Florida electorate, for almost two decades the Republican Party has found a way to dominate district-based elections. Perhaps it is the GOP's impressive success, election-after-election, that has planted the seeds of the party's impending decline? The stark contrast between statewide competitiveness, as reflected best in presidential contests, and Republican hegemony in district-based races, finally drew the attention of an opposition determined to restore electoral balance. In the first election after the enactment of the Fair Districts reforms, Republicans experienced a net loss in the U.S. House, Florida Senate, and Florida House. Although midterm elections, like the one in 2014,[5] tend to be kind to Florida Republicans because, among other things, more voters who fit the profile of the GOP turn out (i.e., seniors, Anglos, and higher income voters), time does not appear to be on the party's side.

Demographic change, especially the remarkable growth of the non-Cuban Hispanic population in Central Florida, is the most palpable sign that Republican hegemony is receding from its 2010 high-water mark. Indeed, the exploding Puerto Rican population in the Orlando area alone will ensure that Florida districts exhibit marked malapportionment well before the next decennial redistricting becomes effective in 2022. Similarly, the population growth generated by Florida's newcomers arrives with a profile of political proclivities that generally favors the Democratic Party.[6]

Reading the political tea leaves, it is a reasonable position to expect Florida Republicans to have their majority status in the U.S. House and state legislature reduced as the next reapportionment nears. For one, the 2014 ruling by Tallahassee Circuit Court Judge Terry Lewis in *Romo v. Detzner*, ensures that the congressional map for 2016 will be significantly different from the current one favored by Republicans. In addition, by 2022 we should expect to have a much better understanding of how the courts interpret Florida's redistricting reform measures, which are clearly doing no favors for the current GOP majority.

Nevertheless, these pronouncements are made with the humble realization that political handicappers frequently suffer embarrassment and ridicule for getting things totally wrong. Regardless, prognostication is not the aim of these concluding remarks. Like elections, redistricting will occur into perpetuity, and the beauty of a representative democracy is that the future state of partisan competition will be decided by Florida's voters.

Appendix A

Additional Tables

Table A.1. Fair Districts coalition partners and grassroots petition gatherers

AARP of Florida	Florida State Conference NAACP
ACLU of Florida	Florida State Council of Machinists
AFL-CIO Florida	Florida Voters Coalition
AFSCME Florida	Florida Women's Consortium
Alliance for Retired Americans—Florida	Florida Young Democrats
American Votes	IBEW Florida
American Federation of Teachers	International Brotherhood of Electrical Workers
Broward Teachers Union	International Brotherhood of Teamsters
Clean Water Action	International Union of Operating Engineers
Common Cause	League of Women Voters
Communication Workers of Florida	Longshoremen Florida
Democracia Ahora	National Council of Jewish Women
Democratic Clubs	National Education Association
Democratic Executive Committees	Organizing For American Volunteers
Dolphin Democrats	People for the American Way Foundation
Duval Teachers Association	PIRG—Florida
EMILY's List	Progress Florida
Equality Florida	Ruth's List
Florida Association of Counties	SEIU
Florida Building Trades	SEIU Florida
Florida Black Caucus of Local Elected Officials	SEIU Florida Retirees
Florida Carpenters Union	Sheetmetal Workers International Union
Florida College Democrats	Sierra Club Foundation
Florida Conservation Alliance Institute	Space Coast Progressive Alliance
Florida Consumer Action Network	Teamster Joint Council 75
Florida Education Association	UAW Retirees of Florida
Florida Fair Elections Coalition	United Auto Workers Florida
Florida League of Cities	United Auto Workers International
Florida League of Mayors	United Postal Worker Retirees
Florida Legislative Black Caucus	United Teachers of Dade
Florida Pipetrades Council	United Transportation Union
Florida School Board Association	Volusia Teachers Association

Table A.2. Redistricting public hearing schedule, 2011

City	Date	Time*	Location
Tallahassee	6/20	1–4, 6–8 PM	412 Knott Building
Pensacola	6/21	10 AM–1 PM	WSRE-TV Jean & Paul Amos Performance Studio
Fort Walton Beach	6/21	6–9 PM	Ft. Walton Beach High School
Panama City	6/22	10 AM–1 PM	Gulf Coast Community College
Jacksonville	7/11	2–4, 6–8 PM	Florida State College at Jacksonville Downtown Campus
St. Augustine	7/12	8–11 AM	Flagler College
Daytona Beach	7/12	6–9 PM	News Journal Center at Daytona State College
The Villages	7/13	8 AM–12 PM	Colony Cottage Recreation Center
Gainesville	7/13	6–9 PM	Santa Fe College
Lakeland	7/25	2–5 PM	Polk State College
Wauchula	7/26	8–11 AM	Hardee County Civic Center
Wesley Chapel	7/26	6–9 PM	Wiregrass Ranch High School Gym
Orlando	7/27	6–8 PM	Bob Carr Performing Arts Center
Melbourne	7/28	10 AM-1 PM	Brevard County Government Center at Viera
Stuart	8/15	6–9 PM	Blake Library
Boca Raton	8/16	10 AM–1 PM	Florida Atlantic University
Davie	8/16	6–9 PM	Broward College Central Campus
Miami	8/17	10 AM–2 PM	Miami Dade College Wolfson Campus
South Miami	8/17	6–9 PM	Florida International University College of Law
Key West	8/18	4–7 PM	Florida Keys Community College
Tampa	8/29	4–8 PM	Jefferson High School Auditorium
Largo	8/30	8–11 AM	EpiCenter at St. Pete College
Sarasota	8/30	6–9 PM	New College Harry Sudakoff Conference Center
Naples	8/31	8–11 AM	Naples Daily News Community Room
Lehigh Acres	8/31	6–9 PM	Veterans Park Gymnasium
Clewiston	9/1	8–11 AM	Hendry County Health Department

* = or until completion of meeting, whichever is first.

Table A.3. Minority and female composition of Florida's congressional and state legislative delegations after 2010 and 2012

Office	Category	After 2010			After 2012		
		Democrat	Republican	Total	Democrat	Republican	Total
U.S. House							
	Blacks	3	1	4	3	0	3
	Hispanics	0	3	3	1	2	3
	Women	4	2	6	5	1	6
State senate							
	Blacks	6	0	6	6	0	6
	Hispanics	0	3	3	1	3	4
	Women	7	7	14	6	6	12
State house							
	Blacks	18	0	18	21	0	21
	Hispanics	3	9	12	4	9	13
	Women	12	15	27	15	13	28
Total		53	40	93	62	34	96

Notes: Data on blacks are from the Florida State House and Senate websites and the Joint Center for Political and Economic Studies; data on Hispanics are from the NALEO Educational Fund; data on women are from the Center for American Women and Politics. Blacks and Hispanics are exclusive categories, but obviously women may be African American or Latino.

Table A.4. Partisan composition of Florida delegations before and after the last two decennial redistrictings

Office	2000 elections	2002 elections	2010 elections	2012 elections
U.S. House	65% (15R, 8D)	72% (18R, 7D)	76% (19R, 6D)	63% (17R, 10D)
State senate	63% (25R, 15D)	65% (26R, 14D)	70% (28R, 12D)	65% (26R, 14D)
State house	64% (77R, 43D)	68% (81R, 39D)	68% (81R, 39D)	62% (74R, 46D)
Total seats	183	185	185	187

Notes: Data present the Republican percentage of each Florida delegation with the total number of Republicans and Democrats displayed respectively in parentheses. Data are from the Florida Division of Elections.

Appendix B

Data Sources

This appendix lists some of the primary sources used by contributors in their analyses of Florida redistricting. Although far from exhaustive, many sources were necessary for building datasets because the state of Florida did not produce a comprehensive database for the 2012 redistricting. The rationale was that compliance with the Fair Districts amendments meant that certain information (racial data and party registration data) should not be made accessible if it could in fact be used to further a partisan gerrymander. See appendix C for a technical explanation of the comprehensive database created for Florida's precincts.

(1) Election returns and registration—Florida Division of Elections. Florida's official election data provided at the precinct and district level. Official party registration numbers are made available at the state, county, and precinct levels.

(2) District population data—MyDistrictBuilder. MyDistrictBuilder is a website created by the Florida House of Representatives. It contains multiple sources of data at various levels of political geography (districts, VTDs, precincts, and blocks).

(3) Comparisons of redistricting plans—public mapping project. Micah Altman and Michael P. McDonald are the principal investigators of this open-source and publicly accessible redistricting program that allows one to create their own redistricting maps and analyze them based on a host of demographic and political criteria.

(4) Data on proposed and passed Florida redistricting plans—Florida Senate. The Florida Senate produced a website with population data and shapefiles for proposed and passed redistricting plans for the U.S. House, state senate, and state house.

(5) Shapefiles—Florida Senate, U.S. Census Bureau, and John Guthrie. The Florida Senate makes available district shapefiles for 2012 and going back to the 1990s on an archived website with what they refer to as FREDS data (Florida Redistricting Electronic Data System). The U.S. Census Bureau makes available district shapefiles for all states' passed legislative and congressional plans. Finally, John Guthrie, the staff director for the Florida Senate, made available the shapefile for the 2012 Florida precincts.

(6) Turnout, party registration, and demographics—Florida voter file. The Florida voter file contains individual level data on the population of Florida's registered voters. In addition to an indicator of whether an individual voted in an election year, the data include party registration, age, race and ethnicity, and gender.

Appendix C

Data Compilation

RICHARD MCKENZIE

The primary objective was to develop a comprehensive database of voter precincts used in the 2012 Florida election cycle that contained the following information for each precinct:

- Unique identification information for the precinct (precinct ID, county, etc.)
- District values for 2010 and 2012 from the following legislative branches of government for each precinct:
  U.S. House
  state house
  state senate
- A coded value used to identify a precinct as split between at least two districts within the same branch of government, or as wholly contained within one district
- Voter return data from the 2012 primary and general elections for each precinct.

The acquisition, validation, and analysis of precinct boundary, congressional district, census, cadastral, and voter return data was necessary to achieve the objective. Given the geographic nature of the aforementioned datasets, the data were compiled and analyzed in ArcGIS Desktop (version 10.1 SP1) software.

Data Collection

The data were collected from two primary sources: (1) The Florida voter file and (2) 2012 precinct level election returns. The voter file was accessed shortly after the 2012 election. This source contains demographic and turn-out information for all voters registered for the 2012 elections. Since the data are provided at the individual level, they were aggregated up to the precinct (the primary unit of analysis). All 67 Florida counties delivered their 2012 election results by precinct to the Florida Division of Elections. Because these data were delivered in various formats, they had to be trans-posed into a single accessible data matrix.

Preprocessing

In order to develop a uniform dataset of legislative districts, a CSV file con-taining the GEOID along with the 2010 and 2012 U.S. House, state house, and state senate district values for each census block (2010 boundaries) for the State of Florida was joined to an Esri shapefile containing the 2010 census block boundaries for the state of Florida. The join was based on GE-OID values that were present in both datasets. Doing so provided a single-source shapefile to generate legislative district boundaries for each of the three branches used in the analysis. This process is further discussed in the analysis section of this appendix. Additionally, the census block shapefile and the precinct shapefile were imported into an Esri feature dataset within a file geodatabase. This process converted the two shapefiles into feature classes and allowed for the correction of topological errors present in both shapefiles.

Initial Validation

Before any analyses were conducted to determine if a precinct was split between two or more legislative district boundaries from the same branch of government, special attention was paid to the topological validity of the 2012 precinct feature class and the 2010 Census Block feature class contain-ing the legislative district identifiers. This process was performed using the topology editing tools found in ArcGIS Desktop. Each feature class under-went separate topological validation using the following rules:

- The feature class must not have gaps.
- The feature class must not have overlapping features.

Another topology validation was conducted after removing the topological errors from the individual feature classes in order to correct obvious topological errors between the two sets of boundaries. The topology rule used is the equivalent of the following:

- The boundary of a feature in the precinct feature class must be covered by the boundary of a feature in the census block feature class.

The second round of topology validation provided a way to identify and adjust precinct boundaries that were not covered by a census block boundary (either due to the precinct boundary being drawn at a different scale of geography, parcel level for example, or a precinct boundary that was drawn without taking any other set of boundaries into consideration). The total number of census blocks identified as split between two or more precinct boundaries did not prove to be significant enough to impact any further analysis. This method produced a total of 509 out of 484,481 census blocks with a cumulative population of 104,716, or 0.006 percent of the state's entire population (when calculated from the census block feature class). This was further supported with the *official* release of an Excel document containing the entire list of split census blocks (split between two or more boundaries), which revealed that the actual reported number of split census blocks for the state was 1,021 out of 484,481 with a cumulative population of 148,248, or 0.008 percent of the state's entire population.

Analysis

Upon completion of the initial stage of topology validations, a new feature class was created from the census block feature class containing the legislative district information. Using the Dissolve geoprocessing tool in ArcGIS Desktop the features of the new feature class were based on every combination of the following seven attributes:

- County
- State house, state senate, and U.S. House district number, 2012
- State house, state senate, and U.S. House district number, 2010

Additionally, population values from each census block were aggregated to the district combination level. This was done in order to distinguish between the district combinations that have no population and the district combinations that have a population greater than zero. As expected, the generation of the district combinations created a new topological problem. There were instances where the 2012 precinct boundaries did not share a boundary with the newly created district combination boundaries, thus making it necessary to run a second round of topology edits on the 2012 precinct boundary feature class. The following topology rule was applied to the precinct feature class:

- The boundary of a feature in the precinct feature class must be covered by the boundary of a feature in the district combination feature class.

District combinations with no population were treated as non-impacting on the process of determining whether or not a precinct was split between two or more district combinations. Any boundary of a precinct feature that was not covered by a district combination boundary was adjusted if, and only if, there was no population associated with the district combination. This was done in order to reduce the number of split district combination features (with regard to the precinct boundary feature class) without transferring population estimates from one precinct to another.

The next step in the analytical process was to create a feature class in which the spatial representation of the features was determined by the intersection of the district combination feature class and the newly aligned 2012 precinct boundary feature class. Using the Intersect geoprocessing tool in ArcGIS Desktop to produce it, each feature in the new feature class was comprised of every unique combination of the following attributes:

- County
- State house, state senate, U.S. House, 2012
- State house, state senate, U.S. House, 2010
- Precinct ID, 2012

Performing the intersection between the precinct boundary and the legislative district combination feature classes resulted in a total of 8,740 unique combinations. Performing the intersection between the precinct boundary and the legislative district combination feature classes also rendered the aggregated population values invalid; this is because there is no way to apportion the population of a legislative district combination feature that was split by two or more features. Therefore, the population field that carried over from the legislative district combination feature class was deleted from the feature class of precinct and legislative district combinations.

It was necessary to provide some sort of population value for each feature in the precinct-legislative district combination feature class in order to continue with the analysis, so population totals (along with land area and water area totals) were calculated for each feature in the precinct-legislative district combination feature class by using the Spatial Join geoprocessing tool in ArcGIS Desktop. The following is a list of the parameters used in the process:

- Target features: the precinct-legislative district combination feature class
- Join features: the centroid points of the 2010 U.S. Census Block feature class
- Join operation: a one-to-one spatial join
- Field mapping options: for each target feature, keep all attribute information from the target features as is, and calculate the sum of the following fields from the join features attribute information:
  population
  land area
  water area
- Match option: any join feature must be completely contained within the target feature

After the spatial join was performed, the precinct-legislative district combinations could be organized into two different categories:

- Features with an estimated population
- Features with an unknown population estimate

The features that have an unknown population estimate were the result of a null spatial join between the precinct-legislative district combinations and the census block centroids. Of the 8,740 unique combinations, 34 had null population values. Given the relatively small number, the null-valued precinct-legislative district combinations were extracted from the feature class and were manually examined to determine if there was any evidence to suggest that some sort of population was present within the boundary of the feature. Features that appeared to have no population present and were *not* an entire precinct (that is, the precinct ID was unique to the feature in question) were removed from the null-valued feature class.

The remaining null-valued precinct-legislative district combination features were added back to the rest of the precinct-legislative district combination features using the Merge geoprocessing tool in ArcGIS Desktop. In order to remain spatially consistent with the other feature classes used in the analysis, the features that were removed from the null-valued precinct-legislative district combination feature class were replaced with features that had no precinct, district, or population information associated with them.

With every possible precinct-legislative district combination accounted for and compiled into a single feature class, it was then time to start the migration of the compiled data from the precinct-legislative district combination feature class back into the original 2012 precinct boundary feature class. The first step was to remove any portions of a split precinct in the precinct-legislative district combination feature class that had a population estimate of zero and restore the boundary of the remaining split precinct back to the original precinct boundary by applying the following topology rule:

- The boundary of the precinct-legislative district combination feature class must be covered by the boundary of the original 2012 precinct feature class.

The topological errors that were the result of precinct actually being split by a legislative district were marked as exceptions. Additionally, a field was added to the topologically verified precinct-legislative district combination feature class. It was populated with the concatenation of a feature's county abbreviation and precinct ID (Precinct 45 in Alachua County would be ALA-045, for example). This field was used to identify correctly each precinct feature while distinguishing between precincts in different counties with the same precinct ID. The same field was also added to the original precinct feature class and to every voter return dataset. The final complete feature class containing every combination of 2010 and 2012 state house, state senate, and U.S. House district combined with 2012 voter precinct and county boundaries had a total of 8,126 unique combinations; which is 1,868 more than the 6,258 features in the 2012 precinct feature class.

Assigning Split Precinct Values to Election Voter Return Data

Prior to the assignment of split precincts in the voter return data, the individual combinations of the complete feature class containing every combination of 2010 and 2012 state house, state senate, and U.S. House district combined with 2012 voter precinct and county boundaries needed to be aggregated to the district level of geography. This was achieved by using the Dissolve geoprocessing tool in ArcGIS Desktop. The feature combinations in the feature class were aggregated based on the following fields:

- County
- Precinct number
- Legislative district (one branch at a time)
- Unique key (the precinct-county combination)

In addition, population estimates were calculated for each feature by summing the population estimate values of the feature combinations. The process was repeated for each legislative branch, producing a total of six new feature classes.

To ensure that the new precinct-individual district combinations were still topologically valid, each of the six new feature classes were converted into points (centroids of their polygon features) using the Feature to Point geoprocessing tool in ArcGIS Desktop and then intersected with the original 2012 precinct feature class using the Intersect geoprocessing tool in ArcGIS Desktop. The result was six new point feature classes that contained all of the attribute information from the feature classes used in the intersections. The new point feature classes were added to an ArcMap map document, where a field calculation was performed to verify that, for each feature in the new point feature class, the unique key from the original precinct feature class matched the unique key from the precinct-individual district combination feature class. There were no instances where the two unique keys did not match. Copies of the precinct-individual district combination feature classes were made and the features that had a population estimate of zero or null were removed.

Using the unique key fields, a relationship class was created between each of the precinct-individual district combination feature classes and their corresponding voter returns in ArcGIS Desktop. A total of nine relationship classes were created (one per set of returns per legislative branch). For each set of returns, a query was made on the related records that isolated non-split precincts (2012 districts) with election results from the rest of the return data. The queried records from the voter returns and the corresponding precinct-individual district feature class were exported into separate tables (both in DBF format). A summary table was then created for the exported records from the precinct-individual district feature class with the purpose of calculating the sum of features per unique key. Any unique key with a feature count greater than 1 would indicate that the precinct was split between at least two 2010 legislative districts for that branch of government.

The next step was to join the exported records from the precinct-indi-

282 · Appendix C

vidual district combination feature class to the related voter returns that were also exported. This was done in ArcGIS Desktop using the Join function. The two sets of exported records were joined based on the unique key values found in both sets of records. Joining the two sets of exported records made it possible to assign 2010 district values for each precinct in the 2012 voter returns with the Field Calculator function in ArcGIS Desktop. The join between the two sets of exported records was removed and another join was created between the exported voter returns and the summary table containing the precinct feature count values. The records that had a feature count that was greater than 1 were selected and their 2010 district values were changed to 0.

The same process of assigning 2010 district values was applied to the precincts that were split between at least two 2012 legislative districts. Upon completion, both sets of exported voter return records were merged backed together and re-sorted in ascending order. The entire process was repeated for each set of voter returns.

Additionally, all precincts had their assigned 2012 district values for each legislative branch validated against the general election voter return records. This was achieved by examining the returns to see if a precinct had voter returns with a sum greater than 0 from more than one contest per legislative branch of government. If a precinct did report returns with a sum greater than 0 from more than one contest in a single branch, the 2012 legislative district value was identified as 0 for being split between more than one contest and the legislative branch was identified as 1 for being split. For example, in Alachua County, the 2012 General Election voter returns indicate that precincts 11 through 15 are all split for one, and only one, legislative branch. Therefore, the district value for the legislative branch where the multiple contests were reported would be 0 and the corresponding split precinct value would be 1.

Conversely, if the 2012 district value of a precinct was identified as technically being split but there were only returns with a sum greater than 1 in one contest, the corresponding district value was changed from 0 to the appropriate district value.

Chamber Switching Precinct Retention

The process of identifying the number precincts retained when a legislator moved from the state house to the state senate (with the exception of Mike Fasano moving from the state senate to the state house) during the 2012 election cycle was made possible by possessing the feature class containing every combination of 2010 and 2012 state house, state senate, and U.S. House district combined with 2012 voter precinct and county boundaries. Using the Select by Attributes function in ArcGIS Desktop, a query was performed on the aforementioned feature class that identified the precincts that contained the 2010 state house district values and the 2012 state senate district values for the candidate in question (for Fasano the query performed was for the 2010 state senate districts and the 2012 state house districts). The selected records were extracted into a new feature class and then aggregated to the precinct-district level using the Dissolve geoprocessing tool in ArcGIS Desktop. The aggregation of features was necessary to avoid redundant precinct values. This could be due to either the precinct being split by more than one district from the U.S. House of Representatives or by having multiple null valued precincts in the selection. Therefore, the extracted features were aggregated based on the following attributes:

- County
- Precinct ID
- State house district in question
- State senate district in question

Appendix D

Maps

This appendix displays four sets of maps (figures D.1–D.4) created by Richard McKenzie. The first set of maps (figure D.1) display the two proposed Florida Senate plans for the 2012 elections. The map on the left side was struck down by the Florida Supreme Court and replaced by the map shown on the right.

Figure D.2 shows the partisan composition of Florida's congressional districts in 2002 (on the left) and 2012 (on the right). Districts won by Republicans are shaded dark gray and districts won by Democrats are shaded light gray.

Figure D.3 shows the partisan composition of Florida's state senate districts in 2002 (on the left) and 2012 (on the right). Districts won by Republicans are shaded dark gray and districts won by Democrats are shaded light gray.

Figure D.4 shows the partisan composition of Florida's state house districts in 2002 (on the left) and 2012 (on the right). Districts won by Republicans are shaded dark gray and districts won by Democrats are shaded light gray.

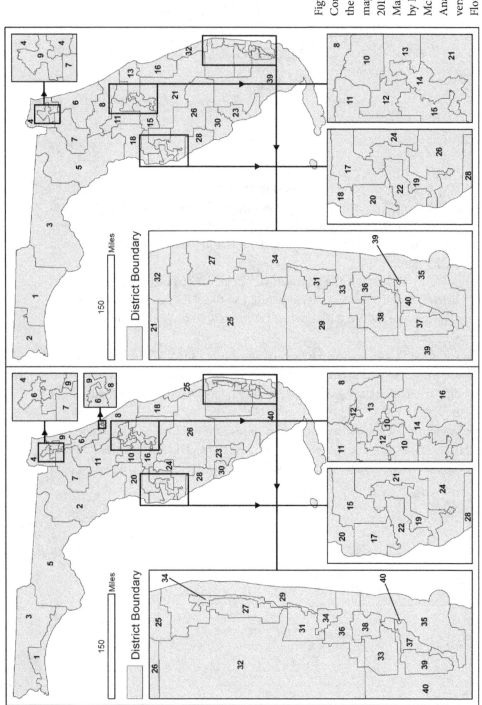

Figure D1. Comparison of the state senate maps for the 2012 elections. Map created by Richard McKenzie, GIS Analyst, University of South Florida.

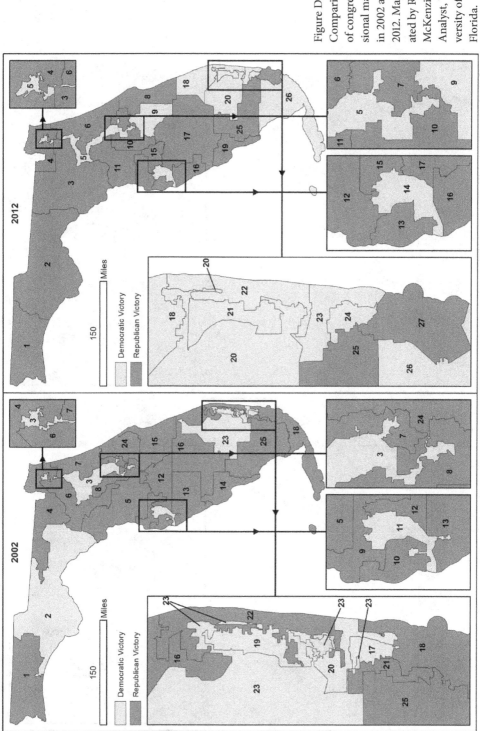

Figure D.2. Comparison of congressional maps in 2002 and 2012. Map created by Richard McKenzie, GIS Analyst, University of South Florida.

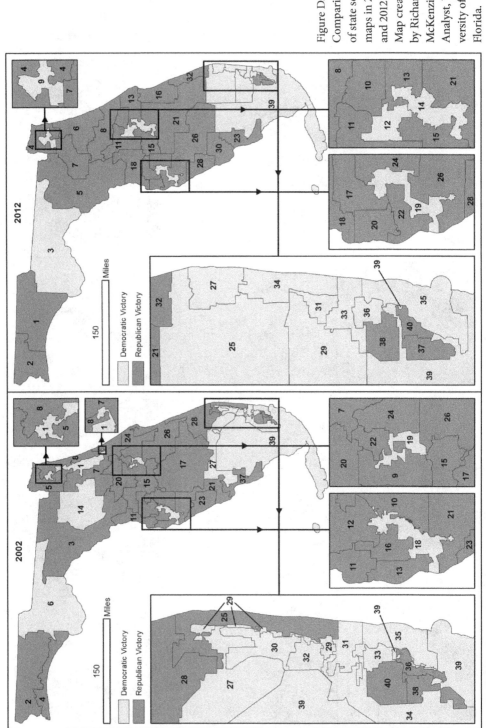

Figure D.3. Comparison of state senate maps in 2002 and 2012. Map created by Richard McKenzie, GIS Analyst, University of South Florida.

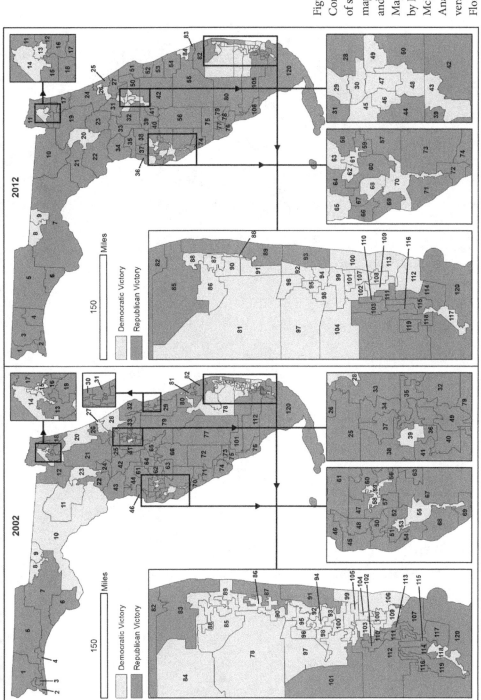

Figure D.4. Comparison of state house maps in 2002 and 2012. Map created by Richard McKenzie, GIS Analyst, University of South Florida.

Notes

Foreword

1. Qtd. in MacManus, "Art and Politics of Reapportionment and Representation in Florida: An Overview," in *Reapportionment and Representation in Florida*, 1–16.

2. Colburn, *From Yellow Dog Democrats to Red State Republicans*.

3. For constitutional language and related court statements, see *In re 2012 Joint Resolution of Apportionment*, No. SC 12–460.

4. MacManus, ed., *Reapportionment and Representation*, and MacManus, ed., *Mapping Florida's Political Landscape*.

Introduction: Redistricting in Florida

1. Bullock, *Redistricting*.

2. Qtd. in Fenno, *Home Style*, 11–12.

3. See Ansolabehere, Gerber, and Snyder, "Equal Votes, Equal Money," 767–77.

4. See Miller and Canak, "From 'Porkchoppers' to 'Lambchoppers,'" 341–66.

5. Specifically the eleven former Confederate states of Alabama, Arkansas, Florida, Georgia, Louisiana, Mississippi, North Carolina, South Carolina, Tennessee, Texas, and Virginia.

6. See table 2.1, Bullock, *Redistricting*, 30.

7. Qtd. in Bullock, *Redistricting*, 43.

8. Population data for Florida's 1962 congressional districts were obtained from University of Colorado professor E. Scott Adler's website: sobek.colorado.edu/~esadler/Congressional_District_Data.html. A map of Florida's 1962 congressional districts can be accessed from UCLA Professor Jeff Lewis' website on United States Congressional District Shapefiles: https://github.com/JeffreyBLewis/congressional-district-boundaries.

9. Data from table 28, Carver and Fiedler, "Florida: A Volatile National Microcosm," 361. As Carver and Fiedler point out, "between 1958 and 1970, the senate grew from 38 seats to 44 to 48, and the house from 95 to 112 to 119. The senate's current size of 40 and the house's current size of 120 date from 1972," 361.

10. Although not a change that affected congressional redistricting, I would be remiss not to acknowledge the significance of the elimination of multimember districts in the Florida Legislature in 1982. This change generally benefited African American candidates

and Republicans, and both groups not surprisingly were strong advocates of the reform. See Lenz and Pritchard, "Florida Legislators' Perceptions," 134–38.

11. For an account of the pressure that the DOJ put on several Southern state legislatures to create majority-minority districts, see Cunningham, *Maximization*.

12. Carver and Fiedler, "Florida," 362.

13. Florida U.S. House District 3, a majority black district represented by Democratic African American representative Corrine Brown, snakes its way in and out of territory stretching from Jacksonville to Orlando. A victim of court decisions that invalidated districts drawn for the overriding purpose of furthering a racial gerrymander (see *Shaw v. Reno* 1993; *Miller v. Johnson* 1995; *Bush v. Vera* 1996), before the 1996 U.S. House elections District 3 was redrawn with a majority white population and Corrine Brown managed to win reelection (she continues to serve in Congress representing what is now Florida U.S. House District 5). The other two majority black districts, both located in South Florida (Districts 17 and 23), were not declared unconstitutional gerrymanders and therefore were not altered for the 1996 elections. For an excellent review of the controversy and electoral consequences surrounding Florida District 3 (and two Georgia congressional districts), see Voss and Lublin, "Black Incumbents, White Districts," 141–82.

14. For example, see Earl and Merle Black, *Rise of Southern Republicans*; Hill, "Does the Creation of Majority Black Districts Aid Republicans?" 384–401; McKee, *Republican Ascendancy in Southern U.S. House Elections*; Petrocik and Desposato, "Partisan Consequences," 613–33.

15. Qtd. in Carver and Fiedler, "Florida," 362.

16. On the relationship between redistricting and political conditions, see McKee, "Political Conditions," 623–50; Hood and McKee, "Unwelcome Constituents," 203–24; McKee, "Effects of Redistricting," 122–33.

17. For insight on the 2010 congressional elections, see Abramson, Aldrich, and Rohde, *Change and Continuity*. For evidence of the significant changes to the partisan composition of numerous state legislatures in the wake of the 2010 elections, see the data and analyses provided by the National Conference of State Legislatures: www.ncsl.org/.

18. A fair criticism of this type of analysis is that redistricting typically prompts retirement when an incumbent's district is dismantled by dividing it into so many pieces that the redrawn percentage is exceedingly high, no matter where the representative chooses to seek reelection. There is little question that some districts in 2012 were dismantled (especially in the state house) and further complicating matters is that several legislators were term-limited. This type of investigation is beyond the scope of the current assessment because, by definition, the redrawn computation is made on the basis of incumbency. Nonetheless, an analysis of the reasons for open seats is worthy of investigation and, as shown in chapter 7, incumbent retirements were in fact more likely in the case of districts that contained higher percentages of redrawn constituents (lower carry-forward populations).

19. For instance, there is no question that redistricting ended Karen Thurman's congressional tenure and greatly contributed to the defeat of Allen West. Republican state senator Ellyn Bogdanoff lost to a fellow incumbent, Democrat Maria Sachs in District 34 and although Bogdanoff carried the precincts she represented prior to redistricting (55.2 percent), she did very poorly in her redrawn precincts, garnering just 40 percent of the vote (and a paltry 25.5 percent in the precincts that neither Bogdanoff nor Sachs

represented before redistricting) and this accounts for her loss (data are from an analysis conducted by the author). For some of the other defeated incumbents, redistricting was less consequential, as explained in chapters 9 (state legislative elections) and 10 (congressional elections).

20. Florida voters approved term limits for state legislators in 1992. For additional information, see the Ballotpedia websites on the Florida Senate and Florida House: http://ballotpedia.org/Florida_State_Senate#Term_limits; http://ballotpedia.org/Florida_House _of_Representatives.

Chapter 1. Before the Lines Are Drawn: Congressional Apportionment in Florida

1. Eighth Census, United States—1860. Instructions to U.S. Marshals, 14.

2. Gibson and Jung, *Historical Census Statistics on Population Totals by Race.*

3. By opinion of the U.S. Attorney General, see 39 Op. Att'y. Gen. 518 (1940).

4. Mills, *Americans Overseas.*

5. This is also due to frequent but slight changes to those included in the overseas count. See Mills, *Americans Overseas.*

6. Franklin v. Massachusetts, 500 U.S. 788 (1992).

7. Louisiana v. Bryson, 132 S. Ct. 1781 (2012).

8. Department of Commerce v. United States House 525 U.S. 326 (1999).

9. Jefferson also argued that the Hamilton method did not have a common divisor, and thereby did not treat all the states fairly. He argued that this also violated the Constitution. See Balinski and Young, *Fair Representation*, 10–22.

10. Kromkowski, *Recreating the American Republic.*

11. Farrand, ed., *Records of the Federal Convention of 1787.*

12. Hamilton, Madison, and Jay, *Federalist Papers.* For an online version, see http://thomas.loc.gov/home/histdox/fedpapers.html.

13. Eagles, *Democracy Delayed.*

14. Reapportionment Act of 1929, ch. 28, §22, 46 Stat. 21, 26 (codified as amended at 2 U.S.C. §2a (2006)) (stating that the number of representatives will be apportioned to states from the existing total number of representatives). This was later recodified with the Apportionment Act of 1941. The only exception is the brief increase to 437 seats to accommodate the admission of Alaska and Hawaii into the Union.

15. Much of this discussion is informed by the seminal work of Balinski and Young, *Fair Representation.* But also see Gaines and Jenkins, "Apportionment Matters," 849–57, and Crocker, *House of Representatives Apportionment Formula.*

16. Note that the definitions of quotient and quota are not consistently used across the apportionment literature.

17. Balinski and Young, *Fair Representation.*

18. Ibid., 14–15.

19. Ibid., 60–66.

20. The Hamilton Method was later reintroduced as the Vinton Method in the 1840s after its new sponsor, Representative Samuel F. Vinton (W-OH). In addition, Representative William Lowndes (DR-SC) introduced another version of a ranking method in the 1820s, but it never gained serious support.

21. Given the 1790 Census apportionment populations, any TIDS in between 32,139 and 33,158 would also generate a U.S. House with 105 seats.

22. Balinski Young, *Fair Representation*, 23–35.

23. The Hill method was later formalized and advocated by Edmund V. Huntington (a professor of mechanics and mathematics at Harvard University).

24. Balinski and Young "Quota Method of Apportionment," 701–30; Balinski and Young, "Apportionment Schemes and the Quota Method," 450–55; Balinski and Young, "On Huntington Methods of Apportionment," 607–18; Balinski and Young, "Jefferson Method of Apportionment," 278–84; Balinski and Young, "Webster Method of Apportionment," 1–4.

25. Edelman, "Getting the Math Right," 297–346.

26. Crocker, *House of Representatives Apportionment Formula*.

27. U.S. Department of Commerce v. Montana, 503 U.S. 442, 460–66 (1992).

28. Balinski and Young, *Fair Representation*, 76.

29. Act of Nov. 15, 1941, ch. 470, 55 Stat. 761, 761–62 (codified as amended at 2 U.S.C. §2a [2006]), amending the Reapportionment Act of 1929 to specify that apportionment will exclusively follow the "method of equal proportions."

30. See "Adams-Onís Treaty of 1819," Texas A&M University website, http://www.tamu.edu/faculty/ccbn/dewitt/adamonis.htm.

31. See the brief history of Florida at the Florida Department of State website, http://www.flheritage.com/facts/history/summary.

32. Congressional Record, 28th Congress, Session II, Chapters 47, 48: 742–43.

33. McCarty, Poole, and Rosenthal, "Congress and the Territorial Expansion," http://www.voteview.com/recentpapers.asp. Its precise apportionment population is not, to the author's knowledge, available. Iowa had 132,573 resident individuals.

34. Ladewig and Jasinski, "On the Causes and Consequences," 89–107; and Ladewig, "One Person, One Vote, 435 Seats," 1125–56.

35. Shaw, "Electoral College," 463–76.

Chapter 2. New Rules for an Old Florida Game: The 2012 Legislative and Congressional Redistricting Process

1. An earlier version of this history can be found in Dye, Jewett, and MacManus, *Politics in Florida*.

2. Myres, *One Man, One Vote*.

3. Price, "Florida," 81–97.

4. Baker v. Carr, 369 U.S. 186 (1962). See also Reynolds v. Sims, 377 U.S. 533 (1964), and Wesberry v. Sanders, 376 U.S. 1 (1964).

5. Maggiotto et al., "Impact of Reapportionment," 101–21.

6. MacManus, ed., *Reapportionment and Representation in Florida*.

7. The legislature attempted to draw district lines to comply with *Baker v. Carr* three times in the early 1960s, but each plan was invalidated by the federal courts. Finally, the federal court took the unusual step of invalidating the results of the fall 1966 elections, hurriedly drew their own district maps complying with one person, one vote, and required special elections in the spring of 1967.

8. Jewett, "Republican Strength," 1–18.

9. Skene, "Reapportionment," in *Florida Handbook, 2005–2006*, 177–95.

10. Thornburg v. Gingles, 478 U.S. 30 (1986).

11. Johnson v. DeGrandy, 512 US 997 (1994).

12. For a thorough review of all issues affecting redistricting in Florida in 1992 through 2001, see MacManus, ed., *Mapping Florida's Political Landscape*.

13. Shaw v. Reno, 509 U.S. 630 (1993); Miller v. Johnson, 515 U.S. 900 (1995).

14. Joni James, "In Win for GOP-Led Legislature, Panel OK's Redistricting Plan," *Miami Herald*, 10 July 2002.

15. Some of the description of requirements and process in this section is taken from MacManus et al., *Politics in Florida*, 201–8.

16. It was rejected for covering too many subjects (an independent redistricting commission and single-member districts) and for being misleading (the ballot summary called the commission non-partisan when its membership was actually to be selected in a partisan fashion).

17. See Aaron Deslatte, "Judges Uphold Fair District Standards as Constitutional," *Orlando Sentinel*, 31 January 2012.

18. Florida Constitution, Article III, Section 20.

19. JoNel Newman, "Voting Rights in Florida, 1982–2006: A Report of RenewtheVRA. org," March 2006, www.aclufl.org/issues/voting_rights/FloridaVRA2.pdf.

20. Shelby County v. Holder, 570 U.S. ____ (2013).

21. Dara Kam, "Scott Holds Up Federal Approval of Redistricting Amendments; Democrats Outraged," *Palm Beach Post*, 25 January 2011.

22. Letter from Andy Bardos, Special Counsel to the Senate President, and George Levesque, General Counsel to the Florida House of Representatives, to T. Christian Herren Jr., Chief of the Voting Section, Civil Rights Division, United States Department of Justice, 29 March 2011.

23. Florida House of Representatives Staff Analysis of Bill # CS/HB 6005 PCB CRS 12–06, Establishing the Congressional Districts of the State, 30 January 2012, 14–16.

24. Associated Press, "Critics Bash Florida Lawmakers' Redistricting Process," *Tampa Tribune*, 21 June 2011.

25. If the legislature is still in session when the bill is sent to the governor's office then the governor must act within a week. If the bill is sent at the end of session and the legislature adjourns then the governor has 15 days.

26. See press releases issued by the Florida House and the Florida Senate, 3 February 2012, www.myfloridahouse.gov/Sections/HouseNews/preview.aspx?PressReleaseId=496, and www.flsenate.gov/Media/PressRelease/Show/Senators/2010-2012/District26/Press Release/PressRelease20120210090519959.

27. Mark Mathews, "Members of Congress Told Not to Try to Influence New Districts," *Orlando Sentinel*, 9 July 2011.

28. The Buzz (staff, *Tampa Bay Times*), "Emerging Thinking on 'Retrogression;' Florida Redistricting's Big Word," *Tampa Bay Times*, 28 November 2011.

29. All quotations in this paragraph in Aaron Deslatte and Kathleen Haughney, "Critics Immediately Challenge Lawmakers' Redrawn Districts," *Orlando Sentinel*, 9 February 2012.

30. See "Order Denying Motion for Summary Judgment, Judge Terry P. Lewis, in the Circuit Court of the Second Judicial Circuit in and for Leon County, Florida, 30 April 2012."

31. See *In Re: Senate Joint Resolution of Legislative Apportionment 1176*, SC12-1, Supreme Court of Florida, 9 March 2012.

32. Mary Ellen Klas, "Florida Senate's 'Drawing for Districts' Show," *Tampa Bay Times*, 22 March 2012.

33. See *In Re: Senate Joint Resolution of Legislative Apportionment 2-B*, SC12-460, Supreme Court of Florida, 27 April 2012.

34. The U.S. Justice Department letter granting preclearance to the legislatively drawn maps can be found at http://censusvalidator.blob.core.windows.net/mydistrictbuilder-data/forDOJ/2012.04.30_DOJApproval_HSC.pdf.

35. Parts of the congressional analysis in the upcoming sections can also be found in Jewett, "'Fair' Districts in Florida," 111–36.

36. Congressional district information taken from the "Florida House of Representatives Staff Analysis of Bill # CS/HB 6005 PCB CRS 12-06, Establishing the Congressional Districts of the State, 30 January 2012." House district information is taken from "Florida House of Representatives Final Bill Analysis of SJR 1176 (HJR 6001, HR 6011), 9 March 2012." Senate district information is taken from "Florida House of Representatives Final Bill Analysis of CS/SJR 2-B, 26 March 2012."

37. Aaron Blake, "Breaking Down the Florida GOP's Redistricting Map," *Washington Post*, 26 January 2012.

38. See "Florida Holds the Record for Redistricting Incumbents Together, Will Weatherford Says," *Politifact Florida*, 13 April 2012, http://www.politifact.com/florida/statements/2012/apr/13/will-weatherford/florida-holds-record-redistricting-incumbents-toge/.

39. Mary Ellen Klas, "Redistricting Maps Make History with Unprecedented Scramble for House Seats," *Tampa Bay Times*, 27 March 2012.

40. Aaron Deslatte, "Florida Senate Passes Redistricting Plan," *Orlando Sentinel*, 22 March 2012.

41. Ibid.

42. Ibid.

43. Ana M. Valdez, "Bogdanoff, Sachs Face Off in the State's Only Senate Race between Two Incumbents," *Palm Beach Post*, 3 October 2012.

44. See appendix table A.3 for the total number of African Americans, Hispanics, and women in Florida's U.S. House, state senate, and state house delegations after the 2010 and 2012 elections.

45. Matt Dixon, "Judge Allows Congressional Maps to Stand," *News Service of Florida*, 30 April 2012.

46. See Steve Bosquet, "Florida Supreme Court: Lawsuit Opposing Senate Redistricting Plan Can Proceed," *Tampa Bay Times*, 11 July 2013.

47. John Kennedy, "Groups Tell Florida High Court that GOP Skewed District Lines for Political Edge," *Palm Beach Post*, 9 May 2013.

48. See *Orlando Sentinel* Interactive Redistricting Map, February 2012, www.orlandosentinel.com/news/politics/os-gfx-redistricting-2010-maps,0,6525157.htmlpage.

Chapter 3. The Law and Politics of Florida Redistricting in State and Federal Court

1. McKenzie, "Beyond Partisanship?"

2. See Vieth v. Jubelirer, 541 U.S. 267 (2004).

3. Brown v. Thomson, 462 U.S. 835 (1983). The Supreme Court announced the rule by stating, "in the past, this Court has recognized that a state legislative apportionment scheme with a maximum population deviation exceeding 10 percent creates a prima facie case of discrimination," 850.

4. In *Brown*, the U.S. Supreme Court upheld a Wyoming House of Representatives plan that had a maximum deviation of 89 percent!

5. See Larios v. Cox, 542 U.S. 947 (2004); see also McKenzie, "Influence of Partisanship.

6. Karcher v. Daggett, 462 U.S. 725 (1983).

7. Shelby County v. Alabama, 133 S. Ct. 2612 (2013). In theory, Congress could change the coverage formula of Section 4 to comply with the Supreme Court's concerns, and that would resurrect the powers of the Department of Justice in Section 5, but Congress currently appears in no hurry to do such a thing.

8. 42 USCS §1973.

9. Johnson v. DeGrandy, 512 U.S. 997 (1994).

10. Thornburg v. Gingles, 478 U.S. 30 (1986), 47.

11. Under the VRA, the Justice Department can also initiate a Section 2 lawsuit against a state or political division.

12. According to the language in *Thornburg*, to sustain an action, "[f]irst, the minority group must be able to demonstrate that it is sufficiently large and geographically compact to constitute a majority in a single-member district. . . . Second, the minority group must be able to show that it is politically cohesive. . . . Third, the minority must be able to demonstrate that the white majority votes sufficiently as a bloc to enable it . . . usually to defeat the minority's preferred candidate," 50–51.

13. The VRA does not specifically require states to draw minority influence districts. These are districts where a minority group could constitute a significant portion of the population of the district (perhaps 40 percent), but they are not enough for a majority. Florida is not required by federal law to draw an influence district, even if one were possible.

14. See Concerned Citizens of Hardee County v. Hardee County Board of Commissioners, 906 F.2d 524 (11th Cir. 1990); see also Hopkins, "Comment: The Minority Coalition's Burden of Proof," 623–54. The Fifth Circuit also allows for minority plaintiffs to institute Section 2 lawsuits based on a political subdivision's failure to create coalition districts.

15. *Thornburg*, 51.

16. Ibid.

17. See Greiner, "Re-Solidifying Racial Bloc Voting," 447–97.

18. *Thornburg*, 79; *Johnson*, 1011.

19. In this totality-of-the-circumstances test, the *Thornburg* court listed many of the senate factors in their opinion. Those factors are the following: "the history of voting-related discrimination in the State or political subdivision; the extent to which voting in the elections of the State or political subdivision is racially polarized; the extent to which the State or political subdivision has used voting practices or procedures that tend to enhance the opportunity for discrimination against the minority group, such as unusually large

election districts, majority vote requirements, and prohibitions against bullet voting; the exclusion of members of the minority group from candidate slating processes; the extent to which minority group members bear the effects of past discrimination in areas such as education, employment, and health, which hinder their ability to participate effectively in the political process; the use of overt or subtle racial appeals in political campaigns; and the extent to which members of the minority group have been elected to public office in the jurisdiction. . . . The Report notes also that evidence demonstrating that elected officials are unresponsive to the particularized needs of the members of the minority group and that the policy underlying the State's or the political subdivision's use of the contested practice or structure is tenuous may have probative value. . . . The Report stresses, however, that this list of typical factors is neither comprehensive nor exclusive," 44–45.

20. *Johnson*, 1016–17.

21. Ibid., 1019.

22. LULAC v. Perry, 548 U.S. 399 (2006).

23. McKenzie, "Influence of Partisanship."

24. Section 4 of the VRA is located in the U.S. Code at 42 USCS §1973b; Section 5 is at 42 USCS §1973c.

25. These counties are Collier, Hardee, Hendry, Hillsborough, and Monroe. Any changes in election laws that affected these counties, including statewide apportionment plans, required Justice Department approval.

26. Beer v. U.S., 425 U.S. 130 (1976); Reno v. Bossier Parish School Board, 520 U.S. 471 (1997); and Reno v. Bossier II, 528 U.S. 320 (2000).

27. For example, if a covered jurisdiction had 5 existing majority-minority districts and then created only 4 such districts in a new plan, that plan could be deemed retrogressive. The *Beer* standard seemed to change after *Georgia v. Ashcroft*, 539 U.S. 461 (2003). Congress more or less restored the old *Beer* standard in its reauthorization of the VRA in 2006.

28. See Texas v. U.S., 831 F. Supp. 2d 244 (2012). Intentional discrimination in election law is oftentimes harder to prove than discriminatory effect.

29. See 42 U.S.C. §1973a(c); see also Crum, "Voting Rights Act's Secret Weapon," 1992–2038.

30. For the current litigation on congressional districts, see *Romo v. Scott,* No. 2012-CA-00412 (Fla. Cir. Ct., Leon County), and for the challenge to the state senate plan, see *League of Women Voters of Florida v. Detzner*, No. 2012-CA-002842 (Fla. Cir. Ct., Leon County).

31. Sanchez v. King, 550 F. Supp. 13 (D.N.M. 1982); Jeffers v. Clinton, 740 F. Supp. 585 (E. D. Ark. 1980).

32. Crum, "Voting Rights Act's Secret Weapon."

33. Josh Gerstein, "Justice Department Challenges North Carolina Voter ID Law," *Politico*, 30 September 2013.

34. Shaw v. Reno, 509 U.S. 630 (1993).

35. Katherine Inglis Butler, "Redistricting in a Post-Shaw Era," 137–270.

36. Bush v. Vera, 517 U.S. 952 (1996); Shaw v. Hunt, 517 U.S. 899 (1996); Butler, "Redistricting in a Post-Shaw Era," 206–7. See also *Miller v. Johnson*, 515 U.S. 900 (1995), for the initial language by the court regarding the use of race as a "predominant" factor.

37. McKenzie, "Influence of Partisanship."

38. Swann v. Adams, 378 U.S. 553 (1964); Swann v. Adams II, 383 U.S. 210 (1966); Swann v. Adams III, 385 U.S. 440 (1967).

39. Swann v. Adams, 263 F. Supp. 225 (1967).

40. Recently, the Court ruled that the initial review conducted automatically within 30 days of the adoption of the state legislative redistricting plan should not preclude later legal challenges to the plan in state trial courts if the challenges revolve around fact-intensive issues that were not or could not be considered in the initial Florida Supreme Court review. See Florida House of Representatives v. League of Women Voters of Florida, 118 So. 3d 198, 204–7 (2013).

41. *In Re: Apportionment Law Appearing as Senate Joint Resolution Number 1305*, 263 So. 2d 797 (1972), 806–7. In this case, the state supreme court upheld the use of multi-member districts under the Florida Constitution. The reality today, however, is that while multimember districts in Florida are in theory constitutional, such districts have been used historically in the South to dilute the voting power of minorities, and thus any future Florida redistricting plan that employed multi-member districts would be subjected to heavy scrutiny under the federal Voting Rights Act as well as the new state constitutional amendments that adopt legal theories commensurate with the VRA.

42. See *In Re: Constitutionality of House Joint Resolution 1987*, 817 So. 2d 819 (2002). In this case, the court warned, "Lake Okeechobee stretches to the limits our language that a district drawn across a body of water does not violate the contiguity requirement," 828.

43. Ibid., 824.

44. In the case of *In Re: Senate Joint Resolution of Legislative Apportionment 1176*, 83 So. 3d 597 (2012), the Court noted, "With the advent of the Fair Districts Amendment, the Florida Constitution now imposes more stringent requirements as to apportionment than the United States Constitution and prior versions of the state constitution," 598–99.

45. Ibid.

46. In the case of *In Re: Senate Joint Resolution of Legislative Apportionment 1176*, while the Court majority states that any "level" of intent (whether malevolent or not) would not be "acceptable," it also concedes that the constitutional language, "by its express terms . . . prohibits intent, not effect," 617.

47. Ibid., 618. The court also said that intent may be inferred by examining traditional redistricting principles contained in Subsection (b), "Where the shape of a district in relation to the demographics is so highly irregular and without justification that it cannot be rationally understood as anything other than an effort to favor or disfavor a political party, improper intent may be inferred. In making this assessment, we evaluate the shapes of districts together with undisputed objective data, such as the relevant voter registration and elections data, incumbents' addresses, and demographics, as well as any proffered undisputed direct evidence of intent."

48. See Article 4, Part 2, Sec. 1(14)(f) of the Arizona Constitution.

49. See *In Re: Senate Joint Resolution of Legislative Apportionment 1176*, 619–20.

50. Ibid., 620 and n23; to back up this practice, the court cited numerous other states which also require their line-drawers to comply with the VRA.

51. Ibid., 620.

52. Ibid., 628.

53. The subservience of equal population requirements to Subsection (a) in the Florida

Constitution seems untenable in terms of current federal constitutional law, given the paramount importance federal courts give to equal population, particularly with respect to congressional districts, but the Florida Supreme Court dances around this inherent contradiction in their 2012 opinion.

54. See *In Re: Senate Joint Resolution of Legislative Apportionment 1176*, 635, the court identified two quantitative measures as helpful in reviewing compactness criteria: the Reock method (circle-dispersion measurement) and the Area/Convex Hull method. The broad reading of this clause allows any future state supreme court to apply the law almost however they see fit.

55. Ibid. In determining what considerations consist of geographic boundaries, the court stated, "We accept the House's view of geographical boundaries that are easily ascertainable and commonly understood, such as 'rivers, railways, interstates, and state roads.'"

56. See Lloyd, "Separating Partisanship," 413–20. Lloyd was the first scholar to try to disaggregate the partisan influences on judging in electoral disputes from ideological ones. He considered a judge's partisan motivations as distinct from ideological motivations, an important nuance that is often lost on some judicial behavioralists, particularly those with a more Rochesterian strategic outlook on judicial behavior.

57. Graves, "Competing Interests," 267–84; Kopko, "Partisanship Suppressed," 301–24; McKenzie, "Influence of Partisanship"; Cottrill and Peretti, "Gerrymandering from the Bench?" 261–76.

58. Segal and Spaeth, *Supreme Court*; Pritchett, *Roosevelt Court*.

59. McKenzie, "Influence of Partisanship."

60. Lodge and Tabor, "Three Steps," 183–213; Bartels, "Beyond the Running Tally," 117–50.

61. Baum, *Judges and Their Audiences*; McKenzie, "Influence of Partisanship."

62. Baum, *Judges and Their Audiences*; McKenzie, "Influence of Partisanship"; Epstein and Knight, *Choices Justices Make*.

63. Langer, *Judicial Review in State Supreme Courts*.

64. McKenzie, "Beyond Partisanship?"

65. In the 1972 state supreme court case, the issue was more about whether multi-member districts were allowed (focusing on the "overlapping territory" language following "contiguity"), and no one appeared to claim that any of the state legislative districts were not contiguous.

66. In *In Re: Constitutionality of Senate Joint Resolution 2g* (1992), 597 So. 2d 276, the court declared, "Contiguity does not require convenience and ease of travel, or travel by terrestrial rather than marine forms of transportation," 279.

67. In McKenzie, "Influence of Partisanship," it is found that plaintiffs who tie political gerrymandering claims to equal population claims are more successful in getting federal courts to strike down those plans even though the political gerrymandering claims themselves are never sustained.

68. See McKenzie, "Beyond Partisanship?"

69. Ibid.

70. A number of justices appear as more than one observation in the dataset because they appear in multiple redistricting cases. Thus, the votes of these justices who appear

twice are not independent observations. To account for this problem, the model employs robust standard errors, clustered around the judge.

71. In this model, judges facing same party plans or nonpartisan court-drawn plans represent the baseline or comparison group. There are only six judge observations that face court-drawn nonpartisan plans—all occurring in cases in the federal courts.

72. Higher scores represent more liberal justices. See Brace, Langer and Hall, "Measuring the Preferences," 387–413.

73. *In Re: Senate Joint Resolution of Legislative Apportionment 1176*, 83 So. 3d 597 (2012).

74. Ibid., 672.

75. Ibid., 691. Lewis went on to smugly state, "Contrary to the suggestion by the dissent, there is no joy or pleasure in this exercise; we follow the constitution as the will of the people of Florida."

76. See, for example, *Burris v. Ryan* (1994), 158 Ill. 2d 469 at 471, or *Voinovich v. Ferguson* (1992), 63 Ohio St. 3d. 198 at 214, or *Terrazas v. Ramirez II* (1992), 1992 Tex. LEXIS 1, 28–29.

77. *In Re: Senate Joint Resolution of Legislative Apportionment 1176*, 83 So. 3d 597 (2012), 698, quoting Justice Blackmun's concurring and dissenting opinion in *Webster v. Reproductive Health Services* (1989), 492 U.S. 490, 552, 109 S. Ct. 3040, 106 L. Ed. 2d 410.

78. 89 So. 3d 872.

79. Florida House of Representatives v. The League of Women Voters of Florida, 118 So. 3d 198 (2013).

80. Matt Dixon, "Lawyers in Voter-Redistricting Suit Make Their Cases to the Florida Supreme Court," *Florida Times-Union*, 16 September 2013; see also Carolina Bolado, "Fla. Justices Seem Open to Limited Redistricting Depositions," *Law360*, 16 September 2013, http://www.law360.com/articles/471702/fla-justices-seem-open-to-limited-redistricting-depositions.

81. See Cox and Miles, "Judging the Voting Rights Act," 1–54.

Chapter 4. Drawing the Line: Public Support for Amendments 5 and 6

1. The language of Amendments 5 and 6 was identical, except that Amendment 5 pertained to "legislative" districts while Amendment 6 pertained to "congressional" districts. Although substantively the same, the amendments were separate to avoid violating Florida's strict single-subject rule for ballot initiatives, which is embodied in Article III, Section 3 of the state constitution. Amendment 5's legislative districting standards were codified in Article III, Section 21, and Amendment 6's congressional standards were codified in Article III, Section 20.

2. Dara Kam, "Fair Districts Ad: Politicians Like Bank Robbers and Foxes in the Hen House," *Palm Beach Post*, 11 October 2010.

3. Tolbert, Smith, and Green, "Strategic Voting," 92–109.

4. Gaffney v. Cummings, 412 U.S. 735 (1973).

5. Martinez v. Bush, 234 F. Supp. 2d 1275, 1312 (S. D. Fla. 2002).

6. Ibid., 1340.

7. Smith and Fridkin, "Delegating Direct Democracy," 333–50.

8. Joni James, "6 Words May Block Overhaul of Redistricting," *St. Petersburg Times*, 23 August 2005.

9. McDonald, "A Comparative Analysis of Redistricting Institutions in the United

States, 2001–02," 371–95; Carson and Crespin, "Effect of State Redistricting Methods," 455–69.

10. The signature requirement for a citizen initiative to qualify for the ballot in Florida is 676,811. On January 22, 2010, the Florida Division of Elections verified 686,016 signatures for Amendment 5 and 681,562 signatures for Amendment 6 and certified the initiatives for the 2010 ballot.

11. Fair Districts Now, "How Has Redistricting Been Done in the Past?"

12. Adam C. Smith, "Florida's Ballot Initiative to Ban Gerrymandering Starts to Draw Foes," *St. Petersburg Times*, 30 August 2009; Mary Ellen Klas, "Charlie Crist's Redistricting Stance Riles Republicans," *Miami Herald*, 21 May 2010.

13. See, for example, Matt Dixon, "Corrine Brown, NAACP at Odds Over Redistricting Amendments," *Jacksonville Times-Union*, 1 October 2010; and American Civil Liberties Union of Florida, "FL Fair Districts and People over Politics Community Forum, USF Tampa Area," 30 September 2010.

14. Allison Ross, "PAC Opposed to Amendments 5, 6 Musters $3.8 Million in a Month," *Palm Beach Post*, 30 October 2010.

15. Cristina Silva, "Incumbents Hard to Beat," *Politifact Florida*, 24 June 2010, http://www.politifact.com/florida/statements/2010/jun/24/fair-districts-florida/incumbents-hard-beat/.

16. Deirdre Macnab and Pam Goodman, "Amendment 7: Fair Districts, Not Poison Pill, Are Needed," *Sun Sentinel*, 6 June 2010.

17. Randy Schultz, "Endorsement: YES on Amendments 5, 6: Let Voters Pick Politicians," *Palm Beach Post*, 1 October 2010; "Fair Redistricting to Reshape Politics," *Tampa Tribune*, 28 September 2010; "'Fair Districts' Will Strengthen Democracy," *St. Petersburg Times*, 28 September 2010.

18. Ron Littlepage, "Yes to Fair Districts Idea; No to Votes on Comp Plans," *Jacksonville Times-Union*, 20 September 2010; See also, Mary Ellen Klas, "Lawmakers Challenge Florida Redistricting Proposals," *Miami Herald*, 20 September 2010.

19. Bianca Fortis, "Former Florida Secretary of State Browning leads Republican-Bankrolled Anti-Fair Districts Group," *Florida Independent*, 22 October 2010.

20. Becky Bowers and Aaron Sharockman, "Opponent of Amendments 5, 6 Claims 'Liberal, Out-of-State' Donors Have Spent Millions" *Politifact Florida*, 31 October 2010, http://www.politifact.com/florida/statements/2010/oct/31/protect-your-vote/opponent-amendments-5-6-claims-liberal-out-state-d/.

21. Aaron Deslatte, "Congressional Critics of Fair Districts Florida Go Off on Amendments," *Orlando Sentinel*, 11 January 2010.

22. "Protect Your Vote," Campaign Contributions, Florida Division of Elections, 31 October 2010.

23. Adam C. Smith, "Florida's Ballot Initiative to Ban Gerrymandering Starts to Draw Foes," *St. Petersburg Times*, 30 August 2009.

24. According to the Florida Division of Elections, there were 4.63 million registered Democrats and 4.04 million registered Republicans in the 2010 election.

25. Lane Wright, "Amendments 5 and 6: The Battle of Less Bad," *Sunshine State News*, 25 October 2010.

26. Aaron Deslatte, "Legislators Set Aside Millions to Defend Redistricting," *Orlando Sentinel*, 4 May 2011.

27. Catherine Whittenburg, "Florida Redistricting Attracts Amendments, Lawsuits," *Tampa Bay Times*, 31 May 2010.

28. Ron Word, "Software Will Help Draw District Lines," *Gainesville Sun*, 16 March 2010.

29. Howard Troxler, "House Passes 'Clarifying' Amendment to Fair Districts," *St. Petersburg Times*, 26 April 2010.

30. On the same day it removed Amendment 7 from the ballot, the Supreme Court denied a challenge to the validity of Amendments 5 and 6. See Marc Caputo and Lee Logan, "Judge Blocks Florida Legislature's Redistricting Amendment from November Ballot," *St. Petersburg Times*, 9 July 2010; Lee Logan, "3 Amendments Kept Off Florida Ballot," *Miami Herald*, 1 September 2010.

31. John Kennedy, "U.S. Reps Sue to Block Redistricting Amendment," *Sunshine State News*, 26 May 2010.

32. The Voting Rights Act of 1965, as part of a broader effort to abolish racial discrimination in voting, mandates that "no voting qualification or prerequisite to voting" can be "applied . . . in a manner which results in a denial or abridgement of the right of any citizen . . . to vote on account of race or color." Some studies have shown that minorities are more likely to engage in the political process and more likely to be satisfied with government if they reside in a majority-minority district. See Barreto, Segura, and Woods, "Mobilizing Effect," 65–75; Marschall and Ruhil, "Substantive Symbols," 17–33. What is less clear from the literature is whether descriptive representation actually leads to greater substantive representation for minorities. See Cameron, Epstein, and O'Halloran, "Do Majority-Minority Districts Maximize Substantive Black Representation in Congress?" 794–812; Bratton, "Effect of Legislative Diversity on Agenda Setting," 115–42; Grose, "Disentangling Constituency," 427–43.

33. Corrine Brown et al. v. State of Florida et al., U.S. Court of Appeals for the 11th Circuit, No. 11-14554. See also Aaron Deslatte, "Bipartisan Duo Blasts Efforts They Say Will Destroy Minority Congressional Districts," *Orlando Sentinel*, 12 January 2010.

34. Florida Department of State: Division of Elections, "Standards for Legislature to Follow in Legislative Redistricting," 16 July 2010.

35. Tolbert, Smith, and Green, "Strategic Voting."

36. Bowler and Donovan, "Reasoning About Institutional Change," 455–76; Bowler, Donovan, and Karp, "Why Politicians Like Electoral Institutions," 434–46.

37. Tolbert, Smith, and Green, "Strategic Voting."

38. Anderson and Tverdova, "Winners, Losers, and Attitudes," 321–38; Anderson et al., *Losers' Consent*.

39. Fougere, Ansolabehere, and Persily, "Partisanship, Public Opinion, and Redistricting," 325–47.

40. We would like to thank Jill Hanauer and Project New America for providing us access and use of these polling data, http://www.projectnewamerica.com/.

41. The Harstad statewide survey oversampled 101 Latinos and 102 African Americans.

42. Each respondent was read the ballot summary for either Amendment 5 or Amendment 6. The respondent was then asked, "If the election were today, how would you vote

on this amendment—would you definitely vote yes, probably vote yes, probably vote no, or definitely vote no?"

43. The African American majority-minority congressional districts were the 3rd, 17th, and 23rd.

44. The African American majority-minority state senate districts were the 1st, 29th, and 33rd. The African American majority-minority state House districts were the 8th, 14th, 15th, 39th, 55th, 59th, 84th, 93rd, 94th, 103rd, 104th, 108th, and 109th.

45. The Latino majority-minority congressional districts were the 18th, 21st, and 25th. The Latino majority-minority state senate districts were the 36th, 38th, and 40th. The Latino majority-minority state house districts were the 102nd, 107th, 110th, 111th, 112th, 113th, 114th, 115th, 116th, 117th, and 119th.

46. We ran logistic regression models (not shown) to test for any significant relationships between a host of predictor and control variables (including party, race, majority-minority district residence, and minority representation, among others) and support for Amendments 5 and 6. Universally across our models, including models restricted by race, no combination of independent variables predicted support for either Amendment 5 or 6 (our dependent variables) at any commonly accepted level of significance. We interpret this as further evidence of the broad-based support across demographics we saw for the Fair Districts Amendments in our bivariate relationships.

47. The counties from which we gathered election data therefore were Alachua, Broward, Clay, Duval, Lake, Marion, Miami-Dade, Orange, Pinellas, Putnam, Seminole, and Volusia.

48. The case *Brown v. State of Florida* was filed on 3 November 2010. See also Ben Smith, "Florida Districting Fight Heads to Court, As Expected," *Politico*, 3 November 2010.

49. The argument at this point would seemingly be that Amendments 5 and 6 violate the U.S. Constitution and the Voting Rights Act of 1965 because they are themselves now a part of the state constitution, having been codified in Article III.

50. Brandon Larrabee, "Judge Upholds Fair Districts Amendment," *News Service of Florida*, 9 September 2011.

Chapter 5. Redistricting in Florida: Loud Voices from the Grassroots

1. Mary Ellen Klas, "Before the Ink Dries on Florida's Redistricting Maps, Lawsuits Fly," *Miami Herald*, 9 February 2012.

2. Florida Senate Hearing Reports, www.flsenate.gov/Session/Redistricting/Hearings.

3. Florida House of Representatives Public Information Office, "OPI Pulse: 2012 Redistricting," 1 February 2012, PublicInfo@myfloridahouse.gov.

4. Matt Dixon, "2 Lawsuits Follow Florida Senate's Final Passage of Redistricting Maps," *Florida Times-Union*, 9 February 2012.

5. King, Feltey, and Susel, "Questions of Participation," 317–26.

6. See for example Stivers, "Public Agency as Polis," 86–105; Delli Carpini, Cook, and Jacobs, "Public Deliberation," 315–44; Roberts, "Public Deliberation," 315–53; Irvin and Stansbury, "Citizen Participation," 55–65.

7. King, Feltey, and Susel, "Questions of Participation," 319.

8. Citizen participation has been an integral part of government at all levels for over 50 years, beginning with the War on Poverty's Economic Opportunity Act of 1964 that

established the Community Action Program calling for "maximum feasible participation" for those excluded or ignored by government. See Roberts, "Public Deliberation," 321, and Crosby, Kelly, and Schaefer, "Citizens Panels," 170–78.

9. Roberts, "Public Deliberation," 326.

10. Ibid., 341.

11. Ibid., 337.

12. King, Feltey, and Susel, "Questions of Participation," 319.

13. Hayes and McKee, "Participatory Effects," 1006–23.

14. Walters, Aydelotte, and Miller, "Putting More Public in Policy Analysis," 349–59.

15. Stivers, "Listening Bureaucrat," 364–69.

16. Checkoway, "Politics of Public Hearings," 566–82; Lando, "Public Hearing Process," 73–82; Adams, "Public Meetings," 43–54; Innes and Booher, "Reframing Public Participation," 419–36; Irvin and Stansbury, "Citizen Participation," 55–65; King, Feltey, and Susel, "Questions of Participation."

17. Checkoway, "Politics of Public Hearings"; Roberts, "Public Deliberation."

18. Checkoway, "Politics of Public Hearings," 575.

19. Rosener, "Citizen Participation," 457–63; Kweit and Kweit, *Implementing Citizen Participation in a Bureaucratic Society.*

20. The senate website detailed how the process would work and what citizen input should be directed toward influence:

> The Legislature will draw lines following the standards in Amendments 5 and 6 and traditional redistricting principles not inconsistent with those standards. *To this end, Legislature encourages public testimony directed to following points:* (1) The full implementation of the protections afforded by the Amendments to racial and language minorities, including continuance of the Legislature's long-established policy to preserve or enhance the number of performing minority districts; (2) The various measures of compactness, from geometric calculations to a broad consideration of how communities relate to one another, for example through commerce, transportation, and communication—in order to promote the creation of effective representational units; (3) The feasibility of using political and geographical boundaries in the formation of districts, in light of other standards such as the equality of district populations, the protection of racial and language minorities, and compactness; and (4) To the extent not inconsistent with the Amendments, the desire to preserve the cores of existing districts or the proper placement of communities of interest in districts, as determined by local circumstances and voter preferences.

21. Florida House of Representatives Office of Public Information. "OPI Pulse: 2012 Redistricting," 1 February 2012, http://mydistrictbuilder.wordpress.com.

22. Senator Don Gaetz, *Redistricting Committee, Florida Legislature; Transcription of Public Hearing, Florida State College Jacksonville Downtown Campus, Jacksonville, FL, July 11, 2011,* http://www.flsenate.gov/PublishedContent/Session/Redistricting/Hearings/5/LR-836-JACKSONVILLE-2PM-STATE.pdf.

23. Representative Will Weatherford, *Redistricting Committee, Florida Legislature; Transcription of Public Hearing, Florida State College Jacksonville Downtown Campus, Jacksonville, FL, July 11, 2011,* http://www.flsenate.gov/PublishedContent/Session/Redistricting/Hearings/5/LR-836-JACKSONVILLE-2PM-STATE.pdf.

24. King, Feltey, and Susel, "Questions of Participation," 319.

25. Roberts, "Public Deliberation," 326.

26. Florida House of Representatives Office of Public Information, "OPI Pulse: 2012 Redistricting."

27. Checkoway, "Politics of Public Hearings."

28. King, Feltey, and Susel, "Questions of Participation," 323.

29. Roberts, "Public Deliberation," 331.

30. King, Feltey, and Susel, "Questions of Participation."

31. Arnstein, "Ladder of Citizen Participation," 216–24.

32. Walters, Aydelotte, and Miller, "Putting More Public in Policy Analysis," 354.

33. Ibid., 353.

34. Irvin and Stansbury, "Citizen Participation," 57.

35. Walters, Aydelotte, and Miller, "Putting More Public in Policy Analysis," 357.

36. Irvin and Stansbury, "Citizen Participation," 58.

37. Rosener, "Citizen Participation."

38. Checkoway, "Politics of Public Hearings."

39. Crosby, Kelly, and Schaefer, "Citizens Panels," 171.

40. Walters, Aydelotte, and Miller, "Putting More Public in Policy Analysis," 355.

41. The Public Hearing Data Base was created by the authors from public comments made at 26 public hearings for the purpose of statistical analysis.

42. Twenty-nine people spoke at multiple hearing sites (24 people spoke twice; 2 three times, 2 four times, and 1 person five times for a total of 67 multiple appearances out of 1,368 (4.9 percent). Among the 29 "multiple speakers," 16 appeared as private citizens, 4 for ACLU, 2 for LWV, 1 a county supervisor of elections, 1 for LULAC, and 5 for a combination of private citizen-some other affiliation. These multiple speakers were included in the database because their responses were often not identical, reflecting different recommendations and concerns at different hearing sites.

43. The Legislative Map Drafts Reaction Data Base was created by the authors for the purpose of statistical analysis from public comments submitted to the house and the senate between November 28, 2011, and January 31, 2012, in reaction to preliminary maps drawn and released by both chambers.

44. Florida Senate written submissions, www.flsenate.gov/PublishedContent/SESSION/HOME/REDISTRICTING2012/PUBLICCOMMENTS/Email_Comments_PCBs.pdf; Florida House written submissions, http://mydistrictbuilderplanexplorer.wordpress.com/public-comment-on-legislative-proposals/.

45. As of this writing, the legislature has not distributed any quantitative analysis of the public comments received. However, the house has acknowledged that, "Redistricting Committee Members and staff focused their attention on applying the public testimony provided to draw the proposed maps." The report identified several common prescriptions made by the public: "(1) Keep counties and municipalities whole when possible to give more voters the chance to elect candidates from their own county increasing their voice in elections; (2) ensure that specific populations within communities, have a meaningful voice in elections; and (3) Comply with the new standards established by Amendments 5 and 6 of the Florida Constitution." See Florida House of Representatives Office of Public Information, "OPI Pulse: 2012 Redistricting." The lack of a database meant that one had to

be created by this research team, often from rather limited information. By the house's own admission, the written public comments posted were not comprehensive.

46. According to the legislature, there were more signed up to speak, but some ended up not doing so for various reasons and others submitted written comments rather than make public statements.

47. The counties not represented are Bradford, Calhoun, DeSoto, Dixie, Franklin, Gulf, Hamilton, Holmes, Liberty, Madison, Suwannee, and Washington. Forty percent of the speakers did not identify their county of residence.

48. Any group that was part of the coalition conducting the petition drive to put Amendments 5 and 6 on the November 2010 ballot, any group that endorsed the Fair Districts amendments, or any group that joined in the litigation challenging the constitutionality of the Florida Legislature's approved congressional and state legislative redistricting plans.

49. Deborah Clark, Pinellas County Supervisor of Elections, *Redistricting Committee, Florida Legislature; Transcription of Public Hearing, EpiCenter at St. Petersburg College, Largo, Florida, August 30, 2011,* http://www.flsenate.gov/PublishedContent/Session/Redistricting/Hearings/22/LR-918-LARGO-STATE.pdf.

50. Representative Will Weatherford, *Redistricting Committee, Florida Legislature; Transcription of Public Hearing, Gulf Coast Community College, Panama City Florida, June 22, 2011,* http://www.flsenate.gov/PublishedContent/Session/Redistricting/Hearings/4/LR-764-PANAMA%20CITY-STATE.PDF.

51. Aaron Deslatte, "Cannon: Florida House Will Appeal Fair Districts Ruling, *Orlando Sentinel,* 29 September 2011, articles.orlandosentinel.com/2011-09-29/news/os-cannon-to-appeal-fair-districts-ruling-20110929_1_fair-districts-congressional-district-maps-congressional-boundaries.

52. Of the 239 speakers who complained about public comment coming before maps were drafted, 11 percent specifically cited incumbent protection as the real reason behind this decision, while 5 percent viewed it as evidence of "making a mockery of the citizen-approved Fair Districts amendments."

53. Senator Don Gaetz, *Redistricting Committee, Florida Legislature; Transcription of Public Hearing, Bob Carr Performing Arts Center, Orlando, Florida, July 27, 2011,* http://www.flsenate.gov/PublishedContent/Session/Redistricting/Hearings/13/LR-843-ORLANDO-STATE.pdf.

54. Amy Sherman, "Weatherford Denies $30 Million Pot Exists for Redistricting," *PolitiFact Florida,* 28 June 2011, www.politifact.com/florida/statements/2011/jun/28/will-weatherford/weatherford-denies-30-million-pot-exists-redistric/.

55. Carolyn Woods, City of Atlantic Beach Commissioner, *Redistricting Committee, Florida Legislature; Transcription of Public Hearing, Florida State College Jacksonville Downtown Campus, Jacksonville, FL, July 11, 2011,* http://www.flsenate.gov/PublishedContent/Session/Redistricting/Hearings/5/LR-836-JACKSONVILLE-2PM-STATE.pdf.

56. Mary Lou Woods, *Redistricting Committee, Florida Legislature; Transcription of Public Hearing, Flagler College, St. Augustine, FL, July 12, 2011,* http://www.flsenate.gov/PublishedContent/Session/Redistricting/Hearings/6/LR-830-ST%5B1%5D.AUGUSTINE-STATE.pdf.

57. Representative Will Weatherford, *Redistricting Committee, Florida Legislature;*

Transcription of Public Hearing, WSRE-TV Jean & Paul Amos Performance Studio, Pensacola, FL, June 21, 2011, https://www.flsenate.gov/PublishedContent/Session/Redistricting/Hearings/2/LR-762-PENSACOLA-STATE.pdf.

58. Representative John Legg, *Redistricting Committee, Florida Legislature; Transcription of Public Hearing, Veterans Park Recreation Center, Lehigh Acres, FL, August 31, 2011*, http://www.flsenate.gov/PublishedContent/Session/Redistricting/Hearings/25/LR923-LEHIGHACRES.pdf.

59. Betsy Barfield, Jefferson County Commissioner, *Redistricting Committee, Florida Legislature; Transcription of Public Hearing, 412 Knott Building, Tallahassee, FL, June 20, 2011*, http://www.flsenate.gov/PublishedContent/Session/Redistricting/Hearings/1/LR-761-TALLA-1PM-STATE.pdf.

60. Sheri Morton, *Redistricting Committee, Florida Legislature; Transcription of Public Hearing, Bob Carr Performing Arts Center, Orlando, Florida, July 27, 2011*, http://www.flsenate.gov/PublishedContent/Session/Redistricting/Hearings/13/LR-843-ORLANDO-STATE.pdf.

61. In the Florida House of Representatives' brief to the Florida Supreme Court defending the house redistricting plan, fifteen different measures of compactness were reported.

62. Gepsi Metellus, *Redistricting Committee, Florida Legislature; Transcription of Public Hearing, Miami Dade College, Wolfson Campus, Miami, Florida, August 17, 2011*, http://www.flsenate.gov/PublishedContent/Session/Redistricting/Hearings/18/LR-861-MIAMI-STATE.pdf.

63. Patrick Manteiga, *Redistricting Committee, Florida Legislature; Transcription of Public Hearing, Jefferson High School Auditorium, Tampa, Florida, August 29, 2011*, http://www.flsenate.gov/PublishedContent/Session/Redistricting/Hearings/21/LR-901-TAMPA-1-STATE.pdf.

64. Alex Belloa, *Redistricting Committee, Florida Legislature; Transcription of Public Hearing, 412 Knott Building, Tallahassee, Florida, June 20, 2011*, http://www.flsenate.gov/PublishedContent/Session/Redistricting/Hearings/1/LR-761-TALLA-1PM-STATE.pdf.

65. Joan Carver, *Redistricting Committee, Florida Legislature; Transcription of Public Hearing, Florida State College Jacksonville Downtown Campus, Jacksonville, FL, July 11, 2011*, http://www.flsenate.gov/PublishedContent/Session/Redistricting/Hearings/5/LR-836-JACKSONVILLE-2PM-STATE.pdf.

66. Mary Jane Arrington, Osceola County Supervisor of Elections, *Redistricting Committee, Florida Legislature; Transcription of Public Hearing, Bob Carr Performing Arts Center, Orlando, Florida, July 27, 2011*, http://www.flsenate.gov/PublishedContent/Session/Redistricting/Hearings/13/LR-843-ORLANDO-STATE.pdf.

67. Current state law prohibits the drawing of state legislative districts until the year in which the redistricting takes place, in this case 2012.Yet, there is not such a prohibition against congressional districts. The senate released a single congressional map while the house proposed three. See *Orlando Sentinel* blog, *Political Pulse*, http://blogs.orlandosentinel.com/news_politics/2012/01/house-advances-three-congressional-maps.html.

68. Ibid.

69. The actual number of responses entered into the data base was 634. The other responses were merely described as mirroring the others.

70. Florida Senate written submissions, www.flsenate.gov/PublishedContent/SESSION/HOME/REDISTRICTING2012/PUBLICCOMMENTS/Email_Comments_PCBs.

pdf; Florida House written submissions, mydistrictbuilderplanexplorer.wordpress.com/public-comment-on-legislative-proposals/.

71. Florida House of Representatives Office of Public Information, "OPI Pulse: 2012 Redistricting."

72. MacManus et al., "Redistricting 2012," 84–87.

73. Initially, a federal district court ruled against Brown and Diaz-Balart on 9 September 2012. A federal Court of Appeals upheld the trial court verdict on 31 January 2012.

74. For example, the revised house map changed its initial proposal to split the unincorporated area of Estero and kept it together instead in response to citizen input. See Ben Wolford, "Together Again: New House Redistricting Maps Keep Estero Whole," *Naples Daily News*, 27 January 2012. Similarly, rather than putting Sarasota and most of Manatee counties into separate congressional districts, revised maps in both houses ended up keeping the counties together. See Jeremy Wallace, "Sarasota and Manatee May Share One District," *Sarasota Herald-Tribune*, 29 January 2012. Keeping cities and counties together, compactness, and minority representation were the most common reasons given for revisions to the initially proposed maps.

75. On 9 February 2012, a suit was filed in state court (Florida Circuit Count, Leon County) challenging the congressional plan based on Fair Districts constitutional standards. The complaint argued that the plan was "brazenly drawn with an unlawful intent to favor a political party and incumbents, sacrificing objective tier-two criteria of compactness and adherence to natural boundaries in the process. . . . The Plan was drawn without a proper analysis of minority voting rights from the outset." Under Florida law, state legislative plans are automatically sent to the Florida Supreme Court for review and on 9 March 2012, the Florida Supreme Court approved the state house plan but struck down the state senate plan because 8 of the 40 districts violated some elements of the Fair Districts amendment. The state legislature then redid the senate map and, on 27 March 2012, passed SJR 2-B (a revised senate plan), which was approved by the Florida Supreme Court. The house, revised senate, and congressional district plans were all pre-cleared by the U.S. Department of Justice on 30 April 2012, allowing elections under the new plans to be held in 2012. Democrats gained seats in Congress (4), the Florida Senate (2), and the Florida House (5). On 5 September 2012, the senate plan was again challenged in state court (Florida Circuit Court, Leon County) by the League of Women Voters of Florida, Common Cause, and the National Council of La Raza. The groups charged that five senate districts (three in the Tampa area, 17, 19, and 22) and two in the Orlando area, 10 and 13) were drawn to protect a GOP majority and that Districts 22 (see Hillsborough and Pinellas Deslatte, "Fair Districts Groups Challenge Florida Senate Maps," *Orlando Sentinel*, 6 September 2012) and 13 (downtown Orlando) were not compact enough. See James Call, "New Lawsuit Challenges Senate Redistricting," *Florida Current*, 5 September 2012; Steve Bousquet, "Group Files Lawsuit over Court-Approved Senate Redistricting Maps," *Tampa Bay Times*, 5 September 2012. For a good review of the litigation chronology, see Justin Levitt, "All About Redistricting," http://redistricting.lls.edu/cases-FL.php#FL.

Chapter 6. Paradoxes of Political Reform: Congressional Redistricting in Florida

1. Hirsch, "United States House of Unrepresentatives," 179–216.

2. McDonald, "Re-Drawing the Line," 99–102.

3. Olga Pierce and Jeff Larson, "How Democrat's Fooled California's Redistricting Commission," *ProPublica*, 21 December 2011.

4. Chen and Rodden, "Unintentional Gerrymandering," 239–69.

5. Gronke and Wilson, "Competing Redistricting Plans," 147–76; Johnson et al., *Restoring Competitive Edge*; McKee, Teigan, and Turgeon, "Partisan Impact," 308–17; McDonald, *Midwest Mapping Project*.

6. Altman and McDonald, "Promise and Perils," 69–112.

7. Altman and McDonald, "A Half-Century of Virginia Redistricting Battles," 771–831.

8. Swann v. Adams, 378 U.S. 553 (1965).

9. Dauer, Maggiotto, and Koven, "Florida," 74–81. For a discussion of Florida's historical provisions for state legislative and congressional redistricting, see McKay, *Reapportionment*, 300–303.

10. Lund v. Mathas, 145 So. 2D 871 (Fla. 1962).

11. Wesberry v. Sanders, 376 U.S. 1 (1964).

12. Gong v. Bryant, 230 F. Supp. 917 (S. D. Fla 1964).

13. Thornburg v. Gingles, 478 U.S. 30 (1986). See also *Bartlett v. Strickland*, 556 U.S. 1 (2009), which requires the demonstration district to be at least 50 percent minority voting age population.

14. Hirsch, "United States House of Unrepresentatives."

15. Grofman, Koetzle, and Brunell, "An Integrated Perspective," 457–70.

16. "Supreme Court Kills Ballot Measure Meant to Let Voters Change Redistricting," *Associated Press*, 23 March 2006.

17. Florida Division of Elections, "Proposed Constitutional Amendments to Be Voted On, November 2, 2010," updated version (09-01-10).

18. *Advisory Opinion to Attorney General re Standards for Establishing Legislative District Boundaries*, 2 So. 3d 175, 191 (Fla. 2009).

19. Dawn Roberts v. Corrine Brown, No. 10-1362.

20. Gary Fineout, "Groups File Suit on Redistricting Ballot Measure," *Miami Herald-Tribune*, 22 May 2010.

21. Dawn Roberts v. NAACP, No. 10-1375, 13.

22. Florida Department of State, Division of Elections, "November 2, 2010, General Election, Official Results, Constitutional Amendment."

23. Aaron Deslatte, "Scott Enters Redistricting Fight," *Orlando Sentinel*, 25 January 2011.

24. League of Women Voters, et al. v. Scott, 4: 2011-cv-10006.

25. John Kennedy, "Update: Amends 5 & 6 Sent to Justice Department After GOP Delay," *Palm Beach Post*, 29 March 2011; Mark Matthews and Aaron Deslatte, "DOJ Has Approved Fair Districts Amendments," *Orlando Sentinel*, 31 May 2011.

26. Diaz-Balart v. Scott, No. 1:10-CV-23968 (S. D. Fla.) and No. 11-14554 (11th Cir.).

27. *In re: 2012 Joint Resolution of Apportionment*, No. SC12-1.

28. *In re: Senate Joint Resolution of Legislative Apportionment 2-B*, No. SC12-460.

29. League of Women Voters of Florida v. Detzner (LWV II), No. 2012-CA-002842.

30. Romo v. Scott, No. 2012-CA-000412 (Fla. Cir. Ct., Leon County) and No. 1D12-5280.

31. Altman, Mac Donald, and McDonald, "Pushbutton Gerrymanders?" 51–66.

32. Altman and McDonald, "Promise and Perils."

33. Altman and McDonald, "A Half-Century."

34. "Florida Legislature Unveils Redistricting Software." Press release from Florida House of Representatives, office of Speaker Tom Feeney, July 12, 2001.

35. Plans for the post-2000 redistricting obtained at the Florida Senate website archive, archive.flsenate.gov.

36. MyDistrictBuilder software available at www.floridaredistricting.org.

37. District Builder software available at www.flsenate.gov/Session/Redistricting/sign _up.cfm.

38. Ibid.

39. See "63 Public Submissions of Florida Redistricting Maps!" and "Milestone: 100 Proposed Redistricting Maps from Floridians," Florida House Redistricting Committee blog, mydistrictbuilder.wordpress.com/2011/09/11/63-public-submissions-of-florida -redistricting-maps, and mydistrictbuilder.wordpress.com/2011/10/20/milestone-100 -proposed-redistricting-maps-from-floridians.

40. Altman and McDonald, "A Half-Century."

41. Altman and McDonald, "BARD," 1–28.

42. Chen and Rodden, "Unintentional Gerrymandering." See also, Hendrick Hertzberg, "Mandate with Destiny," New Yorker, 3 December 2012.

43. Replication data for all of the analyses conducted are available from Altman and McDonald, "Replication Data for Paradoxes of Political Reform: Congressional Redistricting in Florida," http://dx.doi.org/10.7910/DVN/26556; Program on Informatics, MIT Library [Distributor] V1 [Version].

44. "Redistricting Data," U.S. Census Bureau website, www.census.gov/rdo/.

45. See "Open Data and Code for MyDistrictBuilder," Florida House Redistricting Committee blog, mydistrictbuilder.wordpress.com/opendata.

46. Cox, "Partisan Fairness," 751–802; McDonald, "Regulating Redistricting," 675–79.

47. Shaw v. Reno, 509 U.S. 630 (1993), for example.

48. Niemi et al., "Measuring Compactness," 1155–81; Altman, Districting Principles.

49. For a discussion of the Cox and Schwartzberg measure, see Niemi et al., "Measuring Compactness." For a demonstration of the equivalence of this with other alternative measures, see Altman, Districting Principles, chapter 2.

50. We also examine plans that respect what are known as census places, and find a high correlation between plans that respect county boundaries and census place boundaries. For the sake of brevity, we present analysis of county splits only.

51. Thornburg v. Gingles, 478 U.S. 30 (1986). While this landmark case describes a federal Voting Rights Act Section 2 challenge, similar principles apply to measuring racially polarized voting in Voting Rights Act Section 5 litigation. For a comprehensive review of statistical methods to measure racially polarized voting, see Gary King, Solution to Ecological Inference Problem.

52. In calculating these statistics, we follow the Office of Management and Budget Bulletin no. 00-02 (9 March 2000) that a race, such as black, includes all persons who identify themselves to the decennial census as black alone or in combination with another race. Hispanic is tallied from a separate ethnicity question. Persons who identify themselves Hispanic and black are counted more than once by this method.

53. The methods have been used in academic, practical, and legal arenas. For the par-

tisan fairness measure, see Stokes, *Legislative Redistricting by New Jersey Plan*; Grofman and King, "Future of Partisan Symmetry," 2–35; Kousser, "Estimating the Partisan Consequences," 521–41. For the political competition measure, see *In Re 2001 Redistricting Cases* (Case No. S-10504).

54. The student redistricting competition used the 2009 gubernatorial election to evaluate partisan balance and competition. Precinct level election returns for the 2009 governor's election are highly correlated with other recent statewide elections (all correlation coefficients greater than .95), including the 2008 presidential election. Although not a component of this analysis, we are ultimately interested in comparing Virginia with other states, an effort which requires a common metric such as the national election for president.

55. A ten point range is often used by political scientists to identify a competitive election, e.g., Mayhew, "Congressional Elections," 295–317. For a discussion of a more precise measure of what constitutes a competitive district, see McDonald, "Redistricting and District Competition," 222–44. We have not used more advanced techniques to measure the range that would constitute a competitive district for Florida elections as it requires intensive analysis of legislative elections.

56. We included one plan, identified as hpubc0003 on the legislature's website, which did not assign two zero-population census blocks.

57. Altman and McDonald, "A Half-Century."

58. Scott Maxwell, "Follow the Money: Pols Try to Undermine Your Vote," *Orlando Sentinel*, 17 November 2010.

59. Identified by the legislature as plan hpubc0150.

60. Identified by the legislature as plan hpubc0159.

Chapter 7. Running with Uncertainty: Candidate Emergence during Redistricting in Florida

1. We wish to thank Alexandra Cockerham-Groom for assistance in data collection for this project.

2. See House Rule 15.3(b) and Senate Rule 1.361. Also, see the National Conference of State Legislatures website, www.ncsl.org/research/elections-and-campaigns/limits-on-contributions-during-session.aspx.

3. Matt Dixon, "Candidates Await New Maps; Florida Redistricting Process Throws More Uncertainty into Political Races," *Florida Times-Union*, 2 October 2011.

4. George Wilkens, "Republican Dan Raulerson Begins His Run," *Tampa Tribune*, 1 February 2012.

5. William March, "Dems See Some Gain in Florida Contests but Party Members Point to Difficulty in Recruiting Candidates," *Tampa Tribune*, 10 June 2012.

6. George Bennett, "Is Legislature Dragging Feet on Redrawing Maps?" *Palm Beach Post*, 17 August 2011.

7. Madison, "Federalist #44," 277–84.

8. See Canes-Wrone, Brady, and Cogan, "Out of Step, Out of Office," 127–40; Stone, Maisel, and Maestas, "Quality Counts," 479–95.

9. Jackson, "A Reassessment of Voter Mobilization," 331–49; Coleman and Manna, "Congressional Campaign Spending," 757–89.

10. Jacobson, *Politics*, 123–25; Kaid, "Paid Television Advertising," 34–36.

11. See, for example, Stimson, MacKuen, and Erikson, "Dynamic Representation," 542–65.

12. Data on U.S. House elections from 1970 to 2012 were generously provided by Gary C. Jacobson, University of California at San Diego.

13. Jacobson, *Politics*, 38–41.

14. These numbers exclude incumbents running against each other due to redistricting and incumbents defeated in primary elections.

15. Florida Division of Elections, book-closing statistics, general election 2008, election.dos.state.fl.us/voter-registration/statistics/elections.shtml#2008.

16. George Bennett, "Boundary Rules Boost Democrats' Hopes," *Palm Beach Post*, 10 January 2011; William March, "Dems See Some Gain," *Tampa Tribune*, 10 June 2012.

17. Carson, Engstrom, and Roberts, "Redistricting," 283–93; Kazee, "Deterrent Effect," 469–80; Maestas et al., "When to Risk It?" 195–208.

18. Herrnson, "National Party Decision Making," 301–23; Maestas, Maisel, and Stone, "National Party Efforts," 277–300.

19. Gordon S. Black, "A Theory of Political Ambition," 144–55; Rohde, "Risk Bearing and Progressive Ambition," 1–26; and Maestas et al., "When to Risk It?"

20. Ansolabehere, Snyder, and Stewart, "Old Voters, New Voters," 17–34.

21. Florida Division of Elections, "2011 Candidate and Campaign Treasurer Handbook," elections.myflorida.com.

22. Florida Constitution, Article III, Section 15(c).

23. For the 2012 election, candidates seeking office as a state representative or senator who opt to pay the filing fee were required to pay $1,782 for those affiliated with a political party. Like their counterparts running for state office, federal representatives may also pay a filing fee to get their name on the ballot: $10,440 for those claiming party affiliation (2012 *Federal Qualifying Handbook*, 9). For those opting to qualify by collecting signatures, the number required varies according to the position sought: for U.S. House office seekers, 2,298 signatures are required; for state senators, 1,552, and for state representatives, 518. See election.dos.state.fl.us/publications/pdf/2011/2011CandidatePetitionHandbook.pdf.

24. Dixon, Matt Dixon, "Candidates Await New Maps; Florida Redistricting Process Throws More Uncertainty into Political Races," *Florida Times-Union*, 2 October 2011.

25. Maestas et al., "When to Risk It?"

26. Stone, Maisel, and Maestas, "Quality Counts," 479–95.

27. Ansolabehere, Snyder, and Stewart, "Old Voters, New Voters."

28. Stone, Maisel, and Maestas, "Quality Counts."

29. Ansolabehere, Snyder, and Stewart, "Old Voters, New Voters."

30. For example, candidate Spence in U.S. House District 3 was defeated in the primary, but we coded him as an incumbent that filed even though the general election was technically a non-incumbent race. Similarly, in Florida House District 42, the GOP incumbent withdrew because of scandal, but he was on the ballot for the primary election.

31. Jacobson, *Politics*; Maestas and Rugeley, "Assessing the 'Experience Bonus,'" 520–35.

32. Maestas et al., "When to Risk It?"

33. Florida Division of Elections, "2011 Candidate and Campaign Treasurer Handbook."

34. Comparison to 2008 is similar to 2012 with regard to the Democratic presidential

nominee (Obama), while simultaneously controlling for potential presidential coattails effects; see Ferejohn and Calvert, "Presidential Coattails," 161–68.

35. Box-Steffensmeier, "A Dynamic Analysis," 352–71.

36. One of the concerns when running a proportional hazards model is the violation of the proportionality assumption: the assumption "that the effects of covariates are constant over time" (Box-Steffensmeier and Zorn, "Duration Models," 973). As a result, we conducted a pair of tests and found that four of the controls (challenger of the same party, male candidate, and the U.S. House and Florida Senate dummies) did violate this assumption. We corrected for this by interacting the offending variables with a logged time variable (see Box-Steffensmeier and Zorn, "Duration Models"). Despite this correction, neither the carry-forward population variable nor the increase in unbalanced registration variable was statistically significant at conventional levels. For the sake of simplicity the original model is presented here. The results of this alternative specification are available upon request.

37. All other variables held constant at their means. The difference between incumbents and challengers is statistically significant at $p < .01$. The difference between challenger and open seat candidates is not statistically significant.

Chapter 8. The Participatory Consequences of Florida Redistricting

1. Aaron Blake, "Democratic House Candidates Winning the Popular Vote, Despite Big GOP Majority," *Washington Post*, 9 November 2012.

2. John Sides and Eric McGhee, "Redistricting Didn't Win Republicans the House," *Washington Post*, 17 February 2013.

3. Gelman and King, "Enhancing Democracy," 541–59; Yoshinaka and Murphy, "Paradox of Redistricting," 435–47.

4. Jacobson, *Politics*.

5. See Downs, *Economic Theory*; Cox and Munger, "Closeness," 217–31.

6. See Hayes and McKee, "Participatory Effects," 1006–23; Hood and McKee, "Stranger Danger," 344–58; McKee, "Redistricting and Familiarity," 962–79.

7. Hayes and McKee, "Participatory Effects."

8. Winburn and Wagner, "Carving Voters Out," 373–86.

9. Hayes and McKee, "Participatory Effects."

10. Hayes and McKee, "Intersection of Redistricting," 115–30.

11. Sekhon and Titiunik, "When Natural Experiments," 35–57.

12. Hayes and McKee, "Participatory Effects."

13. Winburn and Wagner, "Carving Voters Out."

14. Hayes, Hood, and McKee, "Redistricting and Turnout."

15. Keele and White, "Role of Information."

16. Winburn and Wagner, "Carving Voters Out."

17. Hayes, Hood, and McKee, "Redistricting and Turnout."

18. Keele and White, "Role of Information."

19. Hayes and McKee, "Intersection."

20. Republican state senator Mike Fasano was term limited in 2012, and therefore he sought a state house seat.

21. Hayes and McKee, "Participatory Effects"; Hayes and McKee, "Intersection."

22. Hayes and McKee, "Intersection," 120.

23. The number of candidate returns for the presidential contest is not uniform across Florida counties, but the maximum number of separate returns (including write-in votes) is thirteen. In all three district-based offices (U.S. House, state senate, and state house), the maximum number of separate returns (including write-in votes) is four. Thus, to create the dependent variable for voter roll-off, in some precincts we have aggregated the presidential votes in up to thirteen separate columns in the dataset and aggregated the lower office votes in up to four separate columns. See appendix C for a technical explanation of how this dataset was constructed.

24. We would have liked to consider the effects of redistricting on participation when the race and ethnicity of voters in the redrawn precincts and the race and ethnicity of the incumbent seeking reelection are considered as variables, but because of data limitations, it is not a feasible approach (there are not enough precincts to place any confidence in this type of analysis). Past research (see Hayes and McKee, "Intersection") finds that black populations will exhibit higher roll-off rates when these populations are redrawn, but when African American precincts are placed into districts with a black representative, the shared racial identity reduces the negative influence of redistricting on participation. The number of so-called racially homogeneous precincts in Florida (i.e., where African American turnout is greater than or equal to 95 percent) is much too small (N = 9) to perform this type of analysis. In addition, with respect to Latinos, there is not one precinct in Florida that exhibits a rate of Hispanic turnout greater than or equal to 95 percent.

25. For vote returns data, see Florida Division of Elections website, doe.dos.state.fl.us/elections/resultsarchive/index.asp.

26. Similar to the data displayed in table 8.2, for these bivariate correlations we exclude the ten districts with the chamber switching incumbents featured in table 8.3.

27. The spending variable is divided by $100,000.

28. The models presented in tables 4 and 5 were generated using the xtreg command in Stata 11.

Chapter 9. Elections in a Brave New World: Reform, Redistricting, and the Battle for the 2012 Legislature

1. Robert Draper, "League of Dangerous Mapmakers," *Atlantic Magazine*, October 2012. Draper provides a good overview of the political motives and environment in today's redistricting battles.

2. Born, "Partisan Intentions," 305–19; Cain, "Assessing," 320–33; Niemi and Winsky, "Persistence of Partisan Redistricting Effects," 565–72; Masket, Winburn, and Wright, "Gerrymanderers Are Coming!" 39–43.

3. Mayhew, *Congress;* and Tufte, "The Relationship," 540–54.

4. For analysts who observed a bump, see Born, "Partisan Intentions." For analysts finding no real advantage, see Niemi and Abramowitz, "Partisan Redistricting," 811–17.

5. See Butler and Cain, *Congressional Redistricting*, for a good discussion of commission incentives. For other work on the role of commissions, see Carson and Crespin, "Effect of State Redistricting Methods," 455–69; Winburn, "Does it Matter if Legislatures or Commissions Draw the Lines?" 137–60; and Masket, Winburn, and Wright, "Gerrymanderers Are Coming!"

6. Winburn, *Realities of Redistricting*.

7. This process involves overlaying the old and new maps onto the state's precincts (or census blocks, tracts, or voting tabulation districts) and determining the location of each unit in the old and new maps. With the demographic and population data from each precinct, I determine the amount, in terms of population, of each old district that goes into the new districts. This creates a breakdown for the new districts by their old district component parts. The state of Florida provides this breakdown on their redistricting website.

8. Cox and Katz, *Elbridge Gerry's Salamander*.

9. Gelman and King, "Enhancing Democracy," 541–59; Gaddie and Bullock, *Elections to Open Seats*; Kousser, "Estimating the Partisan Consequences," 521–41. The results of this model allow for a check on the influence of redistricting as suggested by Gaddie and Bullock, "Political Consequences."

10. Kousser, "Estimating the Partisan Consequences."

11. Katie Sanders, "Florida Holds the Record for Redistricting Incumbents Together, Will Weatherford Says," *Politifact Florida*, 13 April 2012.

12. Mary Ellen Klas, "Redrawn Senate Map Passes House, Scramble for Seats Begin," *Tampa Bay Times*, 27 March 2012.

13. See Schaffner, Wagner, and Winburn, "Incumbents Out, Party In?" 396–414.

14. Klas, "Redrawn Senate Map Passes."

15. Patricia Mazzei, "Rep. Ana Rivas Logan Says Rival Campaign Worker Is Defaming Her by Telling Voters She's 'Bad Mother,'" *Miami Herald*, 7 August 2012.

16. Lloyd Dunkelberger, "Democrats Hope Redistricting Results in Seat Gains," *Gainesville Sun*, 10 June 2012.

17. Ibid.

18. Weatherford was only becoming Speaker due to the surprising loss of Speaker-in-waiting, Chris Dorworth. Therefore, the comments come tinged with a bit of irony. "Redistricting, Amendments, Create More Competition," *Associated Press*, 9 November 2012.

19. Jason Garcia, "Dorworth, In Line to Be House Speaker, Now in Danger of Losing His Seat Altogether," *Orlando Sentinel*, 7 November 2012.

20. Spending data obtained from *Follow the Money* website, www.followthemoney.org/database/.

21. Scott Maxwell, "Chris Dorworth's Defeat Was Florida's Political Story of the Year," *Orlando Sentinel*, 27 December 2012.

Chapter 10. Effects of Redistricting in Congressional Elections

1. Four of the Democrats lost general elections, one lost in the primary, one retired, and the seventh switched to the GOP. For analyses of the controversial Texas "re-redistricting," see McKee and McKenzie, "Analyzing Redistricting Outcomes," 95–146; McKee, Teigen, and Turgeon, "Partisan Impact of Congressional Redistricting," 308–17; McKee and Shaw, "Redistricting in Texas," 275–311.

2. The legislative maneuvering that produced the DeLay plan is set forth in great detail in Bickerstaff, *Lines in the Sand*.

3. Aaron Blake, "'Fairness' in Florida and How It Could Help Democrats," *Washington Post*, 17 February 2011.

4. Ibid.

5. Aaron Blake, "Breaking Down Florida GOP's Redistricting Map," *Washington Post*, 26 January 2012.

6. Alan Byrd, qtd. in Kenric Ward, "Hold Onto Your Seat: Redistricting Has John Mica Seeking New Home," *Sunshine State News*, 1 February 2012.

7. "Mica Seeks Reelection in District 7," http://www.micaforcongress.com, 2 February 2012.

8. Joshua Miller, "Republicans Expect Ugly Florida Primary," *Roll Call*, 8 May 2012.

9. Rosalind S. Helderman, "More Intra Party Incumbent Fights than Ever," *Washington Post*, 24 July 2012.

10. Tia Mitchell, "Tea Party Galvanizes Florida GOP Primary," *Tampa Bay Times*, 8 August 2012.

11. Mark Lane, "Lessons from Primary Weren't Expected," *Daytona Beach News-Journal*, 17 August 2012.

12. Bill Thompson, "Stearns Left with Plenty of Campaign Cash after Defeat," *Gainesville Sun*, 17 August 2012.

13. Matt Dixon, "Republican Primary a Bitter Election: Newly Drawn U.S. House District 3 Candidates Tear Each Other Down," *Florida Times-Union*, 3 August 2012.

14. Timothy Gibbons, "Bachmann, Ryan Support Stearns," *Florida Times-Union*, 30 June 2012.

15. Matt Dixon, "Cliff Stearns Was Outworked by Challenger Ted Yoho, Many Say," *Florida Times-Union*, 15 August 2012.

16. Matt Dixon, "Cliff Stearns Was Outworked by Challenger Ted Yoho, Many Say," *Florida Times-Union*, 15 August 2012; Alex Leary and Brittany Alana Davis, "Horse Doctor Unseats Stearns," *Tampa Bay Times*, 16 August 2012.

17. Although a corner of Levy County had been in Stearns's old district, for these calculations it is included among those added to the district rather than among the ones that Stearns had previously represented. However, even if Levy were included among Stearns's previous counties, while the numbers would differ by approximately 1,200, the bottom line remains the same. Stearns succeeded in the area he had previously represented but lost his seat because of a poor showing in the areas added through redistricting.

18. Greg Allen, "After Beating Allen West, House Freshman Faces New Fight," *National Public Radio*, 26 December 2012.

19. Ibid.

20. Lizette Alvarez, "Politics Can Be a Dirty Business. And Then There Are House Races in Florida," *New York Times*, 25 October 2012.

21. Scott Hiaasen and Patricia Mazzei, "Charges in District Helped Lead to Rep. David Rivera's Defeat," *Miami Herald*, 7 November 2012.

22. Citizens for Responsibility and Ethics in Washington, http://crewsmostcorrupt.org/mostcorrupt.

23. Manny Garcia and Marc Caputo, "Rivera Ran Secret Campaign, Stenard Tells FBI," *Miami Herald*, 25 September 2012.

24. For a detailed treatment of the sophisticated Obama voter identification and mobilization effort, see Sasha Issenberg, *Victory Lab*.

25. Patricia Mazzei and Amy Sherman, "In South Florida Congressional Races, David

Rivera Loses to Joe Garcia, Allen West Appears to Fall to Patrick Murphy," *Miami Herald*, 7 November 2012.

26. Scott Hiaasen and Patricia Mazzei, "Charges in District Helped Lead to Rep. David Rivera's Defeat," *Miami Herald*, 7 November 2012.

27. I have chosen to consider District 22 the new district gained through redistricting. One could make the case that District 18 should be considered the new one as it contained less of the old 22nd than did the new 22nd. I, however, have chosen to follow the incumbent Allen West, so that the district in which he chose to run, the 18th, is treated as a continuing district while the open seat in the 22nd I have designated as a new district.

28. Barone and Ujifusa, *Almanac of American Politics*, 323.

29. Ibid.

30. Duncan, ed., *Congressional Quarterly's Politics in America*, 384.

31. Kyle Trystad, "Lois Frankel Launches Bid Against Allen West," *Roll Call*, 21 March 2011.

32. Mack's wife, Mary Bono Mack came up short in her bid for an eighth term in her southern California district.

33. The comparison for Allen West is District 22 for 2010 with District 18 for 2012.

34. Florida does not report votes for uncontested races, so the uncontested Republican and Democratic incumbents' votes are not included in either calculation. Two Democratic districts in which the only opposition came from third party candidates and two districts in which the only GOP opposition came from third party candidates are included in the first but not in the second calculation.

35. "Head of Arizona Redistricting Commission Fired," *National Public Radio*, 2 November 2011.

36. For multiple examples of the majority party drawing plans so that pairs or even triplets of minority party incumbents had to fight for a single seat, see Gaddie and Bullock, "From *Ashcroft* to *Larios*," 997–1048.

37. Pritchard, "Changes in Electoral Structures," 62–70.

Conclusion: The Never-Ending Story

1. Presidential vote data were obtained from the Federal Election Commission, www. fec.gov/pubrec/fe2012/federalelections2012.shtml. The subtitle to this concluding section has been devised with apologies to a movie of the same name that fascinated the author when he was a boy.

2. Rossiter, *Parties and Politics in America*.

3. Without a doubt no other state has a U.S. House delegation that elects the likes of a Ted Yoho, Alan Grayson, Debbie Wasserman Shultz, Daniel Webster, Alcee Hastings, Mario Diaz-Balart, Corrine Brown, Ileana Ros-Lehtinen, Joe Garcia, and Steve Southerland—just to name ten of the 27-member delegation who clearly run the gamut in terms of demographic backgrounds, political viewpoints, and representational styles.

4. Zac Anderson, "Migration to Florida Regaining Momentum," *Herald-Tribune*, 5 January 2013.

5. In the 2014 Florida midterm elections, Republican governor Rick Scott defeated his Republican-turned-Independent-turned-Democratic challenger and former governor, Charlie Crist, by a mere 64,267 votes, which amounts to a 1.1 percentage-point victory

margin. Data obtained from Florida Division of Elections website, http://enight.elections.myflorida.com/StateOffices. In the U.S. House contests two incumbents lost, but the partisan division was not changed from 2012 (17 Republicans and 10 Democrats) as one losing incumbent was a Democrat (Joe Garcia-FL 26) and the other was a Republican (Steve Southerland-FL 2). The partisan division of the Florida Senate remained 26 Republicans and 14 Democrats. It was in the Florida House where the Republican midterm tide manifested itself. Accounting for one vacancy immediately before and after the midterm house contests, the Florida House delegation shifted from 74 Republicans and 45 Democrats to 82 Republicans and 37 Democrats (see National Conference of State Legislatures website, http://www.ncsl.org.) Overall, the 2014 election results in Florida reinforce the contention that the state will continue to move in a Democratic direction since minority voters (especially Latinos) exhibited lower turnout than non-Hispanic whites in this cycle versus in 2012, and their participation will undoubtedly increase in 2016 as their share of the electorate continues to grow.

6. Most of Florida's in-migrants hail from the deep blue northeastern United States. See McKee, *Republican Ascendancy in Southern U.S. House Elections*.

Bibliography

Abramson, Paul R., John H. Aldrich, and David W. Rohde. *Change and Continuity in the 2008 and 2010 Elections*. Washington, D.C.: CQ Press, 2011.

Adams, Brian. "Public Meetings and the Democratic Process." *Public Administration Review* 64 (2004): 43–54.

Altman, Micah. *Districting Principles and Democratic Representation*. Pasadena, Calif.: California Institute of Technology, 1998.

Altman, Micah, Karin Mac Donald, and Michael P. McDonald. "Pushbutton Gerrymanders? How Computing has Changed Redistricting." In *Party Lines: Competition, Partisanship and Congressional Redistricting*, edited by Bruce Cain and Thomas Mann, 51–66. Washington, D.C.: Brookings, 2005.

Altman, Micah, and Michael P. McDonald. "BARD: Better Automated Redistricting." *Journal of Statistical Software* 42 (2011): 1–28.

———. "A Half-Century of Virginia Redistricting Battles: Shifting from Rural Malapportionment to Voting Rights and Participation." *University of Richmond Law Review* 47 (2013): 771–831.

———. "The Promise and Perils of Computers in Redistricting." *Duke Journal of Constitutional Law and Public Policy* 5 (2010): 69–112.

Anderson, Christopher J., Andre Blais, Shaun Bowler, Todd Donovan, and Ola Listhaug. *Loser's Consent: Elections and Democratic Legitimacy*. Oxford, UK: Oxford University Press, 2005.

Anderson, Christopher J., and Yuliya V. Tverdova. "Winners, Losers, and Attitudes about Government in Contemporary Democracies." *International Political Science Review* 22 (2001): 321–38.

Ansolabehere, Stephen, Alan Gerber, and James Snyder. "Equal Votes, Equal Money: Court-Ordered Redistricting and Public Expenditures in the American States." *American Political Science Review* 96 (2002): 767–77.

Ansolabehere, Stephen, James M. Snyder Jr., and Charles Stewart, III. "Old Voters, New Voters, and the Personal Vote: Using Redistricting to Measure the Incumbency Advantage." *American Journal of Political Science* 44 (2000): 17–34.

Arnstein, Sherry R. "A Ladder of Citizen Participation." *Journal of the American Institute of Planners* 35 (1969): 216–24.

Balinski, Michel L., and H. Peyton Young. "Apportionment Schemes and the Quota Method." *American Mathematical Monthly* 84 (1977a): 450–55.

———. *Fair Representation: Meeting the Ideal of One Man, One Vote*. Washington, D.C.: Brookings, 2001.

———. "On Huntington Methods of Apportionment." *SIAM Journal on Applied Mathematics—Part C* 33 (1977b): 607–18.

———. "The Jefferson Method of Apportionment." *SIAM Review* 20 (1978): 278–84.

———. "The Quota Method of Apportionment." *American Mathematical Monthly* 82 (1975): 701–30.

———. "The Webster Method of Apportionment." *Proceedings of the National Academy of Sciences* 77 (1980): 1–4.

Barone, Michael, and Grant Ujifusa. *The Almanac of American Politics: 1994*. Washington, D.C.: National Journal, 1993.

Barreto, Matt A., Gary M. Segura, and Nathan D. Woods. "The Mobilizing Effect of Majority-Minority Districts on Latino Turnout." *American Political Science Review* 98 (2004): 65–75.

Bartels, Larry M. "Beyond the Running Tally: Partisan Bias in Political Perceptions." *Political Behavior* 24 (2002): 117–50.

Baum, Lawrence. *Judges and Their Audiences: A Perspective on Judicial Behavior*. Princeton, N.J.: Princeton University Press, 2006.

Bickerstaff, Steve. *Lines in the Sand: Congressional Redistricting in Texas and the Downfall of Tom DeLay*. Austin: University of Texas Press, 2007.

Black, Earl, and Merle Black. *The Rise of Southern Republicans*. Cambridge, Mass.: Harvard University Press, 2002.

Black, Gordon S. "A Theory of Political Ambition: Career Choices and the Role of Structural Incentives." *American Political Science Review* 66 (1972): 144–55.

Born, Richard. "Partisan Intentions and Election Day Realities in the Congressional Redistricting Process." *American Political Science Review* 79 (1985): 305–19.

Bowler, Shaun, and Todd Donovan. "Reasoning about Institutional Change: Winners, Losers and Support for Electoral Reforms." *British Journal of Political Science* 37 (2007): 455–76.

Bowler, Shaun, Todd Donovan, and Jeffrey A. Karp. "Why Politicians Like Electoral Institutions: Self-Interest, Values, or Ideology?" *Journal of Politics* 68 (2006): 434–46.

Box-Steffensmeier, Janet M. "A Dynamic Analysis of the Role of War Chests in Campaign Strategy." *American Journal of Political Science* 40 (1996): 352–71.

Box-Steffensmeier, Janet M., and Christopher J. W. Zorn. "Duration Models and Proportional Hazards in Political Science." *American Journal of Political Science* 45 (2001): 972–88.

Brace, Paul, Laura Langer, and Melinda Gann Hall. "Measuring the Preferences of State Supreme Court Judges." *Journal of Politics* 62 (2000): 387–413.

Bratton, Kathleen A. "The Effect of Legislative Diversity on Agenda Setting: Evidence from Six State Legislatures." *American Politics Research* 30 (2002): 115–42.

Bullock, Charles S., III. *Redistricting: The Most Political Activity in America*. Lanham, Md.: Rowman & Littlefield, 2010.

Butler, David, and Bruce Cain. *Congressional Redistricting: Comparative and Theoretical Perspectives*. New York: Macmillan, 1992.

Butler, Katherine Inglis. "Redistricting in a Post-Shaw Era: A Small Treatise Accompanied by Districting Guidelines for Legislators, Litigants, and Courts." *University of Richmond Law Review* 36 (2002): 137–270.

Cain, Bruce. "Assessing the Partisan Effects of Redistricting." *American Political Science Review* 79 (1985): 320–33.

Cameron, Charles, David Epstein, and Sharyn O'Halloran. "Do Majority-Minority Districts Maximize Substantive Black Representation in Congress?" *American Political Science Review* 90 (1996): 794–812.

Canes-Wrone, Brandice, David W. Brady, and John F. Cogan. "Out of Step, Out of Office: Electoral Accountability and House Members' Voting." *American Political Science Review* 96 (2002): 127–40.

Carson, Jamie L., and Michael H. Crespin. "The Effect of State Redistricting Methods on Electoral Competition in United States House of Representatives Races." *State Politics and Policy Quarterly* 4 (2004): 455–69.

Carson, Jamie L., Erik J. Engstrom, and Jason M. Roberts. "Redistricting, Candidate Entry, and the Politics of Nineteenth-Century U.S. House Elections." *American Journal of Political Science* 50 (2006): 283–93.

Carver, Joan, and Tom Fiedler. "Florida: A Volatile National Microcosm." In *Southern Politics in the 1990s*, edited by Alexander P. Lamis, 343–76. Baton Rouge: Louisiana State University Press, 1999.

Checkoway, Barry. "The Politics of Public Hearings." *Journal of Applied Behavioral Science* 17 (1981): 566–82.

Chen, Jowei, and Jonathan Rodden. "Report on Computer Simulations of Florida Congressional Districting Plans." Expert report for plaintiffs in *Romo v. Scott*, 15 February 2013.

———. "Unintentional Gerrymandering: Political Geography and Electoral Bias in Legislatures." *Quarterly Journal of Political Science* 8 (2013): 239–69.

Colburn, David R. *From Yellow Dog Democrats to Red State Republicans: Florida and Its Politics since 1940*. Gainesville, Fla.: University Press of Florida, 2007.

Coleman, John J., and Paul F. Manna. "Congressional Campaign Spending and the Quality of Democracy." *Journal of Politics* 62 (2000): 757–89.

Cottrill, James B., and Terri J. Peretti. "Gerrymandering from the Bench? The Electoral Consequences of Judicial Redistricting." *Election Law Journal: Rules, Politics, and Policy* 12 (2013): 261–76.

Cox, Adam B. "Partisan Fairness and Redistricting Politics." *New York University Law Review* 70 (2004): 751–802.

Cox, Adam B., and Thomas J. Miles. "Judging the Voting Rights Act." *Columbia Law Review* 108 (2008): 1–54.

Cox, Gary W., and Jonathan N. Katz. *Elbridge Gerry's Salamander: The Electoral Consequences of the Reapportionment Revolution*. Cambridge, UK: Cambridge University Press, 2002.

Cox, Gary W., and Michael C. Munger. "Closeness, Expenditures, and Turnout in the 1982 U.S. House Elections." *American Political Science Review* 83 (1989): 217–31.

Crocker, Royce. *The House of Representatives Apportionment Formula: An Analysis of Proposals for Change and Their Impact on States*. CRS Report R41382. Washington, D.C.: Congressional Research Service, 2010.

Crosby, Ned, Janet M. Kelly, and Paul Schaefer. "Citizens Panels: A New Approach to Citizen Participation." *Public Administration* 46 (1986): 170–78.

Crum, Travis. "The Voting Rights Act's Secret Weapon: Pocket Trigger Litigation and Dynamic Preclearance." *Yale Law Journal* 119 (2010): 1992–2038.

Cunningham, Maurice T. *Maximization, Whatever the Cost: Race, Redistricting, and the Department of Justice*. Westport, Conn.: Praeger, 2001.

Dauer, Manning J., Michael A. Maggiotto, and Steven G. Koven. "Florida." In *Reapportionment Politics: The History of Redistricting in the 50 States*, edited by Leroy Hardy, Alan Heslop, and Stuart Anderson, 74–81. Beverly Hills, Calif.: Sage, 1981.

Delli Carpini, Michael X., Fay Lomax Cook, and Lawrence R. Jacobs. "Public Deliberation, Discursive Participation, and Citizen Engagement: A Review of the Empirical Literature." *Annual Review of Political Science* 7 (2004): 315–44.

Downs, Anthony. *An Economic Theory of Democracy*. New York: Harper and Row, 1957.

Duncan, Phil, ed. *Congressional Quarterly's Politics in America 1994: The 103rd Congress*. Washington, D.C.: CQ Press, 1993.

Dye, Thomas R., Aubrey Jewett, and Susan A. MacManus. *Politics in Florida*. Tallahassee: Florida Institute of Government, 2007.

Eagles, Charles W. *Democracy Delayed: Congressional Reapportionment and Urban-Rural Conflict in the 1920s*. Athens: University of Georgia, 1990.

Edelman, Paul. "Getting the Math Right: Why California Has Too Many Seats in the House of Representatives." *Vanderbilt Law Review* 59 (2006): 297–346.

Epstein, Lee, and Jack Knight. *The Choices Justices Make*. Washington, D.C.: CQ Press, 1997.

Farrand, Max, ed. *Records of the Federal Convention of 1787*. Vol. II: 644 (Sept. 17, 1787). New Haven, Conn.: Yale University Press, 1911.

Fenno, Richard F., Jr. *Home Style: House Members in Their Districts*. New York: HarperCollins, 1978.

Ferejohn, John A., and Randall L. Calvert. "Presidential Coattails in Historical Perspective." *American Journal of Political Science* 28 (1984): 127–46.

Fougere, Joshua, Stephen Ansolabehere, and Nathaniel Persily. "Partisanship, Public Opinion, and Redistricting." *Election Law Journal: Rules, Politics, and Policy* 9 (2010): 325–47.

Gaddie, Ronald Keith, and Charles S. Bullock, III. *Elections to Open Seats in the U.S. House: Where the Action Is*. Lanham, Md.: Rowman and Littlefield, 2000.

———. "From *Ashcroft* to *Larios*: Recent Redistricting Lessons from Georgia." *Fordham Urban Law Journal* 34 (2006): 997–1048.

———. "The Political Consequences of an Uncontrolled Redistricting." Paper presented at the Annual Meeting of the Southern Political Science Association, New Orleans, 2005.

Gaines, Brian J., and Jeffery A. Jenkins. "Apportionment Matters: Fair Representation in the U.S. House and Electoral College." *Perspectives on Politics* 7 (2009): 849–57.

Gelman, Andrew, and Gary King. "Enhancing Democracy Through Legislative Redistricting." *American Political Science Review* 88 (1994): 541–59.

Gibson, Campbell, and Kay Jung. *Historical Census Statistics on Population Totals By Race, 1790 to 1990, and By Hispanic Origin, 1970 to 1990, For the United States, Regions, Divisions, and States.* Working Paper Series no. 56. Washington, D.C.: Government Printing Office, 2002.

Graves, Scott E. "Competing Interests on State Supreme Courts: Justices' Votes and Voting Rights." *American Review of Politics* 24 (2003): 267–84.

Greiner, D. James. "Re-Solidifying Racial Bloc Voting: Empirics and Legal Doctrine in the Melting Pot." *Indiana Law Journal* 86 (2011): 447–97.

Grofman, Bernard, and Gary King. "The Future of Partisan Symmetry as a Judicial Test for Partisan Gerrymandering after *LULAC v. Perry.*" *Election Law Journal: Rules, Politics, and Policy* 6 (2007): 2–35.

Grofman, Bernard, William Koetzle, and Thomas Brunell. "An Integrated Perspective on the Three Potential Sources of Partisan Bias: Malapportionment, Turnout Differences, and Geographic Distribution of Party Vote Shares." *Electoral Studies* 16 (1997): 457–70.

Gronke, Paul, and J. Matthew Wilson. "Competing Redistricting Plans as Evidence of Political Motives: The North Carolina Case." *American Politics Quarterly* 27 (1999): 147–76.

Grose, Christian R. "Disentangling Constituency and Legislator Effects in Legislative Representation: Black Legislators of Black Districts" *Social Science Quarterly* 86 (2005): 427–43.

Hamilton, Alexander, James Madison, and John Jay. *The Federalist Papers.* New York: Signet Classics, 2003.

Hayes, Danny, M. V. Hood III, and Seth C. McKee. "Redistricting and Turnout in Black and White." Paper presented at the Annual Meeting of the Midwest Political Science Association, Chicago, 2011.

Hayes, Danny, and Seth C. McKee.

———. "The Intersection of Redistricting, Race, and Participation." *American Journal of Political Science* 56 (2012): 115–30.

———. "The Participatory Effects of Redistricting." *American Journal of Political Science* 53 (2009): 1006–23.

Herrnson, Paul S. "National Party Decision Making, Strategies, and Resource Distribution in Congressional Elections." *Western Political Quarterly* 42 (1989): 301–23.

Hill, Kevin A. "Does the Creation of Majority Black Districts Aid Republicans? An Analysis of the 1992 Congressional Elections in Eight Southern States." *Journal of Politics* 57 (1995): 384–401.

Hirsch, Sam. "The United States House of Unrepresentatives: What Went Wrong in the Latest Round of Congressional Redistricting." *Election Law Journal: Rules, Politics, and Policy* 2 (2003): 179–216.

Hood, M. V., III, and Seth C. McKee. "Stranger Danger: Redistricting, Incumbent Recognition, and Vote Choice." *Social Science Quarterly* 91 (2010): 344–58.

———. "Unwelcome Constituents: Redistricting and Countervailing Partisan Tides." *State Politics and Policy Quarterly* 13 (2013): 203–24.

Hopkins, Chelsea J. "Comment: The Minority Coalition's Burden of Proof under Section 2 of the Voting Rights Act." *Santa Clara Law Review* 52 (2012): 623–54.

Innes, Judith E., and David E. Booher. "Reframing Public Participation: Strategies for the 21st Century." *Planning Theory and Practice* 5 (2004): 419–36.

Irvin, Renée A., and John Stansbury. "Citizen Participation in Decision Making: Is It Worth the Effort?" *Public Administration Review* 64 (2004): 55–65.

Issenberg, Sasha. *The Victory Lab: The Secret Science of Winning Campaigns.* New York: Crown, 2012.

Jackson, Robert A. "A Reassessment of Voter Mobilization." *Political Research Quarterly* 49 (1996): 331–49.

Jacobson, Gary C. *The Politics of Congressional Elections.* New York: Pearson, 2009.

Jewett, Aubrey. "Republican Strength in a Southern Legislature: The Impact of One Person, One Vote Redistricting in Florida." *American Review of Politics* 21 (2000): 1–18.

———. "'Fair' Districts in Florida: New Congressional Seats, New Constitutional Standards, Same Old Republican Advantage?" In *The Political Battle over Congressional Redistricting,* edited by William J. Miller and Jeremy D. Walling, 111–35. New York: Lexington Books, 2013.

Johnson, Douglas, Elise Lampe, Justin Levitt, and Andrew Lee. *Restoring the Competitive Edge: California's Need for Redistricting Reform and the Likely Impact of Proposition 77.* Claremont, Calif.: Rose Institute of State and Local Government, Claremont McKenna College, 2005.

Kaid, L. L. "Paid Television Advertising and Candidate Name Identification." *Campaigns and Elections* 3 (1982): 34–36.

Kazee, Thomas A. "The Deterrent Effect of Incumbency on Recruiting Challengers in U.S. House Elections." *Legislative Studies Quarterly* 8 (1983): 469–80.

Keele, Luke, and Ismail White. "The Role of Information Costs in Voter Turnout." Typescript, 2010. In author's possession.

King, Cheryl Simrell, Kathryn M. Feltey, and Bridget O'Neill Susel. "The Questions of Participation: Toward Authentic Public Participation in Public Administration." *Public Administration Review* 58 (1998): 317–26.

King, Gary. *A Solution to the Ecological Inference Problem: Reconstructing Individual Level Behavior from Aggregate Data.* Princeton, N.J.: Princeton University Press, 1997.

Kopko, Kyle C. "Partisanship Suppressed: Judicial Decision-Making in Ralph Nader's 2004 Ballot Access Litigation." *Election Law Journal: Rules, Politics, and Policy* 7 (2008): 301–24.

Kousser, J. Morgan. "Estimating the Partisan Consequences of Redistricting Plans-Simply." *Legislative Studies Quarterly* 21 (1996): 521–41.

Kromkowski, Charles A. *Recreating the American Republic: Rules of Apportionment, Constitutional Change, and American Political Development, 1700–1870.* New York: Cambridge University Press, 2002.

Kweit, Mary G., and Robert W. Kweit. *Implementing Citizen Participation in a Bureaucratic Society.* New York: Praeger, 1981.

Ladewig, Jeffrey W. "One Person, One Vote, 435 Seats: Interstate Malapportionment and Constitutional Requirements." *Connecticut Law Review* 43 (2010): 1125–56.

Ladewig, Jeffrey W., and Mathew P. Jasinski. "On the Causes and Consequences of and Remedies for Interstate Malapportionment of the U.S. House of Representatives." *Perspectives on Politics* 6 (2008): 89–107.

Lando, Tom. "The Public Hearing Process: A Tool for Citizen Participation, or a Path Toward Citizen Alienation?" *National Civic Review* 92 (2003): 73–82.

Langer, Laura. *Judicial Review in State Supreme Courts: A Comparative Study.* Albany: State University of New York Press, 2002.

Lenz, Timothy O., and Anita Pritchard. "Florida Legislators' Perceptions of the Change to Single-Member Districts." *State and Local Government Review* 23 (1991): 134–38.

Lloyd, Randall D. "Separating Partisanship from Party in Judicial Research: Reapportionment in the U.S. District Courts." *American Political Science Review* 89 (1995): 413–20.

Lodge, Milton, and Charles Tabor. "Three Steps toward a Theory of Motivated Political Reasoning." In *Elements of Reason: Cognition, Choice, and the Bounds of Rationality,* edited by Arthur Lupia, Matthew D. McCubbins, and Samuel L. Popkin, 183–213. New York: Cambridge University Press, 2000.

MacManus, Susan A., Joanna Cheshire, Tifini Hill, and Susan Schuler. "Redistricting 2012: Five Lessons Learned." *Quality Cities* 86 (2012): 84–87.

MacManus, Susan A., Aubrey Jewett, Thomas R. Dye, and David J. Bonanza. *Politics in Florida.* Tallahassee: Florida Institute of Government, 2011.

MacManus, Susan A., ed. *Mapping Florida's Political Landscape: The Changing Art and Politics of Reapportionment and Redistricting.* Tallahassee: Florida Institute of Government, 2002.

———, ed. *Reapportionment and Representation in Florida: A Historical Collection.* Tampa: University of South Florida, 1991.

Madison, James. "Federalist #44." In *The Federalist Papers,* by Alexander Hamilton, James Madison, and John Jay, 277–84. New York: Signet Classics, 2003.

———. "Federalist #55." In *The Federalist Papers,* by Alexander Hamilton, James Madison, and John Jay, 338–42. New York: Signet Classics, 2003.

Maestas, Cherie D., Sarah A. Fulton, L. Sandy Maisel, and Walter J. Stone. "When to Risk It? Institutions, Ambitions, and the Decision to Run for the U.S. House." *American Political Science Review* 100 (2006): 195–208.

Maestas, Cherie D., L. Sandy Maisel, and Walter J. Stone. "National Party Efforts to Recruit State Legislators to Run for the U.S. House." *Legislative Studies Quarterly* 30 (2005): 277–300.

Maestas, Cherie D., and Cynthia R. Rugeley. "Assessing the 'Experience Bonus' through Examining Strategic Entry, Candidate Quality, and Campaign Receipts in U.S. House Elections." *American Journal of Political Science* 52 (2008): 520–35.

Maggiotto, Michael A., Manning J. Dauer, Steven G. Koven, Joan S. Carver, and Joel Gottlieb. "The Impact of Reapportionment on Public Policy: The Case of Florida, 1960–1980." *American Politics Quarterly* 13 (1985): 101–21.

Marschall, Melissa J., and Anirudh V. S. Ruhil. "Substantive Symbols: The Attitudinal Dimension of Black Political Incorporation in Local Government." *American Journal of Political Science* 51 (2007): 17–33.

Masket, Seth E., Jonathan Winburn, and Gerald C. Wright. "The Gerrymanderers are Coming! Legislative Redistricting Won't Affect Competition or Polarization Much, No Matter Who Does It." *PS: Political Science and Politics* 45 (2012): 39–43.

Mayhew, David R. *Congress: The Electoral Connection.* New Haven, Conn.: Yale University Press, 1974.

———. "Congressional Elections: The Case of the Vanishing Marginals." *Polity* 6 (1974): 295–317.

McCarty, Nolan M., Keith Poole, and Howard Rosenthal. "Congress and the Territorial Expansion of the United States." Working paper, 1999, http://www.voteview.com/recentpapers.asp.

McDonald, Michael P. "A Comparative Analysis of Redistricting Institutions in the United States, 2001–02." *State Politics and Policy Quarterly* 4 (2004): 371–95.

———. *Midwest Mapping Project*. Fairfax, Va.: George Mason University, 2009.

———. "Redistricting and District Competition." In *The Marketplace of Democracy*, edited by Michael P. McDonald and John Samples, 222–44. Washington, D.C.: Brookings, 2006.

———. "Re-Drawing the Line on District Competition." *PS: Political Science and Politics* 39 (2006): 99–102.

———. "Regulating Redistricting." *PS: Political Science and Politics* 40 (2007): 675–79.

McKay, Robert B. *Reapportionment: The Law and Politics of Equal Representation*. New York: Twentieth Century Fund, 1965.

McKee, Seth C. "The Effects of Redistricting on Voting Behavior in Incumbent U.S. House Elections, 1992–1994." *Political Research Quarterly* 61 (2008): 122–33.

———. "Political Conditions and the Electoral Effects of Redistricting." *American Politics Research* 41 (2013): 623–50.

———. "Redistricting and Familiarity with U.S. House Candidates." *American Politics Research* 36 (2008): 962–79.

———. *Republican Ascendancy in Southern U.S. House Elections*. Boulder, Co.: Westview Press, 2010.

McKee, Seth C., and Mark J. McKenzie. "Analyzing Redistricting Outcomes." In *Rotten Boroughs, Political Thickets, and Legislative Donnybrooks: Redistricting in Texas*, edited by Gary A. Keith, 95–146. Austin: University of Texas Press, 2013.

McKee, Seth C., and Daron R. Shaw. "Redistricting in Texas: Institutionalizing Republican Ascendancy." In *Redistricting in the New Millennium*, edited by Peter F. Galderisi, 275–311. Lanham, Md.: Lexington Books, 2005.

McKee, Seth C., Jeremy M. Teigen, and Mathieu Turgeon. "The Partisan Impact of Congressional Redistricting: The Case of Texas, 2001–2003." *Social Science Quarterly* 87 (2006): 308–17.

McKenzie, Mark Jonathan. "Beyond Partisanship? Federal Courts, State Commissions, and Redistricting." PhD diss., University of Texas, Austin, 2007.

———. "Beyond Partisanship? An Analysis of Judicial Decisions on Redistricting in State Supreme Courts." Paper presented at the Annual Meeting of the Midwest Political Science Association, Chicago, 2010.

———. "The Influence of Partisanship, Ideology, and the Law on Redistricting Decisions in the Federal Courts." *Political Research Quarterly* 65 (2012): 799–813.

Miller, Berkeley, and William Canak. "From 'Porkchoppers' to 'Lambchoppers': The Passage of Florida's Public Employee Relations Act." *Industrial and Labor Relations Review* 44 (1991): 341–66.

Mills, Karen M. *Americans Overseas in U.S. Censuses*, Technical Paper no. 62. Washington, D.C.: Government Printing Office, 1993.

Myres, Sandra L. *One Man, One Vote: Gerrymandering vs. Reapportionment*. Austin, Tex.: Steck-Vaughn, 1970.

Niemi, Richard G., and Alan I. Abramowitz. "Partisan Redistricting and the 1992 Congressional Elections." *Journal of Politics* 56 (1994): 811–17.

Niemi, Richard G., Bernard Grofman, Carl Carlucci, and Thomas Hofeller. "Measuring Compactness and the Role of a Compactness Standard in a Test for Partisan and Racial Gerrymandering." *Journal of Politics* 52 (1990): 1155–81.

Niemi, Richard G., and Laura R. Winsky. "The Persistence of Partisan Redistricting Effects in Congressional Elections in the 1970s and 1980s." *Journal of Politics* 54 (1992): 565–72.

Petrocik, John R., and Scott W. Desposato. "The Partisan Consequences of Majority-Minority Redistricting in the South, 1992 and 1994." *Journal of Politics* 60 (1998): 613–33.

Price, Hugh Douglas. "Florida: Politics and the 'Pork Choppers.'" In *The Politics of Reapportionment*, edited by Malcolm E. Jewell, 81–97. New York: Atherton Press, 1962.

Pritchard, Anita. "Changes in Electoral Structures and the Success of Women Candidates: The Case of Florida." *Social Science Quarterly* 73 (1992): 62–70.

Pritchett, C. Herman. *The Roosevelt Court: A Study in Judicial Politics and Values, 1937–1947*. New York: Macmillan, 1948.

Roberts, Nancy. "Public Deliberation in an Age of Direct Citizen Participation." *American Review of Public Administration* 34 (2004): 315–53.

Rohde, David W. "Risk Bearing and Progressive Ambition: The Case of Members of the United States House of Representatives." *American Journal of Political Science* 23 (1979): 1–26.

Rosener, Judy B. "Citizen Participation: Can We Measure Its Effectiveness?" *Public Administration Review* 3 (1978): 457–63.

Rossiter, Clinton. *Parties and Politics in America*. Ithaca, N.Y.: Cornell University Press, 1960.

Schaffner, Brian F., Michael W. Wagner, and Jonathan Winburn. "Incumbents Out, Party In? Term Limits and Partisan Redistricting in State Legislatures." *State Politics and Policy Quarterly* 4 (2004): 396–414.

Segal, Jeffrey A., and Harold J. Spaeth. *The Supreme Court and the Attitudinal Model Revisited*. New York: Cambridge University Press, 2002.

Sekhon, Jasjeet, and Rocío Titiunik. "When Natural Experiments are Neither Natural nor Experiments." *American Political Science Review* 106 (2012): 35–57.

Shaw, James Evan. "The Electoral College and Unstable Congressional Apportionment." In *Direct Popular Elections of the President and Vice President of the United States: Hearings on S. J. Res. 28, 96th Congress, 1st Session, 463–76, March 27, 30, April 3 and 9, 1979*. Washington, D.C.: Government Printing Office, 1979.

Skene, Neil. "Reapportionment." In *The Florida Handbook, 2005–2006: 30th Biennial Edition*, edited by Allen Morris and Joan Perry Morris, 177–95. Tallahassee, Fla.: Peninsular Publishing, 2005.

Smith, Daniel A., and Dustin Fridkin. "Delegating Direct Democracy: Interparty Legislative Competition and the Adoption of the Initiative in the American States." *American Political Science Review* 102 (2008): 333–50.

Stimson, James A., Michael B. MacKuen, and Robert S. Erikson. "Dynamic Representation." *American Political Science Review* 89 (1995): 542–65.

Stivers, Camilla. "The Listening Bureaucrat: Responsiveness in Public Administration." *Public Administration Review* 54 (1994): 364–69.

———. "The Public Agency as Polis: Active Citizenship in the Administrative State." *Administration and Society* 22 (1990): 86–105.

Stokes, Donald E. *Legislative Redistricting by the New Jersey Plan*. New Brunswick, N.J.: Fund for New Jersey, 1993.

Stone, Walter J., L. Sandy Maisel, and Cherie D. Maestas. "Quality Counts: Extending the Strategic Politician Model of Incumbent Deterrence." *American Journal of Political Science* 48 (2004): 479–95.

Tolbert, Caroline J., Daniel A. Smith, and John C. Green. "Strategic Voting and Legislative Redistricting Reform: District and Statewide Representational Winners and Losers." *Political Research Quarterly* 62 (2009): 92–109.

Tufte, Edward R. "The Relationship between Seats and Votes in Two-Party Systems." *American Political Science Review* 67 (1973): 540–54.

Voss, D. Stephen, and David Lublin. "Black Incumbents, White Districts: An Appraisal of the 1996 Congressional Elections." *American Politics Research* 29 (2001): 141–82.

Walters, Lawrence C., James Aydelotte, and Jessica Miller. "Putting More Public in Policy Analysis." *Public Administration Review* 60 (2000): 349–59.

Winburn, Jonathan. "Does it Matter if Legislatures or Commissions Draw the Lines?" In *Reapportionment and Redistricting in the West*, edited by Gary Moncrief, 137–60. Lanham, Md.: Lexington Books, 2011.

———. *The Realities of Redistricting: Following the Rules and Limiting Gerrymandering in State Legislative Redistricting*. Lanham, Md.: Lexington Books, 2008.

Winburn, Jonathan, and Michael W. Wagner. "Carving Voters Out: Redistricting's Influence on Political Information, Turnout, and Voting Behavior." *Political Research Quarterly* 63 (2010): 373–86.

Yoshinaka, Antoine, and Chad Murphy. "The Paradox of Redistricting: How Partisan Mapmakers Foster Competition but Disrupt Representation." *Political Research Quarterly* 64 (2011): 435–47.

Contributors

Micah Altman is director of research and head scientist, Program on Information Science for the Massachusetts Institute of Technology Libraries.

Travis A. Braidwood is assistant professor of political science at Texas A&M University–Kingsville.

Charles S. Bullock III is Richard B. Russell Professor of Political Science at the University of Georgia.

Joanna M. Cheshire holds a bachelor's in political science and a master's in public administration from the University of South Florida and is public affairs director at Children's Board of Hillsborough County, Florida.

Joseph T. Eagleton holds bachelor's and master's degrees in political science and a juris doctor from the University of Florida. He is currently an attorney in Tallahassee, Florida.

Danny Hayes is associate professor of political science at George Washington University.

Tifini L. Hill holds a bachelor's in political science and a master's in public administration from the University of South Florida and is a senior fiscal analyst in the City of Tampa Budget Office.

M. V. Hood III is professor of political science at the University of Georgia.

Aubrey Jewett is associate professor of political science at the University of Central Florida.

Jeffrey W. Ladewig is associate professor of political science at the University of Connecticut.

Susan A. MacManus is Distinguished University Professor of Political Science and Public Administration at the University of South Florida.

Cherie D. Maestas is Marshall A. Rauch Distinguished Professor of Political Science at the University of North Carolina at Charlotte.

Michael P. McDonald is associate professor of political science at the University of Florida.

Seth C. McKee is associate professor of political science at Texas Tech University.

Mark Jonathan McKenzie is associate professor of political science at Texas Tech University.

Richard McKenzie is a geographic information system analyst at the University of South Florida Library.

Susan C. Schuler is president of Susan Schuler and Associates, a full-service marketing research company with special expertise in quantitative and qualitative research design, statistical analysis, and reporting.

Daniel A. Smith is professor of political science at the University of Florida.

Jonathan Winburn is associate professor of political science at the University of Mississippi.

Index

FLORIDA GOVERNMENT AND POLITICS

Series editors, David R. Colburn and Susan A. MacManus

Florida has emerged today as a microcosm of the nation and has become a political bellwether in national elections. The impact of Florida on the presidential elections of 2000, 2004, and 2008 suggests the magnitude of the state's influence. Of the four most populous states in the nation, Florida is the only one that has moved from one political column to the other in the last three national elections. These developments suggest the vital need to explore the politics of the Sunshine State in greater detail. Books in this series will explore the myriad aspects of politics, political science, public policy, history, and government in Florida.

The 57 Club: My Four Decades in Florida Politics, by Frederick B. Karl (2010)

The Political Education of Buddy MacKay, by Buddy MacKay, with Rick Edmonds (2010)

Immigrant Prince: Mel Martinez and The American Dream, by Richard E. Fogelsong (2011)

Reubin O'D. Askew and the Golden Age of Florida Politics, by Martin A. Dyckman (2011)

Red Pepper and Gorgeous George: Claude Pepper's Epic Defeat in the 1950 Democratic Primary, by James C. Clark (2011)

Inside Bush v. Gore, by Charley Wells (2013)

The Failure of Term Limits in Florida, by Kathryn A. DePalo (2015)

Conservative Hurricane: How Jeb Bush Remade Florida, by Matthew T. Corrigan (2015)

The Failure of Term Limits in Florida, by Kathryn A. DePalo (2015)

Jigsaw Puzzle Politics in the Sunshine State, edited by Seth C. McKee (2015)